Watching the World Die

Watching the World Die

Nuclear Threat Films
of the 1980s

MIKE BOGUE

McFarland & Company, Inc., Publishers
Jefferson, North Carolina

ISBN (print) 978-1-4766-9101-5
ISBN (ebook) 978-1-4766-5070-8

LIBRARY OF CONGRESS AND BRITISH LIBRARY
CATALOGUING DATA ARE AVAILABLE

Library of Congress Control Number 2023040538

Front cover illustration by Todd Tennant

Printed in the United States of America

*McFarland & Company, Inc., Publishers
Box 611, Jefferson, North Carolina 28640
www.mcfarlandpub.com*

In memory of Rick Gore

Acknowledgments

While only one author's name might appear on a book cover, multiple people have helped that author bring the book to life.

Many thanks to Mark Matzke, who patiently read my manuscript and provided a wealth of thoughtful suggestions.

Thanks also to Thomas Kent Miller, who offered constructive suggestions on how to improve my book's opening for readers unfamiliar with the nuclear threat movie genre.

Much appreciation to J.D. Lees, longtime editor of *G-FAN Magazine*, who painstakingly analyzed my manuscript on multiple levels, causing me to rethink the book's presentation and purpose. His insights made the book better.

Appreciation as well to John LeMay for his appraisal of my manuscript.

And a final thanks to artist Todd Tennant, who provided moral support as well as this book's haunting cover.

Table of Contents

Preface

On January 13, 2018, state representative Matthew LoPresti grabbed his two young daughters, placed them in the bathtub and told them to pray. He and the rest of Hawaii had received an emergency warning about an inbound ballistic missile. LoPresti recalls thinking, "I was going between *this doesn't really feel real* and *this is actually what it would feel like*. It's unbelievable that weapons would bring this kind of destruction."[1]

Thirty-eight minutes later, Hawaii's Emergency Alert System confessed they had made a mistake: There was no inbound missile. Amazingly, a worker had accidentally triggered the alarm. His blunder had caused thousands of Hawaiians to panic, many probably assuming they had 20 minutes before impact, the approximate amount of time for a North Korean missile to reach Hawaii. Upon learning of the mistake, Representative LoPresti said his fear turned into anger.

This incident shows that the threat of nuclear weapons remains relevant almost 80 years after the United States bombed Hiroshima and Nagasaki and decades following the end of the Cold War. During the 1980s, tensions between the United States and the Soviet Union heightened, and nuclear threat movies made between 1980 and 1990 reflected the discord. This book covers these films.

The description of a nuclear threat movie covers (1) movies that depict nuclear terrorism, nuclear extortion, nuclear theft or any combination thereof; (2) movies that depict or speak of destruction by nuclear weapons on a small or large scale. This includes films portraying a post-nuke apocalyptic environment; and (3) movies in which an extraordinary nuclear aspect either is the plot or is a substantial part of the plot. This includes movies in which radiation has mutated humans, animals or both.[2]

This three-part definition covers movies released theatrically or direct to video, plus films made for TV and exclusively shown on television. This includes ABC's groundbreaking *The Day After* (1983)[3] as well as the BBC's chilling *Threads* (1984). In addition, the movies surveyed hail from both the East and the West. I saw the majority of these movies during the 1980s when I was a young adult. Some alarmed me, given the distinct possibility of nuclear war during that decade.

This work does not cover documentaries, news specials or other non-fiction presentations concerning the nuclear threat. For this reason, I do not include films such as 1980's *If the Bomb Drops…* and 1982's *The Atomic Cafe*.

In addition, this tome excludes nuke comedy films, including but not limited to 1981's *Modern Problems*, 1981's *Super Fuzz*, 1982's *Runaway Nightmare*, 1984's *The Toxic Avenger* (along with its two 1989 sequels), 1985's *Spies Like Us*, 1986's *Radioactive Dreams*, 1986's *Class of Nuke 'Em High*, 1987's *Cherry 2000* and 1988's *Hell Comes to Frogtown*.

Further, several 1980s movies featured a post-apocalyptic setting that is not a post-nuke one. In fact, I've discovered that though some online descriptions of generic post-apocalyptic films mention nuclear war, the movie doesn't. Such non-nuke post-apocalyptic films are excluded.

Since this book covers the nuclear threat movies of the 1980s, you may wonder why it extends through 1990. As the late Bill Warren wrote in the preface to his classic *Keep Watching the Skies!*, "[T]rends don't watch calendars."[4] He extended his own survey of 1950s science fiction movies from 1950 to 1962, because 1950s-type SF movies continued through the early '60s. This work takes a similar path: Though nuclear threat movies of the '80s did begin in 1980, Cold War anxieties continued through early 1990.

This work is pertinent on a number of levels. For one, while many nuclear war books have been published, not one has exclusively spotlighted the nuclear threat movies of the 1980s. Cold War anxieties of the 1950s and '60s had abated by the '70s. But in the '80s, Cold War fears again reached white hot urgency, with America and Russia poised on the brink. The nuclear threat movies of the 1980s capture and reflect society's Cold War anxieties, and for that reason this book has historical value.

In addition, a potential nuclear exchange between superpowers arguably remains civilization's biggest threat. Few worried about nuclear weapons during the 1990s, but in the 2020s, the possibility of a nuclear attack on either a small or large scale has increased. The international situation, especially involving North Korea, China and Russia, remains unstable. For example, in 2019, Russian state television listed U.S. military facilities targeted by Russian nuclear weapons.[5] In 2020, Russian President Vladimir Putin championed a policy in which Russia might use nuclear weapons in response to a large-scale conventional attack.[6] More recently, in 2022, Russia invaded the Ukraine, and President Putin threatened to possibly use nuclear weapons in this war.[7] This work reminds us that nukes didn't vaporize after the Cold War. They still exist and could still cause untold destruction.

For my coverage of these films, I have gone to the primary sources—the movies themselves. In each entry, I cover the plot, one or more technical aspects, a personal evaluation, and the film's nuclear threat aspect.

In most cases, my synopses don't mention the actors' names, since the cast listing is at the top of each entry. However, in the cases of particularly important nuclear threat movies and/or nuclear threat movies with large casts, I do include the actors' names. Examples include *Virus, Malevil, World War III, The Day After, Special Bulletin, Testament, WarGames, Threads, Dead Man's Letters, Miracle Mile* and *By Dawn's Early Light*.

In addition to watching the films, I have used popular culture books, genre periodicals and scholarly articles dealing with nuclear issues. I have also consulted the Internet cautiously (no Wikipedia entries). The book is organized chronologically in order of release. The films are organized alphabetically within each year.

An old adage goes, "Those who cannot remember the past are condemned to repeat it." Therefore, we need to look back at the nuclear threat movies of the 1980s. Many of them portray events that could have happened then—and some that could still happen now. Skeptical of a nuclear threat playing out today? Ask Hawaii state representative Matthew LoPresti what he thinks.

Introduction

In the 1950s, if a buddy said, "Hey, let's go watch a nuke movie!," you'd have to trek to the local cinema or drive-in movie theater.

But during the 1980s, you could sit in the comfort of your living room and watch many of the decade's nuke movies on TV. The proliferation of cable television and multiple channels in the '80s made this possible, often allowing nuke films to get the widest achievable audience. Thus, ABC's November 20, 1983, broadcast of *The Day After* had an estimated 100 million viewers.[1]

The 1980s nuclear threat movies surveyed in this book fall under four categories: (1) plausible near-future scenarios; (2) post-apocalyptic action adventures; (3) comic book tales; and (4) monster yarns.

Plausible near-future scenarios comprise the most important 1980s nuclear threat movies. Some are limited in scope, either by design or financial necessity. For example, *Special Bulletin* concerns a small nuclear attack in Charleston, South Carolina. *Testament* makes clear a nuclear war has happened across the United States, but the film focuses solely on the Wetherly family in Hamelin, a small California suburb. *WarGames* teases viewers with a potential nuclear war.

Unlike *Special Bulletin* and *Testament*, many plausible '80s nuclear war scenarios broadened their focus. Examples include *The Day After* and *Threads*. In these films, we see widespread destruction. *Threads* even shows England thirteen years after the attack, a bleak landscape inhabited by a handful of humans who've been reduced to medieval subsistence.

The second category of 1980s nuke movies examined in this book is the post-apocalyptic action adventure. These have little to no interest in a plausible post-nuke world, but rather use the setting as an excuse for exploitation, many patterned after 1979's *Mad Max*. More often than not, the films were R-rated and gloried in gratuitous violence and sex. A good example is 1982's *The Aftermath*. A more palatable example is 1983's *Yor, the Hunter from the Future*, a PG item that includes no sex or nudity but does feature gore.

The third category: comic book tales. This grouping includes actual superheroes and the nuclear threat such as 1987's *Superman IV: The Quest for Peace* and also super-beings such as the psionic characters in 1988's *Akira*. But the category also becomes a catch-all for films such as 1984's *Dreamscape* and the same year's *Red Dawn*, movies too over-the-top to be considered plausible near-future scenarios, but that work nicely as cinematic graphic novels.

The book's fourth and final category is the monster yarn. America made several of these in the 1950s,[2] as did Japan. In the 1980s, non–Japanese nuke monster movies include offerings such as 1984's *C.H.U.D.* Japan supplied two such films: 1984's *Godzilla* (Americanized and released in the U.S. as *Godzilla 1985*) and 1989's *Godzilla vs. Biollante.*

For readers who would like to watch films from any or all of these categories, the good news is that most (but, alas, not all) are available on the Internet.

I hope you will find much food for thought in the nuke film explorations. And after reading the book, should you find yourself watching one of the entries such as *The Day After* or *Threads* and deem the angst overwhelming, just remind yourself, "It's only a movie." For now.

CHAPTER ONE

Cold War Jitters

The '50s vs. the '80s

In October 1962 at the height of the Cuban Missile Crisis, a second-grade teacher in St. Petersburg, Florida, ran up and down the classroom aisles saying, "We're all going to die! We're all going to die!" The students were terrified.[1]

This anecdote epitomizes the fear Americans in the '50s and early '60s harbored regarding atomic weapons. For most of those folks, the question wasn't *if* Russia and America would fight a nuclear war, but *when*. For example, in the 1950s, the Federal Civil Defense Administration circulated tens of millions of copies of the pamphlet *Survival Under Atomic Attack*.[2] And in 1961, President John F. Kennedy championed the need for fallout shelters, provoking a panic to build one's own shelter fast.[3]

Next, the Cuban Missile Crisis galvanized American citizens during October 1962, and the U.N. Secretary General declared, "The very existence of mankind is in the balance."[4] During this nuclear crisis between the United States and the Soviet Union, for the first time in history, the U.S. went to DEFCON 2 (one step away from nuclear war).[5] You and I are probably here today because in 1962, Soviet Premier Nikita Khrushchev and American President Kennedy worked out an agreement that prevented World War III.

Leap to the 1980s, when once again, the Cold War grew heated. Political rhetoric breathed fire, such as President Ronald Reagan referring to the Soviet Union as "the evil empire." The Nuclear Freeze movement gained traction in America, and in 1982 staged the nation's biggest anti-nuke rally—an estimated one million protestors in New York City.[6] Across the country, local communities voted in droves for Nuclear Freeze resolutions.[7]

Americans from 1950 to 1965 (which we will abbreviate as simply "the '50s") and from 1980 to 1990 (which we will abbreviate as "the '80s") vaulted fear of an atomic apocalypse to the top of the charts. Hence, we will compare these two time periods of heightened nuclear terror.[8]

But what about the late 1960s and the 1970s? Why not include them in our comparison? Because the period from 1966 to 1979 saw relatively few nuclear threat films. By the late '60s, public interest in nuclear war had waned; the number of magazine articles, newspaper pieces, novels and non-fiction books dealing with the issue had plummeted from their early '60s peak to just a quarter of that number by the late '60s.[9] Other pressing American issues—the Civil Rights Movement, the Vietnam War—had stepped into the spotlight and moved the nuclear issue to the margins. From 1966 to 1979, the public gave little thought to World War III.

However, in the '80s—as in the '50s—public interest in the nuclear issue exploded.[10] Newspaper and magazine articles dealing with nuclear war jumped to levels unseen since the early '60s.[11] In addition, bookstores brimmed with nuclear threat novels and non-fiction books, which also jammed drugstore paperback racks.[12] In the '80s, as in the '50s, nuclear war was once again urgent and newsworthy, its 1966–79 drop in public interest over.

That said, was the atomic cinema of the '50s similar to but also different than the atomic cinema of the '80s?

Before we take a look, a caveat: Don't worry if the titles of the 1950s or 1980s nuclear threat films seem unfamiliar. Many of the 1980s nuke movies only played on TV or were released directly to video; few saw theatrical release. In addition, today in the 21st century, the 1950s is a distant decade whose films rarely turn up on mainstream television.

Speaking of which, during the Cold War anxieties of the '50s, monsters and mutants ruled the nuke genre. Various oversized critters served as metaphors for The Bomb. Subcategories included big bugs, such as the giant ants of 1954's *Them!*; giant humans, such as 1957's *The Amazing Colossal Man*; and prehistoric behemoths, such as 1956's *Godzilla, King of the Monsters!* (the Americanized version of 1954's Japanese *Gojira*). But in the 1980s, almost all nuke movies excluded overgrown arachnids and their colossal cousins.

In addition, human-sized radiation-spawned mutants abounded in the '50s, ranging from the atomic ape-man of 1958's *Monster on the Campus* to the homicidal amphibians of 1964's *The Horror of Party Beach*. In the '80s, only a few human-sized mutants appear, such as the radioactive terror in 1983's *The Being*.

Also, 1950s nuke films tended to keep things antiseptic, generally eschewing depictions of radiation sickness or other physical trauma. Exceptions exist, such as the radiation burn makeup used in 1955's *Day the World Ended*. But most early nuke films went the way of 1959's *On the Beach*, which doesn't show radiation sickness. In addition, when the film's submarine crew visits post-nuked San Francisco and San Diego, the buildings are untouched, the streets deserted. Given the magnitude of radiation that would have stricken people, a few bodies should be lying around. In addition, how could these two cities still be standing?

On the other hand, nuke films of the '80s refused to shy away from post-nuke property devastation. Both 1983's *The Day After* and 1984's *Threads* show ICBM-wrought destruction. In *The Day After*, that of Lawrence, Kansas, and Kansas City, and in *Threads*, Sheffield, England.

Also unlike '50s nuke films, some '80s atomic movies clinically depict physical trauma. True, some '80s apocalyptic films, such as 1984's *Countdown to Looking Glass*, build up to the moment of the nuke attack, then end. Meanwhile, 1983's *Testament* generally takes a discrete route, though it still communicates the horror of death by radiation poisoning. Two key nuke threat films go even further: During its final 30 minutes, *The Day After* shows two of the main characters suffering advanced stages of radiation poisoning. And *Threads* pulls out all the stops, explicitly depicting not just radiation sickness, but also burns and all manner of physical damage.

In addition to being less graphic than 1980s nuke movies, 1950s nuke films tend to be more hopeful. A good example is 1962's *Panic in Year Zero!* Even 1962's downbeat *This Is Not a Test* allows that the two young people have perhaps survived the nuclear blast by taking refuge in a mine shaft. And 1964's *Fail-Safe*, for all its grimness, results in the nuclear destruction of only two cities. However, *On the Beach* eschews optimism and instead depicts humankind's complete annihilation.

Indeed, *On the Beach* serves as the precursor to 1980s nuke threat movies, which tend to be more fatalistic than most of their predecessors. Three of the best examples of *On the Beach*'s '80s children are *Testament*, *The Day After* and *Threads*. These films, especially *Threads*, offer a future riddled with hardship and ending in despair. Hope is but a distant memory.

Still, both '50s and '80s nuke films share one thing: nuclear war's enormity. In the early nuke movies, the main characters understand the gravity of their situation. The same holds true for the folks in 1980s nuke films.

Another similarity: For the most part, both '50s and '80s nuke films portray average people as the main characters, folks whose economic means rarely exceed those of the middle class. In most cases, these folks also happen to be white. For example, if we look at the major '50s nuke films, an African American appears in a significant role in only four of them: 1951's *Five* (Charles Lampkin), 1959's *The World, the Flesh and the Devil* (Harry Belafonte), 1964's *Dr. Strangelove* (James Earl Jones) and the same year's *The Horror of Party Beach* (Eulabelle Moore).

African American representation gradually increased. For example, 1983's *Special Bulletin* includes a black news correspondent (J. Wesley Huston), and the same year's *The Day After* features a young African American family, though we only see the father (William Allen Young) and mother (Fay Hauser). Steve James appears in 1982's *The Soldier* as the only black member of Ken Wahl's team of four operatives and gets a fair amount of screen time. Meanwhile, Meshach Taylor has a thankless role in 1990's *Ultra Warrior*. Woody Strode adds some much-needed class to 1984's *The Final Executioner*. And Fred Williamson is featured in both 1983's *The New Barbarians* and 1988's *Delta Force Commando*.

James Earl Jones brings affability to Admiral Greer in 1990's *The Hunt for Red October* as well as dignity and heart to his American general in 1990's *By Dawn's Early Light*. The always reliable Paul Winfield is good as the world-weary cop in 1984's *The Terminator*. Bernie Casey plays James Bond's good friend Felix Leiter in 1983's *Never Say Never Again*. And Tina Turner excels as the amoral Aunty Entity in 1985's *Mad Max: Beyond Thunderdome*.

Of note is that in 1959's *The World, the Flesh, and the Devil*, Harry Belafonte had top billing. Two '80s nuke films feature an African American in the lead: 1984's *Time Bomb* (Billy Dee Williams) and 1988's *Iron Eagle II* (Louis Gossett, Jr.).

When we look at gender, no '50s nuke movies featured a female as the main protagonist; like most women in 1950s films, they played supporting roles. Yet *Testament* and *Threads* feature strong women as the lead characters. Still, for both of them, World War III brings sorrow upon sorrow.

What about visual depictions of nuclear war? In the '50s, nuke films rarely show war but instead suggest it using stock footage. However, 1952's *Invasion USA* employs some city miniatures when an A-bomb drops on New York City. Also, 1960's *The Time Machine* uses miniatures when London gets nuked. Japan used special effects to depict a nuclear war in Toei's black-and-white *The Final War* (1960) and Toho's color *The Last War* (1961). *The Last War* serves up an elaborate atomic obliteration of Tokyo, as well as quick shots of other world capitals getting nuked.

In the '80s, as in the '50s, few films depict a nuclear war. Even if they do, as in 1983's *The Day After*, much of the footage is stock of nuclear tests conducted in the U.S.

years earlier, somewhat surprising since *The Day After* had a $7.5 million budget, a fair amount in those days. Meanwhile, despite its low budget, *Threads* does show some miniatures effectively destroyed when Sheffield gets nuked.

Another intriguing comparison between the atomic films of the '50s and '80s is the post-nuke movie that occurs 15 or more years after a nuclear war. For the '50s, a few films qualify, one of the best being 1956's *World Without End*, which takes place several centuries in the future and depicts Earth brimming with underground human survivors and above-ground humanoid mutants.

However, the '80s includes a wealth of post-nuke films that occur 15 or more years after a nuclear war. Many style themselves after 1979's *Mad Max* and/or 1981's *Escape from New York*. A typical example is 1987's *Steel Dawn* with Patrick Swayze.

Despite the differences between the nuke films of the '50s and '80s, fear permeates them all. The better-made nuclear threat movies of both periods, such as *On the Beach* and *Testament*, can induce a visceral chill. This momentary shudder, be it for one second or one hour, forces us to acknowledge that nuclear weapons will probably be used sooner or later. We can ignore this gut response, wave it away as though it's a bad dream, resume our day-to-day routine. But if that white light ever flashes through our office, or our bedroom, or our backyard, fear will vomit the following reality into our brain: The jig is up.

CHAPTER TWO

*   *   *

1980

The Children

DIRECTOR: Max Kalmanowicz; WRITERS: Carlton J. Albright, Edward Terry; CINEMATOGRAPHER: Barry Abrams; MUSIC: Harry Manfredini; EDITOR: Nikki Wessling; PRODUCER: Carlton J. Albright.
CAST: Martin Shakar (John Freemont); Gil Rogers (Sheriff Billy Hart); Gale Garnett (Cathy Freemont); Shannon Bolin (Molly).
PRODUCTION: Albright Films; 1980; 93 minutes; rated R.

* * *

By the 1980s, radiation was finished as a means to animate a movie's menace—or was it? *The Children*, a low-budget exploitation thriller from 1980, proves this notion wrong.

A radioactive gas cloud leaks from a nuclear power facility and drifts into the path of a school bus, turning the five children aboard into zombified killers. They don't eat flesh; instead, they roast their victims alive. Sheriff Billy Hart finds the bus, the driver and kids missing. Meanwhile, one of the mutated kid wanders home, and his touch turns an adult into a burned corpse.

Thinking the kids might have been kidnapped, Sheriff Hart organizes a roadblock. Meanwhile, two of the other zombified children return home and barbecue their families.

Sheriff Hart and John Freemont find missing kid Janet, who soon morphs into a zombie (we know because her fingernails turn black). Before she escapes, her touch burns Sheriff Hart's arm.

John and Sheriff Hart speed to John's house. There, a mutated child touches John's hand, burning it. Sheriff Hart shoots her point blank, but the bullets have no effect.

Zombified Paul kills Cathy's young son and pursues her. John shoots Paul, to no avail. Then in a grisly touch, Sheriff Hart uses a sword to chop off Paul's hands. Paul collapses, dying, the fingernails on his amputated hands turning from black to normal. John slays another mutated child by cutting off one of her hands.

John and Sheriff Hart track down the remaining zombified children and amputate their hands, killing them. However, once Sheriff Hart gets in his squad car, a child zombie who still has one of her hands fries him with her touch. John discovers Hart's corpse and dismembers the zombified child. The terror seems to be over.

Cathy, who is pregnant, gives birth to her and John's new baby. John recoils upon seeing the newborn's black fingernails.

Movies have periodically plugged into the maxim "Kids can be little monsters" with chillers such as 1956's *The Bad Seed* and 1993's *The Good Son*. *The Children* is another such film, albeit one maimed by a low budget and inferior execution. Despite a subpar script, the actors are competent. The film itself, however, moves unevenly, and the scenes in which the children roast their victims are unconvincing.

The means of defeating the monster kids—cutting off their hands—vaults to the top of the bad taste meter. Perhaps we should feel fortunate that the protagonists don't cut off the children's feet and heads as well. Equally unsettling, little Clarkie, probably only five or six years old, gets fried by one of the kid zombies, but at least his death occurs offscreen.

Like the otherworldly children in 1960's *Village of the Damned*, the tykes in *The Children* often act and move as one. Also, once their hands are amputated, they emit a strange animal wail. This casts an almost supernatural aspect upon the kids—not really a problem since the movie centers on cheap shocks instead of logic.

The film's nuclear threat connection takes a stab at relevance. The radioactive gas cloud turns the kids into monsters, perhaps a metaphor for the potential dangers of nuclear power, or perhaps more specifically, for the mutations that radiation can produce in children in the womb.

Most of the reviews were unfavorable. In a July 9, 1980, *Washington Post* review, Gary Arnold wrote, "[T]he ugly economy of this situation is softened by the amateurish writing and playing, invariably so klunky that even the most vicious imtimations [*sic*] tend to be reduced to desperate nonsense."[1]

The film is rated R for language, adult content and violence. Somewhat ironically given the title, this movie is not for kids, or pretty much anyone else.

*   *   *

The Lathe of Heaven

DIRECTORS: Fred Barzyk, David Loxton; WRITERS: Roger E. Swaybill, Diane English, based on the novel by Ursula K. Le Guin; MUSIC: Michael Small; CINEMATOG-RAPHER: Robbie Greenberg; EDITOR: Dick Bartlett; PRODUCERS: Carol Brandenburg, Fred Barzyk.

CAST: Bruce Davison (George Orr); Kevin Conway (Dr. William Haber); Margaret Avery (Heather LeLache).

PRODUCTION: Public Broadcasting Service (PBS), Taurus Film, Thirteen/WNET; U.S.-German; 9 January 1980; 105 minutes; not rated.

*   *   *

Let's get this out of the way: The special effects in *The Lathe of Heaven* resemble graphics from a 1970s video game. But the effects scenes are few, and special effects aren't everything in a science fiction film, especially one powered by ideas involving consciousness, ethics and nuclear war.

Four years after dreaming himself away from the nuclear destruction of Portland, Oregon, George Orr seeks a cure for his "effective dreams" that literally change reality. At first his therapist, Dr. William Haber, doubts Orr's claim. But with the help of the "Augmentor" which allows Haber to see a patient's dreams, Haber discovers that Orr is telling the truth: When he dreams of the sun beating down on a rainy day, the rain stops, the clouds clear and the sun shines. But only Orr and Haber remember the previous reality before Orr's dreams transformed it.

Haber decides he must use Orr's ability for humankind's good. While Orr is under hypnosis, Haber tells Orr to dream of an elaborate institution devoted to Haber and his studies—and it happens. Next, Haber tells a sleeping Orr to dream of more room for the world, an end to overpopulation. Orr's lawyer, Heather LaLache, observes this session, and along with Haber and Orr, she sees that he has dreamed of a plague that has wiped out three quarters of the world's populace. Haber asks a sleeping Orr to dream "peace on earth," and Orr dreams of a space alien invasion to unite the world. Later, Haber tells a sleeping Orr to dream of a world without racism, "in which there is no color problem." Everyone turns gray.

Later, feeling he's done with Orr, Haber attempts to employ the power of effective dreaming for himself. Orr steps into Haber's dream and stops him, creating chaos. The resulting world appears to be a hodgepodge of Orr's dreams, such as the existence of aliens but also the effects of partial destruction—a muted version of nuclear ruin—due to, as a nurse says, "the night that everything fell apart." Haber is now mute and confined to a wheelchair, but Orr realizes Haber knows what has happened.

The Lathe of Heaven is buoyed by its feast of intriguing ideas but diminished by its famine of special effects. Costing only $250,000, the PBS telemovie couldn't effectively depict an alien invasion, relying on visuals primitive even for the time. Attempts to show dream transformations of architecture are likewise deficient, using various shots of modern buildings united with a clashing music score to suggest something grand. But the viewer may be unimpressed.

The story's dramatics are so well-done that the scarcity of spectacle only mildly

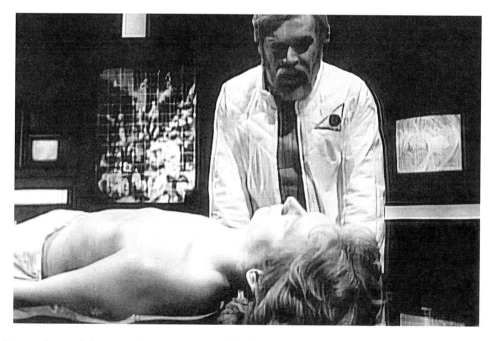

Dr. William Haber (Kevin Conway, standing) leads George Orr (Bruce Davison) into an "effective dream" in 1980's *The Lathe of Heaven* (PBS). Orr's effective dreams become reality, and Dr. Haber is obsessed with using Orr to create a better world.

damages the film. Involved with the characters of George Orr, Dr. Haber and George's girlfriend Heather LaLache, the viewer becomes mesmerized by the film's unfolding examination of consciousness, reality, ethics and the human condition. You want George Orr to "win," and he does, albeit not in the way he would have chosen.

In the movie, Haber's god-like ambitions emerge as he realizes he can harness Orr's "gift" for his own purposes. Haber assumes he has the moral and ethical maturity to remake society into a better world. His attempts to have Orr resolve overpopulation and create world peace backfire, but Haber blames Orr, not himself. The horror of six billion people dying because Orr's dream-created plague "solved" overpopulation fails to deter Haber. Like many a misguided leader drunk with self-importance and blinded by rationalization, his misdeeds multiply.

A therapist ironically in denial, he exploits Orr without guilt. Indeed, Haber's first dream request reveals his stark self-centeredness: the establishment of a magnificent, opulently appointed institution in his name.

Meanwhile, Orr wants to be rid of his god-like power. He realizes that Haber, not he, is the man with the problem. At first passively complying with Haber's manipulation, Orr eventually decries his exploitation.

Interestingly, one of Orr's dream solutions meets Haber's approval—that of "solving" racism by converting everyone's skin color to gray. But what implications would that have regarding the brutal history of racial slavery? The notion that turning everyone gray would rid the world of racism is naïve at best.

Of interest is the nuclear war environment that begins the movie. Orr, dying from radiation exposure, dreams himself out of this nightmare into an alternate reality. But near the end, Orr says everything that's happened since he dreamed himself out of the nuclear war world is a dream. The movie only vaguely follows up on this revelation, and the film doesn't end with the world in atomic shambles. Yet the story implies its opening situation may be the worst environment Orr could find himself in, one so apocalyptic and terrifying that he gladly resorts to effective dreaming to escape. Notably, he doesn't embrace most of his other effective dreams. In addition, the climactic jumble of Orr's dreams contains echoes of his nuclear nightmare, such as the huge fissures in the concrete.

Most reviews were positive. Richard Scheib said the film "treats Ursula Le Guin's book with a great deal of faithfulness. *The Lathe of Heaven* hums along with a genuine conceptual dazzle."[2]

Chris Barsanti called it "a highly cerebral affair (in an era when the commercial networks, not to mention major studios, mainly brainstormed over how to best rip off *Star Wars*)."[3]

If you allow for its low budget, *The Lathe of Heaven* is a thought-provoking science fiction film, one implying nuclear war may be the ultimate nightmare.

*   *   *

Nightmare City

DIRECTOR: Umberto Lenzi; WRITERS: Antonio Cesare Corti, Luis María Delgado, Piero Regnoli; MUSIC: Stelvio Cipriani; CINEMATOGRAPHER: Hans Burman Sanchez; EDITOR: Daniele Alabiso. PRODUCERS: Luis Méndez, Diego Alchimede. CAST: Hugo Stiglitz (Dean Miller); Laura Trotter (Dr. Anna Miller).

PRODUCTION: Dialchi Film, Lotus Films Internacional, Televicine S.A. de C.V.; Italian; 1980; released 11 December 1980 (in Italy); released 18 November 1983 (in the U.S.); 88 minutes; rated R. Alternate title: *City of the Living Dead.*

* * *

Radiation sends *Nightmare City*'s zombies into the world with the desire to drink the blood of the living, thus replenishing red blood cells. In addition, it's made them superhuman, almost indestructible. They are also smarter than the average mutant, wielding tools to kill and maim ordinary humans. But one zombie cliché remains intact: You can only stop them by shooting them through the brain.

The zombies initially burst onto the scene from a military transport plane and immediately go into slaughter mode, taking an occasional break from mutilation and mayhem to slurp a drink from a victim's gaping wounds. They overrun major portions of an Italian city and sabotage the power plant. The military appears helpless.

The movie follows a handful of characters, primarily journalist Dean Miller and Dr. Anna Miller, who have many hazardous scrapes. At the end, a helicopter attempts to rescue them from atop a roller coaster while Dean fends off zombies. Dean escapes, but Anna can't hold onto the rope and falls, dying. Of course, the movie died long before this downbeat finale.

The zombies sport some of the worst makeup ever seen in a professional horror movie; it looks like mud mixed with hair gel. Multiple closeups of the zombies' faces only call attention to the fakery. As for gore, the movie employs so much, you figure the filmmakers must have paid a fortune for stage blood. Most of the plasma pumps from humans who ineptly fight back, often just standing there screaming while a zombie sinks a meat cleaver into their neck.

In desperation, the movie fumbles for profundity in a conversation between Dean and Anna. She claims the zombies' advent is somehow part of the "human cycle," because we "create and obliterate, until we destroy ourselves." This third-rate philosophizing isn't enough to redeem this fiasco. Nor is the "It was all a dream" ending stolen from many a previous tale.

Nightmare City is rated R for good reason: The graphic violence is almost non-stop. The film doesn't have high aspirations, but due to its poor script, ham-fisted direction and crude bloodletting, it fails to meet the standards of even an average low-budget shocker.

* * *

Nuclear Run

DIRECTOR-WRITER: Ian Barry; MUSIC: Andrew Thomas Wilson; CINEMATOGRAPHER: Russell Boyd; EDITOR: Tim Wellburn; PRODUCER: David Elfick.

CAST: Steve Bisley (Larry Stilson); Arna-Maria Winchester (Carmel Stilson); Ross Thompson (Heinrich Schmidt); Ralph Cotterill (Gray); Hugh Keays-Byrne (Eagle); Patrick Ward (Oates).

PRODUCTION: Palm Beach Pictures, Film Victoria, The Australian Film Commission; Australian; 1980; not rated. Alternate title: *The Chain Reaction.*

* * *

Before we plunge into a project, concerned parties may caution us to "test the water." But in 1980's Australian-made thriller *Nuclear Run*, testing the water literally can mean the difference between life and death.

An earthquake in rural Australia causes a nuclear waste facility's pipes to burst. Scientist Heinrich Schmidt risks his life to shut off the flow, becoming fatally contaminated. With only three days to live, he warns of radiation seeping into the water table, but the facility opts to cover up the accident.

Heinrich escapes and takes refuge with a rural couple, race car driver Larry Stilson and nurse Carmel Stilson. However, he has developed amnesia and can't remember what he wanted to warn people about. The facility sends the ruthless Gray and his cohorts to find Heinrich and stop him. Anti-nuke scientist Oates races to find Heinrich as well.

Gray and his men find Heinrich, now suffering from advanced radiation poisoning. They also apprehend Larry and Carmel, who have become radioactive after swimming in a lake. Larry dons a hazmat suit, disguising his identity, and holds a gun on Gray just before he and Carmel escape in Larry's racing truck. Gray follows in a high-speed car chase ending in Gray's death.

Oates alerts the media, and a news helicopter buzzes overhead. The water table contamination cover-up has been blown wide open.

Nuclear Run paints a dark picture of both governmental and industrial authorities. The film's paranoia is almost tangible. The waste disposal company is indifferent to Heinrich's sacrifice and impending death, only wishing to cover up the truth about the contamination. If they have to waste some civilians along the way—such as the hapless telephone operator oblivious to why she is being murdered—so be it.

Gray, the company's hit man (expertly played by Ralph Cotterill), embodies the

Hazmat-suited Larry Stilson (Steve Bisley) holds a gun on ruthless corporate operative Gray (Ralph Cotterill) in 1980's *Nuclear Run* (Palm Beach Pictures et al.). Gray is determined to cover up dangerous radiation leakage that has contaminated the water table.

company's ruthlessness: He has no problem threatening to have one of his men blow off the top of Carmel's head if Larry doesn't cooperate.

The other cast members fare well. Ross Thompson imbues the confused Heinrich with vulnerability. As Carmel, his nurse, Arna-Maria Winchester is believable. Steve Bisley plays the race car hero with appropriate machismo.

The amnesia angle detracts from the thriller storyline. Amnesia in movies or TV, melodramatic as well as unlikely, is usually relegated to soap operas. The film gains nothing from making Heinrich forget the recent past.

Ominous moments abound, such as the company's technicians garbed from head to foot in white hazmat suits, faceless invaders exploring Larry and Carmel's homestead as though it were a foreign and possibly toxic world. There is also tension when Larry tosses a hideously malformed fish on the lake bank, followed by him and Carmel immersed in the water, unaware the lake water is radioactive. This foreshadows the possibility that after drinking contaminated water, hundreds or thousands of Australians will make Geiger counters crackle.

Despite the dark subject matter and the power of the forces arrayed against Heinrich, Oates, Larry and Carmel, *Nuclear Run* gives viewers an upbeat ending. Still, you wonder about Larry and Carmel's ultimate fate.

Unrated, the film includes a surprising amount of nudity of both Larry and Carmel. Seeing these characters in the buff adds nothing to the story, and apparently exists only for exploitation purposes. While the film is unrated in the U.S., the nudity, brief sex (between the married Larry and Carmel), language and violence would likely earn the film an R. It's definitely not kid-friendly.

Nuclear Run had the misfortune of coming out in 1980 after 1979's *The China Syndrome*, both movies containing similar subject matter.[4] Of course, *China Syndrome* was Hollywood "A" budget all the way, boasting popular stars Jane Fonda and Jack Lemmon and enjoying a major promotional campaign. In terms of gloss, obviously a budget-strapped Ozploitation thriller like *Nuclear Run* couldn't compete.

Reportedly, *Nuclear Run*, known as *The Chain Reaction* in Australia, received mixed reviews in its homeland. American critics Mick Martin and Marsha Porter called the movie "an engrossing drama."[5]

The Chain Reaction, or *Nuclear Run* as it's known in the U.S., is that rare 1980s nuke movie boasting a credible premise rather than a post-nuke wasteland awash in motorcycles, car crashes and leather-studded heroes.

* * *

Virus

DIRECTOR: Kinji Fukasaku; WRITERS: Koji Takada, Gregory Knapp, Kinji Fukasaku; based on the 1964 novel *Fukkatsu no hi* by Sakyo Komatsu; MUSIC: Kentarō Haneda (alternate score), Tero Macero (international version); CINEMATOGRAPHER: Daisaku Kimura; EDITOR: Akira Suzuki; PRODUCER: Haruki Kadokawa.
CAST: Masao Kusakari (Dr. Shûzô Yoshizumi); Tsunehiko Watase (Yasuo Tatsuno); Sonny Chiba (Dr. Yamauchi); Kensaku Morita (Ryûji Sanazawa); Toshiyuki Nagashima (Akimasa Matsuo); Glenn Ford (President Richardson); George Kennedy (Admiral Conway); Robert Vaughn (Senator Barkley); Chuck Connors (Captain McCloud); Bo Svenson (Major Carter); Olivia Hussey (Marit).

PRODUCTION: A Haruko Kadokawa Films Production in association with the Tokyo Broadcasting System (TBS); released in Japan by Toho on 28 June 1980; 155 minutes; not released theatrically in the U.S. but sold to cable television and released to home video: TV version runs 93 minutes; VHS version runs 108 minutes; Japanese-language version with English subtitles released to home video in 2006 at 155 minutes; rated PG. Alternate titles: *Virus: Day of Resurrection*; *Day of Resurrection*.

* * *

What's a film called *Virus* doing in a book about nuclear threat movies? Because along with its global plague, it tosses in worldwide nuclear destruction—even though the majority of that world has already died.

East German agents steal a deadly virus called MM88 from the U.S. The plane carrying the pathogen crashes in the Italian Alps. Once exposed to air, the virus, dubbed "the Italian flu," permeates Europe and the Soviet Union, killing millions. Senator Barkin (Robert Vaughn) discovers that the United States created the virus and informs the president (Glenn Ford). The forecast is grim: The virus may kill every human and every vertebrate animal on Earth.

But the virus is dormant at cold temperatures, specifically under minus 10 degrees Celsius, so President Richardson calls Antarctica's Palmer Station and advises them to stay put so they'll survive the plague. Richardson, Barkin and war hawk General Garland (Henry Silva) die, but the latter activates America's Automated Reaction System (ARS) designed to retaliate against the Soviet Union if nuclear missiles rain on America.

In Antarctica, at a gathering chaired by Admiral Conway (George Kennedy), the various international groups meet to determine how to move forward. They get a call from a Soviet sub whose men are infected with the virus; Conway regretfully tells them they cannot land in Antarctica. The sub commander ignores the order, but a British sub overseen by Captain McCloud (Chuck Connors) fires a torpedo at the Soviet sub, destroying it. Because Captain McCloud and his men have been submerged since before the plague hit, Conway invites them to join the Antarctica community.

Only 855 men and eight women number among the South Pole group. After a woman is raped, a group discusses the situation. The majority agrees that in the current situation, traditional monogamous sexual relationships are not possible. To ensure the community's survival, the council decides that each woman will sleep with multiple male partners.

Dr. Yoshizumi (Masao Kusakari), a Japanese scientist, determines that an earthquake will soon ravage North America's East Coast. This quake will set off both the American and Soviet ARS programs, which will fire nuclear missiles at predetermined targets. Antarctica's Palmer Station is one of the Soviet targets.

All eight women and several men evacuate to a deserted freighter. Yoshizumi and Major Carter (Bo Svenson) embark to Washington, D.C., to shut down the ARS; Yoshizumi's departure devastates Mirat (Olivia Hussey), for she and Yoshizumi are in love.

Captain McCloud's British sub ferries Yoshizumi and Carter to D.C. The two men give themselves an experimental plague vaccine before rushing to the ARS control center. The quake hits, resulting in Carter's death. Yoshizumi can't stop the ARS system in time, and the missiles launch.

Yoshizumi survives and, over a period of years, makes his way to the southern tip of South America. There, the women and some male survivors of the Antarctica group are living. Mirat spots Yoshizumi on the beach and rushes to greet her beloved. (What are the odds Yoshizumi would have found the Antarctica survivors? Slim to none?)

As Stuart Galbraith wrote, "*Virus* was an ill-fated attempt to enter the international market—a disaster film released just as the once popular genre was dying."[6] Toho had enjoyed two homegrown disaster movie hits in the 1970s with 1973's *Submersion of Japan*[7] and 1974's *The Great Prophecies of Nostradamus*.[8] But *Virus*, its estimated budget $16 million (then the most expensive Japanese movie to date), failed to deliver. Even worse, despite its American stars, the movie bypassed U.S. theatrical distribution, going directly to TV and later to home video.

Regarding the American cast, their presence both helps and hinders. In the latter category, Chuck Connors makes only a modest attempt at a British accent, even though he's supposed to hail from the U.K. While usually good, Connors fails to convince as the sub commander. However, the other American actors are capable. Occasionally, a scene is played badly—at one point, George Kennedy's Admiral Conway shouts, "Yes, this is stupid!" in a situation that wouldn't call for such vehemence.

Another issue with *Virus* is that both the American TV and home video versions were cut, the former running 93 minutes, the latter 108 minutes, though the original is 155 minutes. The 155-minute version with English subtitles is now officially available on *YouTube* (with ads), and this is the edition of the film interested readers should seek.

Because the movie didn't receive American theatrical distribution, few American reviews exist for the 155-minute version. However, in *Leonard Maltin's 2002 Movie & Video Guide*, Maltin gave this version of the film 2½ out of 4 stars and noted, "Beautiful sequences filmed in the Antarctic, adequate special effects, but overlong and meandering."

Under the direction of Kinji Fukasaku,[9] *Virus* strives to be an end-of-the-world epic in the same vein as 1959's nuclear threat classic *On the Beach*.[10] *Virus*'s first third meets and sometimes exceeds viewer expectations as the pathogen infects the world. The scenes in

Virus, a 1980 Haruko Kadokawa Films' production, features lethal microorganisms much as in 1979's *Plague* (see above, Group 1 Films), yet *Virus* additionally depicts a major nuclear holocaust.

Japan showing panic, disease and death seem alarmingly credible. When the Japanese Antarctica outpost makes radio contact with a five-year-old child in America, they can hear the boy, but he can't hear them. He says his father is sleeping and won't wake up, and that his mother is gone. He also reveals he has his father's gun and knows how to use it. The Japanese try desperately to reach the boy, but the next sound they hear is a gunshot. This vignette chillingly summarizes the horror and tragedy that the MM88 virus has wrought upon the world.

Another scene intended to do the same falters. The Japanese Antarctica crew discovers that the Norwegian outpost crew went crazy and shot themselves to death, with only the pregnant Mirat (Olivia Hussey) surviving. That nearly all of them would resort to suicide or homicide strains credulity.

Virus tackles some interesting social concerns. Given its age, it's intriguing how the film handles the dilemma of 855 men but only eight women. Sylvia has been raped, but the movie bypasses this crime and jumps into discussing a "new morality" due to the many males and few females. It's also telling that most of the members at this meeting are men, although granted, it's one of the women who argues that females must accommodate more than one male partner. But instead of determining who raped Sylvia, and meting out justice, Sylvia's concern is glossed over, meaning the rapist got off scot-free. A newer genre film would (and should) handle this situation differently.

Also, it's curious that all the women except Sylvia acquiesce to the notion of sleeping with multiple male partners. Hard to believe no one would resist for religious or other reasons. In fact, the movie shows the weakness of such a system by depicting Mirat's love for Yoshizumi and indifference to her latest partner.

The nuclear threat aspect of the movie may seem like an afterthought, but it does up the challenge of humankind's continued existence. It's interesting that in *Virus*, both the U.S. and U.S.S.R. have developed the ARS, an automatic means of nuclear retaliation against a first strike. Such a system would be frightening, since it could malfunction or, as in the movie, react to an earthquake rather than a nuclear attack. Any automated means of nuclear counterattack might increase the odds of a nuclear exchange actually happening, as opposed to leaving the situation in human hands.

Upon learning a Soviet ICBM is targeting Palmer Station, one of the Antarctica characters asks, "How long are we to be haunted by our past?" Apparently as long as there are still human beings.

Ironically, as another character later points out, the radiation from the global nuclear exchange has probably destroyed the MM88 virus. Indeed, while the movie ends on a hopeful note, could the small band of survivors truly perpetuate the human race? After all, the film told us the virus destroyed all vertebrate animals, which would damage worldwide ecology.

Of course, even in the 1950s and early 1960s, nuclear threat movies often ended with only a small band of survivors left to replenish the world. Examples include 1951's *Five* and 1955's *Day the World Ended*, both of which offer a post-nuked Adam and Eve to start life anew. Indeed, intentionally or not, *Virus*' finale carries on this tradition. All that's missing is a final credit reading, "There must be no end, only a new beginning."[11]

*   *   *

CHAPTER THREE

1981

Escape From New York

DIRECTOR: John Carpenter; WRITERS: John Carpenter, Nick Castle; MUSIC: John
   Carpenter in association with Alan Howarth; CINEMATOGRAPHER: Dean
   Cundey; EDITOR: Todd Ramsay; PRODUCERS: Larry Franco, Debra Hill.
CAST: Kurt Russell (Snake Plissken); Lee Van Cleef (Police Commissioner Bob Hauk);
   Ernest Borgnine (Cabbie); Donald Pleasence (President John Harker); Isaac Hayes
   (The Duke); Harry Dean Stanton (Brain); Adrienne Barbeau (Maggie).
PRODUCTION: AVCO Embassy Pictures, International Film Investors, Goldcrest
   Films International; 1981; 99 minutes; rated R.

*   *   *

No matter how gritty previous antiheroes may have been, none before *Escape from New York*'s Snake Plissken had decided to nuke the world as a prank. But no director before John Carpenter had ever cast the island of Manhattan as a maximum-security prison either.

In 1997, the president of the United States is en route to Boston for a peace summit with China and Russia, but terrorists force the plane to crash on Manhattan Island, a penitentiary populated by the dregs of society and guarded 24/7. Police Commissioner Hauk recruits war hero turned criminal Snake Plissken to rescue the president in 22 hours. If Plissken fails, micro explosives in his arteries will detonate and kill him. If Plissken completes his mission, he will receive a full pardon.

Once inside Manhattan, Plissken finds the Big Apple has become the Big Hellhole. He fends off underground psychos called "Crazies" as well as other antisocial types brandishing weapons. With the aid of the colorful characters Brain and Maggie, Plissken finds the president is being held captive by the Duke, an imperious type who rules the city and tools about in a chandelier-adorned limousine. The Duke's demand: amnesty for all inmates in return for the president.

After a plethora of bullets, blood and other action movie highlights, including a fight with a giant warrior, Plissken frees the president and delivers him to the authorities. The president will now appear remotely at the peace summit via television, and he will play a cassette tape dealing with nuclear fusion that will prevent war between the superpowers. However, Plissken has switched tapes, and the dumbfounded president finds the *American Bandstand* theme blaring over the speakers. Meanwhile, Plissken takes the real cassette and starts yanking out the tape.

Earlier, Commissioner Hauk had said that what was on the tape could mean "the

Antihero Snake Plissken (Kurt Russell) checks the timer for the micro-explosives planted inside his arteries in 1981's *Escape from New York* (AVCO Embassy Pictures). Set in 1997, the film depicts Manhattan Island as a penitentiary from which Plissken must rescue the United States president.

survival of the human race." But because Plissken's put out with The Man, he decides to give humanity the finger, nuclear annihilation–style. Some may find Plissken's prank "cool," but even in an escapist movie, letting the entire human race buy it because you're disgruntled basically pushes one from antihero to Darth Vader status.

As a sci-fi action movie, *Escape from New York* is technically adept. The production design is terrific, the action on-target. Kurt Russell does fine as the sullen Plissken, a permanent scowl on his face and in his voice. In addition, it's always great to see character actors like Lee Van Cleef (Police Commissioner Hauk) and Donald Pleasence (the president). Isaac Hayes turns in a smooth performance as the Duke. But Ernest Borgnine steals the show as Cabbie, a perennially cheerful survivor who always shows up at just the right time.

Despite all that, the movie feels empty. In fact, I have experienced this same hollow sensibility from other John Carpenter films. Perhaps the director's intent is to appear distant, dispassionate. If so, it just doesn't click with me.

But despite what I think, Carpenter has enjoyed a fan following for decades. He's probably best known for 1978's *Halloween*, arguably his most influential movie, but his other films include the cult favorites *The Thing* (1982) and *Big Trouble in Little China* (1986), both featuring Kurt Russell in the lead. In fact, 1996 saw Russell and Carpenter team again for the *Escape to New York* sequel *Escape from LA*.

Critics largely gave *Escape from New York* positive reviews. Vincent Canby called the film a "brutal, very fine-looking suspense melodrama ... [T]he film works so effectively as a warped vision of ordinary urban blight that it seems to be some kind of hallucinatory editorial."[1] Robert Greenberger gave a more nuanced review, writing, "Carpenter often makes uneven films. This one hits more than it misses."[2]

The movie is rated R for language, adult content and violence. I saw *Escape from New York* in a movie theater in 1981 and found it fairly brutal, but compared to more recent ultra-violent movies, it seems almost restrained.

* * *

For Your Eyes Only

DIRECTOR: John Glen; WRITERS: Richard Maibaum, Michael G. Wilson; MUSIC: Bill Conti; CINEMATOGRAPHER: Alan Hume; EDITOR: John Grover; PRODUCER: Albert R. Broccoli.

CAST: Roger Moore (James Bond, 007); Carole Bouquet (Melina Havelock); Topol (Milos Columbo); Lynn-Holly Johnson (Bibi); Julian Glover (Aristotle Kristatos); Cassandra Harris (Lisl); Jill Bennett (Jacoba Brink).

PRODUCTION: Eon Productions Ltd.; British; released 26 June 1981 (in the U.S.); released 24 June 1981 (in the U.K.); 127 minutes; rated PG.

* * *

James Bond and the nuclear threat were friends long before the 1980s. Three of 007's films—1964's *Goldfinger*, 1965's *Thunderball* and 1967's *You Only Live Twice*—involved permutations of nuclear peril. So given the escalating Cold War tensions in the '80s, it's no surprise the Bond series again plugged into the nuclear threat genre.

During a tongue-in-cheek pre-credits sequence, Bond's arch-enemy Blofeld tries to kill 007 in an out-of-control helicopter. Bond, played by Roger Moore, regains control of the chopper and deposits the terrified Blofeld in a nearby factory smokestack.

After the opening credits, the tone sobers up. *St. Georges*, a British ship, hits a mine and sinks off Albania. The vessel contains the Automatic Targeting Attack Communicator (ATAC), a device that controls all the Polaris nuclear missiles housed in British Polaris submarines. Whoever has the ATAC could fire missiles at any country. Naturally, both Britain and Russia want it.

Bond travels to Greece in hot pursuit, where he meets Melina Havelock, whose parents were murdered by Aristotle Kristatos, a European working for the KGB.

Bond joins forces with Milos Columbo, Kristatos' enemy. Bond and Melina visit the sunken *St. Georges* and recover the ATAC, but Kristatos steals it from them. During an exciting mountaintop monastery climax, Bond gets the ATAC back, and Columbo kills Kristatos. Unfortunately, the helicopter of KGB General Gogol chooses that moment to land. But instead of handing the ATAC over, Bond tosses it off the cliff. Hundreds of feet below, it shatters on impact.

Gogol departs empty-handed, and Bond retires with Melina for an encounter aboard her deceased father's yacht.

The fifth entry for Roger Moore, *For Your Eyes Only* is typical Bond. However, Bond's previous outing, 1979's *Moonraker*, featured elaborate outer space trappings, including an orbital space station and a battle between space Marines and bad guys; it seemed more akin to a fashionable science fiction fantasy than a traditional James Bond thriller. *For Your Eyes Only* takes a more sedate approach, relatively speaking.

To be sure, *For Your Eyes Only* includes the usual amazing stunt work, and kudos to the stunt actors performing these dangerous-looking feats. The other Bond conventions are likewise on display: exotic locations, beautiful women, sneering villains, rugged fights.[3]

The search for the ATAC makes *For Your Eyes Only* qualify as a nuke threat movie, yet you barely hear about the device or its potential for Cold War mayhem. In two other 1980s Bond entries, *Never Say Never Again* and *Octopussy*, the nuke threat is more prominent.

Some fans love Roger Moore's portrayal of Bond, some loathe it. But in *For Your Eyes Only*, Moore's usually flippant 007 barely makes an appearance. He's more restrained here than in his last few Bond entries.

Of course, Moore had cut his teeth on cloak-and-dagger derring-do while on the British TV show *The Saint* (1962–69). In the series, as Simon Templar, Moore turned on the British charm; amusingly, in a 1963 episode, the character pretended he *was* James Bond.[4] Moore's strengths of suavity and humor on *The Saint* likewise became his strengths as James Bond, a role he essayed seven times, starting in 1973 with *Live and Let Die*.

Reviews of *For Your Eyes Only* are mostly favorable. *The New York Times'* Vincent Canby called the film "a slick entertainment." *Starlog Science-Fiction Video Magazine* #1 said, "The producers took a big chance this time, dumping the standard 'supervillain with plans of world domination' plotline…. A welcome, and long overdue, return to what made Bond films great."[5]

For Your Eyes Only ends with a gag involving a parrot on the phone with Margaret Thatcher (Janet Brown), but she thinks it's James Bond. Thatcher thanks Bond and says, "Meanwhile, if there's anything I can do for you…" to which the parrot responds, "Give us a kiss. Give us a kiss." It's a silly bit, one that seems light years removed from the ATAC falling into the wrong hands. But then, that's 007 cinema for you.

* * *

Malevil

DIRECTOR: Christian de Chalonge; WRITERS: Christian de Chalonge, Pierre Dumayet; based on the 1972 novel *Malevil* by Robert Merle; MUSIC: Gabriel Yared; CINEMATOGRAPHER: Jean Penzer; EDITOR: Henri Lanoë; PRODUCER: Claude Nedjar.

CAST: Michel Serrault (Emmanuel Comte); Jacques Dutronc (Colin); Jean-Louis Trintignant (Fulbert); Jacques Villeret (Momo); Robert Dhéry (Peyssou); Hanns Zischler (Le vétérinaire); Pénélope Palmer (Evelyne); Jean Leuvrais (Bouvreuil).

PRODUCTION: Anthea Film, France 2 (FR2), Les Films Gibé; released 13 May 1981 (in France); 120 minutes; French. Alternate title: *Malevil—Die Bombe ist gefallen*.

* * *

What's the first nuclear war movie that comes to mind? If you're an American, it's probably a film in which the characters speak English. The likelihood you thought of a movie spoken in French? Remote. But 1981's *Malevil* is just that: a 1980s nuclear threat movie made by Europeans, specifically the French and German. But while the language may be different, the issues remain the same.

In rural France, Emmanuel Comte (Michel Serrault), the mayor of the small village of Malevil, has invited guests into his wine cellar to sample his current vintage. Just as the wine imbibing starts, the power goes out. There's a deep, rumbling noise, and the earth shakes. The sound becomes deafening, followed by intense heat. A man from above stumbles down the stairs and tumbles to the floor, dead. His clothes are scorched, his face fried. The heat becomes so intense that Emmanuel and his guests pass out.

When everyone in the cellar revives, the mentally challenged Momo (Jacques Villeret) runs outside to find his dog. The landscape, formerly lush and green, is now a mass of scorched earth, and most of Emmanuel's castle house has been demolished. No one says it, but Emmanuel and the others realize a nuclear explosion has taken place, and by implication, a full-scale nuclear war.

The grandmother (Marianne Wischmann) searches for Momo, to no avail. However, someone has stolen Malevil's mare and made off with a pig. Emmanuel and Colin (Jacques Dutronc) find the culprit: none other than Momo, now living in a cave to care for Evelyne (Pénélope Palmer), a young girl blinded by the blast. Emmanuel and Colin return to Malevil with Momo and Evelyne.

Food is scarce, but there are two positive signs: the arrival of honeybees and the birth of a male calf. Water is running low until there's a rainstorm. One character places a camera in the rain, then takes it inside to examine the film; if it is clear, there is no radioactivity. The film is clear, and Emmanuel and his friends celebrate.

Emmanuel and Colin discover strangers raiding their wheat crop and shoot three of them. They spy a nearby train tunnel housing more survivors. Mr. Director (Jean-Louis Trintignant) controls this group, which resembles a religious cult. Cathy (Jacqueline Parent) flees from the tunnel to Malevil, telling them the Director is a monster. Malevil trades milk with the Director for needed medicine. Next, the Director will trade batteries for a pig. The Director insists on Cathy coming back, but she refuses. Malevil is ready to protect her, to which the Director says, "You want war?"

Emmanuel says, "No."

The exchange is made of batteries for a pig.

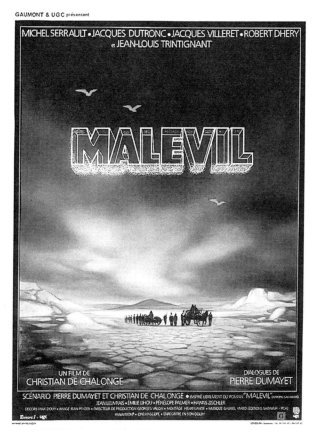

Movie poster for 1981's French-made *Malevil* (Anthea Film) depicting a desolate post–World War III France in which a handful of survivors struggle to stay alive. The movie is based on the best-selling novel *Malevil* by Robert Merle.

The tunnel's combatants attack Malevil, presumably to forcibly take Cathy back to the Director. During the firefight, a tunnel soldier shoots and kills the chemist (Jean Leuvrais), for whom Momo grieves. After the Malevil troops retreat, Emmanuel and Colin encounter survivors who tell them that the Director's plan is to defeat Emmanuel and his forces, then occupy Malevil.

Two survivors take Emmanuel at gunpoint into the tunnel. The Director falls for the scam, and soon Malevil forces rush into the tunnel, but don't have to fire a shot. When the Director belittles the death of a prisoner named Jose, Emmanuel shoots and kills the tyrant.

The people of the tunnel return with Emmanuel and his friends to Malevil. There, life appears to be improving. But out of nowhere, helicopters buzz over Malevil. A loudspeaker tells Emmanuel and his companions, "Regroup quickly for evacuation! Don't take anything with you! You must board immediately!"

The choppers land and the citizens of Malevil climb into them. Once in flight, a loudspeaker tells the Malevil folks, "We are happy to have found you! By an international decision, the destroyed nations' territories are declared uninhabitable zones! These territories will be used for military experiments!" The speaker also tells them that they will be taken to a decontamination center where they will undergo pertinent examinations, presumably of a medical nature.

However, three Malevil folk have chosen not to evacuate inside the choppers and are instead sailing a raft down a river.

If I had to use one term to describe *Malevil*, it would be "low-key." Though concerning a highly important subject, the film resists calling attention to itself: no flashy special effects, no shaky hand-held camera, no atomic sermonizing. Director Christian de Chalonge apparently wanted the subject matter, not the direction, to receive the spotlight.

The actors believably embody their characters. Jacques Villeret imbues the mentally challenged Momo with life. Michel Serrault maintains an even keel as the mayor, a leader called to make difficult decisions in an increasingly difficult world.

Interestingly, none of the characters specifically mentions nuclear war. At one point, Colin asks, "How long since it happened?" But the "it" remains unidentified. In all likelihood, once the Malevil wine basement dwellers recovered from the blast's sound, motion and heat, they would discuss what had happened and determine it had to have been a nuclear blast, presumably meaning a nuclear war had occurred. But the film skirts any such direct dialogue, perhaps to avoid being obvious or preachy.

Also of interest is that we never hear any of the characters talk about knuckling under. In most nuclear threat movies, one of the subthemes is that those who died in the initial blast were the lucky ones. Obviously, the Malevil folks aren't enjoying a summer vacation in the Bahamas, but they carry on, suggesting a theme of resilience over defeatism, maybe even a duty to survive.

Though we see no nuclear explosions, the production design of Malevil's blasted countryside chills as effectively as a horde of mushroom clouds. Gray, bleak and ruined, the landscape suggests a garden tended in Hell. One nice touch has Colin coming upon a half-buried car caked in grime. Likewise, the scorched and broken walls of Malevil display nuclear blight.

One failing of the film is its handling of radiation, specifically the initial fallout. Momo races outside to find his dog, and other Malevil folks wander out into the fallout. Despite this, neither Momo nor anyone else succumbs to radiation sickness. Also, the soil would be irradiated, yet the Malcvil characters have no problem planting and harvesting wheat.

Malevil mostly, but not entirely, eschews physical unpleasantness. For example, shortly after the blast, we do see the scorched face of a blast victim. Likewise, dead horses dot the landscape. But otherwise, *Malevil* relies on the story and its milieu to get across the grim aftermath of nuclear war. For example, the character Evelyne was blinded by an atomic blast, but when she regains her sight, she realizes her mother is dead and breaks down weeping.

Some may find the film's tempo during the middle third too slow. Tightening would have helped. But the movie is well worth watching despite the slow patches.

Malevil's most startling aspect is its ending. Helicopters appear from nowhere to evacuate Malevil's folks to presumably greener, non-nuclear pastures. But prior to this finale, the movie seemed to have already ended with the tunnel people and Malevil folks uniting. Also, the chopper ending leaves many unanswered questions:

Where did the helicopters come from? Somewhere in France? Did the U.N. send them? The chopper loudspeakers tell of "destroyed nations' territories." Who are these destroyed nations? Presumably America and Russia, but who else? France and the rest of Europe? And what kind of "military experiments" will be conducted in these radioactively devastated areas?

Amazon Prime currently offers the movie for rent. That version is subtitled in English. And should subtitles make you squirm in horror, remember: For good films, they're almost always preferable to English dubbing. And they don't take long to get used to. Honest.

Despite its occasionally poky pace, *Malevil* ranks with the better nuclear threat movies of the 1980s. Too bad there's not a sequel to resolve that odd ending, though.

*   *   *

Message from the Future

DIRECTOR-WRITER: David Avidan; MUSIC: Jacob Goldstein; CINEMATOGRAPHER: Amnon Salomon; EDITOR: Ludmila Goliath; PRODUCER: Jacob Kotzky.
CAST: Joseph Bee (FM, Future Man); Avi Yakir (Dr. Dan Ziv-Avi); Irit Meiri (Shelly); Kiichi Sasayama (Miroshi Nabeshima); David Avidan (FM's Superior).
PRODUCTION: Thirteenth Century Films, Jacob Kotzky Productions; Israeli; 1981; 81 minutes; not rated. Alternate title: *A Message from the Future.*

*   *   *

In *Message from the Future*, FM (Future Man) declares, "I am the present. I am the past. I am the salesman." And that's some of the better dialogue.

The film's premise is intriguing: FM time travels from 3005 to 1985 hoping to convince world leaders to start World War III, thus ensuring a better future for humankind. But the movie's execution is horrendous.

After the introduction of FM and his time travel mission, the film switches to a sequence in which a Japanese businessman displays hi-tech robots fighting a speeded-up martial arts match. This impresses his peers.

The movie proceeds at a disjointed clip, zooming here, there and nowhere. Along the way, we witness plenty of (unnecessary) sexual gymnastics between Dr. Ziv and his girlfriend Shelly.

We also see Israel's first official nuclear weapons test; a blackout in New York City and Moscow; a red alert declared by Russia and America; a religious cult whose members strip and wade into the ocean; FM causing major world newspapers to announce his image and mission on the front page; FM zapping two NBC news anchors; a rock group blaring the anthem "Radioactivity"; and a telepathic meeting between FM and world representatives at the U.N. The movie links these episodes poorly, at best.

The movie is unrated; the abundant nudity and sexual activity would net it an R, possibly an X. And most of the nudity objectifies the woman. Of course, nudity doesn't have to devalue women, but here it does.

The movie makes everyone look like idiots. The U.N. scene, in which the representatives start chanting "FM" as though at a pep rally, and then FM leads them in a telepathic chant of "W," becomes mind-numbing.

To their credit, the actors try to make sense of the story and their mostly hopeless dialogue. In addition, the film moves well and, given its low budget, does what it can in the art direction and setting departments. In fact, it resembles low-budget science fiction from the '60s such as 1967's *Journey to the Center of Time*.

Despite the movies' premise, FM's interesting stance ("All wars were started too late") is barely explored. Why would we in 1985 be better off if we started World War III? Apparently, we wouldn't be, but people dozens of years from now would. You can assume the longer the wait for a major nuclear war, perhaps the greater destruction caused due to advancements in nuke-delivery weapons systems and such. But alas, the film doesn't go there.

Dr. Maciej Pietrzak argues that while *Message from the Future* may be lacking in terms of technical expertise, it can be seen as a significant commentary on Israel in the early 1980s.[6] Part of that plays out in the enthusiasm with which the movie greets the success of Israel's first official nuclear test. Instead of fearful, the film's spirit is giddy regarding nuclear weapons. Even World War III doesn't seem off-limits. Still, this fails to explain the "surprise" ending: We learn that FM is actually just a salesman, part of a publicity gimmick staged by a Japanese businessman to hawk the latter's tamp, an electronic device that allows telepathy. But if that's the case, what about all those future things we saw? An attempt to convince the salesman FM that he really was from the future?

Even if Dr. Pietrzak's thesis about the movie shining a light on Israel's geopolitics of the early 1980s is valid, it doesn't mitigate the film's weaknesses. Yet even on its own terms, some seem to like it. For example, on the Internet Movie Database, ratings based on 46 users give the film 5.5 out of 10.

Close to the end of *Message from the Future*, FM holds one hand palm up, fingers splayed, and says, "You don't need more than five fingers to control a solar system, even a galaxy." Then he holds the other hand palm out, fingers splayed, and says, "You don't need more than ten to control the universe." He forgot to add that you don't need more than one to press the off button.

*　＊　＊*

The Road Warrior

DIRECTOR: George Miller; WRITERS: Terry Hayes, George Miller and Brian Hannant; MUSIC: Brian May; CINEMATOGRAPHER: Dean Semler; EDITORS: David Stiven with Tim Wellburn and Michael Balson; PRODUCER: Byron Kennedy.

CAST: Mel Gibson (Mad Max); Bruce Spence (The Gyro Captain); Emil Minty (The Feral Kid).

PRODUCTION: Kennedy Miller Productions; Australian; released 24 December 1981 (in Australia); released 6 May 1982 (in the U.S.); 96 minutes; rated R. Alternate title: *Mad Max 2*.

* * *

The Road Warrior (known as *Mad Max 2* outside the U.S.) set the standard for 1980s post-apocalyptic action movies.

Following a global war that has left the world in shambles, Max (Mel Gibson), a former police officer, roams the Australian wastelands in his supercharged car searching for gas, a scarce commodity. Max clashes with the Gyro Captain, who in exchange for his life shows Max a guarded oil factory. Marauders led by Lord Humungus regularly besiege the installation.

A group of marauders raid cars that have left the factory, and Max brings the one car survivor back to the oil facility. The survivor dies. Marauders attack the facility, and at the end of the assault, Lord Humungus gives the Factory Folk (FF) one day to decide whether to leave the refinery on foot or suffer death at the marauders' hands.

Max tells the FF about a semi-truck he saw earlier which they can use to drive their petrol supply to a place hundreds of miles away. He offers to bring them the truck if they will return his car along with gas. The Gyro Captain takes Max to the truck's location,

An angry Mad Max (Mel Gibson) glares at all comers in 1981's *The Road Warrior* (aka *Mad Max 2*). To his left stands the Feral Kid (Emil Minty), whom Max protects in the film's post-apocalyptic wasteland.

and though Max encounters the Marauders, he gets the truck to the guarded oil factory. He refuses to drive the truck for the FF and instead takes his car and leaves.

Marauders force his car off the road, wrecking it. A Marauder who tries to get gas from Max's mangled auto sets off the car's booby trap, and the vehicle explodes. Via his gyrocopter, the Gyro Captain flies Max to the oil factory. Given the turn of events, the injured Max offers to drive the truck for the FF. Papagallo, the FF leader, accepts his offer.

Max barrels the truck forward while FF autos wait and drive off in smaller vehicles. The parentless Feral Kid has taken a shine to Max and goes with him. When the Marauders attack Max's truck, several FF are killed, including Papagallo. Lord Humungus and the insane Wez die as well. But it turns out the FF carted the gas in oil drums inside their own vehicles, filling the semi tanker with sand.

The Gyro Captain leads the FF and the Feral Kid north. There, the narrator tells us, the Feral Kid became a tribal chief—and that in fact the narrator is the Feral Kid grown up. He says he never again saw Max.

The Road Warrior's filmmakers take the sketchy post-apocalyptic world of 1979's *Mad Max* and enrich it, largely through the opening narration which details society's collapse. Still, the movie offers a vision of the future that is stripped down and uncluttered, one perfect for the various low-budget clones that followed. In addition, *The Road Warrior* established the "look" of post-nuke action movie characters, i.e., studded leather.

Max's characterization is also enhanced from his 1979 portrayal. He remains hard, taciturn and grim, but shows softening around the edges. He carts a mutt called Dog around with him (eventually shot by a Marauder), and he gives the Feral Kid a music box. Though Max attempts to shoo the Feral Kid away, the tyke develops an attachment to the Road Warrior, perhaps sensing the damaged human being hiding behind the tight-lipped swagger.

The film's major attraction is the high-octane action, peppered with amazing (and dangerous) stunt work. This was long before CGI relegated practical effects to the Stone Age. Some critics consider the movie a template for action filmmakers.

Reviews for *The Road Warrior*, both at the time of its release and more recently, are positive. Rotten Tomatoes gives the movie a 94 percent fresh rating based on 53 professional reviews. As just one example from yesteryear, *Starlog Science-Fiction Video Magazine* #1 called the film a "vastly entertaining job well done by everyone."[7]

The Feral Kid may howl like a dog and grunt like an animal, but you may still find him cute. But at least it's the real deal and not a prefab Teletubbies cute.

*   *   *

CHAPTER FOUR

1982

The Aftermath

DIRECTOR-WRITER-PRODUCER-EDITOR: Steve Barkett; MUSIC: John W. Morgan; CINEMATOGRAPHERS: Dennis Skotak, Tom Denove.

CAST: Steve Barkett (Newman); Lynne Margulies (Sarah); Sid Haig (Cutter); Christopher Barkett (Chris); Alfie Martin (Getman); Forrest J Ackerman (Museum Curator); Jim Danforth (Williams).

PRODUCTION: Nautilus Film Company; 1982; rated R. Alternate title: *Zombie Aftermath*.

* * *

As director-writer-producer-editor-star of *The Aftermath*,[1] Steve Brackett embodies independent filmmaker moxie. Unfortunately, his movie suffers from multiple shortcomings.

The nuclear ruins of Los Angeles as depicted in 1982's *The Aftermath* (Nautilus Film Company). Special effects were provided by Robert and Dennis Skotak, who went on to work on bigger-budgeted films such as 1986's *Aliens*, 1989's *The Abyss* and 1991's *Terminator 2: Judgment Day*.

When three American astronauts splash down on Earth, one of them is killed. After the remaining two, Newman and Mathews, are attacked by mutants, they discover the ruins of Los Angeles. Newman finds a dead broadcaster and plays the man's tape, which reveals a double whammy hit the world: nuclear holocaust and biological warfare. Bioweapons created the mutants (the broadcaster called them "mindless, battered monsters"). The mutants will devour humans without a second thought.

Newman and Mathews take refuge in an abandoned mansion. Newman decides he must find out what's "out there," while homebody Mathews stays put. Entering a museum, Newman meets its curator and a young boy, Chris. The curator reveals he will die soon, so Newman takes Chris under his wing.

Newman and Chris are fired upon from a nearby building. Newman overwhelms the shooter and learns that her name is Sarah. She has escaped from Cutter, a ruthless overlord of outlaws who spend their time shooting, torturing and raping innocents. Sarah joins Newman and Chris, and soon she and Newman are romantically involved. While Sarah, Mathews and the freed captives wait in their hideout, Newman takes Chris to get supplies.

Newman returns to find Mathews unconscious and Sarah and the other two females murdered. Newman peels out to stop Cutter and his gang. He dispatches most of Cutter's outlaws; Mathews arrives to help, but Cutter's No. 2 man murders him. Newman tracks No. 2 down and slowly kills him.

Cutter finds Newman and young Chris leaving town. He shoots Newman several times. Chris sneaks up behind the outlaw overlord and shoots and kills him. Newman imparts a few last words to Chris, then dies. Alone, Chris walks down the desert road leading to who knows where.

Astronaut Newman (Steve Barkett) prepares to deliver post-apocalyptic justice in 1982's *The Aftermath*. Barkett not only starred in the low-budget exploitation film, but also produced, wrote, directed and edited.

The Aftermath can't overcome its budgetary constraints. Robert and Dennis Skotak's matte paintings are excellent, but budget-crunching taints almost everything else. The acting is variable as well. Steve Barkett certainly doesn't resemble the usual action hero, yet in some ways, his Everyman looks help. However, the final battle between Newman and Cutter's men goes on too long and fails to convince. Could one man take out all these bad guys single-handedly?

In addition, Barkett apparently wants to embrace two disparate audiences. The family-friendly side of the movie shows Barkett interacting gently with Chris (played by his real-life son) and becoming the boy's mentor. Barkett embodies kindness and sensitivity in these scenes, showing that manliness consists of more than gun-toting proficiency.

On the other squib, the exploitation side of the movie includes, among other things, needless nudity, ugly sexual violence and over-the-top gore. Barkett perhaps hoped these scenes would satisfy exploitation fans who might roll their eyes during the wholesome interludes. In turn, he seemed to hope family-friendly enthusiasts would shut their eyes during the film's graphic scenes.

Certain story aspects appear pointless. The mutants don't add anything to the plot. Sarah uses a laser gun at one point, then it is quickly forgotten.

Fans of the magazine *Famous Monsters of Filmland* (the 1958–82 version) will appreciate Forrest J Ackerman's turn as the museum curator. Though not delivering an Oscar-caliber performance, Ackerman is sincere, and it's interesting to see and hear him while he was still relatively young.

In addition, classic genre fans may get a kick out of seeing Jim Danforth portray the astronaut who dies early in the film. Danforth was an expert at stop-motion animation (which CGI has since superseded), and his efforts can be seen in *Jack the Giant Killer*, *The Wonderful World of the Brothers Grimm* (both 1962), *7 Faces of Dr. Lao* (1964) and *When Dinosaurs Ruled the Earth* (1970).

Sid Haig delivers another first-rate villain as Cutter. No nuance here, just 100 percent meanness. Haig appeared in numerous genre films from the '60s through the 21st century, and passed away in 2021.

Aftermath reviews were mixed, tending towards the negative. James O'Neill wrote, "Dull, unimaginative direct-to-video cheapie."[2] But John Stanley called it a "well-directed-and-edited post-holocaust adventure … a bravura piece of filmmaking."[3]

Steve Barkett worked on a number of other low-budget films during the '80s and '90s. For example, he directed, wrote and starred in 1990's *Empire of the Dark*. On other movies, he toiled in a number of additional capacities, such as stunts and special effects.

The Aftermath shows that life after The Bomb stinks—not exactly headline news—but despite occasional attempts at sincerity, the movie remains basic exploitation fodder.

* * *

Deadline

DIRECTOR: Arch Nicholson; WRITER: Walter Halsey Davis; MUSIC: Brian May; CINEMATOGRAPHER: David Gribble; EDITOR: David Huggett; PRODUCER: Hal McElroy.

CAST: Barry Newman (Barney Duncan); Bill Kerr (William Ashby); Trisha Noble (Gillian Boles); Alwyn Kurts (Jack McGinty); Bruce Spence (Towie).

PRODUCTION: Hanna-Barbera Australia, New South Wales Film Corporation, National Nine Television Network of Australia; Australian; released 2 June 1982 (in Australia); 94 minutes; made-for-TV; in America, released in 1984 by Goodtimes/ Worldvision Home Video.

*   *   *

In 1982's *Deadline*, Australia's National Security Adviser says this about the possibility of an A-bomb exploding in Sydney: "I don't believe there's any threat at all." Of course, the audience knows better and wonders when the Australian authorities will wise up.

An atomic explosion rocks the outback of Western South Wales, the work of extortionists who have set an A-bomb to go off in Sydney if they don't get $100 million in cocaine, heroin and used unmarked currency within 24 hours. The authorities estimate loss of life would be half a million instantly, one million within weeks, and another million due to cancer; evacuation poses problems as well, with a projection of panic deaths in the thousands. National Security Adviser Ashby says the authorities will pay the ransom and keep a lid on the story.

American reporter Barney Duncan investigates a supposed earthquake and discovers that a nuclear explosion caused it. He takes Old Alf, a witness to the explosion, to the Department of Nuclear Medicine. The doctor determines that Old Alf is dying from radiation poisoning. Barney learns that the bomb came not from the government, but from do-it-yourselfers.

When Ashby discovers that Barney knows about the outback explosion, he orders that the reporter be stopped. Barney and his colleague Gillian Boles seek the help of Towie, a computer specialist who finds the address from which the plutonium for the home-made bomb came.

The extortionists order the government to deliver the ransom to an airplane hangar. The authorities comply, and the extortionists take flight. By chance, birds (shades of Alfred Hitchcock) fly near the getaway aircraft, and despite the pilot's attempts to avoid them, the plane crashes into the sea. The Australian authorities don't know this.

Barney and Gillian break into the house of a scientist involved with the home-made bomb and find the device's plans—and the scientist's corpse. Further, they determine that two A-bombs were made, meaning there is one in Sydney that will explode in hours.

After outsmarting two government agents, Barney and Gillian hightail it back to Towie, who processes photos of the scientist's work room. Towie finds the access code to get to the bomb by its phone number, which gives the address where the bomb is located.

Barney, Gillian and Towie rush to a high-rise office containing the bomb, and with only three minutes and 31 seconds before detonation, Towie sets about deactivating the device. However, two armed government agents intrude. One of them shoots Towie, but Barney is able to cut a wire and deactivate the bomb with two seconds to spare.

Ashby orders Barney not to print the story (no doubt fearing it would ruin him and the prime minister), but Barney asserts the public has the right to know. The film ends with Barney and Gillian celebrating their victory with their editor.

Although Australian-produced, *Deadline* has the look and feel of an American made-for-TV movie of the '70s or '80s. The film is competent, and the finale generates tension. Featuring American actor Barry Newman in the lead as Barney is curious; Duncan's nationality has nothing to do with the story, and you assume an Australian actor could have played the part just as well.

Newman has appeared on a number of TV shows as well as movies, both theatrical and made-for-TV. Perhaps his best-known TV work was for the NBC series *Petrocelli* (1974–1976), in which he played a lawyer in an Arizona town. As for theatrical movies, among others, he starred in 1971's cult film *Vanishing Point*. Not to be overlooked is his stage work, nor his nominations for an Emmy and Golden Globe.

As for the film's characters, they are basically stock with a few added dimensions. For example, Duncan is a hard-drinking, hard-driving American reporter who sleeps around but also maintains a fierce fidelity to the truth. Old Alf is a rural victim of the outback nuclear explosion, the sacrificial innocent. We're not surprised, but nevertheless saddened, to hear he will soon die. (What about his dog, left in the car? You assume it dies too, but the movie doesn't say.)

Ashby is clearly a hardcase, looking out for the government's reputation at all costs. Still, he demonstrates ethical limits; tellingly, he does not order that Barney and Gillian be shot, and at film's end, he doesn't have them arrested on trumped-up charges.

The extortionists' fate is unexpected; you don't figure birds—our fine feathered friends—will cause the plane to crash. This demise doesn't satisfy, however, as seeing the authorities arrest the hooligans would have been more appealing.

Reviews of *Deadline* are scarce, but a September 18, 2021, review from *Missionaries of the Sacred Heart* asserted, "While the style of the film is that of the telemovie and the suspense is that of the popular novel, the issues, especially in the light of the 21st century war against terrorism, more real than might have been expected at the time."[4]

By 1982, nuclear extortion had rarely been explored in movies, and rarer still in a non–American film. A nuclear explosion in a major city like Sydney would shock the world, as this would be the first use of nuclear weapons against a civilian population since the 1945 A-bombings of Hiroshima and Nagasaki. Such nuclear nightmares are best left to our sleep.

*   *   *

The Final Option

DIRECTOR: Ian Sharp; WRITERS: Reginald Rose (screenplay), George Markstein (story); MUSIC: Roy Budd; CINEMATOGRAPHER: Phil Meheux; EDITOR: John Grover; PRODUCER: Euan Lloyd.

CAST: Lewis Collins (Captain Peter Skellen); Judy Davis (Frankie Leith); Richard Widmark (Secretary of State Arthur Currie); Edward Woodward (Commander Powell); Robert Webber (General Ira Potter).

PRODUCTION: Richmond Light Horse Productions, Varius Entertainment Trading AG; produced in 1982; British; released in the U.S. on 16 September 1983; 125 minutes; rated R. Alternate title: *Who Dares Wins*.

*   *   *

The Final Option's title serves a dual purpose: both the final option for anti-nuke terrorists who want to bring about nuclear disarmament, and the final option for the authorities who must save the terrorists' hostages.

The government makes it appear that Captain Peter Skellen has gone too far, and thus dismisses him from the Special Air Service (SAS). This allows him to infiltrate the People's Lobby, an anti-nuke group whose leaders are planning a terrorist act. Once he develops a romantic relationship with People's Lobby leader Frankie Leith, she lets him join the group, believing his SAS knowledge will be helpful.

Posing as members of a band, the terrorists crash a dinner party at the American ambassador's house and take everyone hostage. Frankie tells Commander Powell that the government must nuke the Holy Loch Submarine Base within 18 hours or the terrorists will kill the dinner party's guests, including the American Secretary of State.

To ensure that Skellen doesn't betray them, Frankie has ordered People's Lobby operatives to hold his wife and young child hostage. Skellen appears to be helping Frankie, but he's also doing what he can to aid the authorities, who send SAS operatives to kill the terrorists. They successfully carry out this mission. Elsewhere, government operatives rescue Skellen's wife and child.

Apparently, the Iranian Embassy Siege in London in 1980 inspired *The Final Option* (known as *Who Dares Wins* in England). Six terrorists took over the embassy and said that if their demands were not met, they would kill the hostages. They did murder one hostage, after which the SAS moved in and rescued the others. Live television carried this event. In England, it made the SAS famous.[5]

In *The Final Option*, the SAS appear in fictional mode, perfect since the film is a political thriller mixed with action motifs. The pace is brisk, and most of the incidents seem plausible. Judy Davis gives an excellent performance as the terrorist leader who falls for Skellen. She shows real nuance regarding her relationship with Skellen, wanting to believe even at the last that he is on the People's Lobby's side.

One might argue that Skellen seduces Frankie a bit too easily. Given that Skellen is married and has a child, his affair with Frankie also raises ethical questions. How far should a government operative go to complete a mission? Deceit and willingness to kill seem to come with the territory (and we've seen those in plenty of movies), but adultery appears a bit more personal, and on a relationship level, troubling. The movie suggests that Skellen has developed feelings for Frankie when he confronts her at the end, for both pause while looking at each other. An SAS soldier shoots her; Skellen lingers following her death. Skellen and Frankie share no final dialogue.

To its credit, the film's opening establishes that most anti-nuke protesters are not terrorists. In real life, terrorists' demands are usually unreasonable, but the terrorists' demands in *The Final Option* that the authorities nuke a submarine base is absurd. How could the terrorists have thought that the government would order this? That means the terrorists would have slaughtered the dinner guests, which would hardly do much to champion the cause of nuclear disarmament. This would infuriate most of the public and cast a shadow upon legitimate anti-nuke efforts.

Politics appears to have played a part in some critic's appraisals. Because of its conservative viewpoint, some liberals abhor it. *The Boston Globe*'s Michael Blowen called the movie "one of the year's worst films from the most reactionary planks in the Republican platform." He added that those who enjoy it "are those whose idea of a fun evening involves dramatic readings from the classified ads of the periodical *Guns and Ammo*."[6]

On the other hand, Mick Martin and Marsha Porter praised the movie as a "first-rate British-made suspense thriller."[7]

In *The Final Option*, the viewer never really believes the hostages will be killed, much less that the authorities will fire a nuclear missile at a submarine base. Had the terrorists' demands been scaled down, perhaps the film would have generated more tension. But making the nuclear terrorism too real might have soured the audience—or scared them witless.

* * *

Future War 198X

DIRECTORS: Toshio Masuda, Koji Katsubota; WRITER: Kōji Takada; MUSIC: Yokoyama Yuko; CINEMATOGRAPHERS: Hisao Shirai, Michiyo Terao; EDITORS: Yasuhiro Yoshikawa, Yutaka Chikura; PRODUCER: Saburo Yokoi.

CAST: All voice actors: Kin'ya Kitaōji (Mikumo Wataru); Masako Natsume (Laura Gains); Keiichi Noda (Professor Brown); Hidekatsu Shibata (Burt Gains); Yoshio Kaneuchi (President Gibson); Osamu Kobayashi (Secretary of State Girard); Tamio Ōki (Chairman of the Joint Chiefs of Staff McCoy)

PRODUCTION: A Toei Company/Toei Animation film; Japanese; released 30 October 1982 (in Japan); 125 minutes. Alternate title: *Future War 1986; Future War 198X Year.*

* * *

Budgets, by necessity, hamper live-action nuclear war movies. But animated nuclear war films suffer no such economic constraints, a truth borne out in Toei's animated Japanese *Future War 198X.*

In an undisclosed year in the 1980s, Russia kidnaps the American inventor of an orbital antimissile laser defense weapon and puts him in a submarine. To keep the Soviets from prying weapons information from the inventor, America's President Gibson has the Russian submarine destroyed.

In Russia, Defense Minister Bugarin, a hardliner, beefs up forces in East Germany and destroys an American reconnaissance satellite. An East German defector asks for asylum in West Germany, so Russia uses conventional means to kill the pilot. World War III is officially on. The Soviets invade Iran, Saudi Arabia and Oman to capture the countries' oil reserves.

Soviet jets attack Tokyo. America invades Cuba. A Soviet submarine launches nuclear missiles on the U.S., so President Gibson launches a nuclear strike against Russia. Defense Minister Bugarin sends more ICBMs America's way. Between 15 and 20 million lives are lost.

President Gibson orders the launching of four satellite laser defense systems. Bugarin hurls even more ICBMs at America, but the U.S. laser defense systems take them out. All but one of the U.S. defense systems is destroyed.

As a result of a spontaneous peace movement, some of the Russian and Warsaw Pact soldiers desert. After Bugarin is killed, there's hope that Russia and America will lead the world from war to peace.

From the get-go, *Future War 198X* intrigues because it's a Japanese film dealing primarily with Cold War era America and Russia. The filmmakers take a pragmatic view of the leadership of both countries, yet the Soviet Union seems the more threatening of the two, primarily because of hardline Defense Minister Bugarin, who presses for a nuclear war while the more moderate General Secretary Orlov argues against it. America's President Gibson seems confident but wary, not trusting Russia. But neither he nor Orlov seem anxious to engage in a war.

Interestingly, the film makes clear that America's greatest interests lie in Europe, not in Asia. Once the war starts, the movie shows that because American military forces have to concentrate in Europe and the Middle East, Japan is left on its own. Arguably, in the 1980s, Japan perhaps viewed itself as "collateral damage" if World War III should occur. *Future War 198X* is based in part on General Sir John Hackett's 1982 novel *The Third World War: The Untold Story*, so this explains its accent on the West rather than the East.

The movie's animation snares attention. The nuclear explosions are stylized but are no less spectacular for it. Destruction of cities is vivid, and the color schemes—the city's dark night scenes followed by brilliant explosions—provide a startling contrast. However, the city destruction could have been less stylized and more detailed. For example, one effective scene shows nuclear heat melting the Eiffel Tower, and these kinds of graphic depictions should have been seen in every major city that got nuked. The war scenes themselves largely depict tanks and jets in combat and become somewhat repetitious, and we don't see many ground troops.

Most of the music score complements the on-screen visuals. But an unnecessary and out-of-place pop song (sporting typical love ballad lyrics) caps the movie, about as appropriate as having Hanson's "MMMBop" cap *Saving Private Ryan*.

For better or worse, *Future War 198X* attempts to leaven its straightforward war plot with two romantic relationships, one between Wataru and Laura, the other between the lesser-seen Michael and Marina. Both end dramatically, one in tragedy, one in hope.

Story-wise, the film blends science fiction with science fact, and even trails into fantasy territory. The film's orbital missile laser defenses echo the Reagan Administration's 1980s Strategic Defense Initiative—dubbed "Star Wars"—which never saw realization. But in the film, these laser defenses play a key role in mitigating nuclear destruction in the United States.

As for the fantasy element, near the film's end, spontaneous civilian demonstrations against war break out. In addition, many soldiers abandon their weapons. This occurs after we see people praying in a church and hear a minister invoke God to turn people's consciences from war to peace, ending his prayer by saying, "In the name of the Father, the Son and the Holy Spirit, let it come to all people all over the world, peace and tranquility. Amen." This prayer seems to actually come true in the film.

Viewers who favor a realistic nuclear war movie will no doubt gnash their teeth at these scenes. Could a simple prayer turn around almost everyone in the world? No doubt most atheists and agnostics would consider such scenes fantasy in the highest—or lowest.

These sequences also fascinate because they unequivocally pull religion into the nuclear war movie genre. Most Western nuke threat movies eschew references, even indirectly, to the spiritual. So it's interesting that a nuke threat movie made in Japan should matter-of-factly reference religion. In fact, given the minister's prayer ending with "in the name of the Father, the Son and the Holy Spirit," the reference appears to be to Christianity, a minority religion in Japan.

Granted, even for those who believe in God, this prayer extending to the entire world may appear far-fetched. After all, how many millions, or billions, of prayers have been said in the cause of peace throughout the centuries, and especially during the 20th century? Yet most (if not all) seem resolutely ignored. Or were they? We did get through the Cold War without a nuclear confrontation.

On the other hand, some may see this appeal to religion as an attempt to tack anti-war sentiments onto a movie that otherwise presents a pragmatic and brutal depiction of a possible World War III. After all, despite the multitudes pressing for peace in the film, Soviet ICBMs get launched towards America, and an orbital defense laser weapon, not prayer, stops the missiles from incinerating millions.

Reviews of *Future War 198X* are hard to find, and online anime sites are mostly unkind. For example, on the *Zimmerit* site, Sean O'Mara said, "Overly convoluted, poorly animated, and excruciatingly long."[8] On the other hand, *Sci-Fi-Central* opined, "[I]t is wonderfully animated and a real gem."[9]

A true rarity, *Future War 198X* offers an Eastern country's view of what a global nuclear war might have looked like during the 1980s. True, both science fiction and fantasy figure into the mix, but this blending sets the movie apart from most of its Western cousins.

* * *

Nuclearvision

DIRECTOR: James Jacobs; WRITERS: James Jacobs, Guenter Seltmann, Peter F. Strauss; MUSIC: James Jacobs, Chidori No Kai; CINEMATOGRAPHER: James Jacobs; EDITOR: Barbara Lischeck; PRODUCER: Guenter Seltmann.
CAST: Peter Ambach (Tom Broken); Jutta Ilzhoefer (Simone); Hans-Dieter Asner (Dr. Selke); Werner Eichhorn (Major Tennhausen); Roland Eisenmenger (Kurt).
PRODUCTION: Robot; West German; 1982; 79 minutes; not rated.

* * *

In *Nuclearvision*, a German filmmaker asks a government official this question concerning nuclear war: "Why do you think that in Germany, the very country most threatened by nuclear war, we only have shelters for three percent of the people in a state of emergency?" This cuts to the heart of the film's urgency, but the movie is, unfortunately, mostly flawed.

The German government commissions German documentary filmmaker Tom Broken to make a film about what citizens can do when a nuclear war is days, hours or even minutes away. In fact, the film will only be shown if a state of nuclear emergency occurs in West Germany.

Broken is appalled at the matter-of-fact manner in which his German "handlers" describe the horrors of Hiroshima. His obsession with the film he's supposed to make causes his wife Simone to become estranged and addicted to TV. Tom tells his "supervisors" he wants out of making the documentary, but they remind him he has signed a contract. During the final third of the film, Tom has a nightmare in which Bertram, the American computer that controls all ICBMs, launches a first strike.

Though well-intentioned, *Nuclearvision* meanders frequently and drinks from the well of pretentiousness one time too many. Still, the film presents the horrors of a nuclear war in a blunt fashion, focusing on the horrendous films of injured and burned Hiroshima survivors following the August 6, 1945, A-bombing of Hiroshima. As the truth about nuclear war's aftermath becomes clearer to Tom, he can no longer avoid the issue. His nightmare at the end of the film falls flat, but the movie nevertheless scores some significant nuke threat points.

Unlike Europe, America is geographically distant from Russia, and so psychologically,

Americans could think of the Soviets' nuclear missiles as "far away," though of course they could strike the U.S. in about 30 minutes, and faster if Soviet submarines launched them. Europeans didn't have this psychological luxury, and for them, the 1980s must have been scary indeed. In *Nuclearvision*, atomic anxiety consumes Tom's life, and Peter Ambach deftly portrays Tom's fear, confusion and anger.

Unrated, the film would probably rate an R for (totally unnecessary) nudity, language and adult content.

Nuclearvision has its moments, but mostly collapses under the weight of its self-conscious artiness.

*   *   *

Parasite

DIRECTOR-PRODUCER: Charles Band; WRITERS: Alan J. Adler, Michael Shoob, Frank Levering; MUSIC: Richard Band; CINEMATOGRAPHER: Mac Ahlberg; EDITOR: Brad Arensman.

CAST: Robert Glaudini (Dr. Paul Dean); Demi Moore (Patricia Welles); Luca Bercovici (Ricus); James Davidson (Wolf); Al Fann (Collins); Vivian Blaine (Miss Daley).

PRODUCTION: An Irwin Yablans and Charles Band production; 1982; distributed by Embassy Pictures; 85 minutes; rated R. Alternate title: *Parasite in 3-D*.

*   *   *

Demi Moore does not list this movie at the top of her résumé. And who can blame her, or any of the other actors doing their best in this typical low-budget 1980s monster film? But actors aside, the star of the show is the titular creature.

In the near future, a nuclear war has taken place. Since then, scientist Dr. Paul Dean has created a virulent parasite. The Merchants, the group that now controls the U.S., want this creature. Paul bolts, but not before one of the two parasites bores into his flesh. The other parasite is sealed in a metal canister.

Demi Moore as Patricia Welles in 1982's monster movie *Parasite* (aka *Parasite in 3-D*).

Paul flees to the desert town of Joshua (population 64), determined to find a way to destroy the parasite. He runs afoul of a local gang, slimy thugs who appear to have been transported from a 1960s biker movie. Led by Ricus, the gang nabs Paul and the parasite-containing canister.

Despite Paul's warnings not to open the container, Ricus lets one of his gang do just that, and the parasite attaches itself to the man. Angered, Ricus beats Paul until he is unconscious. Patricia, a young woman living on her own, brings Paul home to care for him.

Wolf, one of the Merchants, hums into town in a sleek black sports car. He relentlessly searches for Paul, en route amputating an old man's hand and roughing up Ricus and his gang.

Patricia helps Paul set up his medical equipment at her house and he searches for a way to destroy the parasites.

After the parasite-infected gang member dies, the creature embeds itself in one of the women. Ricus rushes her to town to get help. However, the parasite kills her, then dispatches another townie. Paul uses a sonic device emitting high frequencies to kill the parasite inside him. It bursts from his belly, attaches itself to Patricia's arm, then dies and drops to the floor.

Wolf arrives and, after accosting Collins, attacks Paul. The two fiercely battle. The remaining parasite reappears and attaches itself to Wolf, who falls from the second floor to a nearby butane tank. Patricia shoots the tank, causing it to explode and incinerate both Wolf and the parasite.

As noted earlier, the parasite is the star attraction, and it appears appropriately revolting. The film's monster makers clearly patterned its slimy look after the chest-burster from 1979's *Alien*. Oddly, the creature isn't always as well-articulated as you'd expect. For example, in the scene where it drops from the ceiling onto a townie, it appears motionless; it might have been more effective if its mouth had snapped open on the way down.

Stan Winston, James Kagel and Lance Anderson created the monster visuals. Winston went on to a major Hollywood career in special effects. His work on 1984's *The Terminator* elevated his star in Tinseltown; for 1986's *Aliens*, he won an Oscar for Best Visual Effects. In his career, he won a total of four Oscars; in addition to *Aliens*, he won for Best Visual Effects for 1991's *Terminator 2: Judgment Day* and 1993's *Jurassic Park*, as well as a Best Makeup Oscar for *Terminator 2: Judgment Day*. One of his early movies is the fan favorite *Gargoyles*, a 1972 TV movie for which Winston developed multiple monster costumes, receiving an Emmy for his work. He passed away on June 15, 2008, at the age of 62.

To complement the parasite effects of Winston and his two associates, the film offers a generous dollop of graphic violence. For example, we see a dismembered hand briefly twitch, and we see an excruciating closeup of Wolf's charred corpse. Presumably, since producer-director Charles Band assumed that the gore would net the film an R rating anyway, he throws in a topless sequence tailor-made for the word gratuitous.

Fanciers of low-budget genre flicks probably know Band's work. His voluminous filmography (an impressive 300 production credits) extends from the 1970s to the 21st century. The director-producer's work includes theatrical films and also direct-to-video features. His well-known *Puppet Master* series includes an amazing 14 movies. Other well-known Band series include *Subspecies* and *Trancers*.

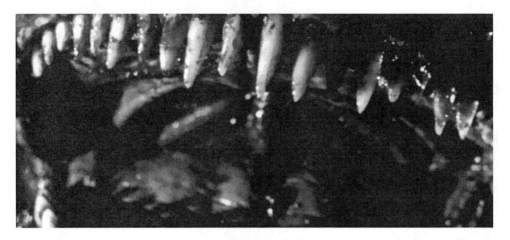

The sharp-toothed mouth of the titular creature in 1982's *Parasite* gets ready to bite into another victim. Stan Winston, along with James Kagel and Lance Anderson, created the film's monster visuals.

In exploitation films, the actors are often considered negligible. Of course, *Parasite* star Demi Moore (who plays Patricia) went on to a hugely successful Hollywood career. Her many films include 1985's *St. Elmo's Fire*, 1992's *A Few Good Men* and 1997's *G.I. Jane*. On a 2019 *The Late Show* appearance, host James Corden asked Moore, "What is the worst movie you have even been in?" She responded, "Actually, that one is easy … *Parasite in 3-D*."[10]

Moore's castmates deliver the goods. As Dr. Paul Dean, Robert Glaudini doesn't look like the hero type, but this makes his casting intriguing. Al Fann, who plays the genial Collins, breathes life into his part, even though he's given little to work with. Fann was an African American character actor who amassed more than 100 film and television credits from the 1970s through the 2000s. He passed away in 2018.

The movie is somewhat vague on a few points. We know a nuclear war of some kind occurred, because Collins tells Paul he left New York City when "all that atomic shit [fallout] started fallin' out of the skies." But we don't know if the nuclear war was limited or large-scale. Also, we have no idea how the Merchants came into power, or what became of the U.S. government.

The film was originally released in 3-D, as you can tell from the various in-your-face camera shots. In a *New York Times* review from March 13, 1982, Janet Maslin wrote, "[3-D] means that the director, Charles Band, is able to make the worm appear to leap at the audience. …The movie winds up more gruesome than scary, especially because the 3-D tricks are both repetitive and infrequent."[11]

As nuclear threat movies go, *Parasite* offers little. Except for a brief dialogue exchange between Collins and Paul, the characters never speak about the nuclear war. But presumably the movie's menace wouldn't have come into being without a nuke exchange.

* * *

The Soldier

DIRECTOR-WRITER-PRODUCER: James Glickenhaus; MUSIC: Tangerine Dream; CINEMATOGRAPHER: Robert M. Baldwin; EDITOR: Paul Fried.

CAST: Ken Wahl (The Soldier); Alberta Watson (Susan Goodman); Jeremiah Sullivan (Ivan); William Prince (The President); Klaus Kinski (Dracha).

PRODUCTION: Embassy Pictures; 1982; 88 minutes; rated R. Alternate title: *Code Name: The Soldier.*

* * *

During the 1960s, James Bond wannabes glutted movie and TV screens. During the 1980s, not so much. But that didn't stop director-writer-producer James Glickenhaus from attempting the 1982 Bondian nuke thriller *The Soldier.*

The film starts with a 007-ish situation: Renegade KGB agents have stolen an American plutonium shipment and created a dirty bomb, which they have hidden in the Saudi Arabian Ghawar Oil Field. They demand that Israel withdraw completely from the West Bank in four days, or else the bomb will be detonated, irradiating 50 percent of the oil fields for the next 300 years.

The American president considers the alternatives, one of which would be for the U.S. to force Israel from the West Bank. But if the oil reserves become irradiated, Western economies may collapse. The CIA director authorizes a super-secret operative known only as The Soldier.

The Soldier's first strategy is none too clever. In Austria, he meets Dracha, a KGB agent, and tells him he thinks renegade KGB agents are afoot, also adding that Dracha is the only person he has told. Naturally, this is an invitation for Dracha and his fellow Russians to assassinate the Soldier, but of course they fail.

The Soldier next tries to contact the CIA director, but the latter is killed by a lamp bomb. Now on the run, the Soldier seeks and gains asylum in the Israeli Embassy, where he learns the U.S. government thinks he killed the CIA director.

With his four fellow super-secret operatives, the Soldier hatches a plan. He sends his intrepid quartet to America where they take over an ICBM silo in Smith Center, Kansas. Then he lets the KGB agents know that unless they deactivate the dirty bomb, his team will launch a nuclear missile at Moscow.

Unbelievably, the Soldier jumps a Porsche over the East Berlin wall (Evel Knievel has nothing on him). He tells a helpful Russian agent that Moscow will shortly become radioactive dust if the dirty bomb isn't deactivated. Of course, the Russian KGB complies, America doesn't go to war with Israel, and the Soldier lives to threaten the globe with World War III another day.

The Soldier mixes comic book aesthetics with political thriller sensibilities. But despite a few good moments, it mostly falls flat. For one thing, unlike James Bond, the Soldier has neither a name nor a number, just a label. His exploits are often 007-ish, such as the scenic Austrian ski chase. And yes, of course he sleeps with the one major female cast member. He also kills without hesitation or apparent remorse.

But his scheme to nuke Moscow if the dirty bomb isn't deactivated is insane, even by comic strip standards. Granted, America forcing Israel from the West Bank would result in untold casualties. And the oil fields becoming irradiated would damage world economies. But blasting Moscow with an ICBM would start World War III, which would result in millions or billions of casualties, plus a living hell for the survivors. Yet this is what the Soldier and his buddies are willing to do.

The Soldier barely gets his ultimatum to Russia in the nick of time. What if he had been delayed ten minutes? What if he had failed to jump the Porsche into East Berlin?

Then Moscow would have been nuked, followed by most of North America, Asia and Europe.

Anyone who would risk the world for a harebrained scheme timed to the last second doesn't deserve our admiration. Indeed, the Soldier and his team almost become the flipside of the film's rogue KGB agents. The movie doesn't show us what happens to the Soldier and his team afterwards. Would America just shrug and say, "Oh, well," letting the Soldier and his buds go their merry way? More likely they would have been tossed into a federal pen.

The Soldier contains several arresting scenes. At the beginning, we see a car ruthlessly run down a woman pushing a baby carriage. But—aha!—she was actually a dastardly enemy agent, and the concerned citizens who rush out to help her are likewise enemy agents who pluck weapons from the baby carriage, which contained a doll instead of a baby. Next we see the Soldier and his teammates, standing in staggered formation side by side, blow the stuffing out of the bad guys. Meanwhile, the Austrian ski chase scene invigorates.

Action, of course, is *The Soldier*'s main attraction. The violence in the first half is extremely graphic, yet becomes less so in the final half. Director Glickenhaus seems to have an infatuation with slow-motion violence, recalling Sam Peckinpah movies of old.

The script is uneven. Too many situations strain credulity, even on a James Bond level. Also, the pallid characterizations need a shot of plasma.

Of course, the story reflects the actual nuclear tensions that dominated the 1980s. While *The Soldier* mostly provides escapism for teenage boys just graduating from G.I. Joe action figures, it occasionally rattles the era's Cold War chains.

Filming on a number of locations gives the movie an expansive feel, similar to globetrotting James Bond movies. The moviemakers actually filmed at Checkpoint Charlie crossing between West and East Berlin.[12]

If you're a country music fan, a very young George Strait briefly appears in a cowboy bar. However, the portrayal of the honkytonk establishment's patrons is less than flattering. Naturally, a huge bar fight breaks out.

Ken Wahl, who plays the Soldier, also appeared in 1979's *The Wanderers* and 1981's *Fort Apache the Bronx* in which he starred as Paul Newman's partner. Wahl is probably best known for the CBS-TV crime drama *Wiseguy* (1987–90).[13] In 1990, he won a Golden Globe for the series as Best Performance by an Actor in a Television Series Drama.[14]

Reviews of *The Soldier* run the gamut. For *The New York Times*, Vincent Canby wrote, "People are shot up, set aflame and otherwise damaged on screen at close range. Everything seems to have been wired to explode on contact except the film itself."[15] In 2018, reviewer Jesse Skeen found more to enjoy: "*The Soldier* has some memorable action pieces accomplished with a low budget."[16]

The Soldier is rated R for language, adult content, brief nudity and violence. Kid stuff? Not really.

The Soldier and his team's intent to nuke Moscow unless Russia disarms the oil field bomb may be nuts, but it reflects 1980s fears that either the Soviet Union or the U.S. might start World War III at any time. And as we know, the Cold War grew even chillier before it experienced a thaw in the late '80s.

*   *   *

Warlords of the 21st Century

DIRECTOR: Harley Cokliss; WRITERS: Irving Austin, Harley Cokliss, John Beech (screenplay); Michael Abrams (story); MUSIC: Kevin Peek; CINEMATOGRA-PHER: Chris Menges; EDITOR: Michael Horton; PRODUCERS: Lloyd Phillips, Rob Whitehouse.

CAST: Michael Beck (Hunter); Annie McEnroe (Corlie); James Wainwright (Jacob Straker); Bruno Lawrence (Willie); John Ratzenberger (Rusty).

PRODUCTION: Lloyd Phillips and Rob Whitehouse; 1982; distributor—New World Pictures; 91 minutes; rated PG. Alternate title: *Battletruck*.

*   *   *

The *Warlords of the 21st Century* poster declares, "After the destruction of World War III comes a new kind of hero!" Well, not that new. In fact, if you've seen *Mad Max* or its various clones, this movie's lone wolf hero Hunter will seem as familiar as a favorite shirt.

In the future, the Oil Wars deplete the world's petroleum resources. Nuclear weapons are employed, so Middle East oil fields seethe with radiation. Things in America aren't much better, as food riots have broken out and martial law has been declared. What's left of the government has left rural America to its own devices, and lawlessness reigns, embodied by renegade Army Colonel Jacob Straker and his motley crew of not-so-merry men. Straker commands a formidable vehicle called Battletruck, which easily overwhelms its enemies.

Battletruck happens upon two traders bearing diesel. When Straker asks where they got it, one of the traders lies, resulting in Straker slitting the man's throat. The other trader happily leads Straker and his men to a supply depot brimming with diesel. In return, Straker has the trader killed.

Straker's daughter Corlie tries to escape from his camp, but Straker's men pursue her. On a spruced-up motorcycle, hero Hunter rescues Corlie. Due to her injured leg, he brings her to a benign community called Clearwater, and the residents take her in. Straker soon comes looking for her. While Straker and his men terrorize Clearwater, Corlie escapes on horseback to Hunter's farm.

Straker and his men attack the farm, but Hunter and Corlie escape. Going back to the now ravaged Clearwater, Hunter asks Rusty to make him an armored vehicle so he can fight Straker's Battletruck. But one Clearwater resident, angry that Corlie didn't tell them the truth about being pursued by Straker, kidnaps her and intends to deliver her to Straker. Hunter pursues them on his cycle, but the renegade resident seriously wounds Hunter with a crossbow.

The renegade delivers Corlie to Straker. Despite his crossbow injury, Hunter makes it back to Clearwater, where Rusty completes the armored vehicle. Against overwhelming odds, Hunter races in pursuit of Corlie. In a fierce struggle, Hunter destroys Straker's diesel supply with a grenade and then manages to get inside the Battletruck. He and Corlie escape, and the out-of-control Battletruck plunges over a cliff, exploding.

Warlords of the 21st Century offers standard post-apocalyptic action. It differs from most in its subgenre by having little graphic violence and no graphic sex or nudity, hence its PG rating. Generally, the movie works. But the pacing sometimes plods. Also, the final battle between Hunter and Straker becomes too much at times. For example,

Hunter landing his motorcycle *inside* Battletruck is less likely than your average amoeba reciting the Gettysburg Address.

James Wainwright gives the villainous Straker a nice, low-key quality, from his calm voice to his toxic affability. He may put his arm around your shoulder, then kill you on the spot. Michael Beck is okay as the loner hero Hunter. It's surprising to see *Cheers'* John Ratzenberger on hand as Rusty the mechanic.

The movie has nice touches here and there. For example, when Rusty apologizes to Hunter for folding under torture, Hunter assures Rusty he would have done the same. And the finale, in which Hunter rides off on horseback, recalls many a Hollywood Western.

One major weakness is Corlie's subplot. When Hunter takes her to Clearwater, she lies and doesn't tell them her father Straker will come looking for her. Later, when asked why she lied, she says that her father would have ravaged Clearwater in search of her anyway. But if she'd told the Clearwater folks the truth from the get-go, perhaps they could have set up defenses in anticipation of Straker's Battletruck. Maybe they could have also secured Hunter's help. But her lie insures that Clearwater doesn't have a chance.

The film posits a lawless post-nuke society in which bad guys predominantly rule. Society has been reduced to subsistence levels, as we see in the activities of the Clearwater community. The movie offers no apparent hope for this state of affairs. Straker, his Battletruck and his thugs are history, but how long until someone takes their place?

But I realize you're not supposed to think too hard about the film's future implications. Whether the finale (in which Hunter gallops away from Clearwater) was supposed to have left an opening for a sequel is unknown. But the film's intent is to be recreation for post-apocalyptic action fans, and on that level, it reasonably succeeds.

But the reviews were less than sensational. Leonard Maltin gave this one two out of four stars: "Routine action film set after WWIII in time of an oil shortage."[17]

* * *

World War III

DIRECTORS: David Greene, Boris Sagal (uncredited); WRITER: Robert L. Joseph; MUSIC: Gil Mellé; CINEMATOGRAPHER: Stevan Larner; EDITORS: Robert L. Kimble, Parkie L. Singh; PRODUCER: Bruce Lansbury.

CAST: David Soul (Colonel Jake Caffey); Brian Keith (Secretary General Gorny); Rock Hudson (President Thomas McKenna); Cathy Lee Crosby (Major Kate Breckenridge); Jeroen Krabbé (Colonel Alexander Vorashin).

PRODUCTION: David Greene Productions, Finnegan Associates, National Broadcasting Company (NBC); broadcast by NBC-TV on 31 January 1982; 209 minutes

* * *

Atomic brinksmanship comes in only one flavor: bitter. The TV-movie *World War III* bears this out, as world leaders, in this case the U.S. president and the Soviet General Secretary, bite off more of the nuclear zeitgeist than either wanted.[18]

A Russian mole takes over a remote Alaskan NORAD station and notifies his Russian contact that the radar will be out for a time. Russian soldiers parachute in to hold the Alaskan oil pipeline "hostage" and sabotage it if America fails to end its grain embargo against the Soviet Union. The Russians clash with the Alaskan National Guard.

Colonel Jake Caffey (David Soul) has become the reluctant Deputy Brigade Commander at Fort Wainright. When the National Guardsmen are reported missing, Caffey heads a search team. They come upon one still-living Guardsman, who says that the Soviet ski troops are moving west. A firefight between the Soviets and Americans ensues.

In Washington, D.C., President Thomas McKenna (Rock Hudson) learns of the Alaskan incident and consults his advisors. Alaska's current inclement weather means that military forces cannot reach the Soviet unit. The president okays a secret armed forces mobilization. Over the phone, he orders Caffey to slow the Soviet troops down.

Caffey informs the remaining National Guardsmen that he will now command them. A Guardsman who grew up hunting in the area surmises where the Soviets are probably headed.

In Moscow, General Secretary Gorny (Brian Keith) learns of the Soviet incursion into Alaska and demands to know its objective. Sculoff (Kai Wulff) tells him it is to force the Americans to end the grain embargo and "save our people from starvation." Hardliner General Rudenski (Robert Prosky) assures Gorny that the Americans will not start a war over the issue.

In Alaska, Caffey and several Guardsmen locate a new launching valve station off the Alaska oil pipeline which houses multiple sections of empty pipeline. Caffey hatches a plan: place the pipes side by side at an angle, have the Guardsmen get into the pipes, then fire at any Soviets they see in their line of fire. Caffey and his men set it up. When the unsuspecting Russians close in, the Americans open fire. A firefight takes lives on both sides.

Soviet Secretary General Gorny (Brian Keith, left) and American President Thomas McKenna (Rock Hudson, right) reach an impasse after butting heads over the two nations' Alaskan conflict in 1982's *World War III* (NBC).

Jim Hardy (Frank Dent), the launching station's manager, tells Caffey that he sends pipe scrapers through the pipeline to remove accumulated dirt and wax for 30 miles until the pipe reaches a new launching station. Caffey reasons that the Russians will likely send flotation charges with remote detonators through the 30 miles of pipeline to destroy it.

Gorny proposes that he and President McKenna meet face to face in Reykjavik, Iceland. At the conference, Gorny and McKenna trade accusations. After a long and heated discussion, the two men arrive at an impasse.

In Alaska, the Soviet troops' political officer informs Colonel Alexander Vorashin (Jeroen Krabbé), leader of the Russian mission, that Moscow says to wait before advancing on the launching station. The American soldiers in the station are almost out of ammo.

President McKenna advances American military readiness to DEFCON 3. He then contacts Caffey and tells him that he (Caffey) and his men are the deciding difference between a "skirmish and World War III."

When the Russians ram an American destroyer in the Arabian Sea, McKenna orders America's military readiness raised to DEFCON 2 (one step away from nuclear war, military forces ready to deploy and engage in less than six hours). Gorny speaks with Colonel Vorashin in Alaska and tells him that he and his unit must seize control of the launching station before the weather clears, adding he hopes to avoid a nuclear war. Colonel Vorashin is troubled by this revelation.

In Moscow, General Rudenski informs Gorny that Soviet Backfire bombers are flying to the U.S. Pacific Coast. Gorny pleads with General Rudenski to cancel this escalation, but Rudenski, clearly calling the shots, assures Gorny the Americans won't raise their military readiness status.

In Alaska, the Russians and Americans engage in another firefight. The Russians exact a terrible toll. Colonel Vorashin asks to speak, unarmed, with Caffey. Vorashin says their leaders have a larger conflict in mind, implying nuclear war. He urges Caffey to join him in ending war by agreeing to a cessation of hostilities. Caffey and Vorashin move to shake hands, but a Russian political officer lobs a hand grenade in their midst, killing them.

In Russia, Gorny is en route to a concert when his limousine explodes. On the phone, President McKenna, expecting to speak with Gorny, instead finds himself talking to hardliner General Rudenski. Both men refuse to withdraw their planes of war. Rudenski tries to convince McKenna that Russia will pull back from the brink, and McKenna says the U.S. will do the same.

However, Rudenski contends that the president does not believe Rudenski's overtures for peace. Also, McKenna must seek a special Congressional committee's approval before he can launch a first strike, but Russia has no such restrictions. Rudenski authorizes a nuclear attack.

McKenna believes the KGB has killed Gorny and that Rudenski has no intention to call back Russia's Backfire bombers. Foregoing the special Congressional committee due to time constraints, a tearful McKenna orders a U.S. attack against the Soviet Union.

We see shots of ordinary people experiencing ordinary life around the world as a deep, ominous synthesizer hums, growing louder and more piercing. After a shot of a crimson sun at rest, the screen goes black, the sound reduced to silence.

World War III presents a "big view" of a nuclear war genesis from the vantage point of world leaders (Soviet and American) and military grunts (again, Soviet and American). The movie eschews civilian perspectives, and as such differs from most of its 1980s nuclear threat cousins such as *Testament*, *The Day After* and *Threads*.

The movie also gives a normalized view of Russians. General Secretary Gorny appears to actually want peace, and the soldiers under Colonel Vorashin's command in Alaska appear to be little different than the American National Guardsmen under Colonel Caffey's command. Unlike older nuclear threat films such as 1952's *Invasion USA*, which portray Soviet soldiers as rape-hungry monsters, *World War III* depicts them as ordinary folks who happen to be living under a different regime.

World War III gives us a more traditional Russian villain in the form of General Rudenski, a KGB zealot. While the movie never explicitly says so, it implies that Rudenski ordered Gorny's assassination. Such militant hardliners did, of course, exist in the Soviet Union, though so too did moderates such as Gorny (think Mikhail Gorbachev, Soviet general secretary from 1985 to 1991).[19]

World War III's two world leaders benefit from portrayals by seasoned American actors, Brian Keith as Gorny and Rock Hudson as President McKenna. Hudson appears dignified, approachable and confident, investing the role with gray-haired gravitas.[20] Meanwhile, Keith breaths believability into his portrait of Gorny, a sincere man worried about his mother country's current position and future destination.

The film's other actors are adequate or better. David Soul is on-point as the short-tempered Colonel Caffey. Baby Boomers may remember Soul from the TV series *Here Come the Brides* (ABC, 1968–70) and *Starsky and Hutch* (ABC, 1975–79).[21] Several entertainment veterans in the cast zip in and out. For example, Katherine Helmond (ABC shows *Soap* and *Who's the Boss?*) appears as a journalist who chats with the president. Character actor James Hampton (*F Troop*, many movie and TV show appearances) has a tad more screen time as one of the president's chief advisors.

World War III director Boris Sagal was killed in an accident a short time after production began. David Greene replaced him. It was originally aired over two nights. Part 2 becomes more intense than Part 1, as well as more chilling. As Part 2 moves inexorably to the point of no return for the two superpowers, the story becomes increasingly ominous. Near the end, showing people living their normal lives resembles the closing minutes of 1964's *Fail-Safe*. When the screen goes black, the sound snuffed out, this stark finale hits home.

The telefilm's theme highlights the peril of miscalculation when it comes to nuclear brinksmanship. For example, early on, General Rudenski reveals himself to be over-confident about the KGB's analysis of America's response to the Russian raid in Alaska. He guarantees Gorny that the Americans will not go to war over the incident, to which Gorny points to a picture of his teenage son and says, "Assure him."

President McKenna's military advisors appear a little less certain than Rudenski, but they nevertheless counsel the president to raise the stakes every time the Soviets make a move. McKenna eventually finds himself ramping up American military readiness to DEFCON 3, and later approaching the point of no return, DEFCON 2.

The notion that either the Americans or Russians might have miscalculated the opposing country's actions during the 1980s is more than conjecture. For example, in 1983, Soviet General Secretary Yuri Andropov feared that the U.S. might be planning a nuclear first strike. Andropov's Operation RYAN ordered the KGB to find evidence to validate Andropov's hunch, so the organization dutifully went about submitting

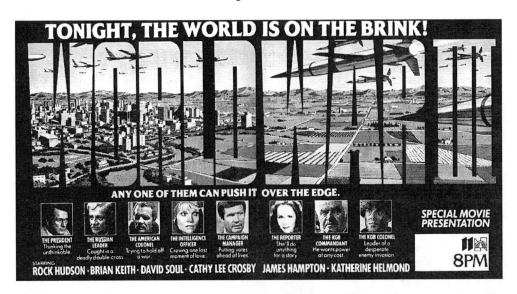

A dynamic (and somewhat misleading) *TV Guide* **ad for** *World War III*'s **debut on January 31, 1982, at 8 p.m. The movie didn't actually show missiles streaking toward a major U.S. city, and the ad exaggerates the roles of James Hampton and Katherine Helmond.**

"evidence," even if they didn't believe it indicated American first-strike intentions.[22] In November 1983, a major NATO military exercise called Able Archer 83 included practices NATO would employ in a nuclear conflict. These maneuvers gave the Soviet leadership the willies, apparently confirming that the U.S. might indeed be planning a first strike.[23] Yet the U.S. had no such intentions. Both sides failed to understand the viewpoint of the other, and this miscalculation could have caused a nuclear war not unlike that portrayed in *World War III*.

The movie depicts two parallel groups, the leadership of the U.S. and the U.S.S.R. and the ground-level military units of both countries. During their Iceland meeting, McKenna and Gorny find they cannot reach a compromise. Both men exhibit a number of traits that prevent agreement: stubbornness, ego, pride. Compare this impasse with the Soviet Colonel Vorashin and American Colonel Caffey meeting in the Alaskan oil launching station. Vorashin tells Caffey, "Our leaders have much bigger ideas [than this skirmish]."

"I know," Caffey replies. "The end."

Implying it is wrong for their leaders to begin a nuclear war, Vorashin asks Caffey, "Shall we deprive them of our services?"

Caffey says, "Well, at least we can tell them we've done our job and now it's time for them to do theirs."

Vorashin smiles. "We are in agreement."

After brief dialogue about ending war, Vorashin says, "I will say to them, 'I have met my enemy, and he is no longer my enemy, and I will walk out of here.'"

Caffey replies, "This is the end of war."

They reach to shake hands, but the Russian political officer ends their lives with a grenade.

While an interesting sequence, the dialogue between the two officers would likely provoke snickers from real-life career soldiers. Could two professional warriors such as

Vorashin and Caffey come to such a quick decision, one that would end their military careers, land them into prison, and brand them as traitors?

Also, would all of the men under each officer's command go along with their commanders' mutual truce? Probably not. And of course, the Russian political officer isn't about to let their unorthodox agreement stand.

Yet perhaps the writer had in mind that soldiers from opposite sides might come to a rational agreement concerning nuclear war before their national leaders would. Of course, Gorny is assassinated before he can again speak with McKenna. Had Gorny lived, we don't know if he and McKenna might have been able to pry each of their nations back from the brink.

In his January 30, 1982, *Washington Post* review, Tom Shales praised *World War III*: "[I]t is in the thoughtful doomsday vein of films like *Fail-Safe* and *Seven Days in May*." In particular, Shales praised Rock Hudson's performance as "the best acting he's done on the screen since his harrowing performance in the superior sci-fi film, *Seconds*." Further, he lauded Robert L. Joseph for his "tense and crackling script." Shales closed his review by noting, "[T]he picture has the snappy seductiveness of a good paperback political potboiler. Let the record show that *World War III* was very adroitly waged."[24]

As a "before the war" nuke film, *World War III* all too well—and all too convincingly—shows that civilians may not necessarily know what their governments are up to, and once they find out, it may be too late.

War?

It's just a mushroom cloud away.

CHAPTER FIVE

*   *   *

1983

The Being

DIRECTOR-WRITER: Jackie Kong; MUSIC: Don Preston; CINEMATOGRAPHERS: Hanania Baer, Robert Ebinger; EDITOR: David H. Newhouse; PRODUCER: Bill Osco.

CAST: Martin Landau (Dr. Garson Jones); Jose Ferrer (Mayor Gordon Lane); William Osco (Detective Mortimer Lutz); Dorothy Malone (Marge Smith); Ruth Buzzi (Virginia Lane); Marianne Gordon (Laurie); Kent Perkins (Officer Dudley); Murray Langston (Arnold).

PRODUCTION: Bill Osco Production, Cybelle Productions; 1983; 82 minutes; rated R. Alternate title: *Easter Sunday.*

* * *

Featuring one of the most offbeat casts of 1980s sci-fi–horror movies, *The Being* unfortunately doesn't live up to the talents of its various thespians. It does, however, live down to the worst of its subgenre.

In Spuds, Idaho, something attacked several folks at a drive-in movie theater. Detective Mortimer Lutz finds smears of green slime. He gets home to find the green slime in his bed and someone or some*thing* attacking him. He escapes. The mayor hires Dr. Garcon Jones to investigate.

Dr. Jones runs some tests at a nearby nuclear dump site. He tells Lutz and his girlfriend Laurie that a light-sensitive creature is running amok. The radiation at the dump must have created the homicidal creature that's on the loose. The monster turns out to be on the back of Lutz and Jones' vehicle, so both jump from the truck. Lutz shoots the gas tank, and the truck explodes in flames.

Lutz and Jones steal into a chemical warehouse, where the creature kills Jones. Lutz dons a gas mask and lets cyanide gas flow through the warehouse, but the creature attacks him anyway. He throws sulfuric acid at its head, injuring it, and uses an axe to hack it to death.

Back at the waste dump, a hand rises from the earth as a radio DJ announces that Jones' investigation found no cause for alarm. Following this scene, on-screen cards tell us the fate of each major character.

Often tiresome and lurid, *The Being* at least features the interesting cast noted above. Jose Ferrer, who plays the mayor, was a Hollywood veteran who won a Best Actor Oscar for 1950's *Cyrano de Bergerac.* Martin Landau was also well-known for both his movie and television work, appearing with wife Barbara Bain as a regular for the first

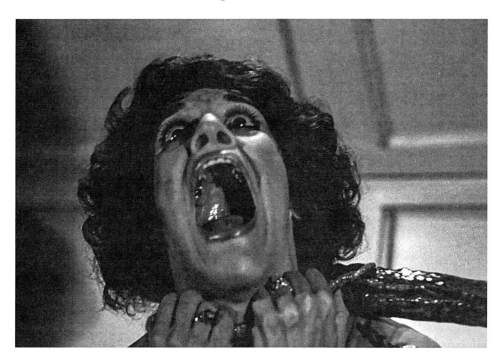

Virginia Lane (Ruth Buzzi) is attacked by the mutant teenager in 1983's *The Being* (Cybelle Productions). The film is a throwback to 1950s movies with monsters created by radiation.

three seasons (1966–69) of the hit TV show *Mission: Impossible*. Science fiction fans no doubt recall his stint with Bain on the syndicated British-made *Space: 1999* (1975–77).[1] Landau went on to appear in several low-budget films such as *The Being* and 1980's *Without Warning*. But in the late '80s, the talented actor found new respect, nominated three times for the Best Supporting Actor Oscar and winning for his performance as Bela Lugosi in 1994's *Ed Wood*.

In addition to Ferrer and Landau, Ruth Buzzi, appearing as the mayor's wife, was a regular on the groundbreaking NBC-TV comedy series *Rowan & Martin's Laugh-In* (1968–73). Marianne Gordon, who plays Detective Lutz's girlfriend Laurie, was for 16 years one of Kenny Rogers' wives, and Dorothy Malone was an Oscar winner.

Beyond that cast, *The Being* offers little. The editing is jagged, the pacing haphazard, the on-screen happenings sometimes confusing. A supposedly humorous subplot about religious folks protesting the opening of a massage parlor in town goes nowhere. To the director's credit, the creature is kept in the shadows for most of the film, but during the climax, we get several up-close looks at the slimy mutant. To the director's discredit, the movie dispenses large dollops of gore and an exploitative topless scene.

Regarding the nuclear threat, *The Being* is a throwback to the mutant movies of the 1950s: Radioactive waste has turned teenager Michael Smith into a homicidal, tunnel-boring monstrosity who bears more than a passing resemblance to 1979's *Alien*. At one point, Dr. Jones comments that other nuclear waste sites around the country may produce more Michael-like mutants. The connection of radiation to the hideous implies nothing good can come of anything radioactive. (Of course, radiation can treat certain cancers.)

Michael's genesis into the mutant remains unclear. Did the radiation turn him into the monster after he was a teenager, or was he already a mutant and the radiation made him even more monstrous?

In the midst of *The Being*'s clutter, the filmmakers do give us one imaginative sequence: Lutz's black-and-white dream featuring him, Dr. Jones, the mayor's wife and the creature.

After the final scene, on-screen cards tell us the cast's fate in a jokey manner. For example, "[Dr.] Garson Jones: was donated to medical science by Mayor Lane." Hilarious, right?

Unsurprisingly, *The Being* has received several unfavorable reviews. Leonard Maltin gave it one and a half out of four stars and bemoaned its "grade-Z script and production."[2] But some reviews seem to like the film. For example, *The Telltale Mind* called it "mindless fun when it comes down to it ... a good time."[3]

I found it mindless, all right, but about as much fun as having a firehose pressure-clean my ears. For me, the phrase "mindless fun" brings to mind innocent nonsense like 1963's *Reptilicus*, not Grade-D sleaze like 1983's *The Being*.

*   *   *

The Day After

DIRECTOR: Nicholas Meyer; WRITER: Edward Hume; MUSIC: David Raksin; music from "The River" by Virgil Thomson; CINEMATOGRAPHER: Gayne Rescher; EDITORS: William Paul Dornisch, Robert Florio; PRODUCER: Robert A. Papazian.

CAST: Jason Robards (Dr. Russell Oakes); Georgann Johnson (Helen Oakes); Kyle Aletter (Marilyn Oakes); John Cullum (Jim Dahlberg); Bibi Besch (Eve Dahlberg); Lori Lethin (Denise Dahlberg); Doug Scott (Danny Dahlberg); Ellen Anthony (Joleen Dahlberg); JoBeth Williams (Nurse Nancy Bauer); Steve Guttenberg (Stephen Klein); John Lithgow (Joe Huxley); Calvin Jung (Dr. Sam Hachiya); Lin McCarthy (Dr. Austin); Rosanna Huffman (Dr. Wallenberg); George Petrie (Dr. Landowska); Jonathan Estrin (Julian French); Amy Madigan (Alison Ransom); William Allen Young (Airman First Class Billy McCoy); Jeff East (Bruce Gallatin); Fay Hauser (Maureen McCoy).

PRODUCTION: ABC Circle Films; broadcast on ABC-TV on 20 November 1983; 122 minutes. The film was released theatrically outside the U.S.: 127 minutes; broadcast on Soviet Union television in 1987.

*   *   *

In an early scene from *The Day After*, a husband and wife discuss whether escalating political tensions in Europe will lead to a nuclear war. Alluding to 1962's Cuban Missile Crisis, the wife says, "It's not gonna happen now."

The husband replies, "Nah. People are crazy, but not that crazy."

After further conversation, the wife says, "What if it does happen? What'll we do?"

The husband has no reply.

Of course, *The Day After* does have a reply, one that caused a sensation in 1983. Aired on ABC the night of November 20, 1983, the film made history by becoming America's highest rated TV-movie, boasting an estimated 100 million viewers.[4]

The storyline follows four Midwestern families as international tensions worsen in Europe. Following the nuclear attack, the film switches exclusively to what becomes of the families.

The Oakes family, the first we see, consists of father Dr. Russ Oakes (Jason Robards), mother Helen (Georgann Johnson) and daughter Marilyn (Kyle Aletter), as well as Allan, a son to whom we are not introduced. The family resides in Kansas City. Marilyn reveals to her father that she is moving to Boston, where her boyfriend will be attending school.

Next, Airman First Class Billy McCoy (William Allen Young) is chopper-bound to one of the missile silos in Missouri near the Hendry family's farm. The Hendry family is comprised of father Dennis (Clayton Day), mother Ellen (Antonie Becker) and two young children.

In the Dahlberg clan, daughter Denise (Lori Lethin) arrives late to her wedding rehearsal with boyfriend Bruce Gallatin (Jeff East). Father Jim (John Cullum) and mother Eve (Bibi Besch) are unamused. Younger daughter Joleen (Ellen Anthony) and son Danny (Doug Scott) shrug it off.

In Kansas City, Dr. Oakes discusses with Helen their daughter Marilyn's plans to leave town. However, a TV special report interrupts their conversation, reporting that East Germany has initiated a blockade of West Berlin.

Airman McCoy and his wife Maureen (Fay Hauser) argue over his being called up on alert and ruining plans to visit her mother with their child Skip. He assures her nothing is going to happen.

On the Dahlberg farm, a special bulletin interrupts the ball game the father is watching, reporting that East Germany has cut off all air traffic to West Berlin. NATO has protested, and the U.S. president puts all American military on Stage II alert. Dr. Oakes and Helen likewise hear this unsettling TV report. They assure each other that a nuclear war simply won't happen—but they don't seem fully convinced.

The hospital staff of the University of Kansas in Lawrence watch in disbelief as nuclear missiles launch toward Russia in 1983's *The Day After* (ABC Circle Films). They know this means Russian ICBMs will soon be hitting the United States.

Two Soviet MiG-25RBs invade West German airspace, firing missiles at a NATO munitions storage facility, also hitting a school and hospital.

At the University of Kansas in Lawrence hospital, Dr. Oakes and a colleague discuss the unfolding international events. Rumor claims Moscow is being evacuated (a rumor confirmed by a radio broadcast), and many Americans are evacuating nearby Kansas City, where Dr. Oakes and his family reside. Dr. Oakes asks his associate, "Do you understand what's going on in this world?"

His associate replies, "Stupidity. It has a habit of getting its way."

The international news continues to grow ominous. The Soviet Union invades West Germany.

At a barbershop, we learn that 150 Minuteman missiles dot the Missouri border, meaning Kansas City is sure to get hit, with nearby Lawrence endangered as well.

A TV newscaster delivers a startling update: Three nuclear weapons have been airburst over Soviet troops invading West Germany. In addition, a nuke has exploded at a regional NATO military headquarters. Next, Russia hits an American Persian Gulf ship, and America retaliates by firing on a Soviet vessel.

Then it happens.

The Hendrys stare in disbelief as a Minuteman missile launches from a nearby silo. Then dozens of other missiles take flight, meaning that in about 30 minutes, Russian missiles will rain on America. Indeed, 300 Soviet ICBMs are bound for the United States.

Panic grips Kansas City. Residents flee into the dubious shelter of basements in municipal buildings. A high-altitude nuclear airburst occurs, resulting in an electromagnetic pulse effect: All electrical circuits burn out. Because of the EMP, on the interstate, Dr. Oakes' car stalls, along with those of his fellow drivers.

A white light flashes across the interstate. A mushroom cloud rises, followed in quick succession by another. A nuclear explosion obliterates Kansas City. We see the X-ray skeletons of residents caught in the blast before they disintegrate. Fire spreads over the city remains, and nuclear winds demolish nearby houses and buildings.

The Hendrys, unable to escape their farm, are destroyed in a nuclear blast that takes out the missile silo nearby. The Dahlbergs take refuge in their basement and survive the blast. However, son Danny looked directly at an explosion and is now blind. All Oakes family members are dead except Dr. Oakes, who walks ten miles into a now nuclear-damaged Lawrence, where he goes to the University of Kansas hospital and takes charge. During his trek, he has been exposed to fallout.

Due to the EMP, the hospital has no electricity, not even backup power. Students have poured into the hospital, many physically uninjured but confused and fearful. Dr. Oakes tells them that those who are uninjured will have to work with the hospital staff for the survival of all. Later, Dr. Oakes and the other doctors discuss emergency plans, deciding to use bottled gas to heat water needed for sterilization.

In the university's Basic Science Building, Prof. Joe Huxley (John Lithgow) has used car batteries to provide a charge for the Geiger counter, and he also broadcasts via radio for any survivors outside Lawrence. He radios Dr. Oakes that the radiation outside is currently under 50 rads an hour (rad = radiation absorbed dose, the amount of radiation a person absorbs), which is dangerous; he notes it won't be safe for students to move outside the hospital until the radiation has decreased to 2 rads per hour.

The Dahlbergs continue to survive in their basement, but someone is walking in the house above. Rifle in hand, Jim confronts the intruder, college student Stephen Klein (Steve Guttenberg). Stephen begs for mercy, says he can help, and offers canned food. Jim reluctantly allows him to enter the basement. Denise gets hysterical, screaming that she can't remember what her boyfriend Bruce's face looks like, and she runs from the house. Stephen assures Jim and Eve he will retrieve her and races outside. Fallout dust covers the landscape, along with dead farm animals. Denise runs into the house, but by this time, both she and Stephen have absorbed a dangerous amount of radiation.

Airman McCoy learns from strangers that Sedalia, where his family lived, has been destroyed He takes a mute stranger along with him, their destination the Lawrence hospital.

At the hospital, people are stealing food and morphine. Dr. Oakes orders tighter security. He also talks to a dispirited pregnant woman two weeks overdue, urging her to have her baby. "You're holding back hope," he says.

The woman replies, "Hope for what? What do you think's gonna happen out there.... We knew the score. We knew all about bombs, we knew all about fallout. We knew this could happen for 40 years. Nobody was interested."

Airman McCoy and his friend make it to the hospital and check in at the admittance table. Both have advanced radiation sickness. McCoy asks the admittance worker, "Is there anything we can do about it?" The worker doesn't respond. Outside, the number of rads per hour has gone down to .4, meaning people in the hospital without serious injuries can now find refuge in other campus buildings.

At the Dahlberg farm, Jim ventures outside to look at his fields. His windmill has collapsed, along with an American flag. He and the family attend an outdoor church service. In an ill-advised attempt to offer comfort, the preacher reads from the Bible's Book of Revelation. Clearly the pastor is in a state of shock. He thanks God for "destroying the destroyers of the earth." During the service, Denise shows symptoms of serious radiation disease.

Stephen says he will take Denise and the blinded Danny to the Lawrence hospital. Stephen promises Jim he will bring them back. After they set out, Danny, bandages still over his eyes, asks Stephen, "What do you see?"

Stephen replies, "Oh, cows. Telephone poles. Usual stuff." Actually, he sees the National Guard loading human corpses from the fields onto a flatbed truck.

Prof. Huxley receives a radio transmission from the U.S. president, speaking to all Americans. He says the U.S. and Soviet Union have declared a ceasefire, and notes that Russia has been devastated as badly as America. He also assures listeners that "America has survived this terrible tribulation," and there has been "no surrender" to America's principles of liberty. He says that the federal government will be working through the states to organize a national recovery.

At the university hospital, Dr. Oakes, now suffering from advanced radiation sickness, can no longer lead or function and is himself hospitalized.

The government provides "tent cities" to the war survivors, and the National Guard delivers food to different camps. But the food is rationed, and a riot breaks out.

In the country, Jim Dahlberg attends a meeting of farmers. An agricultural official gives them instructions that can't reasonably be carried out, and Jim leads the farmers in a show of no confidence. When Jim returns to his farm, squatters have started a campfire and are eating. Jim asks what they are doing there, and one of the squatters dispassionately shoots Jim, killing him, and goes back to his meal.

Stephen finds Denise on a university basketball court teeming with bedridden patients. Denise is losing her hair; Stephen lifts his ball cap to show Denise he has already lost his. He tells her he will take her and Danny back to their parents.

Dr. Oakes, aware he is dying, wants to return to Kansas City and gets a ride aboard a government vehicle. En route, he sees a firing squad shoot looters tied to poles. Kansas City is a mass of rubble, but somehow, Dr. Oakes finds the ruins of his home, in which a family has set up housekeeping. Dr. Oakes orders them to leave. One of the squatters offers food to the doctor, then embraces him as both quietly weep.

The Day After's gestation from idea to event television could itself be the basis for a TV-movie. In the following five paragraphs is the story of that development, all of it taken from a 2018 interview with *Day After* director Nicholas Meyer listed as a bonus feature on Kino Lorber's *Day After* DVD[5]:

ABC executive Brandon Stoddard hatched an idea to make a TV-movie about the aftermath of a nuclear war and asked ABC's Stu Samuels to develop such a project. Samuels hired writer Edward Hume, who penned a script originally titled *Silence in Heaven: The Day After*, later shortened to *The Day After*. Nicholas Meyer, who had scored a major hit as the director of 1982's *Star Trek II: The Wrath of Khan*, was the fourth director ABC approached; he said he read the script and was "duly shaken."

Meyer claims he took the project after his psychoanalyst said this about his hesitation: "Well, I guess this is where we find out who you really are." Meyer said he used this same tactic to hire many of the crew for the film. Nabbing Jason Robards for the lead was an accident: Meyer and Robards happened to be on the same plane; Meyer mentioned he was going to make a movie about nuclear war and asked if Robards was interested. Replied Robards, "Beats signing petitions."

Meyer said he shot the three-hour script intended for a two-night presentation, but believed a one-night movie would be better. For economic reasons, ABC eventually agreed. The Pentagon said they would assist the film by providing equipment and film footage *if* the movie clearly stated that the Soviet Union had started the war. Meyer said, "This was inimical to our purposes, so we declined." Instead, the filmmakers bought and used stock footage.

In the movie, we never know who started the war. Meyer believed the film should not espouse a particular political viewpoint. The goal was to simply show what a nuclear war would be like in Middle America. Further, Meyer saw the project as a public service announcement akin to Smokey Bear, believing *The Day After* could be a "backdoor to the national consciousness through something as innocuous as a TV movie."

After seeing Meyer's cut of the film, ABC executives wept. Nevertheless, they wanted the movie softened. Meyer's editor Paul Dornish refused to recut the movie, and ABC fired him. Meyer likewise refused to recut the movie and left the project for three months. However, he gave an interview in which he said that for *The Day After* (a well-known item at this point), there was "dissension in the ranks." Afterward, Brandon Stoddard called Meyer into his office, and Meyer walked out with 75 or 80 percent of what he wanted put back.

As a film, *The Day After* is divided into three parts: before the holocaust, during the holocaust, after the holocaust. Each section has its own tone and rhythms. The "Before" section makes it clear who the movie is aiming at. During the opening credits, we are treated to a showcase of Middle America—rural fields, small towns, public schools, stockyards, sports stadiums, parks teeming with kids, bikes, dogs, families. The sweeping music could easily have been the score for a Western or family film rather than the soundtrack for a movie dealing with nuclear war and its aftermath.

The "Before" section introduces us to all the main characters, most of them families, in bright, appealing lighting. But as their family stories play out, a dissonant chord sounds: TV and radio broadcasts of international tensions in Europe between East and West Germany. Gradually, these events escalate to the point where the president declares the American military to be on Stage II alert. The viewer knows where the movie's newscasts are headed, yet during this time, the film continues to look like a normal TV-movie, palatable pacing and agreeable visuals intact.

Next comes the "During" section. The pacing picks up with fast camerawork capturing runs on the supermarket, citizens evacuating Kansas City, fighter pilots scrambling into their jets. Finally, we see American ICBMs launched. This is arguably the scariest part of the film. Stunned citizens—farmers, college students, residents—watch as the missiles rocket towards their Russian targets. A stadium full of college students gazes at the soaring missiles, and one of the students ventures, "Like a test, sort of? Like a warning?" Prof. Huxley disabuses her of this delusion.

Jim Dahlberg has his family take shelter in the basement. His wife Eve is in denial, making the beds as though things were normal. Jim has to force her to go to the basement as she goes into hysterics, a disturbing moment. At the now-empty missile silo, a terrified Airman McCoy flees in a military truck. Dr. Oakes speeds down the interstate towards Kansas City, but finds his auto stalling due to EMP effects. The second scariest part in the film occurs: a nuclear explosion's blinding flash baptizes the highway, followed by a gigantic mushroom cloud rearing into the sky like a demonic wraith.

More missiles hit, more mushroom clouds loom, vaporizing Kansas City residents and creating a firestorm. The screen appropriately fades to black; the "During" section is over.

A mushroom cloud looms in the distance over what had been Kansas City in ABC Circle Films' *The Day After*, broadcast on ABC-TV on November 20, 1983. It was seen by an estimated 100 million viewers.

Then the movie switches to the bleakest section: "After." Here, the tone and look of the movie change significantly. Our first sight of a nuke-damaged Lawrence, Kansas, appears to be happening in a grey tableau, fallout spitting about like toxic snow. The tone stays muted throughout this final part of the movie, and grittiness reigns supreme. The pacing becomes almost dream-like at times, appropriate since the film's final hour plays out like a nightmare.

As the "After" section unfolds, we see rampant death and misery from radiation sickness, including burns, sores and hair loss. (But we don't see anyone vomiting, a common effect of radiation poisoning.) We also see hospital staff members struggling to make things work with less than minimal resources. Near the end of this section, the government steps in to deliver food rations and erect tent cities, yet things hardly seem improved.

While the final scene of a stranger weeping with Dr. Oakes in the ruins of the doctor's house may be poignant, it isn't necessarily credible. Kansas City has been obliterated into miles of rubble, so what are the odds that Dr. Oakes could actually locate where his house had once been? Also, surely the radiation levels are high enough that the family squatting in the "house" would die in no time.

The film leaves some plot threads hanging. For example, Stephen says he will take Denise and Danny back to their parents on the farm, but we never see this happen. We do, however, see the father shot and killed. (The film's three-hour work print does show Stephen bring Denise and Danny back to their parents' homestead, but no one greets them. The implication is that along with the father, the mother and little sister have also perished.)

Modern viewers, meaning anyone saturated in post–1993 CGI visuals, may sniff at *The Day After*'s special effects. But for the time, they were thoroughly professional. The reddish-tinted mushroom clouds prove effective, as do the scenes of missiles soaring skyward.

Before *The Day After*, no American film had attempted to show the detailed nuclear destruction of an American city. In 1952, *Invasion USA* showed an A-bomb hit New York City. Similarly, 1960's *The Time Machine* depicted a nuclear attack on London. But both films lack *Day After*'s scope. (It was actually a Japanese film, 1961's *The Last War*, that depicted the detailed nuclear destruction of a city, in this case Tokyo, prior to *The Day After*.)

During the major destruction set piece, the film employs a good deal of stock footage. I was in my twenties when I saw *The Day After* on November 20, 1983, and I had already seen this stock footage of nuclear tests; it had been used in many science fiction movies. The familiarity of these scenes for some members of the 1983 audience somewhat blunted their effect.

Prior to the nuclear destruction sequence, the film uses little music. But you hear almost none following the nuclear attack. This subtly enhances the film's believability and gloom.

During the "After" portion, authority figures seem to be failing the populace. For example, the president gives an address apparently meant to inspire, but in the face of the misery we see and the misery to come, it seems deficient. The minister appears not only to be shell-shocked but also a caricature. Yes, some ministers might give a post-nuke sermon from the Book of Revelation and thank the Almighty for "destroying the destroyers of the earth" (presumably he means the Soviets). But other pastors would attempt to offer compassion and empathy amidst the sorrow and horror.

Speaking of empathy, *The Day After* is family-based, assuming most viewers will relate to this emphasis. We have one upper middle-class family (the Oakes), two rural families (the Dahlbergs and Hendrys) and one military family (the McCoys). However, regarding the McCoys, we see husband Billy and wife Maureen, but not their child Skip. Given that the McCoys are African American, it's too bad we only see Maureen once and never see Skip at all. This story subplot should have been given as much on-screen time as the Oakeses and the Dahlbergs.

ABC heavily promoted *The Day After*. One 30-second promo (available on You-Tube) uses quick cuts of some of the film's compelling moments, with the announcer saying, "Sunday, November 20, a motion picture that takes you beyond imagining." In another promo, people who had seen the film at a preview showing recommended it (big surprise).

A poster for the movie called it "Perhaps the most important film ever made." This lofty statement recalled the blockbuster 1959 nuclear threat movie *On the Beach*, which likewise trumpeted its significance. However, a child of the '50s, *On the Beach* pulled its punches. Everything was antiseptic—no depictions of radiation sickness, corpses or destruction. *The Day After* promised just the opposite, ABC noting that the film's graphic nature might not be suitable for young children. In fact, on November 20, 1983, ABC aired a short introduction to the film by John Cullum (who plays Jim Dahlberg in the movie) urging parental discretion and notifying viewers that a special edition of *Viewpoint*, a news panel hosted by Ted Koppel, would air immediately following the film to discuss its subject matter.

I vividly recall watching this *Viewpoint*, which included some well-known guests: former Secretary of State Henry Kissinger; human rights advocate Elie Wiesel; former Secretary of Defense Robert McNamara; General Brent Scowcroft; scientist Carl Sagan; and conservative commentator William F. Buckley, Jr.[6] Koppel moderated a discussion about preventing nuclear war. Topics included deterrence, "launch on warning," first strikes and the Nuclear Freeze, a hot topic in the early '80s.[7] In a refreshing contrast to the raucous political debates on today's partisan TV news shows, the *Viewpoint* panel showed respect, dignity and civility. Likewise, moderator Koppel never resorted to bullying, shouting or insulting, but instead was a model of decorum.[8]

Early on, Sagan detailed the concept of nuclear winter which he claimed could possibly lead to humanity's extinction. Buckley said this was good news, for if true, it would never be in the Soviet Union's best interests to start a nuclear war. Later, Sagan made this statement about arms escalation: "Imagine a room awash in gasoline, and there are two implacable enemies in that room. One of them has nine thousand matches, the other seven thousand matches. Each of them is concerned about who's ahead, who's stronger."

In hindsight, it's fascinating to hear the 1983 concerns about the near-future of nuclear weapons; often, a *Viewpoint* pundit would speak of what might happen if America was still around 10 or 15 years hence. Fortunately, we know we are still around decades later, though this of course doesn't mean a nuclear war can't happen. Panelist Wiesel spoke of madness becoming a factor: Would an insane dictator use nuclear weapons even if doing so acted against his country's interests?

Prior to the airing of *The Day After*, controversy swirled. In the summer of 1983, the Nuclear Weapons Freeze Campaign and other anti-nuclear groups embraced it, seeing it as a tool to communicate their viewpoints to a wider number of Americans. Among other things, they developed viewer guides, circulated bootleg copies of the movie, organized community events and developed media saturation strategies.[9]

However, many conservatives who championed the policy of MAD (Mutually Assured Destruction) lashed out at ABC. They claimed the film was simplistic and relied on emotions as a response to a possible nuclear war. For example, William F. Buckley said the movie would weaken America.[10] In a similar vein, *National Review* publisher William Rusher fumed that the movie "would generate an ignorant public hysteria at a time when calm resolution to preserve a credible deterrent is called for."[11]

The Day After had a major effect on then President Ronald Reagan. After screening the film on October 10, 1983, he wrote in his diary that it "is powerfully done—all $7 mil. worth. It's very effective & left me greatly depressed."[12] Reagan's official biographer later told director Nicholas Meyer that the only time he saw Reagan become upset "was after they screened *The Day After*, and he just went into a funk."[13]

On November 18, 1983, Reagan received a military briefing regarding a plausible nuclear war scenario. In his autobiography, he wrote,

"In several ways, the sequence of events described in the briefings paralleled those in the ABC movie. Yet there were still some people at the Pentagon who claimed a nuclear war was 'winnable.' I thought they were crazy. Worse, it appears there were also Soviet generals who thought in terms of winning a nuclear war."[14]

Apparently, the movie helped move President Reagan to pursue a serious arms reduction agreement with the Soviet Union. Reagan and Soviet General Secretary Mikhail Gorbachev signed the Intermediate-Range Nuclear Forces Treaty (INF) in 1987.[15] The treaty banned land-based ballistic missiles of short-, medium- and intermediate-range; this resulted in the dismantling of over 2,692 missiles by June 1, 1991.[16]

If *The Day After* has a theme, it is probably hopelessness in the face of such an apocalyptic event. For example, when speaking to a pregnant woman, Dr. Oakes says, "We've got to do everything we can to protect ourselves from the fallout." The woman replies, "What for?" In the Dahlberg basement, daughter Denise asks, "What are we doing down here anyway? It's all over, isn't it?" Later, Eve says, "We're lucky to be alive," to which Jim replies, "We'll see how lucky that is." Ironic, since later we see him shot to death.

Close to the end of the film,

Director Nicholas Meyer (pictured) insisted on making *The Day After* with integrity (Mike Muegel, CC BY 2.0, via Wikimedia Commons).

the pregnant woman speaks of the willing ignorance of the public regarding the possibility of a nuclear war. Dr. Oakes replies, "I can't argue with you," to which the pregnant woman says, "Argue with me. Please. Give me a reason, tell me about hope. Tell me why you work so hard in here." Dr. Oakes: "I don't know."

In essence, along with millions of hapless civilians, nuclear war has vaporized hope. *Testament* (1983), a smaller-scale film with a similar premise, suggests the reason to go on is human decency. Caring for one another to the end is espoused as a reason to live, even when radioactive death is inevitable. (An entry on *Testament* follows later in this chapter.)

In *Starlog Science-Fiction Video Magazine* #1, reviewer Robert Greenberger wrote, "This one will scare you … it shows you the grisly before and after images of Lawrence, Kansas, a typical town facing a nuclear attack … well worth your time."[17] From *Leonard Maltin's 2002 Movie & Video Guide*: "Chilling aftereffects of the catastrophic nuclear bombing of Lawrence, Kansas, in a potent drama…."[18]

In 1983, *TV Guide*'s movie critic Judith Crist wrote, "[*The Day After*] is indeed strong stuff, with the excellent cast keeping it undiluted despite their near-stereotypical roles … [I]t is a tribute to the moviemakers' skills, from special effects to makeup that make the horrors a reality."[19] Fellow *TV Guide* critic Robert MacKenzie opined, "[W]riter Edward H. Hume and everyone else who worked on the film deserve applause for its power and candor."[20] From a late 1990s perspective, *VideoHound's Sci-Fi Experience* called the film "[a] powerful drama … [A] talented cast made the most of the then very topical and frightening material."[21] (Concerning topicality: In the 2020s, everything old has become new.)

Along with the above reviews, plenty of ink, both actual and electronic, has been spilled over *The Day After* from the early '80s to today. Some deride the film as poorly made and, special effects–wise, badly dated. Others applaud its intentions. Folks like me regard it as effective and groundbreaking. But no one can deny that *The Day After* is one of the most important TV-movies ever made, and perhaps the most controversial.

* * *

The Dead Zone

DIRECTOR: David Cronenberg; WRITER: Jeffrey Boam; based on the novel by Stephen King; MUSIC: Michael Kamen; CINEMATOGRAPHER: Mark Irwin; EDITOR: Ronald Sanders; PRODUCER: Debra Hill.

CAST: Christopher Walken (Johnny Smith); Brooke Adams (Sarah Bracknell); Tom Skerritt (Sheriff George Bannerman); Herbert Lom (Dr. Sam Weizak); Martin Sheen (Greg Stillson); Anthony Zerbe (Roger Stuart).

PRODUCTION: Dino De Laurentiis Corporation; 1983; 103 minutes; rated R.

* * *

What if you knew a popular politician was going to start a nuclear war in the near future? For the good of all, would you kill him? Such is the main character's dilemma in 1983's *The Dead Zone*, an adaptation of Stephen King's 1979 novel.

During treacherous weather, schoolteacher Johnny Smith has a car wreck that puts him in a coma. Five years later, he awakens to find his former fiancée Sarah has married and has a child. He also discovers he now has the ability to know certain things about a person's life when he touches them. Sheriff George Bannerman asks Johnny's help to solve a recent murder. Johnny's ability shows him the killer is the sheriff's deputy Frank Dodd. Dodd kills himself.

Johnny begins tutoring Chris, the son of wealthy Roger Stuart. Johnny sees a vision of Chris and two other boys drowning and shares it with Roger, who doesn't believe Johnny and fires him. Chris *does* believe Johnny and stays home. His two friends drown as Johnny foresaw. The fact that Chris didn't drown proves that the future Johnny sees can be changed.

After shaking hands with populist politician Greg Stillson, Johnny sees a future in which Stillson becomes U.S. president and starts an all-out nuclear war. Johnny decides he must kill Stillson before that can happen, even if it means his own death.

The Dead Zone remains one of the best movie adaptations of a Stephen King novel. The film cuts to the chase, not wasting a single shot, yet never seeming rushed. David Cronenberg, the film's director, had up to 1983 been known as a cult filmmaker specializing in uber-gory horror movies such as 1975's *Shivers*, 1977's *Rabid* and 1979's *The Brood*. With *The Dead Zone*, Cronenberg does a directorial about-face: The film takes a low-key, restrained approach, featuring little gore and only a smattering of language, concentrating instead on characterization.

The last third revolves around the moral question of what Johnny should do regarding Stillson. Can he justify the man's murder? He asks his doctor if, given the chance, he would kill Hitler before the Holocaust. The somewhat bemused doctor

After an accident, Johnny Smith (Christopher Walken) can touch someone and predict their future, a talent that plunges him into a nightmarish dilemma in 1983's *The Dead Zone* (Dino De Laurentiis Corporation).

replies in the affirmative, thus unwittingly giving Smith the moral permission he needs.

The acting is first-rate. Walken shines as Johnny, the reluctant bearer of a post-coma "second sense" ability. In his 1983 review, Roger Ebert wrote, "Walken does such a good job of portraying Johnny Smith ... that we forget this is science fiction or fantasy or whatever and just accept it as this guy's story."[22] Ebert added that no King novel had been more successfully filmed.[23]

Walken receives able support from a number of movie veterans: Herbert Lom as his thoughtful doctor, Tom Skerritt as a desperate sheriff, Martin Sheen as Stillson. The other cast members also do first-rate work.

Smith's paranormal ability is never explained, but seems to fall under the domain of fantasy. Not only can he see what's going to happen, he can change it. This gives him an ability no human has ever had. Is it God-sent or Hell-born?

Smith spends the majority of the film viewing his power as a curse. In fact, after the midpoint, he goes into hiding. Yet once he shakes hands with Stillson and foresees the nuclear holocaust, his viewpoint shifts. His life takes on a new meaning when he decides he must kill Stillson before the populist deceiver can become president. In a letter to his former fiancée, Smith writes, "I always thought this power of mine was a curse, but now I can see it's a gift."

His post-coma life has unquestionably been tragic: losing his fiancée, losing his health, losing his privacy. At the end he loses everything, including his legacy and his life, but he saves everyone. What was a curse for Smith turns out to be a boon for humankind.

Smith's second sight vision of Stillson starting World War III is chilling. From his men, Stillson won't take no for an answer, and he calls his launching of America's nuclear missiles "my destiny." After Stillson has pressed the button, the vice-president

Populist politician Greg Stillson (Martin Sheen) acknowledges adulation from his ardent supporters in 1983's *The Dead Zone* (Dino De Laurentiis Corporation). If Stillson isn't stopped, he'll start World War III.

rushes to him and announces that a diplomatic solution has been reached, so war can be averted. Stillson replies, "The missiles are flying. Hallelujah, hallelujah."

True, in present time, Smith's rifle misses Stillson in the auditorium. But Stillson holds up a baby to use as a shield, and a photographer snaps several photos. When Stillson grabs the dying Smith, Smith foresees that Stillson, his political ambitions destroyed, will kill himself.

Does Smith's ultimate sacrifice of every aspect of his life, his total emptying, recall the self-sacrifice of religious figures such as Jesus Christ? Perhaps not intentionally, but this subtext may hold merit. One man (Stillson) seeks to take life, but one man (Smith) gives it.

The Dead Zone garnered mostly positive reviews. In *The New York Times*, Janet Maslin called it "a sad, sympathetic and unsettling movie, quietly forceful but in no way geared to the cheap scream."[24] Leonard Maltin concurred: "Absorbing Stephen King story. ... Walken's moving, heartfelt performance is the core."[25] *VideoHound Sci-Fi Experience*'s editors saw the film as bringing director Cronenberg into more conventional cinematic territory: "[P]lenty of tension, philosophical dilemmas ... the 'mainstream' finally got to see what Cronenberg can do."[26]

The Dead Zone could be considered a peripheral nuke threat movie.[27] Yet the specter of nuclear war haunts the film's final third. No one needs to spell out that an atomic holocaust would mean the end of civilization. That was a truth Americans in the 1980s knew all too well.

*   *   *

Endgame

DIRECTOR: Steven Benson; WRITERS: Alex Carver (screenplay); Steven Benson, Alex Carver (story); MUSIC: Carlo Maria Cordio; CINEMATOGRAPHER: Federico Slonisco; EDITOR: Tony Larson; PRODUCER: Joe D'Amato.

CAST: Al Cliver (Ron Shannon); Laura Gemser (Lilith); George Eastman (Karnak); Gordon Mitchell (Colonel Morgan); Christopher Walsh (Tommy).

PRODUCTION: Filmirage, Cinema 80; Italian; released November 1983 (in Italy); released to VHS via Media Home Entertainment on 23 April 1991 (in the U.S.); 98 minutes; rated R.

*   *   *

Mutants in post-nuke action films usually means the movie eschews realism and enshrines exploitation. Such is the case with the low-budget Italian-made *Endgame*.

Years after a nuclear war, debris, rats and corpses litter New York City, but there are still enough people and technology for the TV game show *Endgame* to ensnare the masses. The show's premise has one or more hunters pursuing a person who acts as the prey, all of the action televised and sponsored by the protein supplement Lifeplus, whose shameless hawking demonstrates that even after World War III, capitalism is still alive and kicking.

Also alive are mutants whom the government guns down at every opportunity. Rod Shannon, seven times an Endgame winner as a hunter, wins his newest match as prey and kills two of his hunters, but spares the third, Karnack. Telepathically, mutant Lilith asks Shannon to guide her and a group of mutants from the city. He agrees and recruits three partners, including strongman Kovack.

En route, Shannon and the others encounter a band of blind homicidal monks (who can "see" thanks to a captive telepathic mutant) and a group of devolved mutants (some ape-like, some with gills and scales). The Bad Mutants kidnap Lilith, but Shannon and Karnack rescue her.

Just when Shannon thinks he's won, government troops under the command of Colonel Morgan round up the good mutants and threaten Shannon's life. Telepathically, Shannon begs young Tommy, the one good mutant with telekinetic powers, to take out Colonel Morgan and his gang of fascists.

Whipping up a windstorm, Tommy directs machine-guns to mow down the government troops, dispatching others with a landslide, crushing others with the military transport vehicle, burning others in fire. As for Colonel Morgan, Tommy makes him aim his gun into his mouth and blow his brains out. This entire well-done sequence recalls the wrath of God visited upon the Nazi villains of 1981's *Raiders of the Lost Ark*.

A helicopter lands to spirit the mutants away (though it doesn't appear as if the chopper has room enough to accommodate them all). Shannon tells Lilith that he can't go with them: "You are the future. I am the present."

Shannon receives gold as his reward for leading the mutants to safety, but his rival Karnack pops up. The two agree to battle it out to see who gets the plunder. Cue freeze frame as they clash.

Extremely low-budget, *Endgame* manages some effective moments, such as Tommy's telekinetic carnage against the bad guys. The opening scenes that present the game show *Endgame* in action are okay, but this motif vanishes during the movie's final half.

Some of the action staging doesn't work. In one scene, three soldiers have their guns trained on Shannon, with a fourth armed soldier to the side, and Shannon somehow shoots them all before even one of them can shoot him.

The business with the blind monks is odd. Are they mutants who are born blind? Or do they blind themselves as part of their initiation into the order? And before they found and bound the telepathic mutant, how did they fight their enemies?

The film somewhat uses the mutants to incur the bigotry of the post-nuke populace. For example, when Kovack learns they are helping mutants escape, he resents it. And of course the government wants to waste them all. The mutants are stand-ins for any marginalized group, but social commentary is not *Endgame*'s strong suit. Still, Prof. Levin briefly speculates on the new society the mutants may bring, one free of deception and ignorance.

As Shannon, Al Cliver appears to be doing his best Clint Eastwood, and he's as hard-bitten as they come. For example, the violent blind monks hold captive a young male mutant whom they force to "see" through their enemies' eyes. When Shannon happens upon the bound mutant, he kills him rather than frees him. I don't think I would want to be a POW with a hardcase like Shannon around.

The makeup on the bad mutants is elemental but fun. The ape-like mutants could have been extras in a *Planet of the Apes* movie. Meanwhile, the silver-skinned fish-men mutants, bearing a smattering of scales on their cheeks and a fin atop their scalps, could have easily fit into a low-budget 1960s horror film (think 1964's *The Horror of Party Beach* or 1966's *Terror Beneath the Sea*).

Endgame was unrated but would probably receive an R for violence, nudity and rape. It resembles many of its Italian post-nuke cinematic cousins and sports the same flaws and excesses. You are forewarned.

* * *

The Exterminators of the Year 3000

DIRECTOR: Jules Harrison aka Giuliano Carnimeo; WRITERS: Elisa Brigatti, Dardano Sacchetti, Jose Truchado Reyes; MUSIC: Detto Mariano; CINEMATOGRAPHER: Alejandro Ulloa; EDITOR: Adriano Tagliavia; PRODUCER: Camillo Teti.

CAST: Robert Jannucci (Alien); Alicia Moro (Trash); Luciano Pigozzi aka Alan Collins (Papillon); Luca Venantini aka Lucas Ford (Tommy); Fred Harris (Crazy Bull).

PRODUCTION: 2T Produzione Film, Globe Film, Film S.r.L.; produced in 1983; Italian-Spanish; released in the U.S. on 4 January 1985; 90 minutes; rated R.

* * *

The Exterminators of the Year 3000 doesn't offer anything revolutionary, but it tries to make good on its own modest terms.

Following a nuclear war, the future is a bleak wasteland in which water is scarce. A settlement has run out of water, and must find some or else. Valiant John sets out to find some, but Crazy Bull and his motoring psychos nab him and demand to know where the H_2O is. John spits in Bull's face—not a suggested negotiating technique—and is killed for his *faux pas*.

Tommy, a young boy from the settlement, teams up with Alien, a cynical, selfish loner out for himself. Crazy Bull has injured Tommy's bionic arm, so Alien takes him to Papillon, a former astronaut, who repairs the limb.

Alien's former lover Trash shows up. She and Alien set out to retrieve water from a warehouse complex. They find the plant and—hurrah!—an abundant water source. But fanatical water cultists attack. Alien and Trash hold their own against the religious zealots.

Then Alien says he plans to sell the water to the highest bidders, and to Hades with Tommy, his precious settlement and humanity in general. Crafty Trash knocks Alien out with a sonic device, fills her tanker with water and peels out. Alien catches up with her in his uber-augmented Exterminator auto, and Trash reveals that Crazy Bull and his sanity-challenged buds are tailing her. In a frenetic finale, Papillon and Tommy arrive to help Trash battle two of the assassins. Alien whittles down Crazy Bull's psycho posse, and kills the big man himself.

But one of the assassins has drained the water from the tanker. The good guys make tracks to the water facility, but one of the water cultists blows the place up. Now what? Rain, of course. And everyone jumps around and shouts as the sky weeps.

The Exterminators of the Year 3000 is, at best, mediocre and, at worst, tiresome. Still, it appears sincere at times, such as the scenes of Papillon's death and Tommy's grieving. But while the auto action may thrill fans of this subgenre, for others it may inspire frequent glances at one's watch.

Rated R for the usual swearing and graphic violence,

* * *

Never Say Never Again

DIRECTOR: Irvin Kershner; WRITERS: Lorenzo Semple, Jr. (screenplay); Kevin McClory, Jack Whittingham, Ian Fleming (story); MUSIC: Michel Legrand; CINEMATOGRAPHER: Douglas Slocombe; EDITOR: Robert Lawrence;

PRODUCER: Jack Schwartzman; UNDERWATER SEQUENCE DIRECTOR: Ricou Browning.[28]

CAST: Sean Connery (James Bond, 007); Klaus Maria Brandauer (Maximilian Largo); Max von Sydow (Blofeld); Barbara Carrera (Fatima); Kim Basinger (Domino Peta-chi); Bernie Casey (Felix Leiter).

PRODUCTION: Taliafilm; British-U.S.; released 7 October 1983 (in the U.S.); released 14 December 1983 (in the U.K.); 134 minutes; rated PG. Alternate title: *James Bond of the Secret Service.*

* * *

When Sean Connery decided to play James Bond again after 12 years, his wife Micheline Roquebrune gave the 1983 Bond film its title *Never Say Never Again*. It was the first Bond movie title that was not also the title of one of the Ian Fleming 007 novels. But it was not the first to deal with the nuclear threat. To some extent, *Never Say Never Again* remakes 1965's *Thunderball*, but the details have changed.

Surgery has altered USAF Captain Jack Petachi's right eye to resemble the U.S. president's right eye, allowing Petachi access to nuclear warhead delivery. From an American Air Force base in England, the retinal scan allows him to arm two Cruise missiles with live nuclear warheads. The criminal organization SPECTRE steals the missiles and demands billions from NATO.

Sent by M to find the missiles, 007 meets SPECTRE agent Maximilian Largo and his lover Domino Petachi. Bond and Largo play a high-stakes 3-D video game that gives increasingly strong electrical shocks to the loser. After Bond wins, he tells Domino that SPECTRE has assassinated her brother, Captain Petachi.

Enraged at Bond kissing Domino, Largo gives her to an Arab seller and imprisons Bond. The intrepid 007 naturally escapes and rescues Domino. The first nuclear warhead SPECTRE has stolen is disarmed.

Bond and his ally Felix Leiter invade Largo's base of operations, but Largo escapes with the live nuclear warhead. Bond tangles with Largo underwater and deactivates the warhead. Using a speargun, Domino kills Largo, her vengeance for Largo having had her brother murdered. As in all James Bond movies, the world is safe for democracy once more, though Bond vows never again to don the mantle of 007. Then he winks at the camera.

Although several actors have portrayed James Bond over the years, for many, Sean Connery, the first Bond, remains *the* 007. His Bond films set the bar for all 007 thrillers to come. Of the six 1960s Bond films, Connery appeared as 007 in five, along with 1971's *Diamonds Are Forever. Never Say Never Again* plays up a graying 007 without apology. Indeed, he seems to be retiring at the end of the film, appropriate since this would be Connery's last Bond.

The film depicts the secret service resources, so abundant in the 1960s Bond movies, impacted by bureaucracy and dwindling interest in the double-O program. For example, Q, who makes the nifty spy gadgets for 007, complains to Bond that budget cuts damaged his department.

As Bond, Connery comes off as smooth as ever, able to believably switch from suave to rugged at a moment's notice. Max von Sydow, who graced a number of director Ingmar Bergman's Swedish dramas, only gets a dollop of screen time as Blofeld, the infamous SPECTRE director. But he seems to enjoy the part.

Klaus Maria Brandauer's take on the villainous Largo is alternately genteel and chilling. Meanwhile, as one of Largo's top operatives, Barbara Carrera is all cyanide and spice and nothing nice as she gleefully dispatches enemies and allies left and right. Given her lavish wardrobe, she must also be raking in an annual seven figure income. On the positive side of the moral ledger, Kim Basinger invests her character Domino with fortitude and smarts, a classy woman far removed from Bimbo-land.

The film makes a laudable move into diversity territory. In the past, white actors had played Bond's friend and ally Felix Leiter. This time out, black actor extraordinaire Bernie Casey fills the CIA agent's shoes.

What about Bond's infamous womanizing? Here it's a bit more restrained than during the 1960s, but only a bit. The classic Bond films didn't include nudity, but they certainly objectified women, often treating them as second-class eye candy good for one thing only. This time, Bond's chief love interest Domino appears more independent than his 1960s paramours. Further, the film's finale suggests that Bond may go the monogamous route with Domino, and perhaps even marry her. Will wonders never cease?

The nuke threat informed three of the 1960s Bond movies. In *Goldfinger* (1964), the title villain wants to irradiate the gold in Fort Knox to raise the value of his personal gold reserves. In *Thunderball* (1965), SPECTRE plans to A-bomb Miami if the authorities don't meet their extortion demands. *You Only Live Twice* (1967) widens SPECTRE's nuclear ambitions: They snatch a Russian *and* an American spacecraft from orbit and plan to nab a second American ship, hoping to provoke the U.S. and the U.S.S.R. to World War III, thereby raising the international heft of an unnamed Asian country (probably China).

Interestingly, SPECTRE demands are less spectacular in *Never Say Never Again* than in *You Only Live Twice*. "All" SPECTRE wants this time is a robust tribute payment or they will detonate the two stolen nukes, one in Middle Eastern oil fields, the other in Washington, D.C. As the foreign secretary tells the panicked

After 12 years, Sean Connery returned as James Bond in 1983's *Never Say Never Again*; 007 has again been pressed into service to thwart the criminal organization SPECTRE, which has stolen two armed nuclear missiles and demands NATO pay billions in ransom.

world leaders, "We are faced with the ultimate nightmare—the abduction of nuclear warheads."

But of course, it's a Bond film, so we never seriously think those nukes will go off. If they did, viewer expectations would collapse. But nuclear terrorism almost always grabs attention as a reliable thriller tease. *Never Say Never Again* cost $36 million but grossed $160 million.[29]

Reviews for the movie are generally favorable. *The New York Times'* Janet Maslin opined, "Mr. Connery ... combines the wry reserve of yesteryear with a hint of weariness that, in the context of the screenplay's insistence on adventure, is genuinely amusing."[30]

But Leonard Maltin wrote, "Connery's stylish performance and self-deprecating humor make his return performance as James Bond ... a real treat—but the film ... is uneven and overlong."[31]

Never Say Never Again has its charms. But to some extent, it's 007 business as usual, the old Bond formula put through its (sometimes shuffling) paces. Sean Connery makes his last take on 007 something special, and the finale indicates an actual change—one for the better—in the character's life.

* * *

The New Barbarians

DIRECTOR: Enzo G. Castellari; WRITERS: Tito Carpi, Enzo G. Castellari; MUSIC: Claudio Simonetti; CINEMATOGRAPHER: Fausto Zuccoli; EDITOR: Gianfranco Amicucci; PRODUCER: Fabrizio De Angelis.
CAST: Timothy Brent aka Giancarlo Prete (Scorpion); Fred Williamson (Nadir); George Eastman (One); Anna Kanakis (Alma); Venantino Venantini (Father Moses).
PRODUCTION: Deaf International Film S.r.l.; Italian; released in Italy on 7 April 1983; released in the U.S. on 13 January 1984; 91 minutes; rated R. Alternate title: *Warriors of the Wasteland.*

* * *

Any movie with characters named Scorpion, Nadir and One can't be all good, and *The New Barbarians* is no exception. It teems with action sequences but still bores the viewer.

The opening card proclaims, "2019. The nuclear holocaust is over." The aftermath has left scattered pockets of humanity, including the Templars, bad guys garbed in white who use their souped-up vehicles to raid caravans. After one such raid, quasi–good guy Scorpion rescues Alma, a woman with a shoulder injury. Nadir, an archer with explosive arrows, more or less teams up with Scorpion.

Meanwhile, One, the leader of the Templars, preaches to his fellow hooligans that the Templars are "the high priests of death." Their purpose is to exterminate humankind, no ifs, ands or buts about it.

Scorpion takes Alma to a religious caravan, where a man known as the wiz treats her shoulder. She elects to stay with the caravan. Its leader, Father Moses, says that due to vehicle maintenance, the caravan can't move for two days.

The Templars once again chase Scorpion, this time capturing him and hauling him to the Templars' camp. Sadistically, One gloats over Scorpion's helplessness and tortures him. Next, the Templars attack the religious caravan, subduing its members.

Three Templars have been assigned to finish Scorpion off, but Nadir dispatches the hapless trio. Scorpion and Nadir attack the Templars. The nefarious One escapes, but Scorpion races after him and uses a car-mounted whirling drill to skewer the Templar leader. One loses control of his vehicle, which crashes and explodes.

Like a faulty fuse, *The New Barbarians* fails to ignite. Many of the frequent action scenes are shown in slow-motion, peculiar since it makes the autos appear ponderous. Graphic violence is kept to a minimum, yet still merits an R rating.

The actors struggle. Fred Williamson as archer Nadir comes off the best, giving his character a dash of charm. With his eye-catching costume, he'd be at home in a superhero movie. Williamson is probably the best-known among the *New Barbarians* cast. In the 1960s, he played professional football and sported the nickname "The Hammer." As an actor, he appeared in an impressive number of films from 1970 to 2019. He has also done TV work.

The rest of the cast is less known. George Eastman's portrayal of One is typical bad guy stuff, his performance lacking the manic verve it needs. As Scorpion, Timothy Brent comes off okay. We do wonder about him when he starts to manhandle Alma, but then he stops and realizes she is injured. From that point on, he sheds his antihero tendencies.

The religious caravan adherents sport curious beliefs. We hear they are prepared to survive seven years after the apocalypse while they follow a signal. Father Moses leads them, but it's unclear whether he was or is a Catholic priest. If he is, his sect's beliefs are more unorthodox than mayonnaise on corn flakes.

The film offers no post-nuke apocalyptic trappings, such as radiation, town or city ruins, or charred landscapes. But the small groups of people suggest the nuclear holocaust was wide-ranging.

Unremarkable in almost every way, *The New Barbarians* offers little, even for fans of *Mad Max* rip-offs, and it's tasteless to boot. Read a good book instead.

*　*　*

Octopussy

DIRECTOR: John Glen; WRITERS: George MacDonald Fraser, Richard Maibaum, Michael G. Wilson; MUSIC: John Barry; CINEMATOGRAPHER: Alan Hume; EDITORS: Peter Davies, Henry Richardson; PRODUCER: Albert R. Broccoli.

CAST: Roger Moore (James Bond, 007); Maud Adams (Octopussy); Louis Jourdan (Kamal Khan).

PRODUCTION: United Artists, Eon Productions, Danjaq; produced by Albert R. Broccoli; British; released 10 June 1983 (in the U.S.); released 6 June 1983 (in the U.K.); 131 minutes; rated PG.

*　*　*

Two James Bond movies in 1983—*Never Say Never Again* and *Octopussy*—must have delighted 007 fans. And both featured Cold War nuke threat plots. But each featured a different Bond: Sean Connery in *Never Say Never Again* and Roger Moore in *Octopussy*.

In the latter, agent 009 dies delivering a rare Carl Fabergé egg to East Berlin's British Embassy. Kamal Khan, a wealthy but shady exile, buys the egg at an auction attended by Bond. Double-O Seven follows the trail to India, where Khan has him captured. Bond overhears Khan speaking to Soviet General Orlov, a war hawk. Bond also meets the mysterious Octopussy, a wealthy manager who presides over a cult of women who work as her agents and participate in her circus. Naturally, she and Bond become romantically involved.

Bond discovers that with Khan's help, General Orlov has planted an A-bomb with a circus that will be entertaining at a U.S. Air Force base in West Germany. The bomb's explosion will be blamed on the Americans (it will have happened on one of their airbases), thus cowing NATO so the Soviets can invade Western Europe, or so the fanatical Orlov hopes.

After a series of vigorous heroics, Bond races to the airbase and, disguised as a clown, steals into the circus' show in progress. With Octopussy's help, he deactivates the device.

Khan has retreated to his palace in India, but Bond and Octopussy find him. He has Octopussy held captive aboard a plane in which he plans to escape, but Bond has other plans. He and Octopussy escape the aircraft, but Khan dies when the plane dashes into a cliff and explodes.

Whatever else one may say about *Octopussy*, no one can say it skimps on action. The film brims with fast-paced derring-do. It must have been quite a workout—sometimes a dangerous one—for the stunt crew. One of the two most elaborate set pieces involves stunt actors running atop a train, fighting each other atop a train, and hanging on to the side of a train for dear life. The second most involved set piece has Bond atop a plane in flight trying to disable the craft and battle one of Khan's henchmen. Roger Moore's doubles should have gotten hazard pay for these death-defying stunts.

The script, acting and direction are all okay, but if you've seen two or three Roger Moore Bonds, you've seen most if not all of it before. Plenty of beautiful women flit here and there, of course. And Maud Adams intrigues as the enigmatic title character Octopussy.

Overall, *Octopussy* takes itself fairly seriously. But when Moore swings on vines and gives the old Johnny Weissmuller Tarzan yell, the camp becomes odious. It doesn't at all fit with the rest of the film's straight-faced action.

It's intriguing how similar the atomic terrorism is in both *Octopussy* and its 1983 competition *Never Say Never Again*. In *Octopussy*, Soviet General Orlov is portrayed as a wild-eyed hawk out of step with Russia's disarmament talks. During his dialogue with Bond, 007 reasons that if Europe thinks the A-bomb that explodes on the U.S. airbase is the result of an American accident, the event will trigger free Europe to unilaterally disarm, thus paving the way for a Russian invasion.

Roger Moore retired his 007 credentials after making one more Bond movie, 1985's *A View to a Kill*. Critics often slammed his Bond films for being too tongue-in-cheek. True or not, they did make money, and Moore did have a following.

Reviews for *Octopussy* are mixed. The *Boston Globe*'s Michael Blowen wrote, "[A]lthough *Octopussy* does capitalize on bigger and better gimmicks, it has a major problem in Moore. He's in his early 50s and a bit too old to be fighting on the top of a train with a saber-swinging Indian or sprinting across a jungle trying to escape from a mob of hunters."[32] On the other hand, Leonard Maltin gave the film three and a half stars: "Grand escapist fare…. Film throws in everything but the kitchen sink for the sake of an entertaining show."[33]

Just as in *Never Say Never Again*, the audience knows the A-bomb will not atomize the circus and the American airbase. Yet it might be interesting to see a parallel universe version of this film in which the circus and airbase suffer nuclear annihilation. Such a movie probably wouldn't have made money, but it would no doubt have taken the Bond series in a new direction, mostly because the A-bomb would have vaporized the intrepid 007.

* * *

Raiders of Atlantis

DIRECTOR: Robert Gold aka Tito Carpi; WRITERS: Robert Gold aka Tito Carpi, Vincent Mannino aka Vincenzo Mannin; MUSIC: Oliver Onions aka Guido, Maurizio De Angelis; CINEMATOGRAPHER: Roberto D'Ettorre Piazzoli; EDITOR: Vincenzo Tomassi; PRODUCER: Edmondo Amati.
CAST: Christopher Connelly (Mike Ross); Marie Fields aka Gioia Scola (Dr. Cathy Rollins); Tony King (Washington).
PRODUCTION: Regency Productions; Italian; 1983; 92 minutes; not rated. Alternate title: *Atlantis Interceptors*.

* * *

According to the overwrought *Raiders of Atlantis*, Atlanteans were homicidal maniacs who slaughtered everything in sight. Yes, that does sound more like a horror movie premise than your average post-nuke adventure framework.

On a large ocean platform, a team of scientists raise a sunken Russian nuclear submarine. But something goes wrong and a huge dome rises from the sea, causing massive waves that destroy the platform. A few scientists survive, and two thieves—Mike and Washington—pick them up. They sail to the nearest island and find the inhabitants have been brutally murdered.

The cause: The Interceptors, Atlanteans who decree that all non–Atlanteans should be killed. According to their leader, "Our civilization does not accept intruders." The latter includes all the protagonists except for Dr. Cathy Rollins. The Interceptors capture her and kill the rest of the cast, save for Mike and Washington. Cathy becomes Atlantisized and starts talking like a robot. But Mike and Washington—and Cathy—escape just in time.

Technically, the film blunders. In the scene in which the ocean platform is destroyed, the special effects and miniature work are subpar. However, the script has more serious problems. The Atlanteans' bloodthirstiness remains a mystery, probably a gambit to kill time and provide opportunities for graphic violence. Interestingly, in addition to their murderous ways, the Atlanteans sport a fashion sense straight out of the Mad Max movies.

Occasionally, the action shows signs of hasty filming. Sometimes there are no squibs, or they don't go off as the heroes gun down the Atlanteans. Often, the violence disturbs, such as the burning of one of the women. The movie's attempts to foster camaraderie among the protagonists sometimes work. For example, a hesitant professor joins in with his fellow protagonists in defending the group, thus winning their friendship and respect.

The nuclear threat tie-in is vague. A scientist says, "The radiation from the submarine caused Atlantis to rise." Near the end, the same scientist neutralizes the sub's missile warheads, thus shutting down Atlantis' power and causing the dome to close and sink back under the sea.

The connection between Cathy and the Atlanteans is bizarre. In Atlantean getup, she cryptically says that the Atlanteans' descendants are coming back. Mike tells her to stop them, and she vanishes, next appearing on multiple screens asking Mike for help. But when Mike and Washington climb into the helicopter to escape, she is inexplicably in the chopper as well.

This unrated movie would get an R for language and graphic violence.

Due to its poorly written screenplay, which fails to explain what the Atlanteans are about, and its lackluster execution, more intent on violence than intrigue, *Raiders of Atlantis* never makes it out of dry dock.

* * *

Rats: Night of Terror

DIRECTOR: Vincent Dawn; WRITERS: Claudio Fragasso, Herve Piccini (screenplay); Bruno Mattei (story); MUSIC: Luigi Ceccarelli; CINEMATOGRAPHER: Franco Delli Colli; EDITOR: Gilbert Kikoine; PRODUCER: Jacques Leitienne.
CAST: Richard Raymond (Kurt); Janna Ryann (Chocolate); Alex McBride (Taurus).
PRODUCTION: Beatrice Film, IMP.EX.CI; Italian-French; 1983; released in the U.S. on 21 February 1986; 91 minutes; not rated.

* * *

"Rats!" was one of Charlie Brown's favorite expressions, but that might have changed if he'd spent five minutes in the post-nuke milieu of *Rats: Night of Terror.*

A nuclear war has ravaged the world, and survivors live underground. But some "new primitives" choose to live on Earth's surface again, despite the risks. Our story relates the (unenviable) fate of one such group. This gang, who appear to have been wardrobed for a Duran Duran music video, happens upon a deserted town in which they discover abundant food, plants and water. Good news, right? Not so fast. Rats who hunt and eat *Homo sapiens* infest the place. With a taste for human flesh, they attack the protagonists, killing them one by one. The rodents pollute the water system and even chew through the tires on the protagonists' motorcycles so our heroes can't escape.

Many rat-gnawed corpses later, figures in hazmat suits emerge from underground, spraying a gas that kills the rats. Only two of our protagonists have survived, both grateful for their rescue. Then one of the hazmat folks takes off his mask, revealing himself to be a rat-human hybrid. Freeze frame on one of the survivors screaming bloody murder.

Rats: Night of Terror attempts to mix elements from 1971's *Willard* with various nature-run-amok films. Numerous horror shots abound: a rat crawls from the mouth of the first victim, rats gnaw bloodily from another victim's torso, *ad nauseam*. But the scares aren't there.

Logic issues abound. For example, while her friends lie in normal beds, one woman zips herself in a sleeping bag she can't unzip when the rats attack her. Why wasn't she in a bed like the others?

The final scene of the man-rat is the obligatory "scare shot" near and dear to horror films. But it doesn't necessarily make sense. If the rat humanoids are on the side of the rats, why did they gas them? Because they wanted to dine on the two human survivors themselves?

If you're familiar with 1950s monster movies, *Rats: Night of Terror* resembles a gross-out version of 1959's *The Killer Shrews*. If you're not familiar with 1950s monster movies, you probably still want to avoid *Rats*. The only terror you may experience is the 91 minutes you can never retrieve.

*   *   *

The Return of the Man from U.N.C.L.E.

DIRECTOR: Ray Austin; WRITER: Michael Sloan, based on the TV series developed by Sam Rolfe; MUSIC: Gerald Fried; CINEMATOGRAPHER: Fred J. Koenekamp; EDITOR: George Jay Nicholson; PRODUCER: Nigel Watts.
CAST: Robert Vaughn (Napoleon Solo); David McCallum (Illya Kuryakin); Patrick Macnee (Sir John Raleigh); Anthony Zerbe (Justin Sepheran).
PRODUCTION: Richard Sloan Productions, Viacom Productions; broadcast on NBC-TV 5 April 1983; 96 minutes; not rated.

*   *   *

James Bond may have reigned as cinema's top movie spy in the 1960s, but on American television, Napoleon Solo ruled as the decade's top secret agent. In the '80s, when TV-movie reunions of vintage TV series were being churned out, Solo and his partner Illya Kuryakin reteamed in *The Return of the Man from U.N.C.L.E.: The Fifteen Years Later Affair*.

THRUSH, an international crime organization, has swiped a nuclear bomb and demands a ransom of $350 million or said device will explode somewhere in the United States. So U.N.C.L.E., the United Network Command for Law and Enforcement, calls back two retired agents, Napoleon, now working in computers, and Illya, now toiling in fashion design.

THRUSH's 1983 resurrection after 15 years is headed by Justin Sepheran, who insists Solo must personally deliver the ransom. Amidst much cloak-and-dagger derring-do, Kuryakin, trapped beneath a nuclear power plant, cheers on an actor with a photographic memory who can disarm the bomb. Meanwhile, Solo and a multitude of U.N.C.L.E. agents besiege THRUSH's Libya headquarters.

Naturally, the bomb is disarmed, Solo and his agents prevail, and that's that—or is it? Solo and Kuryakin repair to a bar, compare career notes, and hear on TV that Air Force One has disappeared. They get a call from U.N.C.L.E.'s current director who asks them, "Are the two of you doing anything for the next few days?"

Happily, this reunion TV movie captures much of the fun spirit of the original 1964–68 series. Campiness intrudes only once, a George Lazenby cameo in which his Aston Martin, with license plate JB, gets Solo out of a tough spot.

Otherwise, the film's humor is honest and stems from Solo and Kuryakin (well-played by Robert Vaughn and David McCallum) trying to adjust to the 1980s. Solo's old U.N.C.L.E. communicator pen beeps early on, startling him at an inopportune moment. He finds his reflexes a bit slower than they were 15 years earlier. In a clever segment, he goes to the tailor shop that used to serve as a front for U.N.C.L.E. headquarters;

the shop owner thinks he's nuts, and Solo realizes that U.N.C.L.E. must have moved. The final shot in which Solo and Kuryakin get the phone call from U.N.C.L.E. is a nice touch.

Leo G. Carroll, who played U.N.C.L.E.'s director Mr. Waverly in the 1960s series, had passed on in 1972. The movie refers to him several times, and one shot highlights his photo. As the spy organization's new head, Patrick Macnee handles the part with his customary British charm.

The stolen nuclear bomb is said to be vastly destructive. But little is made of this, as the movie's atmosphere is friendly, the accent nostalgic. Talk of millions of deaths, radiation burns, fallout and such would have weighed down a project intended to be pleasing. But is it ethical to include a grave menace like a nuclear weapon in a modest entertainment piece? Good question, yet we know that from the '50s on, nukes have been used in comic books and juvenile novels. Perhaps the nuke threat is so deeply embedded in our culture that its use in a children's tale barely merits a shrug. At the same time, this could be a way to take the sting out of thermonuclear reality.

Using a nuclear weapon as a plot device is common in theatrical spy movies, so it's unsurprising it was used in this *Man from U.N.C.L.E.* reunion film. We all know that nukes are bad news, so on a purely plotting basis, it's a great menace to employ.

The Return of the Man from U.N.C.L.E. largely captures the lost '60s—and nowadays, the lost '80s as well. Fans of the old TV series will probably like it, though it may leave others scratching their heads.

* * *

Rush

DIRECTOR: Tonino Ricci; WRITERS: Tito Carpi, Tonino Ricci; MUSIC: Stelvio Cipriani, Francesco De Masi; CINEMATOGRAPHER: Giovanni Bergamini; EDITOR: Vincenzo Tomassi; PRODUCER: Marcello Romeo.
CAST: Conrad Nichols (Rush); Gordon Mitchell (Yor); Laura Trotter (Carol).
PRODUCTION: Biro Cinematografica; Italian; 1983; released in the U.S. in October 1984; 77 minutes; not rated. Alternate title: *Blood Rush*.

* * *

This derivative grade-D action movie attempts to mine 1979's *Mad Max* and 1982's *Rambo: First Blood* for raw material, but winds up producing cartloads of fool's gold instead.

In the desolate post–nuclear war future, the evil minions of Yor capture Rush, amazed that radiation hasn't contaminated him. Yor lords over a compound filled with plant nurseries staffed by unwilling workers guarded by armed soldiers. When you die, you get sent to the fertilizer plant.

Carol, one of the workers plotting against Yor, speaks to Rush in private and begs him to help her and her friends escape. Rush agrees. When the workers revolt, guards capture most of them. Rush escapes and flees into the woods.

To elude Yor and his soldiers, our intrepid hero takes advantage of booby traps, a tractor and the bad guys' atrocious aim to stay one step ahead of them. He commandeers a Jeep and plows it into the compound, shooting scores of Yor's soldiers, as well as (somewhat inexplicably) destroying one of Yor's plant nurseries. Carol helps co-workers escape until one of Yor's soldiers shoots and kills her. The workers beat the guards with clubs.

Rush and Yor square off against each other. After a fierce struggle, Yor falls from a scaffold to his death. Our last image shows a smiling Rush fading into a visual of grass gently blowing in the wind.

Rush suffers not only from a low budget, but also poor storytelling. About midway through the movie, when Rush escapes, you'd swear the sequence in which he continuously battles Yor's soldiers goes on longer than 1956's *The Ten Commandments*. As for the action itself, it is often dubious. We see Rush taking on three, sometimes four guys at a time, and despite the fact they all have rifles, they consistently miss him while he mows them down. The post-nuke setting exists only so we can see Rush savage the bad guys. Yes, we see some (poor) radiation makeup. But you could excise all mention of nuclear war and radiation from the film with little if any threat to the movie's coherence.

I'm sure many stunt doubles got intense workouts filming the action scenes. The pyrotechnics crew was put through their paces as well. Too bad the movie wastes their efforts.

Since the film is dubbed, I can't say much about the acting. But based on facial expressions, some of it appears over-the-top.

*　*　*

Special Bulletin

DIRECTOR: Edward Zwick; WRITERS: Marshall Herskovitz (teleplay); Edward Zwick, Marshall Herskovitz (story); VISUAL EFFECTS: William Feightner; EDITOR: Arden Rynew. PRODUCERS: Marshall Herskovitz, Edward Zwick.

CAST: Ed Flanders (John Woodley); Kathryn Walker (Susan Myles); Christopher Allport (Steven Levitt); David Clennon (Dr. Bruce Lyman); David Rasche (Dr. David McKeeson); J. Wesley Huston (Bernard Frost); Roxanne Hart (Meg Barclay).

PRODUCTION: Ohlmeyer Communications Company, National Broadcasting Company (NBC); broadcast on NBC-TV on 20 March 1983; 105 minutes.

*　*　*

"Are we going to die?" a news reporter asks after a nuclear device has exploded two miles away. This is not the ending the viewer expected from *Special Bulletin*, a TV-movie made to appear as legitimate TV news coverage of domestic nuclear terrorism. For example, in movies such as 1950's *Seven Days to Noon* and books such as 1980's *The Fifth Horseman*, the threatened explosion due to nuclear blackmail is averted. In *Special Bulletin*, it is not.

The film opens with a news flash on fictional network RBS. We see the Coast Guard has waged a firefight with terrorists on a tugboat docked at Charleston, South Carolina. The terrorists won and have abducted news reporter Steve Levitt (Christopher Allport), his camera operator and two Coast Guard members. The terrorists demand and receive a live link from RBS, whose news anchors are John Woodley (Ed Flanders) and Susan Myles (Kathryn Walker). The terrorists release the Coast Guard members.

Dr. Bruce Lymon (David Clennon), the chief terrorist, announces the terrorists' demands: that the 968 detonating modules for nuclear weapons in the Charleston area be delivered to the tugboat by the following evening. Failure to comply will cause the

Two experts race to disarm the anti-tamper devices in a nuclear bomb before it explodes in the Charleston, South Carolina, harbor in 1983's *Special Bulletin*. Insert: Dr. Neils Johanssen (Bernard Behrens) explains to TV viewers the problems two specialists are having.

terrorists to set off a nuclear bomb, which is outfitted with safeguards and booby traps to ensure it will be detonated at the appointed time unless terrorist David McKeeson (David Rasche) disarms it.

The government considers this a hoax, but further investigation reveals Lymon and McKeeson, who claim to have stolen the necessary plutonium, are capable of building a nuclear bomb. In addition, the authorities determine that there is fissionable material aboard the tugboat. The president orders Charleston's evacuation.

Close to the last minute, the government appears to comply with the terrorists, who are jubilant. Two trucks pull up to the tugboat, presumably with the modules. However, a power blackout ensues, a cover for American soldiers who steal aboard the ship and wrest control from the terrorists. Experts turn to the task of disarming the nuclear weapon, but due to the device's safeguards, they fail. The device explodes, resulting in a 23-kiloton nuclear blast that obliterates Charleston. We hear that 2000 died, with many more injured and homeless. The future fate of the irradiated site of Charleston remains unknown.

Not unknown to real-life authorities at the time was the notion of nuclear blackmail. A June 15, 1981, UPI item noted that the Energy Department's security director claimed there had been 75 cases of "nuclear extortion" in the previous five years. Most were attributed to cranks, but the Energy Department considered some serious.[34]

One of *Special Bulletin*'s assets is its believability. Except in the case of Ed Flanders as John Woodley, the TV-movie wisely uses little-known actors instead of well-known stars. This enhances the film's plausibility. Likewise, shooting the movie on video instead of film approximates an actual news program, and the movie's occasional glitches are things that actually happen in live broadcasts. The RBS news set and the demeanor of the journalists, both the two anchors and the correspondents, likewise enhance credibility.

Prior to *Special Bulletin*'s airing on March 20, 1983, NBC executives reportedly panicked over the movie, fearful that viewers would take it as gospel, despite the film's time compressions and planned disclaimers. Director Edward Zwick wasn't happy about NBC's cold feet, but NBC chairman Grant Tinker maintained it was better to "err on the side of responsibility."[35]

Consequently, both before and after commercial breaks, the telecast informed viewers they were only watching a dramatization. Nevertheless, a handful of the TV audience apparently believed the event might be real. According to *The New York Times*, 2,200 viewers in New York, Chicago, Los Angeles, Washington and Cleveland called to ask if the film's nuclear terrorism was actually happening.[36]

In addition to the nuclear issue, the film deals with the world of TV news and its potential complicity in the events it covers. For example, near the beginning, WPIV reporter Steven Levitt runs ever closer into danger as the Coast Guard and terrorists shoot it out. Is this an act of bravery? Or is he thinking more about his career and the need to get a good story at all costs? And what about his hapless camera operator who must accompany him?

Also, by presenting a live feed to the terrorists, has RBS empowered them to hold the city of Charleston hostage? But what alternative would a network have? Should news outlets ignore terrorists? Not a realistic scenario, and not one serving the public. Yet the kind of journalism *Special Bulletin* portrays forges an uncomfortable alliance between exploitation and information. And certainly the commercial nature of news ratings assures the creation and perpetuation of journalist celebrities, a reality that can impede ethical journalism. You can see examples of this on news networks.

When I first saw *Special Bulletin* in 1983, I had assumed the film would end without any nuclear explosions. So I was shocked when the bomb obliterated Charleston. Indeed, this ending rattled me like a sonic boom.

The nuclear detonation stuns the two RBS news anchors into tears and shaky voices. Even the White House administration's press secretary is shocked into submission, offering a subdued declaration of what has happened. Meg (Roxanne Hart), a traumatized RBS reporter on a Navy ship two miles from the explosion, is barely functioning; the blast killed one of her camera operators. She wonders aloud if she, and the others around her, are going to die, presumably from radiation sickness.

The aftermath of the event is as sobering as the explosion itself. We hear about thousands of burn victims, but not enough burn beds in the country to accommodate them. We also hear about half a million who are now homeless, and the reality that Charleston is not only gone, but may forever remain deserted.

You have to wonder what the political and social repercussions would have been in 1983 had the events in *Special Bulletin* occurred. Clearly, the administration would be voted out in a probable landslide, and it's possible the president would be impeached before a new election. Americans would hold terrorists in even greater contempt, especially domestic terrorists. And America would know what heretofore only the nation of Japan had known: a haunted nuclear past.

Would the fear of nuclear attack on American soil (no longer theoretical in the movie) have pushed 1980s Americans to the right or the left? Would more Americans have embraced the Nuclear Freeze movement? Would bilateral disarmament have become even more of a public concern, one on which political elections could be won or lost? A sequel to *Special Bulletin* dealing with these questions might have been intriguing.

Special Bulletin depicts domestic terrorism at a time when most Americans equated terrorism with the Middle East. This telefilm predates by only 12 years the 1995 bombing of the Federal Building in Oklahoma City by domestic terrorist Timothy McVeigh. But *Special Bulletin*'s terrorists consider their actions necessary to force the government to do the right thing; in essence, all is fair in love and war. However, the terrorists putting thousands of innocent lives at risk is unconscionable, and the ending reveals that the tugboat did indeed harbor a live nuclear device. Notably, one anti-nuclear activist in the telefilm distances legitimate nuclear protest efforts from the terrorists' tactics.

The night before the terrorists' deadline, the government orders the evacuation of Charleston. Citizens are confused when police officers go door to door spouting evacuation directives. Roadways are bumper to bumper with vehicles, some stalling or having flat tires; stores are robbed; thousands are forced to evacuate on foot. As African American RBS correspondent Bernard Frost notes, "The Federal Disaster Control Agency had a plan for the evacuation of Charleston, but it proved to be totally inadequate." This implies that civil defense strategies for a nuclear attack in general were deficient, especially for large urban areas.

Many may not think of *Special Bulletin* as science fiction. I would argue that's exactly what it is—and I'm glad. I hope it never becomes science fact. *Starlog Science-Fiction Magazine* #1 (1988) gives the movie four out of five stars, lauding the "excellent cast" and "taut script," and noting, "The film's startling and unnerving."[37]

The telecast reaped six Emmy award nominations and won awards for writing, technical direction/electronic camerawork, video tape editing and Outstanding Drama Special.[38] In addition, director Edward Zwick won the Humanitas Prize, shared with *Special Bulletin* writer Marshall Herskovitz.[39] Zwick would go on to a distinguished record of directing theatrical films, including 1989's *Glory*.

Some consider *Special Bulletin* one of the first "found footage" films, though most of what we see is supposed to be occurring live. The exception is the footage of correspondent Steven Levitt and his unseen camera operator George Takashima as they encounter the Coast Guard's firefight with the tugboat terrorists. In addition, RBS airs tourist-filmed footage of the event.

Special Bulletin differs from most of the films in this book in that it doesn't concern itself with a major nuclear war or its aftermath, but rather with a limited nuclear assault. Fortunately, the telecast's nuclear terrorism theme remains one true in fiction only—at least, so far.

* * *

Stryker

DIRECTOR-PRODUCER: Cirio H. Santiago; WRITERS: Howard Cohen (screenplay); Leonard Hermes (story); MUSIC: Ed Gatchalian; CINEMATOGRAPHER: Ricardo Remias; EDITOR: Bas Santos.

CAST: Steve Sandor (Stryker); Andria Savio (Delha); William Ostrander (Bandit).
PRODUCTION: HCI International, Cinema Vehicles; released in the U.S. on 2 September 1983 by New World; 86 minutes; rated R.

* * *

Stryker is just one of many "lone warrior in a post-nuke wasteland" movies produced during the 1980s.

The opening narration, behind which we see a stock nuclear explosion, tells us, "The last war began in error." The film picks up years later in a desert setting where water has become precious. Delha hails from the Colony, which has an ample supply of H_2O; her mission is to inform the folks who live under the leadership of Trun that water is available. However, the henchmen of the evil Kardis kidnap and torture her to find the Colony's location. Cowboy hat–wearing Stryker and his faithful sidekick Bandit rescue her and spirit her to Trun's people. But Kandis' minions have captured Trun, and one of them uses him as a human urinal. Not to fear! Stryker, Bandit and others rescue the man from further indignities.

Delha leads Trun and his followers to the Colony, where water flows more freely than beer in a Garth Brooks song. Bandit falls in love, but Stryker chooses to remain a loner and sets out on his own. Kardis-led ne'er-do-wells capture him. But little people warriors come to his rescue.

Stryker joins forces with the Colony against Kardis and his venomous commandoes, battling Kardis to the death. Then he picks up a random baby, greets Delha, and appears as ready to go domestic as Robert Reed on *The Brady Bunch*. So much for loners. Last shots: rain gushes from the sky, either tears from Heaven or a quick way to bring this movie to a close. Either way, apparently the finale was meant to suggest a hint of optimism in this post-nuke environment.

Almost everything you see and hear in this made-in-the-Philippines actioner appears to be recycled. Yet the film offers one intriguing idea: Stryker argues that Trun is just like Kardis. However, nothing comes of this potential plot point.

If you're a completist regarding 1980s post-nuke action movies, this might fill your gas tank. Otherwise, you'll be running on empty.

* * *

Survival Zone

DIRECTOR-PRODUCER: Percival Rubens; WRITERS: Percival Rubens, Eric Brown; MUSIC: Nick Labuschagne; CINEMATOGRAPHERS: Vincent G. Cox, Colin Taylor; EDITOR: Mike Chomse.
CAST: Gary Lockwood (Ben Faber); Camilla Sparv (Lucy Faber); Morgan Stevens (Adam Strong); Zoli Marki (Rachel Faber); Ian Steadman (Bigman); Arthur Hall (Uncle Luke); Karl Eric Kostlin (Mark Faber).
PRODUCTION: Commedia Pictures; 1983; 90 minutes; rated R.

* * *

World War III waged with neutron bombs makes all the difference, at least according to *Survival Zone*. Here the buildings in the movie's town seem pristine, nor do we see any other signs of nuclear war—except for the plot.

Following a nuclear holocaust, Ben Faber and his family live on a farm. Though we hear Ben grouse about hungering for a steak, life seems pretty much idyllic. Wife Lucy and daughter Rachel casually shop for clothes in town while Uncle Luke good-naturedly gripes at the family's two horses for not giving him a foal. Lucy speaks of having another baby.

Of course, you know what they say about all good things.

Villainous Bigman leads a cannibalistic motorcycle gang terrorizing the countryside. After assaulting a nunnery and apparently eating the nuns (offscreen), the Cannibal Gang descends upon Ben's farm. Ben and his family hold them off in the daytime. With Ben's permission, Uncle Luke unwisely goes outside to feed the two horses. A cannibal attacks him. Ben gets him into the house, but he dies from his wounds.

Ben and the family leave the house and huddle in the woods that night. There, Ben meets Adam Strong, initially tussling with him, but then realizing that Adam is all right. (With a name like Adam Strong, how could he be otherwise?)

The Cannibal Gang makes themselves at home in Ben's farmhouse, toppling a radio tower and banging on the piano. Despite Lucy's protests, Ben returns to the farm and rigs a building with explosives, which he sets off.

When daylight comes, the cannibals appear to leave the farm. Ben ventures into the house only to find Bigman overtaking him. Bigman demands to know where the women are, and like any good square-jawed hero, Ben spits in his face. Bigman fails to appreciate the gesture and, with the help of his returning henchmen, threatens to chop Ben to pieces bit by bit.

Adam unexpectedly appears, shooting several cannibals. Bigman abducts Rachel in a pickup, but she struggles and manages to tumble out the passenger door. Bigman plows into an explosives shed, blowing up the pickup. But he survives and, with a knife, squares off against the shovel-wielding Adam. After several clumsy swings, Adam manages to whack off Bigman's head. Who knew a shovel could come in so handy?

Survival Zone's small budget works against its ambitions. But the film extols the virtues of the family, even in the face of nuclear war, not unlike a post-nuke version of *The Waltons*.

Gary Lockwood, who plays Ben, seems light years from 1968's *2001; A Space Odyssey*. But he takes his part seriously and, along with his fellow actors, does his best. Film-wise, some of the night scenes are so murky it's hard to tell what's going on. Also, the pacing often lags. Production values are perfunctory.

Surprisingly, for an R-rated film, *Survival Zone* presents little gore. The movie even handles Bigman's beheading scene with restraint. The Cannibal Gang of course has designs on the Faber women, but the film includes no rape scenes or objectifying nudity.

The opening and closing scenes dovetail. At the beginning, we see Adam burying his family; at the end, it appears Adam and Rachel will soon wed. Thus, the family will continue to be the core unit of society even in a post-nuke world. Accordingly, unlike many of its post-apocalyptic kin, *Survival Zone* suggests hope for the future.

*   *   *

Testament

DIRECTOR: Lynne Littman; WRITER: John Sacret Young; based on the short story "The Last Testament" by Carol Amen; MUSIC: James Horner; CINEMATOGRAPHER:

Steven Poster; EDITOR: Suzanne Pettit; PRODUCERS: Jonathan Bernstein, Lynne Littman.

CAST: Jane Alexander (Carol Wetherly); William Devane (Tom Wetherly); Ross Harris (Brad Wetherly); Roxana Zal (Mary Liz Wetherly); Lukas Haas (Scottie Wetherly); Mako (Mike); Gerry Murillo (Hiroshi).

PRODUCTION: PBS, American Playhouse, Entertainment Events; theatrically released by Paramount on 4 November 1983; 90 minutes; rated PG.

*   *   *

If *Testament* had to be tied to an annual calendar event, it would be Mother's Day, for Carol Wetherly, the film's matriarch, soldiers on for her family in the face of overwhelming hardship.

Testament's setup introduces us to the Wetherlys, a typical 1980s American family: father Tom (William Devane), mother Carol (Jane Alexander) and three children. Mary Liz (Roxana Zal) is the oldest, then Brad (Ross Harris), then Scottie (Lukas Haas). They reside in Hamelin, a small California suburb, and Tom commutes to work in San Francisco.

Life proceeds as usual, until that afternoon when the TV goes fuzzy, followed by news that there have been nuclear explosions on the East Coast. The power goes out, and a bright glow flashes through the room.

Carol and her children gather with neighbors at the house of Henry Abhart (Leon Ames), an elderly radio operator. He tells them he has picked up broadcasts from rural America as well as from overseas, but that he gets nothing from the Bay Area or any major American city. He has also been unable to learn what happened; the White House has been silent.

Numbed, the town chooses to function as normally as possible. Resources such as food and gasoline are in short supply. Radiation sickness breaks out. We hear that 1300 townspeople have perished. The police force is thinning out.

Scottie dies from radiation sickness and is buried in the backyard. When Mary Liz perishes, Carol meticulously sews a burial shroud for her.

After Henry Abhart dies, Brad takes over the radio duties, though there is nothing to hear. Carol and Brad take in a mentally challenged boy named Hiroshi (Gerry Murillo), whose father has died. To spare herself, Brad and Hiroshi from the painful death of radiation sickness, Carol has them get in the car in the garage so they can die of carbon monoxide poisoning from the auto's exhaust. But then she cannot go through with it.

The final scene shows Brad's birthday, celebrated with a single candle on crackers. When Brad asks Carol what he should wish for, she says, "That we remember it all, the good and the awful." The film closes with home movie footage of one of Tom's previous birthdays.

Testament was produced for PBS's *American Playhouse*, but Paramount instead released it in theaters on November 4, 1983. A year later, it played on PBS. Theatrical playdates were sparse. The film garnered excellent reviews. Roger Ebert gave it four out of four stars, noting that it made him cry.[40] In addition, 1988's *Starlog Science-Fiction Video Magazine* #1 gave the film its highest rating, declaring it "simply devastating in its humanity."[41] Kim Newman, discussing *The Day After*, *Threads* and *Testament*, called the latter "the most emotionally and intellectually powerful of the three movies."[42] James O'Neill wrote that *Testament* was much better than *The Day After*: "[It's a] beautifully acted and heartbreakingly sad movie that deals with human emotions rather than special FX."[43]

Testament differs from other atomic threat movies of the '80s in that the entire film is seen through the eyes of one family in one suburb. We see no jets or generals, no mushroom clouds or exploding cities, and we don't even hear ominous radio or TV accounts of escalating international tensions. In fact, we never learn what happened. Who started the war? Did it happen due to an accident? We never know, just as the residents of Hamelin wouldn't know.

The 90-minute film's setup (approximately 19 minutes) could be the opening for an entirely different movie. We are introduced to the Wetherlys in a fashion that would be appropriate for a family film. It even sets up a goal for young Brad, to bike to the top of the hill, a feat his father assures him he will eventually achieve. You could have easily seen this sort of thing in TV family dramedies such as *Eight Is Enough* (ABC, 1977–81) or *Family* (ABC, 1976–80)

Then, while Tom toils in San Francisco, the worst happens.

While Carol is listening to answering machine messages and the three children are watching television, a TV news announcer breaks in to declare that nuclear devices have exploded on the East Coast, followed by an Emergency Broadcast System message that the president is about to speak. The TV blinks out, followed by a bright light that flashes through the room, and warning sirens blare. Carol hovers over the children until an eerie glow subsides, but reality has crossed the bridge of no return.

Following a nuclear attack on the United States, Carol Wetherly (Jane Alexander, center) struggles to comfort her children (Roxana Zal, left, and Lukas Haas, right) in 1983's *Testament*. The Wetherly family lives in a California suburb untouched by nuclear blasts, but plagued by fallout.

We know Hamelin is a small town, and after the faraway blast, we see several of its residents, their ages ranging from infants to octogenarians. (Except for the Asian-American Mike (Mako) and his son Hiroshi, we see no people of color.)

One striking aspect of *Testament* is that despite the crisis that has ensnared the town, civility reigns supreme. We hear of scattered lootings, and see one happen to the Wetherlys, but otherwise, bad behavior hasn't broken out. Some nuclear war films depict violence and murder, but *Testament* portrays decency and reserve.

In fact, are the townspeople too well-behaved? Too subdued? For example, the residents we see, including the Wetherlys, continue to live their lives as normally as possible. This includes going on with the children's school play "The Pied Piper of Hamelin." Is putting on this play in the midst of such dire circumstances an act of corporate denial? Are the townspeople still in shock and dealing with their PTSD as well as they can?

Despite the push to retain normalcy, the town's functionality is running down, like a battery losing its charge. Residents begin succumbing to fatal radiation poisoning with an alarming regularity. At a community gathering, we see the police chief, clearly traumatized by his overwhelming responsibilities, comforted by concerned townspeople. At Scottie's backyard funeral, the minister looks shell-shocked, as well he may be if he has attended funerals for the hundreds of townspeople who have died.

The inclusion of a minister does make a nod towards the spiritual, an element missing in most atomic threat movies. Certainly, the notion of being close to death or dying would cause one to consider the afterlife, unless one already has faith. In the case of *Testament*'s residents, perhaps this is another example of their behavioral reserve.

Despite its grimness, *Testament* celebrates the power of family, particularly moms. With Tom absent, Carol holds the family together, metaphorically huddling over them just as she did when the light flashed through the room. She handles Scottie's bafflement and fears gently, and when Mary Liz asks what it's like to make love, Carol answers as

The Pitkins (Rebecca De Mornay, Kevin Costner) bid Carol Wetherly (Jane Alexander, back turned) goodbye in 1983's *Testament*. With their baby dead from radiation poisoning, they are leaving town in hopes of finding "a safe place."

honestly as possible. Brad assumes the role of "man of the house," attempting to take his father's place, and Carol affirms him. She also bears the deaths of Scottie and Mary Liz with as much dignity as possible. As Jane Alexander says in the *Testament* DVD special feature "*Testament* at 20," moms lift trucks off children.[44] The scene of her gently rocking a dying Scottie while both sing a children's song will break all but the stoniest of hearts.

In the film, Tom's possible return to Hamelin represents hope, irrational though it may be in light of the circumstances. Before the nuclear aftermath began, he had left a phone message saying he would get home early. Periodically, the family trusts he will somehow come back, and this anticipated return is tied to the possibility that things can be okay again. But late in the film, Carol hears a phone message Tom left before the power went out that she hadn't previously heard, one in which he says he has to work late. The thought of Tom returning is snuffed out, as are any hopes of things getting better.

Regarding the town as a whole, we can see its transformation from hope to despair through the family of Phil and Cathy Pitkin (Kevin Costner and Rebecca De Mornay). At first, at a community gathering, Phil talks of organizing a kind of Red Cross. Later, Phil and Cathy's baby dies from radiation poisoning. Faced with an increasingly hopeless situation, Phil and Cathy tell Carol they are leaving. "We can't stay here any more," Phil says. "We'll find a safe place."

Cathy adds, "We'll come back just as soon as we can."

Carol wishes them good luck, but it's obvious they won't find a safe place, and that they will never be coming back.

The film understates its horrors. The ordeal of radiation sickness largely occurs offscreen. Also, it's notable that Hamelin isn't accosted by refugees from larger towns, who no doubt would be suffering from radiation exposure and burns. Further, the film ends with Carol, Brad and Hiroshi still alive. It could have showed Brad and Hiroshi perish, followed by Carol succumbing to radiation sickness, probably a lonely vigil with no one to comfort her. A final shot could have shown her dead body. But such a finale might have been overwhelming, and ending the film with the family's home movie of Tom's birthday leaves the viewer with the thought of what once was, but can never be again. This is a subtle reminder that a nuclear holocaust could indeed happen, and that if it did, all the amenities of everyday life we take for granted would vanish forever.

Carol's goal, as well as that of the town as a whole, is to maintain the pre-nuked past as long as possible despite the altered landscape. The past lets Carol and her family endure the post-apocalyptic here and now if only momentarily, such as Carol and Brad dancing to the Beatles' "All My Loving."[45] This moment embodies the undeniable sadness of what is, as well as a fierce stubbornness to accept what will be: the past's demise.

Technically, the film delivers in all departments. James Horner's music score, one of his earliest, aches with longing, appropriately mournful and bittersweet. John Sacret Young's screenplay, based on Carol Amen's short story "The Last Testament," paints a sad but convincing portrayal of a typical American small town succumbing to a nuclear war's aftermath. And Lynne Littman's spare and understated direction serves the cast well.

The acting, both from the adults and the children, shines true. Critic Ebert wrote that Alexander's performance is "the heart of the film."[46] Indeed, she rightfully received an Academy Award nomination as Best Actress. Highly respected, Alexander has won three Primetime Emmy Awards and one Tony Award, along with nominations for four Academy Awards and three Golden Globe Awards. In *Testament*, her character embodies human decency, the film's shining virtue. Is this decency an inherently American trait, or a universally human one? *Testament* suggests both.

Despite its largely subdued nature, the movie allows itself one moment of raw anger: Carol, moaning, clutches dirt and says, "Who did this?" Then she curses them.

So why do Carol and her Hamelin neighbors continue to go on when it's obvious that all—or almost all—of them will soon die? Perhaps because, even at the end, being human means to love and to be loved.

* * *

2019, After the Fall of New York

DIRECTOR: Martin Dolman; WRITERS: Julian Berry, Martin Dolman (story); Julian
    Berry, Martin Dolman, Gabriel Rossini (screenplay); MUSIC: Oliver Onions; CIN-
    EMATOGRAPHER: Giancarlo Ferrando; EDITOR: Eugenio Alabiso; PRODUCER:
    Luciano Martino.
CAST: Michael Sopkiw (Parsifal); Valentine Monnier (Giara); Anna Kanakis (Ania,
    Eurac Captain); George Eastman (Big Ape).
PRODUCTION: Medusa Distribuzione. Nuova Dania Cinematografica, Les Films Du
    Griffin; Italian-French; released on 22 July 1983 (in Italy); released on 7 December
    1984 (in the U.S.); 96 minutes; rated R.

* * *

Unfamiliar with Euracs? They inhabit the Italian-French post-nuke tale *2019, After the Fall of New York*. Inspired by 1981's *Escape from New York* and the *Mad Max* films, this is one of those action movies that manages to sometimes induce boredom despite plenty of violence.

The Pan-American Confederacy and Eurac Monarchy (Europe, Africa and Asia) waged nuclear war in 1999, causing worldwide sterility that persists 20 years hence. The Pan-America president has his men kidnap adventurer–stunt driver Parsifal and directs him to travel to New York, where the only fertile woman in the world exists, and bring her back alive. If Parsifal complies, the Pan-American president promises to reserve him a seat aboard a spaceship that will soon leave for Alpha Centauri. The president assigns Parsifal two Pan-American helpers, Bronx, who knows New York City's geography, and Ratchet, the strongest Pan-American man. In New York City, the trio encounter trouble in the form of unfriendly (to say the least) inhabitants who include, among others, the Rat Eater King.

Euracs capture Parsifal, Bronx, Ratchet and a New York female named Giara. Parsifal escapes with Ratchet and Giara while Bronx stays behind to buy his friends time (and is killed in the process). Our heroes take refuge in an underground domain of little people. The Euracs pop up again, this time sporting sonic weapons that assault the little people like a 120 decibel Who concert circa 1976. Parsifal, Giara, Ratchet and a little person named Shorty escape. They fall in with a rowdy tribe ruled by Big Ape, who joins them in their search.

Shorty leads this motley crew to the subterranean lab where Melissa, the last fertile woman, has been frozen in suspended animation since 1999. Big Ape takes an immediate shine to her, which should have raised everyone's eyebrows, but doesn't. (In private, he impregnates her while she is still unconscious.)

While Parsifal and Ratchet gather scrap with which to armor an old station wagon, Shorty makes himself a decoy and, shockingly, commits suicide to be sure he won't tell the Euracs his friends' location. The station wagon manages (unconvincingly) to escape from New York through the Lincoln Tunnel, but en route, lasers kill Big Ape. Minutes later, Parsifal reveals that Ratchet is a cyborg. Ratchet mortally wounds Giara before Parsifal dispatches him.

Once Parsifal returns to the Pan-American Alaska base, he learns the president is dying and has given Parsifal his place on the spaceship. As it leaves for Alpha Centauri, the last fertile woman on Earth opens her eyes and sees Parsifal, who will soon reveal to her all that has happened in the last 20 years.

2019, After the Fall of New York is typical post-nuke hokum, but it has its plusses. The gloom-draped atomic ruins of New York set a good atmosphere, despite the fact they are clearly models (the static water helps give them away). Other miniatures are enjoyable (if obvious) as well. The acting, as far as one can tell, is passable, though in an English-dubbed film, one can never be sure. One major plus is the intriguing premise: A nuclear war renders survivors sterile, but one fertile woman still exists in the world. Regrettably, the film doesn't really take advantage of this idea.[47]

The characters are basically standard issue Italian post-apocalyptic folks. Parsifal is the hedonistic antihero who in the end does the right thing. Bronx and Shorty are supporting characters called upon to sacrifice themselves for their friends.

Some of the action scenes don't work. One particularly bizarre moment has Big Ape swing his sword and hurl it at three Eurac soldiers—and it slices off all three of their heads! This would be over the top for a Mel Brooks movie, and for a quasi-serious post-nuke melodrama. The movie also dumps plenty of graphic gore on the screen, more than is necessary. In one scene, Bronx uses his mechanical claw-hand to gouge out a villainous Eurac's eyes. Talk about unsightly.

Big Ape's episode with Melissa is troubling. He first knocks out Giara, who has stayed behind to help him "guard" Melissa, and then he has (offscreen) sex with her. He tells Melissa, "You'll make me immortal, carrying my seed." This is clearly rape, yet when Parsifal and Ratchet return from the scrapyard, Giara tells Parsifal, "Everything's fine." She says nothing about having been knocked out (I'm sure the back of her head would still smart), or deducing this could mean that Big Ape has had his way with Melissa. Big Ape does get his comeuppance via Eurac lasers, but the film should have called attention to this sexual assault and offered specific justice for Melissa.

Reviews are scant, but fanciers of post-nuke falderol seemed to appreciate the film. James O'Neill wrote, "Enjoyable trashy Italian-made *Mad Max/Escape from New York* rip…. Lots of gory action keeps this derivative potboiler always on the move."[48]

* * *

2020 Texas Gladiators

DIRECTOR: Kevin Mancuso; WRITER: Alex Carver; MUSIC: Francis Taylor; PRODUCER-CINEMATOGRAPHER: Joe D'Amato; EDITOR: Caesar White.
CAST: Al Cliver (Nisus); Daniel Stephen (Catch Dog); Peter Hooten (Halakron); Sabrina Siani (Maida).
PRODUCTION: Continental Motion Pictures Corp., Eureka Cinematografica; Italian; 1983; 91 minutes; not rated.

* * *

"Firsts" in sports or entertainment are coveted—usually. But 1983's *2020 Texas Gladiators* is the first Italian post-nuke action film to insult Native Americans, not a prized accomplishment.

After a nuclear war, lawless groups terrorize peaceful folks. The self-appointed Rangers oppose these gangs, wiping out one such band of lowlifes. When a Ranger named Catch Dog rapes a woman named Maida, his companions banish him. Nisus feels sorry for Maida, and they leave to start a family in a peaceful community.

Catch Dog and his gang raid this community on behalf of "Black One," a maniacal Nazi type whose troops force the men to work in a mine. They also kill Nisus. But three Rangers free Maida and secure the help of a nearby Native American tribe. Together, they defeat Catch Dog and his gang as well as Black One and his minions. Maida reunites with her daughter, who waves at the departing Rangers.

Let's examine the movie's treatment of Native Americans in the movie's final third. Halakron, a Ranger, attempts to secure the tribe's help, but they refuse. Halakron says, "I was expecting more courage." The tribe explains they have outdated weapons while Black One has advanced weapons, and they would be foolish to face him. Halakron again questions the Native Americans' courage. A fellow Ranger says, "We're just wasting our time here with this bunch of cowardly Indians." This Ranger and a younger tribesman fight to determine whether the Native Americans will assist the Rangers. Of course, the Ranger wins.

As a movie, *2020 Texas Gladiators* embraces confusion. During the first half-hour, scene transitions are shaky, and time passages (in one case, years) are likewise unclear. Logic also wobbles. The film establishes that Black One's troops have transparent thermal shields which protect them from bullets—but for some reason, spears and arrows pass right through the shields.

2020 Texas Gladiators is one of the first Italian post-nuke action movies made in the wake of 1979's *Mad Max* and 1981's *Mad Max 2*. It wants to be a Western, hence the gambling scenes and the Native Americans attacking on horseback with bows and arrows. Also, the Rangers recall the actual Texas Rangers who originated in 1823.

Unrated, the movie ladles on the exploitation grunge (gore, rape, depravity). An R rating would be assured. The best thing about *2020 Texas Gladiators* is its title. The rest stinks.

WarGames

DIRECTOR: John Badham; WRITERS: Lawrence Lasker, Walter F. Parkes; MUSIC: Arthur B. Rubinstein; CINEMATOGRAPHER: William A. Fraker; EDITOR: Tom Rolf; PRODUCER: Harold Schneider.

CAST: Matthew Broderick (David Lightman); Dabney Coleman (Dr. John McKittrick); John Wood (Dr. Stephen Falken); Ally Sheedy (Jennifer Mack); Barry Corbin (General Jack Beringer).

PRODUCTION: United Artists and Sherwood Productions; 1983; 114 minutes; rated PG.

*   *   *

In *WarGames*, high school student David Lightman (Matthew Broderick) asks his computer to play Global Thermonuclear War. "Fine," the computer replies. "All right!"

Broderick exclaims—perhaps not the same reaction 1982's million anti-nuke marchers in New York might have had.[49]

WarGames is one of the few American nuclear threat movies of the 1980s released to theaters; most debuted on TV or went direct to video. At a budget of $12 million, the film had a healthy domestic gross of $74,433,837.[50] Combining thriller and youth movie conventions, *WarGames* wisely plays to its strengths.

Because some soldiers fail to turn the launch key on NORAD nuclear missile drills, computer specialist Dr. John McKittrick (Dabney Coleman) argues that control for a nuclear war should be turned over to the computer WOPR (War Operation Plan Response). Despite protests from General Beringer (Barry Corbin), NORAD does just this, and WOPR continuously runs simulations to learn various nuclear war scenarios.

David, a bright computer hacker, uses his PC to change his high school grades and those of Jennifer Mack (Ally Sheedy). While attempting to track down the phone number for a computer game company so he can download its games, David inadvertently gets into a system that doesn't identify itself. One of the games is called Falken's Maze.

David figures out that the password is the name of Falken's deceased son Joshua, allowing David to play a game called Global Thermonuclear War. David doesn't realize the game is housed in WOPR, and the program's computer displays show NORAD personnel that Soviet missiles have actually been launched. However, David gets out of the game, causing WOPR to terminate the nuclear missile simulation.

From a TV news story, David learns that the Global Thermonuclear War game he thought he was playing is for real. FBI agents arrest David and take him to NORAD,

Teenage computer whiz David Lightman (Matthew Broderick) initiates a game of Global Thermonuclear War with an unknown opponent as girlfriend Jennifer Mack (Ally Sheedy) watches in 1983's *WarGames* (Sherwood Productions). Lightman doesn't realize his opponent is a NORAD computer program that thinks their game of nuclear war is real.

where he insists he is not working with the Soviets and thought he was playing a game. McKittrick doesn't buy his story.

David escapes with a NORAD tour group and, with Jennifer's help, flies to Oregon and meets Dr. Stephen Falken (John Wood) on the latter's island property. David describes what is happening, but Falken refuses to help; the dispirited scientist is convinced an all-out nuclear war is inevitable, so it doesn't matter if it happens the next day or years later.

After Jennifer and David leave, Falken has a change of heart and flies them in his chopper to a Jeep that races to NORAD's Cheyenne Mountain Complex. WOPR indicates full nuclear engagement from the Soviet Union, shifting nuclear readiness to DEF-CON 1: "Nuclear War Imminent." Falken helps convince the NORAD authorities that WOPR is creating an incoming Soviet simulation, so the U.S. chooses not to retaliate.

American bases that WOPR said had been hit by Russian missiles report they are still intact, but WPOR won't let NORAD personnel halt the launch of American missiles. David gets into the system to play tic-tac-toe with WPOR, which teaches the supercomputer the game is futile. Similarly, WPOR runs all nuclear war scenarios against the Soviet Union, determining the game is unwinnable; consequently, it abandons the game. The crisis has ended.

As a thriller, *WarGames* milks every suspense scene to the hilt. For example, when the government Jeep is taking Falken, David and Jennifer to NORAD before the door closes, they make it with seconds to spare. Similarly, when NORAD personnel are waiting to see if Soviet missiles really have hit American military bases, the radio operator says, "This is Crystal Palace. You still on?" He repeats his request, then adds, "Anyone there?" After a few seconds, he hears, "Affirmative, sir." There's probably no reason there would have been a delay, except to heighten suspense. This is not a criticism, just an observation. In fact, director John Badham infuses the film with nail-biting tension.

Memorable characters populate the film. David is the protagonist, and we follow him through juvenile recklessness to insightful action. He and Jennifer are on hand to pull in the "teen crowd," but while David might be a smart aleck, his brash remark to his high school teacher is not without context: The movie has shown us the teacher is a jerk by flashing David and Jennifer's failing grades to the class. Of course, David thinks nothing of flaunting authority, a trait that enables him to inadvertently create the movie's nuclear dilemma. As Jennifer says late in the film, "I told you not to start playing games with that thing." Near the end, when Jennifer asks what WPOR is doing as it runs nuclear war scenarios, David replies, "It's learning." In the film, so is David.

WarGames is the movie that launched Matthew Broderick's career. Three years after *WarGames*, he starred in John Hughes' popular teen flick *Ferris Bueller's Day Off* as an even bigger smart aleck. Broderick soon moved to adult roles, such as his impressive turn as a Union cavalry officer in 1989's *Glory*.

Dabney Coleman is, as always, competent, despite his thankless role of Dr. McKittrick. Also proficient, John Wood gives Dr. Falken an almost permanent look of amusement. As General Jack Beringer, Barry Corbin seems to enjoy himself hugely, epitomizing tobacco-chewing, good ol' boy panache. Corbin knows how to have fun with his character without patronizing him.

As nuclear war films go, *WarGames* is that rare bird in which no nuclear weapons explode. However, catastrophe threatens throughout, though the film's high spirits pretty much telegraph that David and Jennifer are not going to be vaporized before the end credits roll. *WarGames* might be the most entertainment-oriented of all the major 1980s nuke movies, which probably explains its commercial success. It sought to appeal to both teen and adult audiences, and given its healthy box office take, this ploy worked.

In a 2013 interview for *Nuclear Age Peace Foundation*, director Badham talked about his approach to the film: "People don't really want to go to the theater to be lectured to, or frightened in a real way. They like to be frightened by *Jaws* because they're not going in the water.... We were walking a fine line in that movie between how threatening and frightening would we make it."[51] He also responded to a question about whether *WarGames* should have ended with a hint of nuclear menace still out there: "I absolutely understand what you're telling me, and that criticism is very fair. It might have added a whole layer of extra texture and meaning to the film."[52]

Thematically, the movie makes the case that a global nuclear war is unwinnable. As WPOR declares at the end, Global Thermonuclear War is "[a] strange game. The only winning move is not to play." In fact, the film appears to argue that David's recklessness, which almost plunges the world into a nuke war, parallels the recklessness of the United States and Soviet Union in assuming either nation could come out on top following a nuclear exchange. The movie implicitly asks, "Could these two superpowers learn the futility of such a notion in time?" During the Cold War anxieties of 1983, that was a weighty question, the answer far from certain.

The movie also thematically criticizes widespread application of AI, which is what causes WOPR to almost start a nuclear war. In this sense, the film is akin to 1970's *Colossus: The Forbin Project*, in which two supercomputers—one in America, one in Russia—merge and take control of both countries' nuclear arsenals. Colossus also takes charge of humanity, demanding obedience or else. That doesn't happen in *WarGames*, but you pretty much figure that after the movie's end, the control of America's nuclear

General Jack Beringer (Barry Corbin) points at NORAD screens indicating that the Soviet Union has launched a massive ICBM attack on the United States in 1983's *WarGames* (Sherwood Productions). The general initiates DEFCON 1—Nuclear War Imminent.

war machine will be returned to fallible human beings. The film implies that such power is better off in the hands of humanity than automation. As Falken tells General Beringer, "Do the world a favor and don't act like [a machine]." And in fact, it is the general's decision to stand down that saves civilization, whereas we would have perished under WOPR's custody.

As a teen film, *WarGames* gives David's parents short shrift. They appear clueless about their son. For example, we learn he has missed a week of school, yet presumably his parents didn't realize it (although the school would have called them). Once David is arrested, the parents disappear, as though they've abandoned him. This was probably a good move to appeal to the teen audience, but you'd hope real parents would be more involved than this.

Character-wise and of interest to Beatles fans, Jen Chaney informs us that the writers "originally envisioned John Lennon as one of the central characters in *WarGames*, the mysterious Dr. Stephen Falken. When Lennon was killed in 1980, that dream also died...." As an actor, Lennon had appeared in 1966's *How I Won the War*, as well as the Beatles movies *A Hard Day's Night* (1964) and *Help!* (1965). How he would have fared playing Dr. Falken, we can only imagine—in a different context, of course.[53]

WarGames received good reviews, both then and now. RottenTomatoes gives it a 93 percent "Fresh" rating based on 44 professional reviews. The top 11 reviews were written recently, yet remain largely positive. In 2015, Chris Barsanti wrote, "[T]his remains one of the first and best of the cyberflicks.... One of the great Cold War films ... [d]irected with efficient thrills and humor by John Badham."[54]

Speaking of efficiency, *WarGames* played an unexpected role in setting national policy regarding cybersecurity. On June 4, 1983, President Ronald Reagan saw *WarGames*. He asked the chairman of the Joint Chiefs of Staff if the movie's premise was credible. After investigation, the chairman responded, "Mr. President, the problem is much worse than you think." This served as the catalyst for a serious study of cybersecurity, resulting in the national security document NSDD-145, known as "National Policy on Telecommunications and Automated Information Systems Security."[55]

In 2008, MGM released a direct-to-video *WarGames* sequel called *WarGames: The Dead Code*. The only character from the original is Professor Falken (now played by Gary Reineke). This time, the system in question is called RIPLEY, a computer program that deals with terrorists. Nuclear intrigue once again comes into play.

While the original *WarGames*' technology may be dated, its themes remain relevant. We still live under the shadow of potential nuclear war, most likely with Russia or China. And glitches can happen in the real world, such as a 1995 mistake that almost plunged Russia and the U.S. into a nuclear holocaust.[56] Global Thermonuclear War may indeed be a strange game, but that doesn't mean it will never be played.

*   *   *

Yor, the Hunter from the Future

DIRECTOR: Anthony M. Dawson aka Antonio Margheriti; WRITERS: Anthony M. Dawnson aka Antonio Margheriti, Robert Bailey, based on the novel *Yor* by Juan Zanotto, Ray Collins; MUSIC: John Scott; CINEMATOGRAPHER: Marcello Masciocchi; EDITOR: Alberto Moriani; PRODUCER: Michele Marsala.

CAST: Reb Brown (Yor); Corinne Cléry (Kala); Alan Collins (Pag); Carole André (Ena); John Steiner (Overlord); Ayshe Gul (Roa).

PRODUCTION: Diamant, Kodiak Films; released as *Il mondo di Yor* in Italy by Dimant Film/RAI on 3 February 1983, 98 minutes; released as *Yor, the Hunter from the Future* in the U.S. on 19 August 1983, 89 minutes; rated PG.

* * *

Regarding her 1983 review of *Yor, the Hunter from the Future*, Janet Maslin confessed she couldn't sit through the entire movie.[57] Leonard Maltin called it a "[s]hamelessly idiotic muscleman movie."[58] And James O'Neill opined the film "is good for a few laughs but not much else."[59] Despite all that, certain geeks out there may find it enjoyable. I did.

In a prehistoric world, loner Yor searches for his roots. He kills a triceratops-like monster, saving the lives of cave people Kala and Pag (presumably Kala's father or older relative). Blue-skinned barbarians kidnap Kala along with her tribe; in short order, Yor saves Kala and causes a flood that drowns the barbarians (and apparently Kala's people along with them).

Kala and Pag accompany golden-haired Yor into a desert, where he encounters the equally golden-haired Roa, discovering she is from the same race as he (their national anthem must be "Surfin' Safari"). Roa is fatally wounded during a battle with cavemen, but before dying, she tells Yor his birthplace is an island with a magnificent castle on the sea.

Yor, Kala, and Pag meet yet another caveman tribe, and Yor saves some of its children from a sluggish dimetrodon. Later, Yor and friends journey to the forementioned island, and discover that Yor's ancestors are the survivors of a nuclear war that destroyed civilization. (Surprise.) The Overlord rules the island with a band of androids sporting Darth Vader-ish helmets. He hopes to create a superior race with Yor and Kala's help.

Rebels join Yor, Kala and Pag in an attack against the Overlord's minions. An elderly rebel deactivates the Overlord's androids as the island's atomic pile is set to go off. The Overlord battles Yor and tries to stop the pile from exploding. He fails. Yor, Kala, Pag and the surviving rebels escape in a spacecraft. A narrator tells us that Yor hopes to restore peace to the world, laying the groundwork for an apparent sequel that never materialized (no doubt causing film critics the world over to heave a sigh of relief).

Despite *Yor*'s low budget, on April 19, 1983, Columbia wide-released the film in America to 1,425 theaters. The movie performed poorly, taking in only $2.8 million.[60] Perhaps word of mouth killed it? Certainly the unkind reviews couldn't have helped.

No one can deny that the film is amazingly derivative, drawing from *Conan the Barbarian*, *Star Wars* and other then-contemporary SFantasies. In fact, the "plot twist" (Yor lives in a post-nuclear holocaust world) is straight out of Roger Corman's 1958 *Teenage Cave Man*, which featured a Brylcreemed Robert Vaughn as opposed to *Yor*'s blow-dried Reb Brown. As for those who call the film juvenile, I plead no contest.

But the movie boasts an undeniable pulpy spirit, recalling 20th century comic books such as *Mighty Samson*[61] and *Turok, Son of Stone*.[62] In fact, a comic-addicted 12-year-old could have written the storyline. The scant production values, including the fun if primitive animatronic monsters, bring to mind the Italian strongmen movies of the late '50s and '60s, in which heroes such as Hercules battled beasts, barbarians and

A triceratops-like monster attacks Yor (Reb Brown) in the post-nuke world of 1983's *Yor, the Hunter from the Future*, an Italian film that Columbia wide-released to 1,425 American theaters on April 19, 1983.

evil despots. Baby Boomers (such as myself) who grew up immersed in these colorful albeit outrageous fantasies will revel in nostalgia.

Director Antonio Margheriti was no stranger to low-budget genre fare. His '60s science fiction and fantasy output includes 1961's *Battle of the Worlds* (starring Claude Rains), 1964's *Hercules, Prisoner of Evil* and *Devil of the Desert Against the Son of Hercules*, 1965's *War of the Planets* and 1966's *Wild, Wild Planet*. The latter enjoyed a wide release in the U.S. in 1967 and featured a slick ad campaign.

Star Reb Brown is probably best known for bringing Captain America to life in the 1979 TV movies *Captain America* and *Captain America II: Death Too Soon*. He also appears in 1973's *Sssssss*, 1985's *Howling II: Your Sister Is a Werewolf*, 1988's *Space Mutiny* and *Robowar* and 2011's *Night Claws*. Talking about *Yor* in a 2011 YouTube interview, Brown said the film "was hard, it was very hard." He also noted that during the filming in Turkey and Rome, he went from 230 pounds to 205. "I thought I could trust the water," Brown noted, "but you can't!"[63] Mill Creek Entertainment released a Blu-ray of the film in 2018 that includes commentary by Brown.

Some reviewers confess a fondness for *Yor*. John Stanley opined, "Lowbrow fantasy escapism, but energetically on the level of a Saturday serial and hence palatable entertainment."[64]

Even for nostalgia addicts like myself, *Yor* wears thin at times. And the switch from prehistoric settings to *Star Wars* trappings appears more calculated than a quadratic equation. If, like critic Janet Maslin, you should start to watch this movie and find you can't finish it, I bear you no ill will.

CHAPTER SIX

1984

Access Code

DIRECTOR-PRODUCER-EDITOR: Mark Sobel; WRITER: Stanley Richards; MUSIC: Gene Hobson; CINEMATOGRAPHER: Shane D. Kelly.

CAST: Martin Landau (Agency Head); Michael Ansara (Senator Dales); Macdonald Carey (Senator Williams); Michael Durrell (Michael Barnes); Marcia Mueller (Julie Barnes); Michael Napoli (Ben Marcus).

PRODUCTION: Access Productions; 1984; 88 minutes; not rated.

* * *

If you're watching a government conspiracy movie and the stupidity level of both the heroes and the villains reaches 9 on a 1–10 scale, you might be inclined to stop watching. Unless, like yours truly, you're the author of a book on 1980s nuclear threat movies, hence the reason I sat through all 88 agonizing minutes of *Access Code*.

Things begin well, with an unknown outside power seizing control of government computers and almost launching America's nuclear arsenal, but stopping at the last minute. The Agency (that's all it's called) enlists the aid of computer genius and former employee Michael Barnes. Once he drops out of the picture, his sister Julie, also a computer wiz, teams with journalist Ben Marcus to get to the bottom of what turns out to be a far-reaching conspiracy, one utilizing a super-satellite to keep tabs on the populace.

This sounds okay on paper, but on film, the poorly written script prevents audience involvement. Both the government and Julie and Ben do a number of foolish things. For instance: After the Agency is trying to kill them, Julie and Ben just wander onto the computer complex and explore without encountering guards (so much for security), taking time to watch a video in the back of a roomful of conspirators. Then the couple leaves, opening and closing the door so loudly even a hearing-impaired octogenarian would notice it, much less the roomful of conspirators, who don't even stir.

In addition, the film's poor technique impedes the pacing, slowing many sequences to a crawl, including an interminable car chase. Attempts at comedy relief are insulting. To be fair, glimmers of genuine paranoia wink from the movie at times, and the ending tries hard to be both mysterious and menacing—and somewhat succeeds.

The film's opening nuclear threat angle seems promising, and you keep expecting it to pop up again, but alas, it never does.

Unrated, the film (apparently direct-to-video) would probably receive a PG-13 for language and violence.

* * *

C.H.U.D.

DIRECTOR: Douglas Cheek; WRITERS: Parnell Hall (screenplay); Shepard Abbott
  (story); MUSIC: Cooper Hughes; CINEMATOGRAPHER: Peter Stein; EDITOR:
  Claire Simpson; SPECIAL MAKEUP: John Caglione, Jr.; PRODUCER: Andrew
  Bonime.
CAST: John Heard (George Cooper); Daniel Stern (A.J. "The Reverend" Shepherd);
  Christopher Curry (Captain Bosch); Kim Greist (Lauren Daniels); George Martin
  (Wilson).
PRODUCTION: New World Pictures, C.H.U.D. Productions; 1984; 88 minutes; rated R.

* * *

It's not every day a 1980s genre movie gets referenced in a modern horror film by
an acclaimed director, but such is the case for the nuke thriller *C.H.U.D.* In the opening of filmmaker Jordan Peele's 2019 movie *Us*, a VHS tape of *C.H.U.D.* is seen. And this
is more than a mere cameo: *C.H.U.D.*'s themes dovetail with the themes in *Us*. How?
Before we go there, *C.H.U.D.*'s synopsis:

The homeless are disappearing and New York City Police Captain Bosch wants to
know why. Along with soup kitchen manager A.J., Bosch brings his superiors evidence
that nuclear workers are toiling in the sewers and subway tunnels, and that something
down there caused a radiation detector to go haywire and took a bite out of a homeless
person's leg.

After A.J. and Bosch threaten to go to the press, Wilson, the Nuclear Regulatory
Commission administrator, reveals that in the sewers, the government has found a dead
mutant that apparently killed the missing persons. The creature is known as a C.H.U.D.,
Cannibalistic Humanoid Underground Dweller. Wilson plans to kill all the C.H.U.D.s
by filling a portion of the sewers with methane gas.

In the sewers, professional photographer Cooper and A.J. find multiple crates of
radioactive waste the government has secretly stockpiled, the cause of homeless persons
mutating into monsters.

C.H.U.D.s attack and kill everyone in a diner, and reporters flood the scene. Showing that he has no conscience, Wilson orders the sewers sealed and filled with methane gas, despite the fact that Cooper and A.J. are still down there. Captain Bosch drives
a vehicle off the manhole through which Cooper and A.J. hope to escape, but Wilson
shoots the police captain in the chest.

A.J. and Cooper escape to the surface where Wilson tries to run them down with
a truck. A.J. shoots Wilson in the head and his vehicle swerves over the open manhole,
exploding due to the gas in the sewers.

Cooper and his wife Lauren embrace, and A.J. is glad to see that Captain Bosch,
despite his severe gunshot wound, is still alive.

C.H.U.D.'s radiation-created monsters are a definite throwback to the nuke-caused
mutants of the 1950s. In reality, too much radiation simply kills you, but *C.H.U.D.* exists
in the same parallel world as many '50s nuke movies in which radiation morphs humans
into monsters. In fact, just as in many creature features of old, we don't get a look at one of
the C.H.U.D.s until about half an hour into the film. Hearing the Geiger counter click into
high gear summons a welcome nostalgia of long-ago Saturday afternoon monster movies.

However, *C.H.U.D.*'s paranoia breaks with '50s nuke movies. In oldies such as 1954's

Them!, the authorities are the good guys with no ulterior motives. But in *C.H.U.D.*, the government is covering up its stockpile of nuclear waste beneath New York City, oblivious to the deaths and mutations it has caused. Clearly, *C.H.U.D.*'s Wilson, the Nuclear Regulatory Agency administrator, is as bad as bad guys get.

George Martin plays Wilson with an appropriate low-key venality; he looks like the evil twin of *The Lucy Show*'s Gale Gordon. As for the film's heroes, due to photographer Cooper's prominence, we assume he must be the good guy. However, Cooper almost falls apart under pressure, whereas A.J. and Bosch soldier on, performing the actions that result in victory, making them the movie's heroes.

Each of *C.H.U.D.*'s actors shoulder their own weight and then some. This is of paramount importance in a scare film. As Jordan Peele has said, "A horror movie is only as good as the performances of the people that, you know, are witnessing the horror."[1] One standout in *C.H.U.D.* is Christopher Curry as Captain Bosch. A C.H.U.D. has killed Bosch's wife, and Curry displays Bosch's shock and despondency with impressive verisimilitude.

The film intermingles many subplots, but never feels crowded or confused. Also, *C.H.U.D.* moves at a nice pace. It really turns on the graphic gunk during the final third, including closeups of decapitated heads and exposed innards. While explicit violence was nothing new in 1980s horror films, *C.H.U.D.* overdoes it.

In addition, the plot doesn't always convince. For example, in her apartment, Lauren uses a sword to behead a C.H.U.D. What was that sword doing there? Swords, after all, are not common décor in New York apartments. The film should have foreshadowed the blade: Lauren could have asked Cooper to get rid of the saber on the wall, and he could have replied that it's an old family heirloom with which he has no intention of parting.

On the surface, *C.H.U.D.* and the forementioned *Us* seem to have little in common. But thematically, they share a similar subtext. *C.H.U.D.* deals with the homeless, the marginalized bottom of the socioeconomic heap who are literally being forced into the underground; *Us* deals with those beneath the surface who lack the privileges and wealth of those who live topside. In addition, *C.H.U.D.*'s humanoid monsters are out to kill surface-dwellers, just as *Us'* subterranean doppelgängers plan to slaughter their top-dwelling counterparts.[2]

Regarding the nuclear threat, *C.H.U.D.* asserts that radiation physically changes the homeless, a radical exaggeration of the fact that real radiation poisoning can likewise change a person's appearance and damage their health. This also implies that in a dangerous nuclear situation, the marginalized will suffer the most.

C.H.U.D. is rated R for language, adult content and graphic violence. Kids might like the monsters, but parental guidance is advised.

A September 1, 1984, *New York Times* review called *C.H.U.D.* "enjoyable ... in the category of horror films it stands as a praiseworthy effort."[3]

While no classic, *C.H.U.D.* is well-made for what it is, and how many other 1980s horror films get the honor of being Easter egged into a Jordan Peele movie?

* * *

Countdown to Looking Glass

DIRECTOR: Fred Barzyk; WRITER: Albert Ruben; CINEMATOGRAPHER: Miklos Lente; EDITORS: Peter Frank, Leah Siegel, Bernie Clayton; PRODUCER: David Loxton.

CAST: Patrick Watson (Don Tobin); Helen Shaver (Dorian Waldorf); Michael Murphy (Bob Calhoun); Scott Glenn (Michael Boyle).
PRODUCTION: Home Box Office, L&B Productions, Primedia Productions; broadcast on HBO on 14 October 1984; 86 minutes; not rated.

*   *   *

Imagine it's 1984 and you hear this disclaimer before an upcoming HBO movie: "The program you are about to see is based on a war game developed with the help of military experts and advisors. Its purpose is to inform, not to alarm." Hogwash. The program—*Countdown to Looking Glass*—most certainly was designed to alarm, if not outright terrify. And while the movie is of course dated in many ways, its central theme remains uncomfortably pertinent.

Taking the same tack as *Special Bulletin* (1983), most of *Countdown to Looking Glass* consists of a series of news broadcasts, though it also blends in more conventional non-news narrative:

CVN World News Today reports that the U.S. ambassador to Saudi Arabia has been killed, presumably by terrorists. Days earlier, Chile, Argentina and Brazil defaulted on their loans. This wounds the oil-producing nations and causes Oman's economy to tank. Soviet-backed guerrillas seize control of Oman's government.

America sends its military into Saudi Arabia to prevent King Fahd's regime from being overthrown. America insists this is a peacekeeping mission, but a displeased Britain refuses to help. In a countermove, Oman announces it will enforce a toll of $10,000 on any oil ships sailing through the Strait of Hormuz to reach the Persian Gulf. Said vessels refuse to pay the toll. A Kremlin announcement suggests that if America will pull its forces out of Saudi Arabia, Russia will ensure the toll ends. The blockade, say the oil experts, cannot continue indefinitely.

American jets and unidentified aircraft battle over Saudi Arabia, with an American reconnaissance plane shot down, its crew perishing. America sends a fleet of warships to the Persian Gulf: the carrier *Nimitz* accompanied by cruisers, frigates and submarines. CVN news anchor Don Tobin (Patrick Watson) reports that most of these vessels possess nuclear cruise missiles, torpedoes and depth charges.

The U.S. president tells the nation that America must open the Persian Gulf to shipping, adding that he has given the Navy permission to take any steps necessary to accomplish this goal. He also announces that all Selective Service registrants who are 20 years old will be inducted into the military.

White House insider Bob Calhoun (Michael Murphy) shares a top-secret satellite photo with his girlfriend, CVN correspondent Dorian Waldorf (Helen Shaver). The photo shows that two days earlier, Russian forces were massed on the Iran-Russian border; today, they're gone. Dorian pleads for CVN to report this bombshell item, but anchor Tobin says the network cannot do so until two White House sources verify it.

Aboard the USS *Nimitz*, CVN correspondent Michael Boyle (Scott Glenn) reports that American jets are searching for Soviet submarines, believed to be armed with conventional and nuclear weapons, headed for the Strait of Hormuz. Due to the magnitude of the unfolding events, Tobin announces that CVN will now stay on the air 24 hours a day.

The government orders all American nuclear power plants to shut down. In addition, the White House suspends daily press briefings. Shortly thereafter, the Secretary of Defense dies of a heart attack.

In 1984's *Countdown to Looking Glass* (HBO), news correspondent Michael Boyle (Scott Glenn) reports from a U.S. aircraft carrier as Russian and American tensions escalate in the Middle East.

Overseas, a Dutch oil tanker tries to sail past Oman in the dead of night, but either an Omani gunboat or a Russian submarine fires upon it, causing it to explode. In the U.S., thousands attempt to flee major cities, clogging highways. American B-52s take flight en masse. Bob rushes to CVN and asks Dorian to leave with him; he notes that D.C. authorities are being evacuated. Dorian says she loves him, but that she has to stay.

Omani gunboats and U.S. naval forces engage in combat. On the *Nimitz*, CVN correspondent Boyle confirms Russia and America have exchanged nukes. His report fuzzes into static; the *Nimitz* has apparently been nuked.

The American airborne command post, which contains the president and his staff, takes flight, its destination five miles high to avoid destruction and stay in contact with American forces. The CVN network leaves the air, replaced by the Emergency Broadcast System. The last thing we see is a freeze-frame of the president's plane taking off, followed by a high-pitched whine.

Countdown to Looking Glass uses the "news show" format of events unfolding during a newscast but combines it with a more traditional narrative outside the CVN news set. This method is sometimes jarring, as the two forms of presentation don't always gel. *Special Bulletin*, which was solely shown as a newscast, is smoother than *Countdown to Looking Glass*.

But *Looking Glass'* inclusion of actual persons dealing with politics and history enhances its plausibility. For example, when a very young Representative Newt Gingrich is asked to comment on the movie's unfolding events, his response sounds like what a Republican at the time might have said. That's because Gingrich, former presidential candidate Eugene McCarthy and *Looking Glass'* other actual "talking heads" respond to the movie's situation in their own words. According to producer David Loxton, "The commentators were only told what had taken place in the story up to the point of their appearance, and were asked to give their own unscripted analyses of these events, as if they were reporting for a real broadcast."[4]

The movie's credibility is also enhanced by the presence of actual journalists, Eric Sevareid and Nancy Dickerson, as themselves, albeit supposedly working for the fictitious CVN network. In addition, Patrick Watson, who plays CVN anchorperson Don Tobin, was in reality a Canadian journalist and broadcaster.

The rest of the cast includes such familiar 1980s faces as Scott Glenn, Helen Shaver and Michael Murphy. They handle the material well. Fred Barzyk's direction is solid. Visually, the film has less to offer than some '80s nuke movies. But what we do see, such as an exploding ship, convinces. Unfortunately, the sporadic music score calls unwanted attention to itself.

The film paints a respectful picture of American journalists. For example, once a nuclear depth charge has exploded, correspondent Boyle continues to report until the *Nimitz* is apparently nuked itself. And when Bob asks Dorian to come with him to escape the imminent nuclear destruction of D.C., she refuses. He tells her no further broadcasts can help. She says, "Maybe, but I can't leave. I do love you." Anchor Tobin makes clear he will not leave his post until the Emergency Broadcast System breaks in. All three journalists embody a strong ethic to serve the public until the end.

One offbeat touch has the 53-year-old Secretary of Defense dying (offscreen) from a heart attack during White House deliberations. That the pressure of America-on-the-brink decision-making could result in death is, as far as I know, unique in the nuclear threat genre.

Typical for this film genre, the movie starts with trouble overseas that escalates step by step. When there's a spontaneous evacuation from major American cities, and the phone lines become jammed, the point of no return is in sight. You know where the story is going, and there's a distinct dread leading up to the nuclear engagement between the superpowers. When CVN correspondent Boyle is broadcasting from the *Nimitz* and a white light flashes onscreen, followed by static, you know the worst has happened.

The film's last sound, a shrill whir, is ominous. Was this an allusion to 1964's *Fail-Safe* in which the American ambassador in Moscow is on the phone when the Bomb hits, his demise signified by a high-pitched whine over the phone lines?[5] *Looking Glass* appears open-ended,

The DVD cover for 1984's *Countdown to Looking Glass* sports the sardonic tag line "A live special report from the end of the world."

but the viewer is reasonably sure that soon, America will resemble a continent-wide Hiroshima.

The scenario *Looking Glass* presents is complicated, but international events often are. As Eric Sevareid notes, stumbling into war is a process, a series of events, not one sudden massive assault against another nation. Indeed, Admiral La Rocque flatly states, "Any war with the Soviet Union will be a nuclear war."

The viewer can appreciate the pressures the film's scenario puts upon the American leaders. If oil doesn't get to its allies—for example, Japan—grave consequences could follow in these countries, which could further destabilize the international situation. Apparently, this is one of the major reasons the president says, "Our commitment to peace is matched only by our resolve that no nation great or small may hold other nations hostage to its greed for wealth and power."

In addition, when anchor Tobin asks Representative Gingrich if anything is worth risking a nuclear war, Gingrich says, "War is horrible; slavery is worse." During the '80s, this view saw capitulation to the Soviet Union in any capacity as a sacrifice of liberty, implying that the ultimate result would be Soviet subjugation of America. As Gingrich puts it, "Freedom will die."

Still, would the result of a full-scale nuclear war so devastate both Russia and America that civilization in these nations would cease to exist? Tobin tells Eric Sevareid, "Once the players came to the edge of the abyss and looked into it ... they would pull back." Sevareid appears unconvinced. Tobin adds that the apparent oncoming nuclear war is the result of one nation stalking another, "not the peoples of either country."

Regarding people, *Looking Glass* makes a brief nod to the spiritual, unusual in the nuclear threat genre. For example, in Japan, hundreds gather at the Hiroshima Monument. One couple traveled 300 miles to reach this destination, telling a CVN anchor that something told them this is where they should be. Toward the end of the film, Tobin tells his audience, "If there's anything to the power of prayer," now would be a good time to try it. Further, Sevareid declares, "If the present leaders can't intervene in this situation and back up and stop it, then God'll have to forgive them, because there won't be anyone else around to do it."[6]

Countdown to Looking Glass is only a movie. And we all know that in reality, both superpowers avoided a nuclear confrontation during the 1980s. Apparently, clear heads in both countries prevailed, and that is certainly a reason to give thanks.

* * *

Dark Enemy

DIRECTOR-WRITER: Colin Finbow; MUSIC: David Hewson; CINEMATOGRA-PHER: Amos Richardson; EDITORS: Matthew Landauer, Charles Robertson.
CAST: Rory Macfarquhar (Aron); David Haig (Ash); Douglas Storm (Ezra).
PRODUCTION: Children's Film Unit production in association with Goldcrest and Channel Four; released in the U.K. on 17 November 1984; 82 minutes; not rated.

* * *

"There's a dark enemy inside all of us," a Moon Child tells *Dark Enemy*'s hero Aron. "In all our time on Earth, we've made the same mistakes." Such is the core truth this British post-nuke production offers.

At an undetermined time, a group of nature-loving folks, mostly young, share a simple set of rules. They live a commune-like agrarian lifestyle, and they never travel into the forbidden areas. Elders periodically warn the youngsters of dangerous "Moon Dogs" and "Moon Children." One night, some curious youngsters come upon a Moon Child. Aron, a child with initiative, uses a torch to scare it off.

Ash warns Aron not to see the elder Ezra any longer because of Ezra's head sickness (apparently senility). But Aron visits him nevertheless, and soon Ezra dies.

Ash, now the reigning elder, orders Aron, Barnaby and Garth to undergo the Ordeal. The one who returns first from this perilous journey shall become the new leader. But in the middle of the trek, Barnaby and Garth cheat, leaving Aron far behind. But Aron meets a Moon Child who tells him they have the same parents, and that she has been calling to him telepathically (he thought it was the wind). She further shares she was Ezra's friend, but the commune threw her out, and she has secrets from Ezra she wants to share with Aron.

Aron learns that humans existed before the dark time. They coveted other people's possessions and lands, and even wished to own other people. Their greed led to their releasing powerful, destructive magic (nuclear weapons) that ushered in the dark time. But following the dark time, the commune grew, devising rules of sharing to keep its members from growing greedy.

Ash's dog kills the Moon Child, and he falls and dies. Aron arrives back at the commune before Barnaby or Garth. When they return soon thereafter, Garth declares the old rules are over, meaning Aron is not their leader.

Barnaby shows the youngsters Ash's secret stash gathered from beyond the commune. These trinkets, ranging from toys to canned food, dazzle the children. Barnaby promises that if they follow him, he'll take them to a place where they will never have to work again but can play all day, as well as accumulate more magic things.

Defiantly, Aron informs the children of the truth about the past, that terrible spells born of human greed ushered in the dark time. But the children don't care. They pledge allegiance to Barnaby and follow him in quest of the magic land he has promised. Aron refuses to go, so one of the girls gives him her doll to keep him company.

When Aron casts the doll away, its pre-recorded messages go off, getting stuck on the short sentence "I want," which plays over and over and over.

Dark Enemy is a decently made post-nuke story that often plays like a combination of 1963's *Lord of the Flies* and 1958's *Teenage Cave Man*. The revelation that the commune people flourish long after a nuclear war doesn't surprise, but human greed, the film's selected cause of that war, intrigues. The story posits that we turn "wants" into "needs" and thus feel entitled to what other people or other countries have.

However, this oversimplifies the causes of wars. Sometimes, "want" and "need" can blur together. For example, if I want medicine for my seriously ill child, this want is not selfish, but rather compassionate. And it isn't necessarily bad in and of itself to want "magic things" (i.e., technology), especially if I strive for a just society in which all people can partake of techno wonders. For example, the commune would benefit from antibiotics, mechanical transportation, infrastructure and other quality-of-life staples of modern technological societies.

And yes, a country may wage war to possess another nation. But often it is only the aggressor nation that wants to possess a nearby country, not the aggrieved nation, which just wants to be left alone.

The Moon Child tells Aron we all harbor an internal dark enemy. This assertion is remarkably similar to the sin nature Judeo-Christianity teaches exists within us. The film's suggested remedy is to create a small, share-and-share-alike agrarian society that frowns upon desiring more. But given human nature, could such a society exist indefinitely? Or even for long? *Dark Enemy* doesn't think so.

Despite a mostly naturalistic presentation, the movie includes telepathic mutants—the Moon Children—without apology. Notably, the Moon Child's face is disfigured, apparently a birth defect, and she says she and her kind "bear punishment for the past." Speaking of which, the film wisely places the revelation of nuclear war into the context in which the commune dwellers would understand it, i.e., magic and spells rather than science and technology. The final scene in which the doll incessantly repeats "I want" comes off as heavy-handed. But Barnaby's bamboozling the youngsters with promises of more stuff is well-played.

Interestingly, Aron doesn't tell the youngsters Barnaby tried to kill him when Barnaby cut the rope over the river. Why does Aron keep this to himself? Perhaps he doesn't want to smear his fellow Ordeal competitors, even with the truth. Of course, Barnaby's attempted murder argues that humanity may again move into a time of unleashing destructive "magic."

Not as profound as it wants to be, *Dark Enemy* is nevertheless an effective post-nuke tale that intelligently explores human weakness and strength, suggesting that, unfortunately, the former usually wins.

* * *

Dreamscape

DIRECTOR: Joseph Ruben; WRITERS: David Loughery, Chuck Russell, Joseph Ruben; MUSIC: Maurice Jarre; CINEMATOGRAPHER: Brian Tufano; EDITOR: Richard Halsey; VISUAL EFFECTS: Peter Kuran; PRODUCER: Bruce Cohn Curtis.
CAST: Dennis Quaid (Alex Gardner); Max von Sydow (Dr. Paul Novotny); Christopher Plummer (Bob Blair); David Patrick Kelly (Ray Glatman); Kate Capeshaw (Dr. Jane DeVries).
PRODUCTION: Zupnik-Curtis Enterprises, Bella Productions, Chevy Chase Films; 1984; 99 minutes; rated PG-13.

* * *

You've heard it before: If you die in your sleep, you die in real life. Myth or truth? In *Dreamscape*, this maxim proves all too true in a plot to assassinate the United States president before he can initiate nuclear disarmament.

Alex Gardner, a gifted mentalist, joins a dream research project led by Dr. Novotny. Alex enters the dreams of a young boy and coaxes him to kill the Snake-Man, the monster haunting the boy's sleep.

Meanwhile, the president has been having nightmares of nuclear war and plans to lead a disarmament delegation to Geneva. Government agent Bob Blair plots to eliminate the president by having psychic Tommy Ray Glatman invade the president's dream and kill him. Tommy Ray has already killed an elderly lady in her sleep as a "trial run."

Blair has Dr. Novotny killed. Alex evades Blair's guys; getting help from Jane

DeVries, he sneaks into the dream research building and enters the president's nuclear dream—but so does Tommy Ray.

Alex takes on the visage of Tommy's father, whom Tommy murdered years earlier. This distraction allows the president to slay Tommy, thus killing Tommy in real life. To stop Blair from making another attempt on the president's life, Alex enters Blair's dreams and kills him.

Dreamscape combines several movie genres—horror, science fiction, adventure, nuke threat. Arguably, the key concept, that of a psychic entering into another person's dreams, is fantasy rather than science fiction. Would anybody want someone to invade their dreams without consent? Alex does just this when he enters Jane's dream without her permission and makes love to her. Alex's unwanted dreamland intrusion understandably upsets Jane. While perhaps not quite psychic rape (Jane's dream self goes along with Alex's advances), this sequence comes close.

As for the president's nuclear dreams, they appear appropriately nightmarish. Having the president staring at a nuke-ravaged Washington, D.C., from inside a moving train car is ingenious. Also, the Bomb-injured survivors shuffling toward the president is a grisly touch, and the red-tinted landscape and sky suggest death.

The president tells Blair that he thinks the dreams are a purposeful attempt to convince him to engage the Soviet Union with nuclear disarmament talks. If that's the case, who orchestrated these dreams? God? The president? Both?

Also, what will the president do next? Presumably, begin nuclear disarmament negotiations with Russia. And of course, this happened in real life in 1987 when President Reagan and Soviet General Secretary Gorbachev signed the Intermediate-Range Nuclear Forces Treaty, or INF (see the entry on 1983's *The Day After* for more information).

Alex Gardner (Dennis Quaid, right) warns the president (Eddie Albert) that he is having a nightmare of a nuked Washington, D.C. in 1984's *Dreamscape* (Zupnik-Curtis Enterprises).

The film's special effects are somewhat dated but still arresting. The Snake-Man is partially brought to life using stop-motion animation, a technique CGI has supplanted, but one that may bring a smile to many a Baby Boomer's face.

All the actors do creditable work. Christopher Plummer excels, playing the villainous Blair to ice-hearted perfection. Hard to believe this is the same guy who played the sympathetic Captain von Trapp in 1965's *The Sound of Music*. As Alex, Dennis Quaid has a boyish, impudent attitude, but he learns a thing or two about responsibility before movie's end. David Patrick Kelly seems to relish his role of Tommy, a homicidal psychopath exhibiting even less of a conscience than Blair. Max von Sydow imbues Dr. Novotny with fatherly kindness, and Kate Capshaw energizes her underwritten role as best she can.

When the Motion Picture Association of America gave *Dreamscape* an R, the studio appealed the rating, and the MPAA changed it to PG-13.[7] Some (many?) would say an R rating might be well-deserved, given that the film includes rough language, strong sexual content and graphic violence.

Reviews are mostly positive. Rotten Tomatoes gives *Dreamscape* a 78 percent fresh rating based on the reviews of 32 professional critics. In 1988's *Starlog Science-Fiction Video Magazine* #1, Robert Greenberger wrote, "Dreams always make for entertaining movies … [*Dreamscape* is] no exception."[8] But *The New York Times*' Janet Maslin complained that the film "is mostly maladroit, without the kind of high gloss or confidence that might help carry its audience along."[9]

As for nuclear dreams, like *Dreamscape*'s president, I've had a few of my own. In the most realistic of the bunch, I am residing in a motel surrounded by desert. A helicopter lands, and out walk hazmat-suited individuals. They tell me and the other motel residents that strong radiation has swept through the area, and that we can expect to die within the next two weeks. Having read about the agony of radiation sickness, terror stirs my intestines. Of course, before the first symptoms showed, I woke up. But will I be so lucky next time?

* * *

The Final Executioner

DIRECTOR: Romolo Guerrieri; WRITER: Roberto Leoni; MUSIC: Carlo De Nonno; CINEMATOGRAPHER: Guglielmo Mancon; EDITOR: Alessandro Lucidi; PRODUCER: Luciano Appignani.
CAST: William Mang (Alan Tanner); Marina Costa (Edra); Harrison Muller (Erasmus); Woody Strode (Sam).
PRODUCTION: Immagine S.r.l.; Italian; 1984; 95 minutes; not rated.

* * *

Toward the end of *The Final Executioner*, the character Louis says, "I want out of this before I end up dead."

His boss Edra tells him, "Escape, then."

That would also be the audience's option.

The film opens with familiar stock shots of nuclear explosions, plus the havoc they wreak. We also see color volcano footage—presumably a nuclear blast has caused the eruption. Finally, we see two shots of what appears to be either Hiroshima or Nagasaki after they were A-bombed in 1945.

The narrator tells us that post-nuke society has divided into two groups: the rich who have remained uncontaminated from radiation, and the contaminated masses whom the rich consider "target material" they hunt to rid the world of radiation-afflicted individuals.

Scientist Alan Tanner, one of the uncontaminated, discovers that contamination no longer exists for anyone, including "target material." For this, the rich deem him and his wife "expendable" and banish them to the hunting reserve.

Several human hunters stalk Alan, his wife and several other unfortunates, killing most of them. One of the hunters rapes and kills Alan's wife, and another, Erasmus, frees Alan. Edra, the leader of the hunters, shoots Alan. He falls into a river, but survives.

Sam, a lone individual in the wilderness, takes Alan in and nurses him back to health. Sam reveals that before the Catastrophe, he served as a law officer. Alan says he wants justice, so Sam agrees to train him to be an effective avenger. Naturally, Alan passes the training with flying colors. Sam leaves Alan a note along with a handgun and one bullet.

Alan steals into Edra's estate, where the hunters, including his wife's rapist-murderer, reside. He's soon holding three hunters hostage, including Edra's little brother Evan (the boy has been stabbed and is dying). Alan tells one of the hunters to seek medical help for Evan, but instead she tries to escape. Unfortunately for her, Alan has booby-trapped her motorcycle, which explodes.

Eventually, it's Alan vs. Edra and Erasmus. Erasmus wields a sword against Alan. Just as it appears Erasmus will waste him, Alan pulls out the gun Sam left him and kills Erasmus with its one bullet.

Soon Edra has Alan in her sites, literally. But as she prepares to fire, she's shot by Sam the ex-lawman, who has come to Alan's rescue. Sam invites Alan to join him as a fellow law officer, to bring justice to the post-catastrophe world. Alan accepts the invitation.

The Final Executioner adds a few new ideas to the 1980s' Italian action film genre, mixing 1932's *The Most Dangerous Game* and 1974's *Death Wish* into its post-nuke blend. Like Charles Bronson in *Death Wish*, Alan seeks revenge for the rape and murder of his wife. He becomes a one-man killing machine, an equal opportunity avenger who dispatches male and female alike.

Also, the notion of the rich hunting fellow humans recalls *The Most Dangerous Game* on a large scale. The human hunters all appear to be dastardly villains with no compunctions about murdering their fellow men and women. At least one or two hunters should have had mixed feelings about this practice. Or perhaps Edra's little brother Evan could have questioned it. Instead, the villains, even Evan, are bad guys on the level of *Star Wars'* stormtroopers.

Alan tells Sam that 80 million of the contaminated have been hunted and killed. That suggests millions of the uncontaminated rich. Given that reality, what possible chance do Alan and Sam have of bringing law and order back to the world? But, better to try than fold.

Though not rated, the film would merit an R, partially for graphic violence and partially for an uber-gratuitous sex scene. Definitely not escapist fare for the kids.

Overall, *The Final Executioner* is a routine action film riddled with dull patches. Its one remarkable aspect is the inclusion of African American actor Woody Strode (1914-94) as Sam. Strode was a professional athlete who in 1946 played for the Los Angeles

Rams, but he is probably better known as an actor who appeared in a number of films and television shows for over five decades. Notable films include 1959's *Pork Chop Hill*, 1960's *Spartacus* and especially 1960's *Sergeant Rutledge*, in which he played the lead. Directed by veteran director John Ford, the film dealt with racism head-on, a Hollywood rarity at that time. The studio had wanted Sidney Poitier, but Ford held out for Strode.[10] Strode brings dignity to his role in *The Final Executioner*, but it is definitely one of his lesser films.

The Final Executioner was not the final post-nuke action movie to roll out of Italy. As you will read in successive entries, the number of such movies suggests a fecundity greater than rabbits.

* * *

First Strike

DIRECTOR: Allan Kuskowski; WRITERS: Allan Kuskowski, Dave Hanson; MUSIC: Jan Michael Alejandro; CINEMATOGRAPHER: Glenn Roland, Jr.; EDITORS: Bret Hampton, Jay Melzer, George Verschoor; PRODUCERS: Dave Hanson, Bob Nudo.
CAST: Stuart Whitman (Captain Welch); Paul Mantee (Lieutenant Mitchell); Persis Khambatta (Sylvia Kruger); B.G. Fisher (Boris Petroff).
PRODUCTION: Tekstar Quest International Productions; 1984; 94 minutes; not rated.

* * *

Some 1980s nuclear threat movies are more obscure than Question Mark and the Mysterians' follow-up to their 1966 hit "96 Tears."[11] *First Strike* is such a film. Despite the presence of the well-known actor Stuart Whitman, the movie apparently had few (if any) U.S. playdates.

The nuclear submarine U.S.S. *Cobra* is conducting underwater surveillance off Russia's coast. *Cobra* accidentally fires a torpedo at an approaching Soviet destroyer, but Lieutenant Mitchell remotely defuses it.

Captain Welch commands the *Cobra*, scheduled to conduct a "spy exchange" with Russia. Once aboard the sub, spy Sylvia Kruger kills one of two Russian prisoners and orders Boris Petroff, the second prisoner, to assist her in her double-crossing plan. Both begin shooting the crew as they move through the vessel. Sylvia has planted explosives on the sub's nuclear reactor.

Sylvia gives Boris the list of the codes previously obtained from the CIA. But Boris discovers the codes are not valid. When a crew member breaks into the compartment, he and Boris shoot each other. Sylvia shoots Captain Welch, but he survives.

The Russians realize their plan has gone awry. A nuclear missile from the *Cobra* was to have been fired at Syria, which would then provoke Syria to attack the American fleet with ICBMs provided by Russia. This would give Russia control over the Middle East's oil reserves.

Sylvia's planted explosives go off on the *Cobra*'s reactor, and a crewman has to fix the problem before the sub suffers a meltdown. Realizing what the Russians are up to, Welch orders all torpedoes fired at the Soviets. He dies, but Lieutenant Mitchell carries out his last order. The torpedoes destroy the enemy ships.

Russia chooses to withdraw, and the U.S. also withdraws. The Secretary of State tells Lieutenant Mitchell that he and the *Cobra* crew must "sit tight"; if they showed back up in Norfolk, the Russians would be embarrassed, and there would be too many questions. An onscreen message says the *Cobra* disappeared and may have been reassigned to the CIA, and that no one ever saw the sub's officers and crew again.

Technically, *First Strike* is ragged, perhaps the major reason it didn't receive a general release in America. The acting is variable. Whitman and Mantee are competent as Captain Welch and Lieutenant Mitchell, but B.G. Fisher plays Boris Petroff too broadly. His Russian caricature might have been perfect for *Saturday Night Live*, but deadly for a Cold War thriller that wants to be taken seriously.

The script bristles with clichés. For example, Leon Askin's conniving Soviet Chairman out-villains *Bullwinkle*'s Boris Badenov. The finale, in which the onscreen message tells us the *Cobra* and its crew disappeared, disappoints. At worst, this implies America has these guys stashed away somewhere from which they'll never escape. At best, this implies the crew may have gone the "witness protection" route Navy style, given different names, identities and histories. But that would still mean these men would never again see family and friends. Also, the notion of the *Cobra* being re-assigned to the CIA sounds dubious, to say the least.

The film's special effects vary from good to fair. For the time, the model work is decent. However, the movie's strained budget results in it recycling (twice) one of the most famous stock shots of a hydrogen bomb exploding in the Pacific.

Science fiction fans are probably familiar with Indian-born Persis Khambatta; her most famous role was in 1979's *Star Trek: The Motion Picture* (she was shaved bald to play Lieutenant Ilia, a Deltan navigator). Her other '80s films include *Nighthawks* (1981), *Megaforce* (1982), *Warrior of the Lost World* (1983) and *She-Wolves of the Wasteland* (1988). She died of a heart attack on August 18, 1998. Some sources omit *First Strike* from her career altogether. One example is her Turner Classic Movies write-up, which fails to include the title in her filmography.[12]

Stuart Whitman was a veteran Hollywood actor who appeared in dozens of films, as well as numerous TV shows, running the gamut from Westerns to horror movies. His genre work includes 1971's *City Beneath the Sea* (a failed Irwin Allen TV pilot) and 1972's infamous *Night of the Lepus* (giant carnivorous bunnies on the loose). After his full-speed-ahead career, Whitman retired from acting in 2000. He passed away in 2020 from skin cancer.

While the name Paul Mantee may ring few bells, Baby Boomers may remember him for 1964's *Robinson Crusoe on Mars*. In this engaging science fiction adventure, Mantee plays an astronaut who finds himself stranded on Mars decades before Matt Damon. Mantee passed away in 2013.

First Strike seems to want to compete in the espionage movie big leagues, but its small budget and other flaws strand it in Grade-B territory.

*   *   *

Godzilla aka Godzilla 1985

Godzilla: Japanese Version (1984):
DIRECTOR: Koji Hashimoto; WRITER: Shuichi Nagahara; MUSIC: Reijiro Koroku; CINEMATOGRAPHER: Kazutami Hara; EDITOR: Yoshitami Kuroiwa; SPECIAL EFFECTS: Teruyoshi Nakano; PRODUCER: Tomoyuki Tanaka.
CAST: Ken Tanaka (Goro Maki); Yasuko Sawaguchi (Naoko Okumura); Yosuke Natsuki

(Professor Makoto Hayashida); Ken Okumura (Shin Takuma); Keiju Kobayashi (Prime Minister Mitamura).

PRODUCTION: Toho; released in Japan on 15 December 1984; 103 minutes. Alternate title: *The Return of Godzilla*.

Godzilla 1985: Americanized version (1985):

DIRECTOR: R.J. Kizer; WRITER: Lisa Tomei; CINEMATOGRAPHER: Steven Dubin; EDITOR: Michael Spence.

CAST: Raymond Burr (Steven Martin); Warren J. Kemmerling (General Goodhue); Travis Swords (Major McDonough).

PRODUCTION: New World Pictures; released in America on 23 August 1985; 87 minutes, rated PG.

* * *

Will the real Godzilla please stand up? In the famed monster's long career, he has been pressed into service as a protector of Earth, a hero of Japan and a force of nature. But according to the late Tomoyuki Tanaka, who produced Godzilla's first 22 movies, the King of the Monsters "is the son of the atomic bomb. He is a nightmare created out of the darkness of the human soul. He is the sacred beast of the apocalypse."[13]

Tanaka's quote refers to the original 1954 *Godzilla* (*Gojira*) in which the monster serves as a metaphor for the Bomb, his destruction of Tokyo a stand-in for the 1945 nuclear obliteration of Hiroshima and Nagasaki. As *Village Voice* critic J. Hoberman writes, "Gojira—Godzilla to us—is the great movie monster of the post–World War II period, in part because [director Ishiro] Honda seems to have conceived this primordial force of nature as a living mushroom cloud."[14]

Despite its variable special effects, the original Japanese-language *Gojira, sans* Raymond Burr inserts, brims with moody photography and thermonuclear angst. The film not only glances backward to 1945's A-bombings, but also gazes ahead at what the world may become in the H-bomb age: an ash-ridden tableau where great cities once stood.

In 1984, Toho decided to go back to Godzilla's atomic roots. Godzilla hadn't appeared on movie screens for nine years, and his 1970s films suffered from slashed budgets and camp elements. Toho settled on a script that harkened back to the 1954 original not only in terms of ambience, but also of presentation. The 1984 *Godzilla* would be the only Big G movie since 1954 in which Godzilla did not battle a kaiju opponent.

In another bold move, Toho decided that in the 1984 *Godzilla*'s continuity, only the first Godzilla movie had actually happened. The following 14, in which the Big G battled King Kong, Mothra, King Ghidorah, Mechagodzilla *et al.*, ceased to exist as Godzilla canon.

The plot synopsis for the Japanese language 1984 *Godzilla* follows:

A storm at sea tosses about a Japanese fishing boat. A nearby island erupts, freeing a giant monster. Later, reporter Goro Maki happens upon the vessel and finds the crew dead except for Ken Okumura.

Hospitalized, Ken identifies the giant monster he saw as Godzilla. Goro writes a news story, but his editor suppresses it. Goro visits Professor Makoto Hayashida to discuss the monster.

Elsewhere, Godzilla destroys a Soviet submarine. The Japanese government keeps this secret. The Soviets blame the U.S. for the sub's destruction. To prevent a nuclear confrontation between the superpowers, the Japanese government publicly admits that

Godzilla sunk the sub. Godzilla next attacks a Japanese nuclear power plant, literally "eating" its radiation.

Prime Minister Mitamura meets with the American and Russian ambassadors; both want to use nuclear weapons to destroy Godzilla, even though the monster is in Japanese waters and an atomic explosion could devastate Tokyo. The prime minister convinces the Russians and Americans to forsake their plans to nuke Godzilla. However, Russia has a Soviet freighter in Tokyo Bay whose controls can launch an orbital nuclear missile at Godzilla should the need arise.

As Godzilla approaches Tokyo, the Japanese military throws everything they've got at the Big G, but his atomic ray incinerates their artillery. Also, the kaiju creates a wave that jostles the Soviet ship, causing it to set off a countdown to launch the orbital nuke against Godzilla. An injured Soviet colonel struggles to stop the launch, but dies before he can do so.

Godzilla smashes into Tokyo. Super-X, a military aircraft designed to battle the kaiju, shoots a skyward flare to trick Godzilla into opening his maw, then fires cadmium shells into his mouth. Super-X repeats the process, causing a weakened Godzilla to crash into a skyscraper.

Meanwhile, the orbital Soviet nuclear missile launches toward Tokyo. The Americans fire a missile that intercepts and destroys the Soviet missile. The resulting clouds spark lightning that crackles across Godzilla, reviving him. The kaiju again engages Super-X in battle, toppling a skyscraper onto the craft.

Professor Hayashida has a plan to use an avian homing signal to lure Godzilla to Mount Mihara, which the military will intentionally cause to erupt. The scientist turns on the homing signal, and Godzilla is indeed drawn to Mount Mihara. The kaiju falls into the volcano, and explosives ignite an eruption that engulfs him. Despite the hundreds of deaths and billions in property damage Godzilla has just caused, the prime minister weeps as the kaiju perishes.

Toho had high hopes for Godzilla's 1980s return, anticipating a Japanese box office gross of $12 million. But the film only took in $6.8 million.[15] Consequently, Toho pitched the movie to Hollywood, hoping to get $5 million for distribution rights. American studios weren't interested; reportedly, the highest offer Toho got was $2 million.[16] The studio eventually sold the movie to New World (at one time Roger Corman's film company) for half a million.[17]

New World cut some Japanese footage and filmed new scenes with Raymond Burr reprising his character of Steve Martin from 1956's Americanization *Godzilla, King of the Monsters!* Burr, best-known for the TV series *Perry Mason* (1957–66) and *Ironside* (1967–75), jumped at the chance to play Martin again. "[E]verybody thought I was out of my mind. But it wasn't the large sum of money. It was the fact that first of all, I kind of liked *Godzilla*, and where do you get the opportunity to play yourself 30 years later?"[18] Further, Burr did not see Godzilla as camp, but rather as a serious anti-nuclear metaphor, and you won't find even a centimeter of a tongue in his cheek as he recites his lines.[19]

Following is a look at the American footage New World added to the 1984 *Godzilla*:

The military summons Mr. Martin (the "Steve" was dropped for obvious reasons) because of his earlier experience with Godzilla. Along with a group of American military officers, Martin watches the monster's raid on Tokyo unfold. "Comedy relief" makes its unwanted presence known through the smart-aleck remarks of Major McDonough. Examples:

**A LIST:

> "That's quite an urban renewal program they got goin' on over there."
> "I'd say put a uniform on [Godzilla] and sign him up."
> "Maybe [Godzilla needs] a megadose of horse tranquilizers."

Dr. Pepper was one of the film's sponsors, and the soft drink's placement in the American scenes becomes more rampant than robocalls for an extended car warranty.

Once Godzilla vanishes into Mount Mihara, Martin delivers a heartfelt (if somewhat pretentious) commentary on the monster's demise. Unlike 1956's *Godzilla, King of the Monsters!*, in which clever editing and inserts made Burr appear to be interacting with some of the Japanese characters, Burr takes a completely non-participatory role in *Godzilla 1985*. Not once does he appear to be in Japan or speak with any of the Japanese characters. If the American scenes were dropped from the film, it wouldn't lose dramatic momentum. But for sentimental reasons, it was nice to see Burr return to the Big G series.

New World also chose to drop some of the special effects scenes and to re-shuffle the order of others. Curiously, a nice effects shot of Godzilla reflected in a mirrored glass skyscraper was cut, along with a scene of Godzilla in the background while crowds flee in the foreground. Meanwhile, the Super-X sequence was re-edited. Some non-effects scenes were cut as well.

In Japan in 1984, Toho heavily advertised its new Godzilla feature. One major marketing tool was an 18-foot robotic Godzilla Cybot, designed to perform facial expressions and other movements not possible for a man-in-suit monster. The Cybot cost $475,000.[20] Toho heavily promoted the Cybot in Japan, claiming that the machine "would appear in 70 percent of the special effects scenes."[21] In reality, the Cybot appeared in only a few scenes highlighting Godzilla's facial expressions; the majority of the movie relied on the tried-and-true method of suitmation, with actor Kenpachiro Satsuma emoting inside the heavy costume.

Toho wanted their new Godzilla movie to compete with American special effects extravaganzas, and thus spent $6.25 million on the film, more than they had ever spent on a Godzilla movie before. But while Teruyoshi Nakano's special effects are better than his visuals in Godzilla's 1970s movies, they still run hot and cold. One problem is scale. The miniatures in Godzilla's first 15 movies were built at a 1/25 scale when Godzilla was 50 meters (164 feet). However, Toho wanted to expand Godzilla's height to 80 meters (262 feet) so the towering skyscrapers in the current Tokyo wouldn't dwarf him. That reduced the scale of the miniatures to 1/40.[22] This decreased size especially hurt the credibility of the miniature military vehicles, as well as many of the city miniatures.

Another example of inadequate effects is the giant sea louse found on the fishing vessel. Its flying movements are awkward and unconvincing. New World trimmed these scenes, but they still remain second-rate.

In 1984, tensions between the Soviet Union and the U.S. ran high. This is fleshed out when Godzilla destroys the Soviet sub, but Russia thinks America did it. Still considering the Cold War, it's instructive to note the changes New World made to *Godzilla* to make it more palatable for Reagan-era America. In the Japanese original, both Russia and America have orbital nuclear missile platforms. But in the Americanization, only Russia is depicted as having a space-based nuke.

In the Japanese version, after the Russian ambassador's meeting with Japan's prime minister, a Russian ship officer tells a peer that the government has decided against using nuclear weapons. But in the Americanization, the same officer says, "I've received orders from Moscow to keep our nuclear option open."

Finally, the Japanese version depicts the launching of Russia's orbital nuke to be a mistake that a Russian naval officer tries to prevent. But the Americanization edits the sequence so that it appears as if the Russian officer is trying to make sure the missile *does* launch.

The American version clearly makes the Soviet Union out to be the bad guys. But in the Japanese version, Russia and America are basically depicted as moral equals. For example, ambassadors from both nations call for nuking Godzilla, despite the fact that the kaiju is in Tokyo Bay. At one point, the frustrated American ambassador says, "This is no time to be discussing principles." The prime minister convinces the Russian and American leaders not to use nukes by asking them if they would use nukes if Godzilla attacked Moscow or Washington. As the prime minister says, "Both leaders finally understood."

Some might feel that the film's critique of the Cold War arms race appears befuddled. The Japanese refuse to let the U.S. or Soviet Union use nuclear weapons to destroy Godzilla. Yet when the Soviet nuclear missile is fired at Tokyo from space, the means of stopping it is another nuclear missile, this one fired by the Americans. On the one hand, the movie seems to condemn nuclear weapons per se, but on the other hand, the salvation of Tokyo occurs *because* of a nuclear weapon. Then again, the American and Russian nuke collision creates a radiation storm that revives Godzilla, so perhaps the film is arguing that tragedy will always result from the use of nuclear weapons.

In the book *The Atomic Bomb in Japanese Cinema*, Jason C. Jones argues that just as the Japanese must fight Godzilla alone in the 1954 film, they also fight the kaiju alone in the 1984 *Godzilla*.[23] In the latter film, the U.S. and U.S.S.R. offer help, yes, but only in the form of nuclear weapons that could damage Japan, an all-or-nothing gambit. In this regard, the Soviet Union goes one step further than America by actually having a ship in Tokyo Bay that can launch a nuclear missile at Tokyo from space. So it appears as though, if only incrementally, the U.S. is not as morally deficit in the Japanese version of 1984's *Godzilla* as the U.S.S.R.

Nevertheless, if not for the interference of the superpowers, Japan might have finished off Godzilla. Super-X launches cadmium shells into Godzilla's mouth which seem to kill the atomic dragon. However, radioactive lightning caused by the American missile colliding with the Russian rocket resuscitates him.

While Godzilla is of course a fantasy character, the political debates in 1984's *Godzilla* wrestle with the actual nuclear issues that then threatened the world. Using nukes, even just one, could open a "no man's land." Once escalation started, could a nuclear tit for tat be avoided? Even a limited use of nukes could cause not only loss of life and real estate, but perhaps economic chaos as well. Such would be the result of Tokyo's irradiation.

In Cold War terms, *Godzilla* depicts Japan as being at the mercy of Russia and America. Japan can stand firm on its anti-nuke principles, but it can't influence the political trajectories of either the U.S. or the U.S.S.R. Whatever decisions the superpowers make or conflicts they fight, Japan would not have a say, but it might reap the consequences, certainly in case of a nuclear war.

American critics stomped New World's *Godzilla 1985* flat. Here's an example, from Vincent Canby's 1985 *New York Times* review: "Godzilla, who is supposed to be about 240 feet tall, still looks like a wind-up toy … [There are] lots of references to the lessons to be learned from 'this strangely innocent but tragic creature.'"[24]

Godzilla 1985 was budget-challenged, at $6.25 million costing only a fraction of concurrent American special effects films, among them 1985's *Back to the Future* ($19 million), 1985's *Explorers* ($25 million) and 1984's *2010: The Year We Make Contact* ($28 million).

For a friendly take on the Japanese version, respected movie scholar David Kalat—author of *A Critical History and Filmography of Toho's Godzilla Series, 2nd ed.*—opined, "With some bold decisions and savvy strategies, [producer] Tomoyuki Tanaka and his team had successfully reinvented Godzilla."[25]

Godzilla's next several Toho movies would become less political and more entertainment-oriented. Still, 1989's *Godzilla vs. Biollante* touches on atomic matters. In addition, 1995's *Godzilla vs. Destoroyah* spotlights Godzilla's nuclear aspects, as it is a sequel of sorts to the 1954 original. And 2016's *Shin Godzilla*, which updates the premise of the 1984 *Godzilla*, reignites nuclear threat issues in a more contemporary context. After all, if the famed kaiju *is* the sacred beast of the apocalypse, nuclear threat cinema can never be far behind.

* * *

The Killing Edge

DIRECTOR: Lindsay Craig Shonteff; WRITER: Robert Bauer; MUSIC: John Dinsdale; CINEMATOGRAPHER: Hugh Williams; EDITOR: Derek Hawthorne; PRODUCER: Elizabeth Gray.
CAST: Bill French (Steve Johnson); Paul Ashe (Lenny).
PRODUCTION: unknown; release date: unknown; released in 1984 according to IMDb; 81 minutes; not rated.

* * *

Sometimes a movie is so obscure that even IMDb.com gets the description wrong. For 1984's British-made *The Killing Edge*, IMDb says, "In a post-nuclear-war wasteland, a man searches for his family while trying to avoid deadly killer robots." Well, it *is* a post-nuke world, but no killer robots show up—perhaps a relief to some, a disappointment to others.

Following a nuclear war, Steve Johnson scours the British countryside hunting for his wife and son. He meets a woman who tells him that a paramilitary group called the Terminators have enslaved the valley's few survivors, and they kill anyone who opposes them. Steve and the woman band together. When marauders appear, Steve defeats them, but they kill the woman.

Next Steve stumbles across a work detail guarded by the Terminators and is surprised to see his wife and son among the workers. She runs toward him, but a guard shoots her and the boy. Furious, Steve guns down the guards.

He later meets a young escapee from the Terminators who says Guard #7 had beaten Steve's son. As Steve lies in wait for Guard #7, the Terminator shoots Steve, but he survives. Next, Steve attacks a group of three Terminators, one of them Guard #7. Though shot up himself, Steve manages to kill Guard #7.

Extremely low-budget, *The Killing Edge* strives to create a lawless post-nuke Britain, only partially succeeding. The film takes place in the countryside, sparing the filmmakers any need to create city rubble. But nuclear war appears to have left the rural landscapes untouched.

The acting is fair, with Bill French satisfactory as the lead character. The techno soundtrack smacks of the synthesizer-drenched pop music that dominated 1980s' charts. Sometimes the staging of the action scenes stumbles, such as Steve more than once making himself an easy target. Also, it's amazing that despite suffering multiple gunshots, he keeps chugging along.

One haunting exchange occurs between Steve and a man dying of radiation. Steve tells the man that when the nuclear attack happened, he was on a business trip. The man says, "That sounds funny now, business trip."

The film's story is a standard post-nuke near-future scenario. Midway the narrative changes from a search adventure into a revenge tale. This is fairly typical in post-nuke near-future movies, somewhat recalling 1962's *Panic in Year Zero!*

The Killing Edge is no award-winner, but neither is it the Grade-Z stinker some Internet user reviews claim. But could killer robots have helped? Alas, we'll never know.

*   *   *

Mad Warrior

DIRECTOR: Willy Milan aka Wilfredo Milan; WRITER: Bonnie Paredes; MUSIC: Rogert Rigor; CINEMATOGRAPHER: Vic Anao; EDITOR: Pat Ramos.
CAST: Anthony Alonzo (Rex); Jennifer Kirkham (Raya).
PRODUCTION: JPM Productions; made in the Philippines in 1984; released in the U.S. in 1985; 75 minutes; not rated. Alternate title: *Clash of the Warlords*.

*   *   *

Action doesn't always equal excitement, and this has rarely been truer than in the post-nuke cheapie *Mad Warrior*. It takes place on an island after a nuclear war. An insane warlord, Malzon, rules over a group of warriors in a shoddy encampment, pitting his gladiators against each other in an even shoddier "arena" (a circle of four-foot wooden posts). Why they fight for Malzon is anyone's guess, but maybe the benefits are good. Malzon's top warrior is Rex.

Rex, his young son and a sympathetic woman escape from Malzon's camp. Malzon's goons kill the woman and Rex's son. Raya, a female warrior, comes to Rex's aid, and both wind up in a benevolent settlement run by Raya's father. Malzon's men capture Rex and haul him back to the gladiator arena. There, he battles a number of tough customers amidst high kicks, terse groans and bad staging.

The benevolent settlement folks arrive to battle Malzon's tribe, and they win. Malzon and Rex somewhat unexpectedly square off against each other with light sabers *à la Star Wars*—and no, the movie gave no hint this was coming. After winning, Rex chooses to leave the settlement and go his own way. A displeased Raya says, "You're really crazy. Crazy like a mad warrior."

Of course, the maddest character in this low-budgeter has got to be the evil Malzon. He's given to bouts of maniacal laughter and foaming at the mouth during a full moon (though the movie actually shows us a half moon).

Although only 75 minutes long, *Mad Warrior* feels much longer.

* * *

A Man Called Rage

DIRECTOR: Anthony Richmond; WRITERS: Jaime Comas Gil, Eugenio Benito; MUSIC: Stelvio Cipriani; CINEMATOGRAPHER: Gianni Bergamini; EDITOR: Vincenzo Tommassi; PRODUCER: Paolo Ferrara.

CAST: Conrad Nichols (Rage); Steve Eliot (Slash); Werner Pochath (Victor); Taida Urruzola (Mara); Chris Huerta (Omar).

PRODUCTION: Tiber Cinemat, International Roma, Arco Film Madrid; Italian; 1984; released in the U.S. in October 1986; 90 minutes; not rated. Alternate title: *Rage*.

* * *

Yet another Italian post-nuke action movie, *A Man Called Rage* opens with numerous stock shots of nuclear explosions. Next, commandos capture Rage and take him to an underground facility. There, the benevolent leader tells Rage about Alpha Base, a site that has the uranium reserves and knowledge to decontaminate the Earth.

The leader entreats Rage to find this site, and Rage gives in. His crew consists of Victor, Mara and Omar, a rotund egghead who provides explosives and would-be comedy relief. They journey to the domain of a rogue named Slash and ask him for the maps to the forbidden lands. Slash says he must escort Rage and take his share of the loot. Rage knows Slash is a two-faced lout, so he and his companions steal the maps and "borrow" a truck. Naturally, Slash and his unkempt crew follow them.

En route to Alpha Base, Rage's group encounters some friendly folks on horseback and leave weapons for them. Remember this, it figures prominently in the finale.

Rage and his friends find that Alpha Base is deserted and there's no uranium at all. But Alpha Base does offer important videocassettes (remember, this was the '80s) and books, plant seeds and a Bible that's been preserved in cryonic suspension. Alpha Base's self-destruct component starts, forcing Rage and friends to flee like bandits.

Slash and his evil followers catch up and fighting ensues. The conflict climaxes with Rage's group shooting it out with Slash's commandos from a train. Just when it looks as though Slash will prevail, a group of armed men, some on horseback, some on foot, arrive (shades of the U.S. cavalry). Yes, these are the folks for whom Rage left weapons.

Rage and friends accompany these nomadic saviors as they travel north, which is supposedly decontaminated. There, they will plant the seeds they found in Alpha Base.

Like most post-nuke action flicks, *A Man Called Rage* features plenty of unlikely sights. For example, when Rage and friends come upon Slash's base of operations, it's like Party Central, complete with dancing, flashing lights, scorpion racing (don't ask) and a smiling woman with a serpent.

As for wardrobe, Mara appears to have purchased her combat attire at a Daisy Dukes thrift store. Of course, for the ladies, Rage's sleeveless outfit shows off his biceps. Rage and Mara do not get romantically involved, perhaps the movie's only surprise.

Throwing in the freight train towards the end adds a bit of novelty, but not enough. The climactic shootout, like everything else in this movie, goes on too long. However, one saving grace is the optimistic finale. Also, the movie's veneration of the

Bible is intriguing. But all in all, *A Man Called Rage* is just another Italian post-nuke shoot-'em-up.

*   *   *

Massive Retaliation

DIRECTOR-PRODUCER: Thomas A. Cohen; WRITERS: Larry Wittnebert, Richard Beban; MUSIC: Harn Soper, Paul Potyen; CINEMATOGRAPHER: Richard Lerner; EDITOR: B.J. Sears.

CAST: Christopher Burton (Carl Fredericks); Molly Cohen (Meghan Fredericks); Doug Santana (Peter Fredericks); Alex Drude (Harry Tolliver, Jr.); Lisa Soloway (Kimberly Briscoe); Jason Gedrick (Eric Briscoe); Johnny Weissmuller, Jr. (Deputy Virgil Griffin); Bobcat Goldthwait (Ernie Rust), Karlene Crockett (Marianne Briscoe).

PRODUCTION: Hammermark, One Pass Inc.; 1984; 90 minutes. Alternate title: *Days of Sunshine Past*.

*   *   *

Massive Retaliation's poster exclaims, "Who will live? What will they do to survive?" The art depicts a rifle-toting woman and man, and below them a mushroom cloud looms over a city while a long line of cars exits town. Looks exciting, but suggests a movie somewhat different than the actual film.

Three families, the Briscoes, the Fredericks and the Tollivers, co-own an emergency compound to which they will evacuate if nuclear war breaks out. Jackie Tolliver, a newswoman, discovers (1) that Russia is involved in an evacuation drill and (2) that the Soviets are massing on the Russia-Iran border. She calls Dr. Lee Briscoe, a leader of the tri-family group, and he orders her to tell everyone to pack and meet at the compound at midnight.

They do so, and Lee gives them marching orders for securing the ranch. Meanwhile, Lee's teenage son Eric is bringing the families' kids in a van, but the water pump goes out. He can't buy one because he doesn't have a credit card in his name, so he tries to steal a pump. The merchant pulls a rifle on him.

At the compound, the Emergency Broadcast System voice declares, "This is not a test." The speaker says that Americans are evacuating from urban to rural areas. Given this news, several worry about the kids in Eric's care. Lois Fredericks commandeers a car to get the kids, but her auto hits a mine. Lee and Harry pull her from the vehicle. Harry inadvertently steps on a mine, injuring his leg.

Eric, jailed for trying to steal the water pump, is released by the busy sheriff. Desperate, he steals the sheriff's water pump, installs it in the van and heads for the compound.

At the compound gate, Lee confronts Deputy Virgil Griffin and his crony Ernie Rust. Lee refuses to give them any of the compound's gas. As the hours wear on, Lee scarfs uppers to stay awake. Tensions break out among the women. An alarm goes off, telling Lee that someone is on the compound grounds. Kirk shoots someone, but doesn't know who.

Susie, the Fredericks' employee, is the one who was shot. Although Lee is a surgeon, he refuses to operate on her or give her medicine, insisting that medical treatment must be limited to the three families. Outraged, Lois, once a nurse, treats Susie while Marianne Briscoe shares her medicine.

Kirk hears a transmission claiming that the Pope has declared he will excommunicate any Catholic who takes part in the current U.S.-U.S.S.R. conflict, and there are 783 million Catholics worldwide.

Deputy Griffin and Ernie fly a plane over the compound and contaminate its reservoir. This leaves only enough bottled water for a week, a fact imperiling the group.

Eric drives into the compound with the kids. The families are overjoyed until they see that Deputy Griffin and Ernie are holding guns on the kids. The deputy says someone from the group can visit the children in the van for one minute. Lee volunteers, and once inside the van, he slaps and scolds his son Eric for what Eric has "let" happen.

Deputy Griffin gives the families a half hour to vacate the compound, and threatens to kill one of the kids every 20 minutes after the time limit is up. Lee suggests the families rush the van, even if it means losing one of the kids. After hearing Griffin's warning gunshots, the families take cover across from the van. Lee and Kirk tote weapons. Deputy Griffin grabs one of the kids for cover, and he and Ernie take refuge in an earthen depression. Lee fires and hits Ernie's leg.

Back at the compound, Harry hears over the radio, "An immediate ceasefire was declared moments ago in a joint announcement released by the White House and the Kremlin. Both nations have agreed to continue around-the-clock negotiations to further de-escalate the worldwide crisis." On crutches, Harry hobbles to the families, declaring, "It's over!" Deputy Griffin shoots him. Harry tells everyone about the ceasefire, but Lee calls it Russian propaganda designed to get Americans to lower their guard.

Lee orders Kirk to drop his rifle; Kirk complies, then says, "I understand war. And I know when they're over. This one's over. It was over for us before it began." Walking towards Deputy Griffin, Kirk puts his hands up, but Lee shoots Kirk. Lois knocks the

Movie poster for 1984's *Massive Retaliation* (Hammermark), which concerns three survivalist families who pull together during what appears to be an international build-up to nuclear war. In the film, survivalism is put under the magnifying glass.

weapon from Lee's hands. In unison, Eric and the kids form a circle around Kirk's prone body.

As a survivalist drama (some would say melodrama), *Massive Retaliation* sometimes suffers logic lapses. For example, the three families jointly own a survivalist compound, and one of the key elements of such a refuge would be inaccessibility. But the compound is out in the open, has a paved road, and a gate on that paved road. The Fredericks' employee Susie finds the compound without any problem.

Another issue is adequate preparation. When Deputy Griffin contaminates the reservoir, we discover the protagonists only have enough bottled water to last a week. Given that the reservoir is out in the open, and that fallout could be a hazard via radioactive rain, it's short-sighted to have so little water on hand.

Some scenes meander, such as Eric racing on his bike to the van. The music during this sequence, and during much of the rest of the movie, often falls flat. The quality of the acting varies. As Harry, Michael Pritchard hams it up during his opening scenes. Granted, he's supposed to be the group's resident funny man, but he comes off like an outtake from a *Saturday Night Live* skit.

Comedian Bobcat Goldthwait, as the deputy's crony Ernie, sometimes appears to think he's in a comedy, as when he imitates a flying plane. But laughs are not what a serious nuke movie needs.

The rest of the cast passes muster. Peter Donat, no stranger to playing movie heavies, invests his survivalist character Lee Briscoe with authenticity. He takes the character from being an intellectual survivalist to a hands-on survivalist, one who seriously considers sacrificing one or more of the families' children to wrest control from Griffin. Johnny Weissmuller, Jr., gives a decent performance as the amoral deputy, demonstrating how fast some men might take the law into their own hands when World War III comes.

Massive Retaliation differs from many of its 1980s filmic cousins. For example, some '80s nuke movies briefly touch on survivalist themes, but in *Massive Retaliation*, survivalism is the dominant thread. Also, the film depicts a limited nuclear war. We know nukes have been used, because eyewitnesses report having seen "blinding flashes of light and mushroom clouds" when Soviet and American warships clashed in the Gulf of Oman. Less clear is whether any U.S. or U.S.S.R. cities have been nuked. But the movie ends with a ceasefire between the two superpowers, implying it's possible to stop a limited nuke war, unusual because most nuke movies suggest that after even one tactical nuclear weapon is used, full retaliation can't be far behind.

Another unique touch has the Pope declare he will excommunicate any Catholics who participate in the war. You have to wonder how many Catholics would have resided in the Soviet Union, whereas the U.S. has millions of Catholics, including many men and women in the armed forces. Would such a ploy by the Vatican affect a war between the superpowers? *Massive Retaliation* thinks so.

The movie has an axe or two to grind. While perhaps all nuke threat films imply an antiwar message, *Massive Retaliation* blares it from the rooftops. Even the film's opening credits folk song "Children of the Darkness" makes this clear. Indeed, contrivances mar the story to accommodate antiwar themes. For example, near the end of the film, Eric says, "[The kids and I] can't just sit here." His sister Kim replies, "What are we gonna do without guns?" What they do is form a hand-in-hand ring around the gunshot Kirk. Perhaps this gesture of nonviolent solidarity is supposed to soften Griffin's heart, but the lawman has been pretty merciless up to this point.

It's also clear this peaceful end to the survivalists' drama is meant to echo the ceasefire Russia and America have declared. For example, we hear that there have been mass desertions from both American and Russian armed forces, a key event leading to the superpowers' ceasefire. But how probable is that? We also hear that worldwide peace demonstrations have influenced Soviet and American leaders to declare an end to hostilities. But would either country's leaders really have been impressed with such protests? And could unsanctioned demonstrations have occurred in the Soviet Union in 1984, a time before the relatively moderate Gorbachev took over?

Another antiwar contrivance involves Lee's portrayal. He's apparently intended to be the archetypal survivalist. By the end of the film, he has become a son-slapping caricature willing to shoot friends and sacrifice children. But not all survivalists would necessarily go that far; they don't all have horns.

About an hour into the film, the movie airs the key arguments for and against survivalism in the face of a nuclear war: A gunshot Susie stumbles into the compound's house, causing Lee and Lois to heatedly debate. Lee refuses to treat Susie, so Lois, a one-time nurse, tends her.

In a *Starlog* #190 interview (May 1993), Peter Donat discussed his character: "The guy I play, the doctor, says, 'Look, let the hordes of people in here who want to get in, we'll last for three days, and *all* die. What's the good of that? So, we'll shoot 'em…. I've got a feeling that something like this could still happen someday."[26] Donat seems to sympathize with Lee, as opposed to finding him a villain.

In the film, the compound's group fractures. But both sides have a point. As Lois and Marianne implicitly argue, how can you not help an injured person right in front of you? Maybe you can't help all the Susies in the world, but you can help this one. For example, maybe you can't feed the thousands of children who starve each day, but you can feed a few of them—and if you found a starving child on your doorstep one morning, you wouldn't plead limited resources, even if you were out of work or on a restricted income.

On the other hand, what if you were a senior citizen on a fixed income and found 50 starving children on your doorstep, and only had enough resources to feed half? How would you choose who got food and who didn't? If the 50 children were in a line, and your grandchildren were the last in line, would they number among the half of kids who got food, or would you instead give food to the first 25 children in line, meaning your grandkids would go hungry?

After the argument between Lee and Lois, Lee appears to have won Jackie to his side. But on the other hand, he has lost Kirk, who after having inadvertently shot Susie, appears to want no part in survival that involves random killing or maiming. Similarly, Marianne has turned against him and has joined Lois and Kirk.

The survivalist argument broached in *Massive Retaliation* has graced nuke films of the past. For example, 1955's *Day the World Ended* offers a similar premise: Preparing for a post-nuke world, Paul Birch stores up enough resources for him, his daughter Lori Nelson and her boyfriend. However, against Birch's orders, Nelson lets five more people into their compound. The father in 1962's *Panic in Year Zero!* espouses a similar philosophy. Out with the family on a fishing trip when nuclear war breaks out, he develops a quick disdain for anyone who isn't family.

Since *Massive Retaliation* ends with a ceasefire between the Soviet Union and the United States, you have to wonder what happens to the movie's characters after the final scene. You assume Marianne will seek a divorce from Lee. In addition, Lee, who has shot Kirk, would no doubt be arrested and charged; assuming Kirk died, Lee would be slapped with a murder charge. Likewise, Deputy Griffin and his crony Ernie would probably find themselves in legal hot water. And Kirk may have shot Susie inadvertently, but he still shot her, so you assume he would be charged with manslaughter. More positively, Harry and Jackie would likely reconcile, a process that appears to have already started. And the kids probably wouldn't be going on any more road trips in which Eric was in charge.

If a studio made *Massive Retaliation* today, to keep up with our increasingly nihilistic times, we would probably still see the children stand hand-in-hand around Kirk— followed seconds later by the blinding flash of a nuclear explosion.

*   *   *

Nausicaä of the Valley of the Wind

DIRECTOR-WRITER: Hayao Miyazaki, based on his manga; MUSIC: Joe Hisaishi; CINEMATOGRAPHERS: Koji Shiragami, Yukitomo Shudo, Yasuhiro Shimizu, Mamoru Sugiura; EDITORS: Naoki Kaneko, Tomoko Kida, Shôji Sakai; PRODUCER: Isao Takahata.

CAST (voice cast, Japanese version): Sumi Shimamoto (Nausicaä); Mahito Tsujimura (Jihl/Muzu); Hisako Kyôda (Oh-Baba); Gorô Naya (Yupa); Ichirô Nagai (Mito).

PRODUCTION: Nibariki, Tokuma Shoten, Hakuhodo, Topcraft; Japanese; 1984; 117 minutes; rated PG.

*   *   *

This animated film takes place a thousand years after "the Seven Days of Fire" destroyed the world. The remaining humans are clustered in various communities, some peaceful, some less so. Nausicaä is the princess of the Valley of the Wind, a peace-loving agricultural society. However, the Sea of Decay, the result of humankind's past pollution, edges ever closer.

The Tolmekians are a violent people who attack without cause. They plan to use a Great Warrior from past times to destroy the Sea of Decay's toxic plants and massive insects.

Provoked, angry, whale-sized insects called Ohms charge towards the valley. To defeat the monstrous herd, the Tolmekians employ a Great Warrior from times past; however, it has not yet reached maturation, and after blasting many Ohms, it dies—but the countless Ohms continue their charge.

Nausicaä discovers a baby Ohm is being used as bait to lure the adult insects. She frees the infant and returns it to the Ohms. Sensing her benevolent intentions, the Ohms leave the valley and head back to the Sea of Decay.

One of the key reasons we watch movies is to be transported to other worlds, either in terms of time, situation, geography or all three. The latter is the case for *Nausicaä of the Valley of the Wind*. Intricate backgrounds and foregrounds, as well as strikingly realized flora and fauna, vividly bring the film's animated world to life. Writer-director Hayao Miyazaki's visual artistry seems boundless, yet the story and action corral the film into commercial territory.

The movie's most fascinating denizens are the Ohms—gigantic, armored, caterpillar-like creatures reminiscent of Toho's Mothra in its infant form. Briefly, a flashback shows Ohms razing cities. As a diehard *daikaiju* fan, I wish we'd seen more of this.

Miyazaki's themes include pacifism and environmentalism. Indeed, given its ecological emphasis, *Nausicaä* could be called Earth Day anime. Meanwhile, Miyazaki's pacifist inclinations somewhat belie the onscreen violence; after all, it isn't Flower Power that defeats the villains, but rather weaponry. Yet the film does argue that violence should be used as a last resort.

The "Seven Days of Fire" said to have destroyed the world were clearly nuclear in nature. For example, the first ray the Great Warrior uses to blast the distant herd of Ohms results in a mushroom cloud and a huge wind blast.

Nausicaä of the Valley of the Wind established its writer-director Miyazaki as a major force in Japanese animation; on Rotten Tomatoes, the film gets an 86 percent fresh rating based on 19 professional reviews. Miyazaki went on to helm the critically acclaimed animated movies *Princess Mononoke* (1997), *Spirted Away* (2001) and *Howl's Moving Castle* (2004).

Nausicaä is rated PG for violence, but overall, the film is kid-friendly. Its combination of fantasy and science fiction plays like a fairy tale with the scary parts left in.

* * *

One Night Stand

DIRECTOR-WRITER: John Duigan; MUSIC: William Motzing; CINEMATOGRA-
    PHER: Tom Cowan; EDITOR: John Scott; PRODUCER: Richard Mason.
CAST: Tyler Coppin (Sam); Cassandra Delaney (Sharon); Jay Hackett (Brendan); Saskia
    Post (Eva); David Pledger (Tony).
PRODUCTION: Astra Film Productions Pty Ltd., Michael Edgley International; Aus-
    tralian; released in the U.S. on 5 May 1984; released in Australia on 5 April 1984; 94
    minutes; not rated.

* * *

The Australian poster for *One Night Stand* depicts two couples standing beneath umbrellas, as though such canopies could shield them from bombs. This implies that the movie may be a comedy, which it most assuredly isn't.

On New Year's Eve, Eva meets her friend Sharon at the Sydney Opera House, where Sharon works, after closing. There, Sharon and Eva discover Sam, an American sailor who has gone AWOL and has been hiding in the opera house because he knows war is imminent. Sam announces that World War III has started. Over the radio, we hear that tactical nuclear weapons have been used in East and West Germany; nuclear devices have exploded south of Sydney and at a U.S. military base.

The news shocks Sharon, Eva, Sam and opera house maintenance man Brendan. As they hear more frightening radio broadcasts throughout the next few hours, they struggle to cope. Several think of their parents. They also have a go at the Opera House bar. Gradually, each of them shares memories from childhood, school days and teen years. Later, when each has become slightly sloshed, they play strip poker. Afterward, Sharon and Brendan sleep with each other.

By herself, Eva listens to a TV broadcast and learns that much of Europe—including

London and Paris—have, in the words of the news anchor, "virtually ceased to exist." The station next plays footage from an area northwest of New York City showing screaming nuclear burn victims. In tears, Eva shares what she saw with the others.

Sydney residents are ordered to go to the nearest underground shelter. As Sharon, Brendan, Eva and Sam join the throng heading for this refuge, the cloud-infested sky above is an angry red. Once they are all below, Sharon and Eva are asked to sing a song, and they begin to sing "It Might as Well Rain Until September." The lights go out, followed by the deep rumble of an apparent explosion. People scream. After a blackout, Sharon and Eva finish their song, Sam lights a match, and the screen freezes.

One Night Stand's examination of four young people trying to deal with the imminent end of the world is mesmerizing. At one point, they discuss nuclear war, as if to make the prospect less frightening. Eva asks, "What does radiation do to you?" Sam tells her it causes "a lingering death." Sharon asks if anything can survive. Dryly, Sam says, "Only mutations."

They also try to drown their troubles in drink. It doesn't work. When Brendan inadvertently blasts a rock song (the Easybeats' "Friday On My Mind") over the stage audio system, Eva, Sharon and Sam give themselves over to joyous and chaotic dance. For a time, they lose themselves in the music, just as many do during troubled times. Only thing is, at some point, the music stops.

Memories of both good and bad times help the characters cope, both as individuals and as a quartet. At some level, they apparently can't believe it's all going to end, and this finale might be only hours or minutes away. At one point, Eva wonders what it's like to be dead. Brendan replies, "I thought you believed in God." Eva replies, "I do. Well, I think I do."

Later, after having seen the horrific TV footage of nuclear burn victims, a tearful Eva tells her friends, "Maybe we should pray." Brendan lashes back that the burn victims must have been praying too, and it didn't help them. Eva counters that people, not God, caused the nuclear explosion. But Brendan's case against God immediately takes root, and despite Eva's suggestion, the quartet do not pray. Clearly, their vision of reality does not allow for a divine being, implying that the universe is a capricious, nihilistic beast and that they soon may become victims.

Though much of the movie takes place indoors depicting interactions between the main characters, some of the film's other images are arresting. For example, when the quartet has joined the crowd racing for the shelter, a crimson sky broods overhead, as though the heavens are bleeding. In this scene, *One Night Stand* intersperses images of the flood scenes in 1927's *Metropolis* to imaginative effect.

Some may question the scene in which Eva sees the TV broadcast of burn victims near New York City. Given that a massive number of nuclear explosions have probably occurred in America, technology might be on the fritz. However, the TV anchor does say that after a few minutes, the transmission stopped, implying that more nuclear explosions have ravaged New York.

Near the film's end, the scenes of the New York burn victims are startling given that the movie has spared us the slightest hint of physical carnage. We don't seem to see skin peeling from people's faces, a horrific image Eva later recounts to her friends. However, the screams of the burn victims would unsettle anyone.

One Night Stand offers many quietly effective moments. For example, it takes place on New Year's Eve, and briefly in the background, we hear a forlorn bagpipe playing

"Auld Lang Sine." Many of the main character's memories evoke a restrained poignancy, particularly toward the movie's end.

After the four protagonists take shelter along with hundreds of others, the movie displays a sense of humanity as they huddle together. Sharon and Eva's "It Might as Well Rain Until September" duet humbly attempts to communicate a common bond that all those present share, a token of normality in a gravely abnormal circumstance. The movie's humane sentiments continue through the closing credits, during which we hear "Kumbaya" with no sense of irony, "Give Peace a Chance" and "We Shall Overcome."

Unrated, the film would likely receive an R due to language, adult content, brief nudity and horrific images.

Reviewer Adam Groves wrote that the protagonists

> wind up in a subway tunnel along with hundreds of anonymous refugees while the world is decimated above them. The sense of approaching menace that suffuses these scenes gives *One Night Stand* its power.[27] ...[T]he question isn't if, or even when, the missiles will hit, but rather how horrendous the damage will be when they do.[28]

On the *One Night Stand* poster it says, "As nuclear war breaks out—they've got one night to live the rest of their life." This sentence ably sums up the movie's core. Let's hope that this sentence will never sum up your last night on earth.

* * *

Red Dawn

DIRECTOR: John Milius; WRITERS: Kevin Reynolds, John Milius; MUSIC: Vasil Poledouris; CINEMATOGRAPHER: Ric Waite; EDITOR: Thom Noble; PRODUCERS: Buzz Feitshans, Barry Beckerman.

CAST: Patrick Swayze (Jed Eckert); C. Thomas Howell (Robert Morris); Lea Thompson (Erica Mason); Charlie Sheen (Matt Eckert); Powers Boothe (Lieutenant Colonel Andy Tanner); Brad Savage (Danny).

PRODUCTION: Valkyrie Films, United Artists; 1984; 114 minutes; PG-13. Alternate title: *Ten Soldiers*.

* * *

When *Red Dawn* came out, *The Guinness Book of Records* deemed it the most violent movie ever made, sporting two acts of violence every 60 seconds.[29]

The controversial film posits a near-future in which NATO has disbanded and Mexico has fallen to the Communists. A combination of Cuban, Nicaraguan and Russian troops seize control of the small Colorado town of Calumet. Grabbing firearms and ammo, several teenagers escape to the mountains. From there, under the command of former Calumet quarterback Jed Eckert, they launch a guerrilla campaign against the occupying forces, using the high school's team name Wolverines.

After a Cuban MiG-21 shoots down his fighter jet, Lieutenant Colonel Andy Tanner joins them and recounts the limited nuclear strike that destroyed several key American cities. The Wolverines continue to stage raids, and Andy dies fighting. After several Wolverines have perished, brothers Jed and Matt stage one last raid while Erica and Danny climb over the Rockies and reach Free America. Back in Calumet, both Jed and Matt die.

Red Dawn wants to be an earnest tale of contemporary American freedom fighters, yet its central premise—a handful of teenagers taking on the Communist occupation—fails to convince. The Wolverines become a serious thorn in the enemy's side, despite the latter's legion of soldiers and military weaponry. This may work as a teenager's heroic fantasy, but tanks as a credible scenario.

However, the movie boasts some interesting touches. The transformation of the town's drive-in movie theater to a re-education camp is imaginative. Also, two female teenagers take up arms alongside their adolescent male counterparts, a nod to gender equality.

Red Dawn is one of the few 1980s films to employ a limited nuclear war as opposed to all-out atomic Armageddon. Andy reveals that Soviet nukes took out the missile silos in North and South Dakota as well as key communication cities such as Omaha, Washington and Kansas City. He also says the Russians won't use further nukes on America because they "want to take us in one piece." As to why World War III began, Andy says, "Two toughest kids on the block, I guess." A somewhat world-weary view.

Critics at the time of *Red Dawn*'s release mostly panned it, often along political-ideological lines. For example, in a 1984 *New York Times* review, Vincent Canby says the movie "provides an unusual glimpse into the mind of a certain kind of contemporary archconservative … it exposes for all to see the cockeyed nightmares of those on the lunatic fringe, the self-styled patriots who might even embarrass the members of the John Birch Society."[30]

Red Dawn's politics aside, it's just too over-the-top. Still, it does deal with some

From left to right, Jed Eckert (Patrick Swayze), Robert Morris (C. Thomas Howell) and Matt Eckert (Charlie Sheen) scope out their hometown, wondering if it is enemy-occupied, in 1984's *Red Dawn* (Valkyrie Films). All three are members of the Wolverines, a group of young people fighting against local Communist occupation following a limited nuclear strike against the U.S.

complexities. For example, at one point, Daryl swallows an enemy tracking device which leads the occupation troops to the Wolverines. The Wolverines argue about the merits of shooting Daryl, and one of them asks, "What's the difference between us and them?" To which Jed replies, "Because we live here." This suggests a hardening of soul that war brings, regardless of the rightness of one's cause.

Which brings us to the topic of sacrifice. While *Red Dawn* is too comic book–like for its own good, it gives viewers a taste of what combat soldiers risk: life, limb and sanity. In the case of the movie's young warriors, all but two die.

Red Dawn has attained a cult status, even in the Ukraine. In April 2022, Ukrainian soldiers spray-painted the word "Wolverines" on disbanded Russian tanks and military vehicles.[31] In addition, commentators likened the Ukraine's underdog resistance against Russia to the Wolverines' struggle against the Soviets.[32] Also, in the early part of 2022, *Red Dawn* saw a 500 percent increase in global video-in-demand popularity.[33]

While the guerrilla war theme of *Red Dawn*[34] has found resonance in the Ukraine and other places, hopefully the film's limited nuke war aspect—the strikes on key American cities—will not find counterparts in real life.

* * *

She

DIRECTOR-WRITER: Avi Nesher; MUSIC: Rick Wakeman; CINEMATOGRAPHER: Sandro Mancori; EDITOR: Nicholas Wentworth; PRODUCER: Renato Dandi.

CAST: Sandahl Bergman (She); David Goss (Tom); Quin Kessler (Shanda); Harrison Muller (Dick); Elena Wiedermann (Hari).

PRODUCTION: Continental Motion Pictures, Royal Films B.V., Trans World Entertainment; Italian; 1984; released in the U.S. on 25 December 1985; 106 minutes; not rated.

* * *

She.

If I gave you that movie title and asked what you knew about it, what would you say?

You might give me the lowdown on Hammer Films' 1965 version with Ursula Andress, or Merian C. Cooper's 1935 version with Helen Gahagan. You almost certainly wouldn't tell me about an alleged version of H. Rider Haggard's novel *She* produced in the mid–1980s as an atomic age action flick.

It's "Year 23, After the Cancellation." Friends Tom and Dick struggle to survive in a post-nuke world. The Norks, a nasty bunch, kidnap Dick's sister Hari. While trying to rescue her, Tom and Dick meet a so-called goddess who goes by the name of She. This formidable warrior, and with her second-in-command Shanda, choose to help Tom and Dick.

En route, our heroes encounter vampires who resemble extras from a 1960s British horror film; cult leader Godan, whose eyes can levitate men or women; and mad scientist Rabel, who prattles on about nothing while performing gory experiments. In the end, Tom, Dick and She set booby traps for the villainous Norks, and along with Shanda and her she-warriors, defeat the cads, thus freeing Hari.

She's nuke threat credentials are slight. The movie features touches—or should that be smears—of satire. So is *She* a comedy? No, because its major intent is straightforward adventure. But that doesn't stop the film from showcasing annoying Robin Williams wannabe David Traylor as Xenon.

Weirdest aspect of *She*: The music score was written by Rick Wakeman of rock group Yes fame. (Signature song: "Owner of a Lonely Heart.") And the closing romantic ballad "Eternal Woman" was written and performed by Justin Hayward of the Moody Blues. (Signature song: "Nights in White Satin.")

Unrated, the film would probably receive a PG-13 for violence and adult content.

* * *

The Terminator

DIRECTOR: James Cameron; WRITERS: James Cameron, Gale Anne Hurd; MUSIC: Brad Fiedel; CINEMATOGRAPHER: Adam Greenberg; EDITOR: Mark Goldblatt; SPECIAL EFFECTS: Roger George, Frank DeMarco; SPECIAL TERMINATOR EFFECTS: Stan Winston; PRODUCER: Gale Anne Hurd.

CAST: Arnold Schwarzenegger (The Terminator); Michael Biehn (Kyle Reese); Linda Hamilton (Sarah Connor); Paul Winfield (Traxler); Lance Henriksen (Vukovich).

PRODUCTION: Cinema '84, Euro Film Funding, Hemdale, Pacific Western; 1984; 107 minutes; rated R.

* * *

From the year 2029, two time travelers transport to 1984 Los Angeles. One of them is the Terminator, a cyborg killing machine who plans to murder Sarah Connor; the other is Kyle Reese, a future soldier who's been sent to stop the Terminator. The Terminator initially kills two women named Sarah Connor who aren't the Sarah Connor he's after (he is going by the phone book listings). The cyborg assassin tracks down the real Sarah Connor, but before he can kill her, Reese saves her and they hide in a garage.

Reese explains that in the near-future, an artificial intelligence network called Skynet will trigger worldwide nuclear war. Afterward, Skynet's forces live to kill the surviving humans. Via a time machine, Skynet sent the Terminator back to the 1980s to kill Sarah so she won't give birth to John Connor, the future leader of the resistance movement against Skynet. Reese has time traveled to save Sarah's life, thus ensuring that her son John will be born.

The police capture Reese and Sarah and haul them to the police station (they think Reese is nuts). Soon, the Terminator shows up and wastes virtually every cop at the station. Reese and Sarah escape to a motel. There, Reese tells Sarah that from a photo of her that John gave him, he fell in love with her and has always been in love with her. Lovemaking follows. (Sure, an unstoppable cyborg with murderous intentions may appear at any second—what a perfect time to have sex.)

On a motorcycle, the Terminator shows up once again and chases Sarah and Reese as Reese lobs pipe bombs from their truck. After the truck crashes, the Terminator commandeers a tanker to run Sarah down. But Reese slips a pipe bomb into the truck's hose tube. The tanker explodes in a display of spectacular pyrotechnics, but the Terminator, now a metal skeleton shorn of all human-looking outer covering, is still alive and ticking.

The cyborg assassin follows them into a factory, where Reese shoves a pipe bomb into its midsection, resulting in his death and the cyborg blown in half. The Terminator's severed torso tries to kill Sarah, but she destroys it in a hydraulic press.

Months later, Sarah is pregnant with Reese's son, who will be born to lead a revolt against Skynet.

The Terminator is a fast-paced science fiction thriller jam-packed with action. The stunt work is plentiful and impressive. As time travel movies go, it may be the most violent ever.

Arnold Schwarzenegger nails it as the Terminator—merciless, emotionless, relentless. Michael Biehn and Linda Hamilton also impress as Reese and Sarah, with Hamilton finding inner strength to save the day at the end. Veteran actors Paul Winfield and Lance Henriksen score points as the two world-weary cops who find out the hard way that Biehn is telling the truth.

The special effects shine, though some younger viewers may be somewhat puzzled by the stop-motion animation effects partially used to bring the Terminator's fleshless skeleton to life. Of course, model animation was still standard in the 1980s.

The film's nuke threat angle lies in the unseen nuclear war that Reese tells us Skynet waged. We do see future ruins of Los Angeles, with Reese and fellow human guerrillas doing what they can to resist Skynet's ray-blasting war machines.

The film receives positive reviews. On Rotten Tomatoes, it boasts a resounding 100 percent fresh based on 67 professional critiques. Leonard Maltin gave it three and a half out of four stars and wrote, "Terrific action picture never lets up for a minute—a model for others to follow."[35]

The film is rated R for adult content, sex, nudity, language and graphic violence.

The Terminator's time travel gymnastics may spin heads, but the action sweeps viewers into full-speed-ahead mode.

* * *

Threads

DIRECTOR-PRODUCER: Mick Jackson; WRITER: Barry Hine; CINEMATOGRA-PHERS: Andrew Dun, Paul Morris; EDITORS: Jim Latham, Donna Bickerstaff; VISUAL EFFECTS: Peter Wragg; SPECIAL EFFECTS: Peter Kersey.
CAST: Karen Meagher (Ruth Beckett); Reece Dinsdale (Jimmy Kemp); David Brierley (Mr. Bill Kemp); Rita May (Mrs. Rita Kemp); Nicholas Lane (Michael Kemp).
PRODUCTION: BBC in association with Western-World Television and the Nine Network (Australia); British; premiered on U.K. television on 23 September 1984; premiered on U.S. television on 13 January 1985; 112 minutes; not rated.

* * *

On January 13, 1985, my cat Newt must have thought I was crazy. I let him inside the house trailer the same as always, except my eyes stung. I was weeping, thinking about how in a nuclear war, Newt might die a horrible death. The film I had just watched on Superstation TBS—*Threads*—made this possibility all too clear.

Lest you think I was a boy when I first saw the film, I was actually in my late twenties. And no, I rarely wept over movies of any kind, but this one threatened loved ones. My parents, brother, relatives, friends … and cat.

Of all 1980s nuclear threat films, for me, *Threads* was The Big One. Sure, intellectually I already knew something about nuclear war, and a little over a year before, I had seen ABC-TV's *The Day After*, anything but a walk in the park. Yet *Threads* made a nuclear attack real on a visceral level, and as I was to discover many years later, I was not the only one who thought so.

In Sheffield, England, two young lovers, Ruth Beckett (Karen Meagher) and Jimmy Kemp (Reece Dinsdale), must make an important decision when Ruth reveals she is pregnant. Jimmy tells his parents that he and Ruth plan to wed. Ruth also informs her parents. The Becketts and Kemps meet at Ruth's house.

The Soviet Union invades Iran with the apparent intention of making the Middle Eastern country a satellite. The U.S. sends in troops. Later, an American submarine sinks, and the U.S. blames the Soviets. The American president expresses outrage.

In Sheffield, Ruth and Jimmy look for an apartment. Jimmy seems apprehensive about becoming a father and husband, but Ruth pooh-poohs his trepidation, assuring him all will be well.

The situation between the Soviets and Americans continues to worsen. The president proposes to Soviet leaders that both Russia and America withdraw from Iran. The U.S.S.R. ignores the suggestion, so American B-52 bombers attack a military base in Mashad. In turn, the Soviets launch a nuclear missile that destroys the bombers. America retaliates with a low-yield tactical nuclear weapon that blasts the Mashad base. Russia sinks an American aircraft carrier, and the U.S. blockades Cuba.

In Britain, the government seizes control of the airways and cross-channel ferries. In Sheffield, the municipal emergency committee begins planning for the worst. PSA announcements flood radio and TV. The international situation has cast a shadow over Ruth and Jimmy's plans, and Ruth weeps.

Staying with her parents, Ruth develops severe morning sickness. When her mom tries to call her workplace, the phone is dead. The government has severed all non-essential phone lines. A nuclear attack is imminent.

Near Sheffield, a nuclear missile destroys Finningley Air Force Base. Sheffield's citizens, who can see the mushroom cloud, panic. The Kemps build a lean-to in their home, and the Becketts, including Ruth, take refuge in the basement. The blast hits, scattering wreckage everywhere.

Due to Sheffield's industrial status, a nuclear missile obliterates much of the city and sets the rest on fire. Mrs. Kemp, badly burned, and Mr. Kemp find the body of their young son Michael buried under rubble.

After a few days in the Beckett basement, the grandmother dies. When Mr. and Mrs. Beckett haul the body to the first floor, Ruth escapes into the maelstrom outside. As she stumbles through the rubble-strewn streets, she encounters nightmare sights—a scorched cat, a dead dog, charred human corpses, a woman in shock clinging to a dead infant.

Looters kill the Becketts. Mrs. Kemp also perishes, apparently from her injuries. Mr. Kemp dies from radiation poisoning.

Sheffield continues to deteriorate. The members of the emergency committee, housed in an underground bunker, die from suffocation. Burned and injured residents overwhelm a hospital. The authorities shoot looters and ration the city's meager food supply.

Ruth flees from Sheffield, discovering things are miserable everywhere. Eventually, she gives birth to her baby, naming her Jane.

Ten years later, the incessant need to work the land to survive has exhausted Ruth, and she dies. Three years later, two teenagers rape Jane. Jane has a baby, wrapped in

Rita Kemp (Rita May, left) and Bill Kemp (David Brierley, right) are shell-shocked survivors of a nuclear attack on Sheffield, England, in 1984's *Threads* (BBC). Rita's burns will soon lead to her death; Bill, a victim of radiation poisoning, will die more slowly.

bloody swaddling clothes. When she sees her offspring, she is horrified, and the film freezes before we hear her scream.

Though inspired by *The Day After*, *Threads* is its own nuclear nightmare. Both films use the method of an ever-escalating international situation resonating ominously in the background, eventually affecting the characters. Both also feature characters of varying socioeconomic levels. The countries involved are the Soviet Union and the United States but *Threads* relays its message from a British perspective, one perhaps resentful at times that any nuclear conflict between Russia and America would inevitably pull the U.K. into it.

While flawed in some ways, *Threads* succeeds in its intent to scare viewers out of nuclear complacency. Director Mick Jackson's matter-of-fact tone permeates the movie, giving the pre-war scenes, direct attack scenes and postwar scenes a documentary feel. Despite the film's low budget, its special effects fare well, mixing competent miniatures with stock footage.

In addition, the film uses striking details. You expect shots of charred corpses, but to accentuate the agony of burning to death, we see a lone hand groping from a pile of fiery rubble. The flesh catches fire, and soon individual flames crown the tip of each stiffened finger, like candlesticks in Hell. In addition, when the populace of Sheffield panics, the film shows us the Kemps frantically trying to erect their lean-to—and we hear dozens, hundreds, perhaps thousands of people screaming simultaneously from across the city. In 1985, I had never before heard anything like that in a movie, and it chilled me.

The film teems with memorable set pieces. One of the most effective is that of the post-nuclear attack hospital. Without anesthesia or adequate supplies, the medical staff members valiantly but hopelessly try to tend to the flood of burned, infected and injured Britons pouring through its doors. This place of would-be healing becomes an infirmary of the damned, children and adults wailing as shrapnel is extracted and limbs amputated.

The art direction enhances the post-nuke mood of despair and confusion. Mists often pass across the screen, and ruins exhibit a gray or brownish hue. Shots of blasted areas recall photos of Hiroshima. Sound-wise, a howling wind haunts *Threads'* post-nuke world.

The sober story aids and abets the no-nonsense direction. Sentimentality never enters into the tale. Instead, we have the occasional irony, as early in the film, Ruth assures a concerned Jimmy about their soon-to-be married life: "It'll be lovely. I just know it." Similarly, a quick scene shows Jimmy's younger brother Michael playing with a model of a fighter jet. Also, long after the nuclear attack, we see a poster for life insurance featuring the image of a smiling child with the ad line, "Standard Life for all of your life." Unlike in a more traditional scenario, Ruth and Jimmy do not get back together. Apparently, Jimmy dies during the blast wave (but we don't see this).

The acting is uniformly good, but Karen Meagher as Ruth is a standout. She plays Ruth as a vulnerable individual who nevertheless has a strong survival instinct that kicks in days after the nuke attack. At first, the carnage horrifies her. But she eventually becomes inured to it, her numbness on display during the hospital scenes in which she appears indifferent to the human suffering surrounding her.

One aspect of *Threads'* presentation, the voiceover narration, had director Jackson and screenwriter Barry Hines at odds. Hines felt it unnecessary, but Jackson championed it.[36] In retrospect, the narration does call attention to itself, and arguably might distance audiences, especially younger audiences, from the film.

An important facet of *Threads'* script is that it doesn't cover only a few weeks following the nuclear attack, but 13 years. We see nuclear winter assault the U.K., ushering in freezing temperatures during the summer months and dark skies refusing to yield enough sunlight to ripen the crops. We also see the gradual diminution of Britain in terms of population and technology. One particularly disquieting aspect of this not-so-brave new world is that kids born following the nuclear attack appear unable to form coherent sentences and develop a strange broken English. Ruth's child Jane fits into this category.

One of the key takeaways from *Threads* is how woefully unprepared the U.K. was to handle a nuclear war's aftermath. The government pamphlet "Protect and Survive" offered unrealistic advice on how a family could weather a nuclear strike. *Threads'* emergency committee members, bunkered beneath the city, have received little training or direction on what to do. Sheffield families are in worse shape, as demonstrated by the Kemps' frantic last-minute attempt to build a lean-to shelter.

On the audio commentary for *Threads'* 2018 Severin DVD, director Jackson speaks at length about making the film. He says that one of the difficulties was the small budget. He also harshly criticizes *The Day After* as "a soap opera." Regarding *Day After*'s ending, he says,

Following a nuclear attack on England, survival essentials are rationed. Protestors demand more food while government troops hold them back in 1984's *Threads* (BBC). Many critics consider it to be perhaps the most harrowing nuclear war film ever made.

> The underlying thought of this is that it would all be manageable. At the end of the movie, everything is ruined, you've got Jason Robards still there and you know that just out of the frame about to come in is all the bulldozers and relief efforts and rescue and help, and then it's gonna be okay really, and I thought "That's not telling the truth."[37]

With all due respect, Jackson seems to be misremembering *Day After*'s ending. Near the finale, Robards is dying from radiation sickness. The nuclear attack has completely demolished the Kansas City he returns to, and he finds only radioactive ruins of his home. Nothing is going to be "okay" for him. Also, food and other resources are growing scarce, tenuous government intervention is being overwhelmed, and martial law has gotten severe, as one of the last sights we see is soldiers shooting looters. The final words we hear in the film are from John Lithgow broadcasting over his radio, "Hello? This is Lawrence, Lawrence, Kansas. Is anybody there? Anybody? Anybody at all...?" The movie's finale clearly implies bulldozers will not be arriving any minute to clear the nationwide radioactive rubble and build pristine new cities. At the fadeout, things have gotten worse, and the movie indicates that life will continue its post-nuke downhill slide.

To demonstrate that *Threads* is more truthful than *Day After*, Jackson compares the hospital scenes in each film.[38] However, when we see the *Threads* hospital, over two weeks have passed since the nuclear attack. For *Day After*'s university hospital, only a few days have passed. But soon, resources are running out, morphine is being stolen, staff members are dying, and the facility is inundated. It hasn't reached the horrific level of the hospital in *Threads*, but in a couple more weeks, there probably wouldn't be much difference.

I don't wish to get into a *Threads* vs. *The Day After* argument. ABC-TV kept *Day After* director Nicholas Meyer from making his movie grittier, forcing him to make some compromises. *Threads*, on the other hand, plays like the no-holds-barred docudrama it is. While I consider *The Day After* a worthy if flawed effort, *Threads* remains the gold standard for nuclear war movies. As Jackson points out on the DVD commentary, one thing about *Threads* that hasn't dated is the reality of nuclear weapons and the reality of what they can do.[39] For this reason, *Threads* remains relevant.

The BBC aired *Threads* in the U.K. on September 23, 1984. A few months later, on January 13, 1985, it debuted in America on Superstation TBS. TBS owner Ted Turner introduced the movie by saying, "It is not our intention to frighten, but to inform. Because the more we know about what could happen, the less chance it is that it will happen."[40]

In 1985, *Threads* was nominated for seven British Academy of Film and Television Arts awards and won four: Best Single Drama, Best Design, Best Film Cameraman and Best Film Editor.[41] Leonard Maltin called the movie "unrelentingly graphic and grim, sobering, and shattering—as it should be."[42] In *The Sci-Fi Movie Guide*, Chris Barsanti called *Threads* "unsparing…. The effect on the British populace after being broadcast in 1984 was reportedly almost as traumatic as after American television showed *The Day After*."[43] James O'Neill called *Threads* "[m]aybe the grimmest and most disturbing film of its kind … exceedingly well acted and realistic to a fault."[44]

Summing up the feelings of many reviewers, Paul Whitelaw wrote in *The Guardian*, "[*Threads* is] easily one of the most harrowing things ever to air on television…. Watching it on DVD now … is no less gut-wrenching."[45]

Regarding Whitelaw's comments, some readers who have never seen the film might express skepticism, especially younger viewers. And it's true—if you're looking for an ultimate gross-out movie, something along the lines of 2008's *The Midnight Meat Train* or the *Hostel* film series, *Threads* will probably disappoint you. But consider this: Psychotic serial killers will hunt few of us, but nuclear war, if it happens, will find us all.

The strength of *Threads* lies in part in its graphic nature, yes, but it's the *context* of that explicit imagery that horrifies, its fusion with matter-of-fact verisimilitude that gives the movie its power. As Jackson says, "The real effect of a nuclear war is not what it does to things, to buildings, to cities, it's what it does to society, what it does to people, what it does psychologically."[46]

Threads is a chronicle of what nuclear war could—and probably would—do to society not only in 1984, but also today.

*   *   *

Time Bomb

DIRECTOR: Paul Krasny; WRITERS: Westbrook Claridge (teleplay); Roderick Taylor (story); MUSIC: Sylvester Levay; CINEMATOGRAPHER: Don Reddy; EDITORS: Donald Hoskinson, Donald R. Rode, David A. Simmons; PRODUCER: James McAdams.

CAST: Billy Dee Williams (Wes Tanner); Joseph Bottoms (Daniel "Dan" Picard); Merlin Olsen (Jake Calahan); Morgan Fairchild (Renee DeSalles), Dianne B. Shaw (Cara); Anne Kerry (Tracy).

PRODUCTION: Barry Weitz Films, Universal Television; aired on NBC 25 March 1984; 95 minutes; not rated.

*   *   *

Near the beginning of the made-for-TV *Time Bomb*, an instructor holds up an orange and tells his class that, if it was made of pure weapons-grade plutonium, "it would make a nuclear explosion sufficient to destroy all man-made structures within a radius of .54 miles. It would also kill 80 percent of all lifeforms within the same mile-wide zone." As the movie unfolds, this lesson moves from academic to actual.

Wes Tanner and his friend Jake Calahan will drive an armored transport vehicle with a shipment of weapons-grade plutonium through Texas. Both men previously served in the military. The night before their departure, Wes and his girlfriend Cara and Jake and his wife Tracy dine at a restaurant where they meet hot-headed Dan Picard, who starts a fight. Jake forcibly removes Dan from the restaurant.

The morning of their departure, Wes and Jake are surprised to find that Dan will partner with them in the semi cab. Assuming that it will be an uneventful journey, Wes, Jake, and Dan set out toward their destination.

However, frost-blooded Renee DeSalles commandeers a group of terrorists who stage a fake wreck in their vehicle's path, then steal the freight trailer with the plutonium. DeSalles shoots and kills Jake.

Wes and Dan race cross-country to catch up with the stolen shipment. Once they do, back and forth violence rages between Wes and Dan and the terrorists. The plutonium gets loaded on a plane, but not before Wes has clandestinely climbed aboard. He kills DeSalles and, from a van running parallel to the plane, Dan shoots and kills the pilot. The plane comes to a stop. In a sad finale, Jake's wife Tracy learns her husband has died.

Time Bomb typifies the made-for-TV movies regularly churned out during the 1970s and 1980s. The acting is solid and the action sequences reasonably well-handled. But the film overplays Jake's death scene. Wes spends too much time with Jake, and much as Wes might want to mourn the loss of his friend, his major priority would be to keep that deadly plutonium from leaving the country.

As nuke threat movies go, *Time Bomb* gets points for featuring an African American, Billy Dee Williams, in the lead role. A gifted actor, Williams enjoyed breakout success with the 1971 made-for-TV movie *Brian's Song*, in which he gave a moving performance as fullback Gale Sayers. The movie depicts Sayers' friendship with white teammate Brian Piccolo (James Caan) and Piccolo's death from cancer at an early age. Both Williams and Caan were Emmy-nominated.[47]

Soon thereafter, Williams landed a leading role in 1974's *Lady Sings the Blues*, which starred Diana Ross as legendary blues singer Billie Holiday. In the popular *Star Wars* series, Williams played Lando Calrissian in 1980's *The Empire Strikes Back* and 1983's *The Return of the Jedi*. He continued to appear in prominent roles throughout the '80s, '90s and 2000s.[48]

Time Bomb also features Morgan Fairchild, a definite icon of the 1980s. She became known for playing cold, calculating bad girls like Constance in the TV series *Flamingo Road* (1980–82). In the 1990s, she sometimes lampooned her image, such as when she played Matthew Perry's mother on the sitcom *Friends*.[49]

Time Bomb ends with the terrorists foiled. The movie suggests that if terrorists were to try to steal weapons-grade plutonium in the U.S., government agents would stop them. But what if the transport truck experienced a traffic mishap or, even less likely, was knocked off the highway by a tornado, and some of that plutonium escaped? Of course, that has apparently never happened and, God willing, never will. But if it did....

* * *

Warriors of the Apocalypse

DIRECTOR-PRODUCER: Bobby A. Suarez; WRITERS: Ken Metcalfe (screenplay);
Bobby A. Suarez (story); MUSIC: Ole Hoyer; CINEMATOGRAPHER: Jun Pereira;
EDITOR: None listed.
CAST: Michael James (Trapper); Deborah Moore (Princess Sheela); Ken Metcalfe (High
Priest Guruk); Chito Guerrero (Anuk); Mike Cohen (Doc).
PRODUCTION: A-S Panorama International Film, BAS Film Productions; made in
1984 in the Philippines; released in the U.S. on 7 March 1986; 96 minutes; rated R.
Alternate titles: *Time Raiders*, *Operation Overkill*, *Searchers of the Voodoo Mountain*.

* * *

One hundred fifty years have passed since a devastating war and a new Dark Ages
has descended upon the world. Trapper leads a group of nomads as they struggle to survive this hostile terrain. After fighting rival nomads, Anuk tells Trapper and his group
that he can lead them to a wonderful Mountain of Life.

Trapper decides to follow Anuk. After the nomads trek into the jungle, hostile
natives attack twice, the second time taking them hostage. Anuk helps them escape.
Next, the nomads encounter a group of laughing Amazons who live on the Mountain of
Life. These women seem delighted to see the all-male nomads—except for poor old Doc,
whom the ladies bypass like he was a contagious disease.

Trapper and company meet the mountain's two imperious leaders: Guruk the high
priest and Princess Sheela. Guruk and Sheela don't have the best working relationship,
and before long, sparks fly—literally.

Guruk frees the nomads but they are recaptured and told they can socialize in the
village, but mustn't try to escape again. Under a full moon, a fertility observance tran-
spires—and Sheela has eyes only for Trapper.

Inside the mountain, Doc discovers a refurbished reactor. Guruk tells him it was
designed "to turn a scorched mountain into a lush paradise." Guruk also reveals that
when he dies, the immortality enjoyed by the Amazons and little people will end. Then,
somehow, he hears Sheela's thoughts saying, "I will destroy Guruk. I loathe him, loathe
him, loathe him!" Understandably upset, Guruk warns Trapper that Sheela is evil.

Using laser beams that shoot from their eyes, Guruk and Sheela battle it out, and
Sheela wins. Wasting no time, Sheela displays what a killjoy she can be by wiping out the
village. Later, she laser-beams those trying to escape, but overdoes it to the point that
her overtaxed power kills her. Trapper, who in no time has gotten over his tryst with
Sheela, says he will stay to help rebuild, and the nomads follow his lead.

The best scene in *Warriors of the Wasteland* is the opening stock footage nuclear
explosion that gradually fades to black, an effective visual implying a new Dark Ages.
Otherwise, the movie resembles a "lost world" movie from the black-and-white era.
The major difference is that *Warriors of the Apocalypse* exhibits post–'60s sensibilities, i.e., hedonism to the max. In the past, you'd never have your explorers shack-
ing up with Amazons. But in the '80s, having casual sex was tantamount to getting a
drink of water.

Story-wise, the film posits a curious mixture of science fiction and fantasy. A reactor resides inside the mountain, but Guruk and Sheela also appeal to supernatural
forces. Guruk and Sheela's laser beam battle disappoints, employing elementary special

effects that looked dated even in 1984. Despite all the action, the movie sometimes plods. Worst of all, its depiction of the jungle natives is offensive, implying that post-nuke people of color had socially devolved to a greater degree than whites (i.e., Trapper and his all–Caucasian nomads).

Warriors of the Apocalypse, a relic of its time, is not recommended.

CHAPTER SEVEN

*   *   *

1985

Defcon-4

DIRECTOR-WRITER: Paul Donovan; MUSIC: Chris Young;
CINEMATOGRAPHERS: Doug Connell, Les Krizsan; EDITOR: Todd Ramsay; SPE-
 CIAL EFFECTS: Bruce McKenna, Dave Albiston; PRODUCERS: B.B. Gillian, Paul
 Donovan, Maura O'Connell.
CAST: Tom Choate (Howe); Lenore Zann (J.J.); Maury Chaykin (Vinny); Kate Lynch
 (Jordan); Kevin King (Guideon Hayes); John Walsch (Walker).
PRODUCTION: New World, Salter Street Films; 1985; distributed by New World Pic-
 tures; 88 minutes; rated R.

* * *

Defcon-4 is a movie that starts like gangbusters and collapses midway. The first half is a fairly plausible, sometimes intense near-future thriller. The second half devolves into familiar post-apocalyptic action movie tropes.

Astronauts Howe, Jordan and Walker operate America's "The Nemesis," a secret orbital nuclear weapons platform. The pace aboard the craft appears leisurely, until nuclear war breaks out on Earth. The crew never receives the code to fire their own nukes, but after over a month in space, a renegade program hijacks the Nemesis's computer system and the craft plummets toward Earth. Howe and Walker launch all their weapons, except for one malfunctioning missile; it, like the others, is set to detonate within 60 hours.

The craft experiences a rough landing, and Jordan is knocked cold. The craft has landed with the entry door buried in the sand of a beach. As Walker tries to dig his way out, something drags him through the sand, killing him. After Howe digs himself free, he encounters Terminals—cannibals afflicted with a radiation-wrought disease. Surviv-alist Vinny catches Howe and takes him to his compound.

With Howe and a woman named J.J. in tow, Vinny goes in search of Howe's space-craft. Interrupting their trek, a paramilitary group imprisons all three. Guideon, the group's commander, reveals that his subordinate Boomer initiated the computer pro-gram that brought down the Nemesis, and now he wants to know the whereabouts of American survival bunkers (Howe knows the codes). However, Guideon learns Boomer can supply the necessary password after all, so Guideon has Howe imprisoned.

After a great deal of unpleasantness in Guideon's compound, the merciless des-pot plans to hang Howe, J.J., Vinny and Jordan (captured by Guideon's men when they raided the Nemesis). Howe manages to escape and finds a road grader and weapons. He

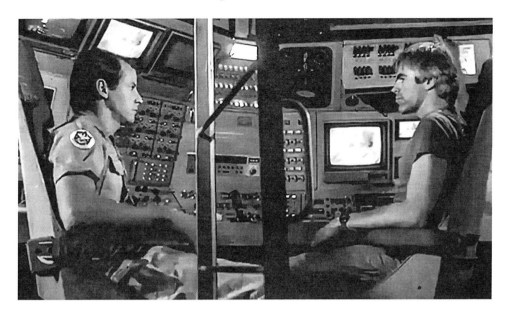

Aboard an orbital nuclear weapons platform, astronauts Howe (Tim Choate, left) and Walker (John Walsh) are rattled when they receive orders to arm their nuclear missiles in 1985's *Defcon-4* (Salter Street Films).

arms Guideon's enemies (everyone except the despot's personal militia) and leads on attack on Guideon's compound.

Guideon attempts to flee aboard a boat, but soon finds himself injured and swimming back to his compound while J.J., Howe and Vinny escape in the sea vessel. At this point, the Nemesis missile explodes, destroying Guideon and his survivalist band.

The first half of *Defcon-4* impresses with its tension and pathos. The raw reactions of the three astronauts convey their disbelief that the world has been plunged into a nuclear war. Howe and Walker's decision to wait until they receive the code War One seems credible; who wants to be responsible for the death of millions?

In a particularly potent scene, Howe receives a radio message from his wife in Oregon. She reveals that while she and her neighbors didn't get hit, radiation has set in, as well as an unknown disease. Hundreds have died in the area, including her baby, whom she says got the disease and was summarily shot and burned. She says her gums are bleeding, and it's obvious she will die soon. This broadcast captures in microcosm the horrors that survivors of a nuclear holocaust would suffer, and Howe's face mirrors his anguish.

The film's second half devotes itself to two post-apocalyptic tropes: crazed cannibals and paramilitary thugs. As the latter's ruler, Kevin King's portrayal of Guideon oozes sleaze. An arrogant kid drunk with power, he wields his authority with a sadism worthy of Josef Mengele. Because we see Guideon do so many rotten things, his instantaneous death by nuclear explosion seems far too merciful. It's never clear how Guideon, who appears to be college age, established power over adult military professionals. At one point, J.J. tells Howe that Guideon "has his ways." Not a convincing explanation.

The other actors manage well. Tim Choate as main character Howe is both believable and sympathetic. Despite its low budget, the movie fares well in all technical aspects, only seriously faltering in the story department.

For the most part, the film is careful not to stray too far into comic book territory. But Howe's climactic assault on Guideon and his men proves less than believable, and seems to belong in a different movie. The finale tells us "The final victory has been won. Mankind can now rest in peace." You mean only one power-mad jerk like Guideon exists following the apocalypse? Not likely, but admirably upbeat. The film could just as easily have ended with Guideon winning. The cannibals appear to be in the film as an afterthought. They don't figure into the plot. There's graphic content, but generally more restrained than in most R-rated films.

As far as audience ratings go, the movie sports an IMDb rating of 4.5 out of 10 based on 2110 votes. Some mainstream critics at the time of release were even less generous. In the April 28, 1985, *New York Times*, Vincent Canby wrote, "The movie ... is busy without being at all interesting."[1] Leonard Maltin's book gave the film a BOMB rating and sniped, "It sounds like an industrial-strength roach killer, and it could use one."[2] According to *TV Guide*, "[The director's] war scenario is frighteningly simple and not the least bit implausible. The film has some weak points, but they barely detract from its overall disturbing effect."[3]

Defcon-4 attempts to strike a balance between credible post-nuke angst and diverting post-nuke action. Unfortunately, the latter topples the film into the standard near-future adventure category. At the midway point, the film could have taken the road less traveled, but instead settled for the road well-trod.

*   *   *

Doomsday Plot

DIRECTOR-WRITER: Allan Levine; MUSIC: Paul Zaza; EDITORS: John Floyd, Kirk Jones, Dave Alcock; PRODUCER: Bev Burrow.
CAST: Jan Taylor (Karen Stachuck); Simon Henri aka Simon Sekulovich (Frank DeNucci); Robert Reece (Chuck Ericson); James Westlake (Arthur Goodly); Tom Nursall (Yuri Alexandrov); Winn Bray (Madame Kutzov).
PRODUCTION: Emmeritus Productions, CHCH-TV; Canadian; 1985; 95 minutes; not rated. Alternate title: *The Edge*.

*   *   *

The Royal Canadian Mounties always get their man, but in the case of *Doomsday Plot*, they always get their bomb—we hope. Especially since the bomb is a suitcase nuke aboard a Canadian passenger airliner.

During the Cold War, America decides to provide neutral Finland with a nuclear weapon, to be delivered via a Canadian passenger plane. A terrorist organization called the Brokerage kidnaps Dr. Wofford, the bomb's creator. Dolby, Wofford's assistant, will be aboard the plane instead, and he will carry the bomb—the TISWEN II—in a suitcase in his lap. A Brokerage terrorist hijacks the plane and orders it flown to Libya. Frank DeNucci, a Canadian agent, punches out the terrorist only to discover that Wofford's assistant Dolby aboard the plane is a Dolby imposter.

Back on the ground, Canadian agent Karen Stachuck, acting head of her secret service unit, discovers the Soviets will shoot down the Canadian plane if it enters Russian airspace, thus starting World War III. Arthur Goodly, a traitor working for the Brokerage, says the kidnapped Wofford will disarm the bomb in return for letting the

Brokerage keep it. After the plane lands back in Canada, the TISWEN II is disarmed and the Brokerage members try to kidnap Karen. She flees from their limo with the bomb. The Canadian agents take out the Brokerage operatives and arrest Arthur. World War III has been averted.

Made for Canadian television, *Doomsday Plot* sports the look and feel of TV-movies. Signs of a rushed production crop up in the staging of fight scenes. Too often, a fist or kick obviously doesn't connect with its intended target, harming plausibility. Commendably, the script piles on the terrible trouble. After we discover that Wofford's assistant on the plane is a lookalike, he accidentally triggers the bomb's timer, meaning it will explode in five hours. This accelerates the tension, complicating the authorities' scramble to remedy the situation.

In addition, the story includes an effective red herring: Russian agent Yuri Alexandrov. You assume he's going to be working for the Brokerage and will betray Karen and her agents, but instead, he remains benign to the end.

However, the script also includes some shake-your-head moments. For example, Karen's boyfriend Dan just happens to decide to reconcile with her as her mission is coming to a close, and his car blocks the Brokerage's limo from escaping—talk about coincidence.

The film's wrap-up wants to be too warm and fuzzy. Karen and Dan are reunited while Yuri walks off with two Canadian agents, the three of them palsy-walsy. But a Canadian agent was shot and killed minutes earlier, so the abrupt change to Happily-Ever-After Land feels inappropriate. But this is just the sort of ending TV dramas once had. The acting works. Madame Kutzov reminds me of *The Wizard of Oz*'s Wicked Witch Margaret Hamilton, though nobody drops a house on her.

Doomsday Plot is watchable, and it's interesting to observe a Cold War storyline unfold from a Canadian perspective.

* * *

Mad Max: Beyond Thunderdome

DIRECTORS: George Miller, George Ogilvie; WRITERS: Terry Hayes, George Miller; MUSIC: Maurice Jarre; CINEMATOGRAPHER: Dean Semler; EDITOR: Richard Francis-Bruce; VISUAL DESIGN CONSULTANT: Ed Verreaux; PRODUCER: George Miller.

CAST: Mel Gibson (Mad Max); Tina Turner (Aunty Entity); Bruce Spence (Jedediah); Adam Cockburn (Jedediah, Jr.); Angelo Rossitto (The Master); Paul Larsson (The Blaster).

PRODUCTION: Kennedy Miller Productions; Australian; released in the U.S. on 10 July 1985; released in Australia 8 August 1985; 107 minutes; PG-13.

* * *

In *Mad Max: Beyond Thunderdome*, one of Bartertown's laws is "Bust a deal, face the wheel." Some Mad Max fans felt this third Mad Max movie had indeed busted a deal by straying too far from the series' roots—and some may have wished they could subject the filmmakers to Bartertown's wheel.[4] But other fans welcomed this expansion of Mad Max's world.

Still wandering in a post-apocalyptic Australia, Max goes to a small community called Bartertown to retrieve camels from the thief who stole them. The town's ruler, Aunty Entity, strikes a deal with Max: If he will kill Master-Blaster, she will see that his camels are returned. Master-Blaster is actually two men: (1) Master, a little person who gives the orders, and (2) Blaster, a burly masked hulk who enforces Master's commands.

Aunty Entity is in a struggle with Master over who runs Bartertown, and he has the advantage because he provides the town's energy via his underground pig-methane plant. Max publicly challenges Master-Blaster, and Aunty Entity arranges a duel in Thunderdome, a roped half-dome in which the two combatants will fight until one is dead.

After a brutal struggle, Max is ready to slay Master, whose mask has been torn off. When Max realizes from Blaster's face that he is mentally challenged, he refuses to slay him. A furious Aunty Entity has Max's hands tied and sends him from Bartertown on a horse. The horse eventually dies from exhaustion, and Max is in a bad way.

Young Savannah Nix finds Max and brings him to the desert oasis in which she lives with other pre-adolescents and teenagers. Many years before, their Boeing 747 had crashed, and their parents left to get help, but never returned. When Max revives, the children believe he is the fabled Captain Walker who has come to fly them to Tomorrow-Tomorrow Land. But Max confesses he's not the man they hope for, and that cities are a thing of the past.

A group of the children set out anyway, and Max catches up with them. Max and the kids sneak into Bartertown to free the imprisoned Master and to gather supplies. They eventually escape in an airplane while Max waits behind. Aunty Entity chooses not to harm Max and lets him go. The airplane takes the children to the nuclear-ravaged

Aunty Entity (Tina Turner), ruler of Bartertown, stands in the midst of the Thunderdome battle area in 1985's *Mad Max: Beyond Thunderdome* (Kennedy Miller Productions). The film takes place in a nuked Australia where society has degenerated into scattered tribes and marauders, as well as loners like Mad Max (Mel Gibson, not pictured).

ruins of Sydney, where the youngsters establish a new society. Meanwhile, Max finds himself once again alone in the desert.

Mad Max: Beyond Thunderdome is an intelligent post-apocalyptic tale that expands the world established in the first two *Mad Max* movies. Civilization has been resurrected, albeit crudely, in the civics of Bartertown. The community has licked the energy problem. And if two men quarrel, the law says: Let them fight to the death in Thunderdome. "Two men enter, one man leaves." This seems to be Aunty Entity's brutal solution to prevent future warfare. In addition, we see the wrecked remains of the Boeing 747 as well as Sydney's nuclear ruins—which appear to be standing fairly well, so we assume it didn't suffer a direct hit.

The children are a sticking point for some *Mad Max* fans. *Beyond Thunderdome* is neatly divided into three segments: (1) Bartertown, (2) the children, and (3) the attempted melding of the Bartertown and children stories. The Bartertown segment overflows with grunge, eccentricity and action, not to mention pig dung.

But the children segment changes tone and aches with melancholy, especially when their shared fable of Captain Walker rescuing them turns out to be no more substantial than a toothpick bicycle. The children section, both in concept and execution, is also undeniably Spielbergian. And while the movie's third section uniting Bartertown and the children is competent enough, before it arrives, you still feel as though you've just watched two separate movies, albeit both worthwhile enterprises.

Mel Gibson turns in good work as Max, and a decent cast ably supports him. Tina Turner is effective as Aunty Entity. In the '80s, her heyday, she had several hit songs, including the iconic "What's Love Got to Do with It."

The post-nuke world trappings intrigue, springing from the first two *Mad Max* movies, from which most '80s post-nuke action movies "borrowed."

The film generally receives positive reviews. Rotten Tomatoes gives it an 81 percent fresh rating based on 54 professional reviews. Roger Ebert gave it four out of four stars and wrote that it was "not only the best of the three Mad Max movies, but one of the best films of 1985."[5]

Despite the downbeat tone of the first two Mad Max movies, *Mad Max: Beyond Thunderdome* adds hope to the mix.

*   *   *

O-Bi, O-Ba: The End of Civilization

DIRECTOR-WRITER: Piotr Szulkin; MUSIC: Jerzy Satanowski; CINEMATOGRA-
   PHER: Witold Sobocinski; EDITOR: Elzbieta Kurkowska.
CAST: Jerzy Stuhr (Soft); Krystyna Janda (Gea).
PRODUCTION: Zespol Filmowy Perspektywa; Polish; 1985; 88 minutes; not rated.

*   *   *

In *O-Bi, O-Ba: The End of Civilization*, an engineer says, "It's good to be there, in that group of expectant people." This could refer to a stadium of sports fans, an audience of moviegoers, or a church of believers. But in *O-Bi, O-Ba*, it refers to a vault of nuclear war survivors.

A year after a nuclear holocaust, hundreds of people reside in the government-created Dome. The Dome shows signs of deterioration, and Soft, the Dome's morale officer, knows the structure will soon collapse. His superiors have created the story that an Ark—presumably a transport plane or spaceship—will arrive to rescue the survivors. But Soft knows this is a myth designed to give the survivors hope. Those who realize the story isn't true call those who believe it "freaks."

Resources are running out and survivors are dying. Soft's boss orders him to recruit an engineer who can repair the Dome. Soft speaks with the engineer and stresses that if the Dome collapses, all will die in a frozen radioactive wasteland. But the engineer sees no reason to repair the Dome. He says, "If we are doomed to Hell, why should we keep the dome?"

Soft's boss berates him for failing to get the engineer on board. But Soft resolves to make the Ark mythos believable. He searches for a Bible, but only finds a cover from which the pages have been torn.

Soft learns about a possible airplane hangar in the Dome, and searches for it in vain. At the end, the Dome collapses, and Soft trudges into the snow outside. There, he sees himself and his deceased girlfriend leaving in a balloon, a final illusion before he shuffles away.

O-Bi, O-Ba: The End of Civilization is a grim film whose art direction expresses decay. The interiors are dingy, and the lighting casts crowd scenes in a drab, washed-out blue. Despite the claustrophobic setting, writer-director Piotr Szulkin keeps the movie mobile.

Striking images abound. For example, Soft's girlfriend Gea has told him that she must practice on a high wire so she can be one of the first to enter the Ark. But when Soft sees her practicing, she loses her footing and falls to her death. A spotlight illuminates her prone body as dozens of gray-robed survivors shuffle around her.

Some residents have carried the Ark myth too far. A man invites Soft to his "Eden," a refrigerated chamber including a miniature Ark which he worships, as well as a glass compartment of dead women whom the man has flash-frozen. This fanatic believes that in the future, he will thaw out the women and perpetuate the human race. Realizing the man is insane, Soft locks him in his chamber and drops the key down a floor grate.

In relation to presenting the Dome as a dispiriting refuge, the film explores the ethics of false hope. From the leaders' perspective, the myth that an Ark will rescue the survivors motivates the latter to carry on. Otherwise, many would give up, succumbing to depression or, in some cases, suicide.

But is it morally right to feed people a lie, even a well-meaning lie? Soft wrestles with this ethical dilemma. He considers anything that will keep people thriving worthwhile. But the engineer who refuses to fix the Dome sees through his reasoning. If the Dome is eventually going to collapse despite any renovations, and the people will then die in a frigid radioactive environment, why postpone the inevitable? Soft tells the engineer, "This repair is your moral duty." The engineer replies, "You know, morality is a passkey. It opens every door, including the one hiding immoral intentions."

In trying to put off the inevitable Dome collapse, the leadership suggests they too believe some unlikely event or agent may arrive to save them all. It's a forlorn hope, perhaps one unconscious in Soft's mind, but is Russian roulette hope better than no hope at all?

Or perhaps Soft, representing the leadership, won't admit what will happen once the Dome collapses: Hundreds of robed survivors will hurry into the snow, searching for an Ark that never came and never will. Some will freeze to death, others will succumb to radiation poisoning. In hours or days, gray-robed corpses will blemish the snow like sores.

As for the Dome, it entails puzzling aspects. The movie tells us it was only built to last one year. Why? Did the government think the survivors would all have died by then? Or was it not possible to build one that would last for many years? Its origin remains mysterious, and the film gives no clue as to whether the Dome's inhabitants are the only survivors left in the world. Certainly someone in the Dome would have tried to establish radio contact with any government or individual still alive. But if they did, we don't hear about it.

Soft's fantasy of him and his girlfriend floating away at the end is both wistful and grave. Soft's hopes, dreams and even reasons for living appear to be sailing aloft with the balloon. The same appears to be true for the Dome itself.

Thematically, the film considers whether hope would even be possible for survivors of a nuclear war, and if so, in what form. No doubt any government left would try to inspire its citizens to carry on. But would this entail pulling the radioactive wool over their eyes? Or would the nuclear war have so shaken the citizens' world that government propaganda would find no foothold? After all, in the weeks following a nuclear holocaust, many (most?) survivors would be dying from a number of causes: radiation poisoning, disease, infection, starvation.

Probably those with religious faith might be the most likely to cling to hope, though paper tiger faith would die a quick death. Some, despite bedrock faith, would no doubt wonder why God had allowed this holocaust and its grim aftermath to happen.

Atheists and agnostics might cling to the hope that survivors could rebuild a better world. But some God-deniers would not believe that meaningful survival following a nuclear holocaust was in the cards.

On Roger.Ebert.com, Michal Oleszczyk writes,

> [*O-Bi, O-Ba* depicts] a post-nuclear wasteland, reigned by political terror and existential loneliness, indicated by the presence of Camus-like protagonists clinging to remnants of human decency…. The set designs and camerawork is [*sic*] consistently impressive, especially in case of Piotr [Witold?] Sobocinski's gliding StediCam.[6]

Perhaps, as the engineer tells Soft, it is good to be among a group of expectant people. Yet we should be clear about the object of that expectation. Is it the real deal, or just funny money?

* * *

The Sea Serpent

DIRECTOR: Gregory Greens aka Amando de Ossorio; WRITER: Gordon A. Osburn aka Amando de Ossorio; MUSIC: Robin Davis aka Manel Santisteban; CINEMATOGRAPHER: Paul P. Cutler aka Raúl Pérez Cubero; EDITOR: Anthony Red aka José Antonio Rojo; PRODUCER: José Frade.

CAST: Timothy Bottoms (Pedro Fontán); Taryn Power (Margaret); Jared Martin (Linares); Ray Milland (Professor Timothy Wallace); Carole James (Jill).

PRODUCTION: Constan Films S.A., Calepas International; Spanish; 1985; 92 minutes; not rated. Alternate title: *Hydra*.

* * *

This attempted revival of the giant monster genre of the '50s and '60s is not without its charms, but it fails due to a lackluster script and meager budget.

An American bomber experiences problems with a nuclear bomb's faulty mechanism. The military honchos don't want nearby Russians to nab the weapon under any circumstances, so they order the bomber to deactivate the bomb and drop it into the Atlantic. The supposedly deactivated bomb explodes once it hits the ocean (a good special effect), bathing a curious reptilian beast in radiation.

The newly revived monster starts devouring hapless victims off the Spanish coast. Pedro, a disgraced sea captain stripped of command (his story of a sea serpent attacking his crew wasn't believed), and Margaret, who saw the serpent consume a friend, join forces with oceanographer Professor Wallace to stop the beast. They choose not to inform the authorities, but take on the creature themselves. Using flare guns and dynamite, they drive the monster away from the coastline, though it's still very much alive. Apparently they figure some other country can worry about the monster chowing down on its locals.

In the movie, radiation appears to revive a dormant creature that was already colossal; if it did bloat the animal's size, it happened offscreen. Regardless, this radiation business is enough to qualify the monster for nuclear threat service.

The Sea Serpent mixes tropes from both 1950s atomic monster movies with 1980s sensibilities. It also tosses in a less than stellar budget, and provides strictly by-the-numbers direction. The result: According to many, unwatchable.

Yes, the film is daft in several ways, such as the story's inconclusive finale. In addition, the screeching monster—often a hand puppet—is less than convincing. But there's something likable here. The monster's attack on a lighthouse appears to be an attempted homage to 1953's *The Beast from 20,000 Fathoms*. Also, the serpent's climactic low-budget rampage, in which it destroys a bridge, derails a train car and smashes a helicopter (all obvious but entertaining miniatures), is undeniably fun, not unlike a kid having his King Kong action figure attack a Lionel train set.

This was one of veteran Hollywood actor Ray Milland's final films. But the film's meager status notwithstanding, Milland's performance as Professor Wallace is professional, and he even seems to enjoy the role. In the latter part of his long career, Milland appeared in many genre movies (such as 1963's *X—The Man with the X-Ray Eyes* and 1972's *Frogs*), and in the '40s and '50s, he rated as an "A" budget star, winning a Best Actor Oscar for 1945's *The Lost Weekend*. Although *The Sea Serpent*, Milland's next-to-last movie, may sink, his accomplishments never will.

* * *

Survival 1990

DIRECTOR-PRODUCER: Peter McCubbin; WRITERS: Gina Mandelli, Peter McCubbin; MUSIC: Tanos; SUPERVISING EDITOR: Kirk Jones.
CAST: Nancy Cser (Miranda); Jeff Holec (John); Craig Williams (Simon).
PRODUCTION: CHCH-TV, Emmeritus Productions; Canadian; 1985; 80 minutes; not rated. Alternate Title: *Survival Earth*.

* * *

They say talk is cheap, and that's certainly the case in this low-budget Canadian post-nuke movie. Talk is almost all it is, which saves on the budget, but plays havoc on the viewer's attention span.

Ten years after a catastrophe has befallen the world, survivors John and Miranda live in a park. John, an intellectual, reads Yeats to Miranda. She remembers nothing before 1986, the year in which civilization went belly-up. Simon the soldier comes along, shoots and eats their dog (sorry, Fido) and joins them. Vandals who whoop like frat boys occasionally harass. Toss a clone of John into the mix for no apparent reason, prepare for one last big gun battle, and that's basically the whole shebang.

The movie doesn't explain "The Fall" which ended society. We know it involved atomics, for John says the Pickering nuclear power plant melted down. Miranda was nearby at the time, and somehow the meltdown wiped her memory and temporarily turned her purple. John says she's a mutant, but she looks as normal as him and Simon.

The opening scenes show images of nuclear power plants, so presumably, several power plants had accidents. In addition, the beginning shows a mushroom cloud, so presumably nukes exploded. Unrated, *Survival 1990* would probably receive a PG-13 for language, adult content, brief nudity and violence.

The movie ends with John, Miranda and Simon happily chattering, John and Miranda telling Simon they need to find him a female. Meanwhile, viewers may feel they need to find another movie.

* * *

Wheels of Fire

DIRECTOR-PRODUCER: Cirio H. Santiago; WRITERS: Frederick Bailey (screenplay); Ellen Collett (story); MUSIC: Chris Young; CINEMATOGRAPHER: Ricardo Remias; EDITOR: George Saint aka Gervacio Santos.
CAST: Gary Watkins (Trace); Laura Banks (Stinger); Lynda Wiesmeier (Arlie); Linda Grovenor (Spike); Joseph Anderson (Scourge).
PRODUCTION: Rodeo; produced in the Philippines; 1985; 81 minutes; rated R.

* * *

Wheels of Fire is the usual: Trace, a Mad Max–type loner, travels the wastelands of a wiped-out world. Scourge and his evil henchmen kidnap Trace's sister Arlie, and Trace fires on all six cylinders to rescue her. Along the way, he meets a group of peaceful folks building a spaceship, but they never get far. In the end, Trace and the good guys win. Or do they?

One aspect of the movie stinks: female abuse. Lynda Wiesmeier is relentlessly exploited in the nude and becomes the villains' involuntary go-to sex slave. Some of the movie's other aspects aren't half bad. Chris Young's music score is evocative. Several of the performances are good, such as Linda Grovenor's turn as Spike. And the action is slam-bang.

Wheels of Fire is rated R for language, adult content, nudity, rape and violence.

* * *

CHAPTER EIGHT

1986

America 3000

DIRECTOR-WRITER: David Engelbach; MUSIC: Tony Berg; CINEMATOGRAPHER: David Gurfinkel; EDITOR: Alain Jakubowicz; PRODUCERS: Menahem Golan, Yoram Globus.
CAST: Chuck Wagner (Korvis); Laurene Landon (Vena); William Wallace (Gruss); Victoria Barrett (Lakella);
PRODUCTION: Golan-Globus Productions; 1986; 92 minutes; rated PG-13.

* * *

Women ruling over men is nothing new in science fiction; for example, it happened in 1958's *Queen of Outer Space*. But this familiar theme rarely elevates women, and such is the case with 1986's *America 3000*.

Nine hundred years after a nuclear war, women dominate men and use many of them as slaves and neutered pets. Korvis is one man who's had enough. He leads fellow plugots (the women's term for men) into a raid on a frau (the future term for women) settlement, stealing food and freeing men.

Injured by a frau, Korvis falls into an underground shaft and discovers a vault packed with weaponry such as laser rifles and hand grenades. He also hears an ancient message meant for the president of the United States, whom 3000 A.D. mythology calls "the Prezeedent," a fabled savior. Slipping on a gold hazmat suit, Korvis masquerades as the Prezeedent and arranges a meeting with frau leader Vena.

Vena's scheming sister Lakella and another frau lead the women to attack the men's camp. Korvis thinks Vena has tricked him, but she swears she didn't and that she too was deceived. She lays down her weapons. This act motivates all the women and men to do the same, ushering in the beginning of a new age and soon, no doubt, a new profession: marriage counselor.

The film supplies a future slang—for example, "nuke" means to kill, "waggos" means crazy, etc. This is an imaginative (if also obvious) touch. It's also nice that the movie does not ape the *Mad Max* style found in so many 1980s low-budget post-nuke action flicks.

When Korvis accidentally activates the computer message meant for the U.S. president hundreds of years earlier, a General Greer informs the president that NORAD computers mistakenly detected incoming missiles and fired back a retaliatory strike at Russia. General Greer ironically says, "We've won it. Caught the Russkies with their pants down."

Given the substandard script and impoverished budget, as a post-nuke action film sprinkled with satire, *America 3000* doesn't click.

* * *

Dead Man's Letters

DIRECTOR: Konstantin Lopushanskiy; WRITERS: Konstantin Lopushanskiy, Vyacheslav Rybakov, Boris Strugatskiy; MUSIC: Aleksandr Zhurbin; CINEMATOG-RAPHER: Nikolai Pokoptsev; EDITOR: T. Pulinoy aka Tatyana Pulina; PRODUC-ERS: Yuri Golynchik, Raisa Proskuryakova.

CAST: Rolan Bykov (Professor Larsen); Vatslav Dvorzhetsky (Pastor); Vera Mayorova (Anna).

PRODUCTION: Lenfilm; released in the Soviet Union on 15 September 1986; Russian; 88 minutes; not rated. Alternate title: *Letters from a Dead Man.*

* * *

A nuclear war movie made in the Soviet Union during the 1980s would be riddled with Soviet propaganda, no?

No.

Dead Man's Letters depicts a grim post-nuke world bereft of political spin, instead

Professor Larsen (Rolan Bykov) wears one of the protective body suits that post-nuke survivors don to venture outside, where rubble and corpses litter the terrain in 1986's Russian-made *Dead Man's Letters.*

appealing to the universal fear of how a nuclear war would affect all countries in both the East and West.

In the film, a nuclear attack in the near future has blasted, burned and polluted a small Russian town, and presumably the entirety of the Soviet Union and world. The few scattered town residents wear protective body suits that include gas masks to go outside, where rubble and corpses litter the terrain. Professor Larsen (Rolan Bykov), a prize-winning physicist, has taken refuge with his wife Anna (Vera Mayorova) in a museum basement along with a handful of other survivors. Anna is sick, and Larsen is nursing her to health, or so he hopes.

Larsen visits an orphanage where the children refuse to speak, perhaps catatonic. A world-weary government representative says the children cannot be evacuated to the central bunker because its resources would be wasted on them. The man's callousness shocks Larsen, but the scene suggests that the war's survivors are becoming increasingly amoral.

Larsen gives Anna a painkiller, then risks breaking a curfew to get her more medicine. A medical friend tells him that painkillers are running out and that an order has gone around that everyone must soon evacuate to the central bunker. Larsen won't hear of it. He insists, without a logical hypothesis, that other people exist elsewhere in the world. Although he can't prove it, he senses it. He acquires a painkiller for his wife and flees during a government black market raid. But when he returns to the museum basement, he discovers his wife, dead. Other museum survivors help him bury her.

During the burial, we hear the text of one of Larsen's letters to his son Eric, apparently killed in the war. He constantly writes letters to Eric, though his son, even if he is alive somewhere, will probably never receive them.

A scholar who has been dictating a fatalistic epitaph to humankind reveals that, due to the hopelessness of the current situation, he plans to commit suicide, and does so. Horror consumes his son.

The orphanage caretaker brings the orphaned children to Larsen, telling him the central bunker has rejected them. Though the caretaker and other survivors evacuate to the central bunker, Larsen chooses to care for the children. When Christmas arrives, Larsen builds the children a skeletal tree festooned with candles.

Soon, a child's voice takes over the narration from Larsen. He explains that Larsen has died, but before death, he insisted other humans still lived outside the town, and he urged the children to leave while they still could. In the closing scenes, the children have banded together and begun a trek into the outside world—their destination, like the fate of the Earth, unknown.

Much of the film is shot in sepia tones, and darkness permeates both the inner and outer environments. The exterior world is a windswept nightmare riddled with ruined buildings and dead bodies.

The film is deliberately paced, frequently relying on its gloomy music score, which often sounds like a constant, brooding reverberation, to accentuate its horrors. Similarly, the acting is subdued. As the film's narrator and main character Professor Larsen, Rolan Bykov is excellent. He appears on the verge of resignation, but his hopes for a future for humankind, however vague, keep him going. Desperate for converts, he preaches this post-nuke gospel to almost everyone he encounters, including the orphaned children.

His wife Anna's illness is never spelled out, but we assume she is dying from radiation poisoning. However, if this is the case, she has no sores, and her hair is intact.

Perhaps director Konstantin Lopushanskiy wanted the nature of her sickness to remain ambiguous.

Like 1983's American-made *Testament*, *Dead Man's Letters* occurs in one small town. But *Testament*'s characters sport no body suits, and hostile weather doesn't dim their daytimes. *Dead Man's Letters* creates a much more claustrophobic environment, as though the entire world has been reduced to the town's handful of survivors. Unlike Larsen, several of the survivors believe they are the last ones, and that hope of others alive somewhere is an illusion.

As in *Testament* and 1983's *The Day After*, the characters don't know how the war started. Yet unlike those two films, this Russian drama posits that the war may have started due to a computer error. Before a missile operator could halt the launch, he choked on his coffee, and thus did not stop the launch in time. Subsequently, he hung himself. We hear Larsen mentally dictate a letter to his son Eric recounting this story, but it is unclear whether this actually happened or if Larsen's memory is malfunctioning. It certainly sounds like an "urban myth."

While *Testament* restrains physical horror, *Dead Man's Letters* spells it out, similar to *The Day After*. Even so, the nastiness we witness in *Dead Man's Letters* appears unclear at times. For example, in search of his son Eric, Larsen ventures through an emergency center in which doctors operate on war-ravaged children. The quick visuals we see repulse us, but we can't always tell just what we have seen. Still, the screams and moans of the children unnerve as much or more than any graphic surgery.

Also similar to *The Day After* and 1984's *Threads*, *Dead Man's Letters* gives us a direct look at World War III's nuclear destruction. First we see the missiles blast off from their silos, the populace panic, the missiles hit. But the film's apocalyptic visuals mix the naturalistic with the ethereal. As the explosions take out whole cities, we hear a woman's voice sing a beautiful aria. Such is the multifaceted approach of *Dead Man's Letters*.

The special effects of the nuclear attack are excellent. Aside from the missiles launching, few of the visuals rely on stock footage. The explosions appear gigantic in comparison to the realistic models they demolish.

Dead Man's Letters never mentions the term "nuclear winter," but the sky is always overcast, the wind always howls, and darkness always permeates. Some characters note how cold it is. When we see the children trekking into the outside world at the end, the landscape appears to be covered with snow.

The film depicts an interior nuclear winter as well, one raging in the soul of Larsen, the main character. Though we hear Larsen's voiceover narration composing letters to his son, we learn little about the son. Anna insists that Eric burned to death, for she saw it in a dream. Larsen maintains that Eric must still be alive somewhere. The letters to Eric we hear Larsen compose help Larsen survive, giving him a reason to soldier on despite the harsh present and perhaps even more dismal future.

Differing from its Western counterparts, *Dead Man's Letters* is that rarity of rarities: a philosophical film that is not pretentious. Throughout, we hear many ruminations on the nature of humankind. One subplot concerns a scholar dictating an essay on humanity's failings that have led to nuclear annihilation. At one point, he says, "We are nothing but presumptuous monkeys." He also notes that the human race has long been mired in a "slow suicide." Yet he adds, "I loved mankind. I love it better now that it no longer exists." The scholar's view of humanity is one of despair, suggesting the absence of God and absolutes—that we are nothing but meat puppets. Accordingly, the scholar chooses to live out his philosophy by calmly killing himself. Still, before he pulls the trigger, he says, "Lord, forgive me."

Dead Man's Letters argues that humankind has a spiritual side. The film depicts its priest with dignity, as one who still champions right and wrong, implying that moral absolutes do exist. Compare this to the shell-shocked pastors of *Testament* and *The Day After*. And while Larsen seems to be putting his faith more in humankind than in God, he still maintains that hope exists, that it must exist—and hope implies meaning, not nihilism.

Yet in the bleak world *Dead Man's Letters* depicts, it's easy to see how a survivor might lose their faith in anything and everything amidst the grime and desolation. Can one continue to be a moral agent in a world that seems to have vaporized civility along with civilization? This is a dilemma most of the best nuclear war films tackle, one with which *Dead Man's Letters* grapples.

The January 27, 1989, *New York Times* offered an insightful critique from Richard Bernstein: "Mr. Lopushanskiy ... achieves a splendid goulishness [sic] with scenes of a remarkable world ... [but] despite its technical virtues, [it] seems just a bit too contrived to truly convince."[1] Kim Newman calls the film "the grimmest possible vision of a functioning post-holocaust society, set in a dingily orange-lit and leaky underground complex where bureaucracy still rules."[2]

Despite its chilling depiction of a post-nuke world, *Dead Man's Letters* insists on remaining hopeful, even if the source of that hope is unclear. Larsen dies feeling he has accomplished something, because the orphaned children will now venture out in the world and perhaps find those other survivors Larsen so passionately insists are there. In this sense, *Dead Man's Letters* is more optimistic than *Testament*, *The Day After* and *Threads*, its major Western counterparts. Or is it, as a detractor might assert, simply more delusional?

*　　*　　*

The Fifth Missile

DIRECTOR: Larry Peerce; WRITER: Eric Bercovici, based on the novel *The Gold Crew* by Thomas N. Scortia and Frank M. Robinson; MUSIC: Pino Donaggio; CINEMA-TOGRAPHER: Cristiano Pogany; EDITORS: Jack Tucker, Maureen O'Connell; PRODUCER: Arthur Fellows.

CAST: Robert Conrad (Commander Mark Van Meer); Sam Waterston (Captain Allard Renslow); Richard Roundtree (Commander Frederick Bryce); Jonathan Banks (Ray Olson); Art LaFleur ("Animal" Meslinsky); Dennis Holahan (Warden); Sergio Fantoni (Pietro); Yvette Mimieux (Cheryl Leary); David Soul (Captain Kevin Harris).

PRODUCTION: Bercovici/St. Johns Productions, Cinecittà, MGM/UA Television; broadcast on NBC-TV on 23 February 1986; 150 minutes; not rated.

*　　*　　*

Despite the presence of four talented lead actors and an offbeat take on the nuke threat genre, *The Fifth Missile* flounders due to script implausibilities and an overlong running time.

The premise: The crew of the U.S. submarine *Montana* is to be tested for their nuclear war readiness should World War III break out. Only three people—Commander

Van Meer, Captain Harris and Commander Bryce—know the alleged nuclear attack will be bogus, and as a safeguard, the four missiles to be fired will all be "blanks," though a fifth missile not to be fired will be real. What could possibly go wrong with such a scenario?

Plenty. Inconveniently (but plenty conveniently for the scriptwriter), paint used on a small interior section of the submarine releases toxic fumes that cause the crew to become edgy and hyper— except for Van Meer, who is secretly taking antidepressants that counteract the paint fumes. The fumes turn Captain Harris into a wide-eyed martinet who believes World War III really has started and seems all too willing to launch all of the sub's missiles. It's up to Van Meer to stop him.

On shore, Van Meer's best friend Captain Renslow figures out what the now crazed Harris might do if he thought a nuclear war was on, so he boards a chopper to shoot down any missiles the *Montana* fires.

The VHS cover for NBC's 1986 telemovie *The Fifth Missile,* a nuke thriller in which the U.S.S. *Montana*'s captain has succumbed to toxic fumes and believes a drill involving a World War III scenario is real—meaning he plans to launch a nuclear missile.

After numerous perils, including the inadvertent death of Commander Bryce, Van Meer triumphs. Still, under Harris' order, the real missile gets fired, then shot down by Renslow's helicopter. The devastated missile crashes into the sea and damages the submarine, which starts to sink; Van Meer and the crew escape, but an injured Harris goes down with the ship.

The Fifth Missile has the feel of a TV movie, which isn't a crime, but deleting 15 or 20 minutes would have helped make it leaner and meaner. However, that wouldn't resolve several story problems. First off, why would any presidential administration be crazy enough to make an actual nuclear sub crew think World War III has broken out? Didn't they consider that one or more of the crew might react recklessly? The movie makes it clear that Van Meer, Bryce and Harris know the test is only a drill. However, only Harris knows the location of the submarine unit that relays bogus World War III messages to the sub, and once he goes bat-crazy, he's obviously not telling. Wouldn't it have made more sense for both Van Meer and Bryce to have known as well? Also, it's a bit fortuitous that Van Meer's antidepressants happen to counteract the toxic paint fumes. And at the end, why in the world does Renslow jump from the helicopter into the frigid sea below? Apparently because Van Meer is his best friend, but Van Meer doesn't need rescuing.

In addition, staging occasionally fumbles. At a couple of points, Van Meer too easily overcomes crewmen holding weapons on him. But due to tight shooting schedules, that sort of thing often happens with TV movies and TV shows.

The film's cast helps keep the movie afloat. Robert Conrad delivers a decent low-key turn as Van Meer, the navy officer who secretly takes antidepressants to cope with his wife's tragic demise. Sam Waterston as Conrad's best friend Renslow is excellent as always. Both are veteran TV players, Conrad best known for CBS's *The Wild Wild West* (1965–69) and Waterston for NBC's *Law & Order* (1994–2010, 2022–).Richard Roundtree delivers a quiet performance as psychiatrist Commander Bryne, and his character is unfortunately killed too quickly.

As the already disagreeable Harris, David Soul twitches into Mr. Hyde territory once the paint fumes take hold. This probably wasn't an easy role to play, but Soul overdoes it at times. However, some of his excesses could be attributable to the director's coaxing.

Reviews were less than stellar. For *The New York Times*, John Corry wrote that the film "seems to be made up of stray pieces of other movies ... *The Fifth Missile* isn't terrific television; it isn't awful television, either. It's just television."[3]

Anyone looking forward to acquiring a copy of *The Fifth Missile* may be disappointed—in the post–VHS age, it's a hard movie to find.

* * *

The Manhattan Project

DIRECTOR: Marshall Brickman; WRITERS: Marshall Brickman, Thomas Baum; MUSIC: Philippe Sarde; CINEMATOGRAPHER: Billy Williams; EDITOR: Nina Feinberg; PRODUCERS: Jennifer Ogden, Marshall Brickman.
CAST: John Lithgow (Dr. John Mathewson); Christopher Collet (Paul Stephens); Jill Eikenberry (Elizabeth Stephens); Cynthia Nixon (Jenny Anderman).
PRODUCTION: Gladden Entertainment; 1986; 117 minutes; rated PG-13.

* * *

No, not *that* Manhattan Project, the one during World War II for which scientists designed the first atomic bomb. This is a 1986 movie in which a gifted high school student builds an atomic bomb of his own and arms it.

In Ithaca, New York, Dr. John Mathewson oversees a bogus nuclear medicine laboratory called Medatomics, whose actual purpose is to process weapons-grade plutonium for the military.

Dr. Mathewson is romancing Elizabeth Stephens, and as part of his amorous campaign, he gives her son Paul a tour of Medatomics. Paul, a brilliant high school student with a streak of arrogance, figures out that Mathewson's facility is secretly processing plutonium. Paul's journalist girlfriend Jenny Anderman helps him pilfer some of the plutonium, which Paul uses to build an atomic bomb he enters in the New York Science Fair.

Paul and Jenny discover that the authorities are looking for them. Paul calls Mathewson and says he will hand over the bomb on one condition: Mathewson must type a statement revealing the truth about Medatomics' real purpose. Mathewson agrees to meet Paul at the lab, where he gives Paul the requested statement.

An FBI agent orders Paul to step away from the unarmed bomb. Realizing this is a ruse to shoot Paul, Mathewson stops the FBI agent. Paul arms the bomb. Mathewson convinces Paul to give him the bomb, which he does, but Mathewson announces to the government and military agents, "I'm taking [Paul] out of here."

Unexpectedly, the bomb starts its countdown sequence. Mathewson and Paul, with help from assorted agents, manage to disarm the device.

As Mathewson and Paul move for the outside door, a Lieutenant Colonel Conroy orders them to stop. Mathewson says the officer can't make him and Paul—and all the people who have gathered outside—simply go away.

The Manhattan Project mixes the then-popular "teen movie" genre with the straight suspense thriller, the same formula that 1983's *WarGames* used. In addition, both feature a "teen couple" as the protagonists: Matthew Broderick and Ally Sheedy in *WarGames*, Christopher Collet and Cynthia Nixon in *Manhattan Project*. In both movies, government authorities chase them. Both also feature a prominent adult scientist who interacts with the teens. Last but not least, both movies spotlight the nuclear issue. *WarGames* threatens the advent of World War III, and while *Manhattan Project*'s threat is less far-reaching, Mathewson nevertheless tells us the homemade atomic bomb could produce a 50-kiloton explosion, which could entail a blast radius of 20 kilometers, or 12 miles.

While *WarGames* succeeded at the box office, *Manhattan Project* bombed (pun intended). With a budget of $10.5 million, the film only made about $4 million in the U.S.[4]

Manhattan Project is edgier than *WarGames*, and this may be one reason it didn't fare as well at the box office. Both films feature somewhat smart-aleck teenage protagonists, but Matthew Broderick's character David Lightman is, appropriately enough, lighter than Christopher Collet's Paul Stephens. Paul appears more rash and more dangerous than David. For example, near the end, Paul intentionally arms his homemade nuclear device, an act that easily could have resulted in the deaths of hundreds or thousands of people.

Paul is, in some ways, a younger version of Mathewson. In an interview, director/-co-writer Marshall Brickman said, "Paul and John [Dr. Mathewson] are really two sides of the same character. They're both child-like, they both are infatuated with gadgets."[5]

And both display a wit that veers toward the offbeat if not the sardonic, both boast intellects the size of pyramids, both maintain a cockeyed view of life, and both salivate over science. Mathewson has let science blind him to the implications of his research. All too happily, he signs away his ethics to indulge his life's work in the fraudulent Medatomics which secretly processes enough weapons-grade plutonium to contaminate the state of New York. Of course, the Ithaca community doesn't know the government is risking its welfare, and Mathewson doesn't seem to notice, until close to the movie's finale.

When Lieutenant Colonel Conroy orders Mathewson to take the armed atomic bomb from Paul, the colonel implies that Paul will then be shot; Mathewson starts to tell Conroy that he is a scientist, not a killer. But Conroy asks him what he thinks

Medatomics is for—his intellectual stimulation? This prompts Mathewson's change of heart: Once he persuades Paul to give him the bomb, he decides to do at least one decent thing before his possible demise: make sure Paul leaves the lab alive. He has finally removed his blinders and sees his complicity with the government's unethical designs for the sellout it has always been.

But is the ending in which Mathewson and Paul leave the lab and Conroy leaves the premises in a helicopter plausible? Would the government let Paul and Mathewson go? Probably not, but in the heat of the moment, maybe.

But assuming the ending is plausible, what next? Paul had, after all, created and armed a nuclear device. Would he avoid all legal penalties? Should he avoid such penalties? This is where the movie might spark debate between different viewers. I argue he should suffer some penalty, as arming the bomb imperiled many lives, an act considerably more dangerous than Paul's usual pranks. It also begs the question "What is Paul capable of in the future, given the "right" circumstances?"

Technically, the film works on most levels. I did find Philippe Sarde's music score inappropriate at times. For example, during the sequence in which Paul is building his homemade atomic bomb, the music appears to have drifted in from a Disney family movie.

The acting is first-rate on all fronts. John Lithgow is a veteran who has proven during his long career that he can do anything—comedy, drama, science fiction. Speaking of the latter, science fiction fans (such as myself) well remember his thespian turns in *The Adventures of Buckaroo Banzai Across the 8th Dimension* and *2010: The Year We Make Contact*, both 1984.

Having won a truckload of acting awards (Emmys, Tonys, Golden Globes, etc.), Lithgow is equally adept at playing good guys or bad guys. *Manhattan Project* calls on him to perform a somewhat complex role, as we watch his character transform from inadvertent villain to intentional hero. In 1985, Lithgow said about the film, "The script appealed to me, and the subject matter was intriguing, too. It's a cut above the teenage science movies that have been filling the theaters this summer."[6]

Marshall Brickman, the film's director, co-writer and co-producer, is largely known for his contributions to comedy. For example, in olden days, he wrote for Johnny Carson's *Tonight Show*. In addition, with Woody Allen, he co-wrote 1973's *Sleeper*, 1977's *Annie Hall* (he and Allen won a Best Original Screenplay Oscar), 1979's *Manhattan* and 1993's *Manhattan Murder Mystery*. He also co-wrote and directed 1980's *Simon* and 1983's *Lovesick*. This explains why *Manhattan Project* has its lighter moments. For example, during a tense scene in which Paul is working to dismantle the armed atomic bomb, he asks those around him, "Anybody have a Philips head screwdriver?" Seven hands with Philips head screwdrivers shoot forward.

So is *Manhattan Project* a thriller dishing occasional jokes, or is it a *Dr. Strangelove* wannabe? Apparently the former. In a John C. Tibbetts interview, Brickman said *Dr. Strangelove* was a "black comedy" and that he wasn't drawn to the genre, but was comfortable lacing his "nuclear fairy tale" with jokes: "Every dark cloud, even if it's coming from Chernobyl, has some kind of humorous lining around it."[7] According to Gerald Jonas,

> Mr. Brickman's original goal in writing *The Manhattan Project* was to make something completely different from what he calls "yak and track" movies, in which dialogue is the main engine of plot. "Jokes are easy," he says. "I wanted character, I wanted to go for the emotions

that the kid feels, that the scientist feels; I wanted the audience to feel the seductiveness of machinery."[8]

Technology's ability to dazzle rates as one of *Manhattan Project*'s more important themes. I admit that over the decades, space technology, both of NASA and now wealthy individuals and non-government companies, has always wowed me. And when it comes to nuclear technology, mushroom clouds have always awed me, though I hope I never see one in real life.

Regarding its main subject, the nuclear threat, the film proclaims that any participation in the creation, maintenance or use of nuclear weapons is bad, and we're talking supervillain-level bad. To some, this may sound reasonable; to others, absurd. But a quick evaluation will reveal that in America, all of us who pay federal taxes are complicit in perpetuating the nuclear threat. That doesn't mean that we can't lobby for verifiable nuclear disarmament of, say, Russia, China, North Korea, Europe and America, as well as champion policies that mitigate nuclear war.

Could a brilliant high school student design an atomic bomb? In 1976, John Aristotle Phillips, a Princeton University junior, became famous as "The A-Bomb Kid" after he designed "a working Nagasaki-class weapon the size of a beach ball."[9] His teacher, Dr. Freeman Dyson, gave him an A but encouraged him to destroy the paper. The U.S. government classified it.[10] So yes, *The Manhattan Project*'s core concept is plausible, even if the elaborate wrapping paper around it may not be.

Reviews of *Manhattan Project* were mixed. Vincent Canby's said that it "tends to neutralize its own serious intentions by being too jokey much of the time and, at other times, too much the teen-age adventure-comedy whose conventions deny the immensity of the horror with which it's concerned."[11] Michael Wilmington asked, "[H]ow do you make a character who wants to build an atomic bomb—for whatever reason—sympathetic? ... Who are you likelier to root for: a guy running around your backyard with an A-bomb or the people trying to stop him?"[12] Roger Ebert loved

Dr. John Mathewson (John Lithgow, right) urges Paul Stephens (Christopher Collet) to hand over Paul's homemade atomic bomb in 1986's *The Manhattan Project* (Gladden Entertainment Corporation). If the bomb goes off, thousands could die.

the film, giving it four out of four stars: "[It's] a *tour de force* ... a tense and effective thriller."[13]

In the relentless march of time, *The Manhattan Project* is one of hundreds of forgotten movies from the latter 20th century. But despite its flaws, it doesn't deserve its obscurity.

*   *   *

The Nuclear Conspiracy

PRODUCER-WRITER-DIRECTOR: Rainer Erler; MUSIC: Eugen Thomas; CINEMA-TOGRAPHER: Wolfgang Grasshoff; EDITOR: Peter Przygodda.
CAST: Birgit Doll (Susan); Albert Fortell (Steve); Mark Lee (David).
PRODUCTION: Atlas International, Reflex Film Ltd.; British-German-Austrian-Australian; 1986; 120 minutes; not rated. Alternate title: *News Report on a Journey to a Bright Future.*

*   *   *

If a woman in black-rimmed glasses calling herself Aunt Ruth should offer to care for your child, run like the wind. She's actually part of a scheme to cover up a nuclear waste crime, and she's not above harming your child if you don't cooperate. Such is the dilemma Susan faces in *The Nuclear Conspiracy.*

Susan's journalist husband David hasn't contacted her in weeks, but in the middle of the night, she gets an anxious call from him. Teaming with photojournalist Steve to find her husband, they pick up David's trail, globe-trotting to Marseilles, New York City, Singapore and Australia.

Their adversaries stay one step ahead of Susan and Steve, killing an important New York lead and having "Aunt Ruth" kidnap Susan's young daughter Julia. Steve makes a deal with the baddies (offscreen), agreeing to keep the information he and Susan uncovered secret, so Susan is reunited with her daughter.

But Susan doggedly goes to Australia to continue tracking David. For pay, an aborigine tells Susan and Steve about a nuclear waste facility under construction in the desert. There, Susan and Steve find David beneath a truck, dehydrated and barely alive.

At a celebration to welcome David back, David spills the truth about the conspiracy. Via helicopters, news journalists fly to the area and a French nuclear representative confesses astonishment. He confirms that the waste is important "as a source of raw materials," and that 95 percent of it is "after reconditioning, totally usable." A journalist says, "Such as in the manufacture as a bomb." The French rep maintains that such waste would not be allowed to fall into the wrong hands.

However, minutes later, it's determined that the steel containers supposedly containing nuclear waste are empty, and who has the waste, nobody knows. Perhaps the "wrong hands"?

The Nuclear Conspiracy plays like an average 1980s political thriller. Occasional moments of menace spark interest, but at 120 minutes, the film is too long, and is often padded by showing Steve's photos as he takes them.

In addition, the film suffers from illogic. The conspiracy was willing to kill Susan and Steve's New York contact, so why not go one step further by killing Susan and Steve? Yes, the conspiracy unwisely tries to kill Susan with carbon monoxide poisoning, but instead, the conspiracy could have simply had Susan shot like the New York contact. Similarly, why didn't the conspiracy make sure David was dead before abandoning him in the desert?

The most surprising and disturbing part of the film involves Steve's character change near the movie's end. We've seen he is conniving, but we don't expect him to sexually assault Susan. His drunkenness is no excuse for this kind of brutality, and it reveals Steve to be a total jerk.

Unrated, the film would probably receive an R for language, sexual assault, and brief nudity.

The Nuclear Conspiracy is a standard nuclear threat thriller with a few outstanding moments.

* * *

The Patriot

DIRECTOR: Frank Harris; WRITERS: Andy Ruben, Katt Shea Ruben; MUSIC: Jay Ferguson; CINEMATOGRAPHER: Frank Harris; EDITOR: Rierhard E. Westover; PRODUCER: Michael Bennett.
CAST: Gregg Henry (Lieutenant Matt Ryder); Simone Griffeth (Sean); Leslie Nielsen (Admiral Frazer); Jeff Conaway (Commander Mitchell).
PRODUCTION: Crown International Pictures, Patriot Productions; 1986; 88 minutes; rated R.

* * *

Matt Ryder, a disgraced Vietnam veteran, finds himself shanghaied to the office of Admiral Frazier, who offers him a deal: His record will be cleared if he retrieves recently stolen nuclear bombs. Like any good action hero, Ryder jumps at the chance. En route, he confronts Navy officer Sean, his former lady love who spurned him, and naturally this leads to the usual R-rated lust, excuse me, I mean love scene.

This angers Sean's boyfriend Commander Mitchell, but it turns out he's involved in smuggling the stolen nuclear bombs, one of which is armed. Ryder and Sean unite to foil the nuke smuggling operation, which comes down to cutting the right wire on the nuclear device to deactivate it; if Ryder cuts the wrong wire, they're toast. Does Ryder succeed?

Mediocre at best, *The Patriot* offers okay action, hit-and-miss performances, and a typical action movie script. The hand-to-hand combat and gun battles are mostly well-staged. Jeff Conaway's transition from naval officer to wild-eyed fanatic seems borderline over-the-top. Gregg Henry as Ryder makes a fair action hero, and Leslie Nielsen is fine as an iconic Navy admiral. Script-wise, there's only one surprise: a chilling scene in which the bad guy in charge of the stolen nukes methodically kills his two comedy relief henchmen.

The movie is rated R for language, adult content, sex, brief nudity and violence.

* * *

Population: 1

DIRECTOR-WRITER: Rene Daalder; MUSIC: Daniel Schwartz; CINEMATOGRAPHER: Keith "KK" Barrett; EDITOR-PRODUCER: Bianca Daalder.

CAST: Tomata Du Plenty; Dino Lee; Helen Heaven; Sheela Edwards.
PRODUCTION: American Scenes; 1986; 72 minutes; not rated.

* * *

Some films defy the familiar movie rating systems. They are so twisted that no numerical rating will do. *Population: 1* is such a movie.

I call it a "movie" in the loose sense only. After all, *Population:1* glories in its incoherency. It is possibly the most self-indulgent and pretentious film I have ever seen, and it should come with a warning label. My guess is that writer-director Rene Daalder would probably welcome my negative appraisal of the film.

Basically, *Population: 1* is a long (72 minute) music video, appropriate since the 1980s was *the* decade of music videos. In the film, the last survivor of a nuclear war in the United States musically chronicles (sort of) his and America's journey from innocence to atomic annihilation. Simultaneously, the man tracks (again, sort of) his love affair with singer Sheela Edwards, who warbles numbers such as "Jazz Vampire" and "I Wanna Hurt."

One of the film's music videos actually works: The song is the catchy "Hard Work," staged cleverly. In addition, there are flashes of imagination throughout. But most of the film is unwatchable dross.

Also, despite the movie's opening shot that claims the film is rated PG, this is definitely R-rated territory. Lots of nudity and bizarre sex stuff.

Population: 1 exhibits art-house posturing à la Andy Warhol. The film's star, Tomata Du Plenty, had been a lead singer for the techno-punk group the Screamers, and musically, the film may remind some of '80s avant-garde bands.

Inarguably, *Population: 1* is different from most 1980s nuclear threat movies. But "different" doesn't necessarily mean "better."

* * *

The Sacrifice

DIRECTOR-WRITER: Andrei Tarkovskij (aka Tarkovsky); CINEMATOGRAPHER: Sven Nykvist; EDITORS: Michal Leszczylowski, Andrei Tarkovskij; PRODUCER: Anna-Lena Wibom.

CAST: Erland Josephson (Alexander); Susan Fleetwood (Adelaide); Allan Edwall (Otto); Guðrún S. Gísladóttir (Maria); Sven Wollter (Victor).

PRODUCTION: Svenska Filminstitutet, Argos Films, Film Four International, Josephson & Nykvist HB, Sveriges Television/SVT2, Sandrew Film & Theater AB; Swedish-French-British; released in Sweden on 9 May 1986; released in the U.S. on 26 September 1986; 149 minutes; rated PG.

* * *

Most 1980s nuke threat movies are easy to follow, but such is not the case with *The Sacrifice*. Directed by the celebrated Andrei Tarkovsky (renowned for 1972's science fiction epic *Solaris*), *The Sacrifice* is a nuclear war drama that takes a strange turn from the conventional.

Living on an island off Sweden, Alexander is celebrating his birthday. He spends time with "Little Man," his young son who is temporarily mute due to a recent operation. Alexander regales Little Man with a long monologue.

Several folks—family and friends—gather at Alexander's house for his birthday; Alexander's wife Adelaide sends house servant Marta home.

Via low-flying jets and radio reports, Alexander and his guests learn they are on the eve of World War III. Adelaide comes unglued and must be sedated. The electricity and phones go out. Alexander tells God he will give up his family, including Little Man, and destroy his house if God will undo the nuclear madness.

Otto tells Alexander that for this to happen, Alexander must sleep with Marta, the house servant who has retired to her home. Otto says she is an authentic witch. Alexander has sex with Marta, both of them hovering above the bed, as Marta tries to quell Alexander's fear.

Alexander wakes up on the same couch in his house he went to sleep on. But now the power is on, and the phone has a dial tone. Alexander takes this to mean that God has honored his oath, so while everyone is gone from his house, he sets it aflame. His horrified family and friends come running. Ambulance attendants subdue Alexander and take him away, presumably to a mental ward.

It's tempting to dismiss *The Sacrifice* as a pretentious art film. Various art film tropes are present and accounted for: existential monologues, long static takes, religious references, obscure symbolism. In fact, initially, I was going to say the film is 1955's *Day the World Ended* as directed by Ingmar Bergman.

But that's unfair. The movie, despite its lapses, is sincere and earnest. At the time he made the film, Tarkovsky was ill, and in fact he died on December 29, 1986, a few months after *The Sacrifice*'s release. The movie wrestles with mortality and meaning, just as Tarkovsky may have done in real life. One patch of dialogue seems to sum up human experience: "We live. We have our ups and downs. We hope. We wait for something."

That God's granting of Alexander's oath to renounce all his loves requires him to sleep with his maid Marta is, to say the least, odd. Perhaps Marta is looked at as an innocent of sorts, a guileless mediator between God and Man (in this case, Alexander). Of course, the movie is European, so sex is virtually required to take place somewhere along the way. As a plot device, this floating sexual union appears both outré and tasteless, even if it is intended to be metaphoric.

When Alexander awakens and the power is on, this recalls to some extent James Stewart getting to live his life again in 1946's *It's a Wonderful Life*. Only in Alexander's case, he destroys everything in his life—his house, his relationship with his family, his sanity. This is disturbing, implying that God requires Alexander not just to sacrifice himself but loved ones as well. This sounds a lot like the Old Testament God, and of course, the religious allusions in *The Sacrifice*, save for the witch, are Christian in nature.

The film also stands foursquare against technology. In an early monologue, Alexander says, "As soon as we make a scientific breakthrough, we put it to use in the service of evil." This may be a popular view, but the truth is more complex. In and of itself, technology is, like the laws of nature, neither good nor evil. We can use it to do terrible things, such as employ nuclear weapons, or we can use it to do helpful things, such as provide life-saving cures for infants.

The nuclear war hints in *The Sacrifice* are few, but potent. The low-flying jets roaring over the house set glasses rattling, an intrusion of the new normal into the old normal.

The Sacrifice has a dreamlike quality. Perhaps the episode with the witch was all a dream. After all, we see Alexander fall asleep on the couch, and when he wakes up (after his tryst with the witch), all signs of an oncoming World War III have vanished. So perhaps only the pre-dream and post-dream segments "really" happened.

As for this day being Alexander's birthday, perhaps his carrying out his end of the bargain with God—his house burning and relationship severing—serves as a "new birth" for him. His sacrifice has assured that all (except his closest relations) can live just as they did before the intrusion of World War III. And yes, despite my misgivings, I appear to be doing art film analysis.

The film received highly positive critiques. Rotten Tomatoes gives it an 86 percent fresh rating based on 42 professional reviews. The film is rated PG for adult content and brief nudity.

While not everyone's cup of nuclear war angst, *The Sacrifice* has something to say.

*　*　*

A State of Emergency

PRODUCER-DIRECTOR: Richard C. Bennett; WRITERS: Ray Cunneff, Tom Guggino; MUSIC: Georges Garvarentz; CINEMATOGRAPHER: Willy Kurant; EDITOR: Catherine Kelber.
CAST: Martin Sheen (Alex Carmody); Fionnula Flanagan (Dianne Carmody); Tim Pigott-Smith (Father Joe Ryan); Ken Parrish (Peter Firth).
PRODUCTION: EsTar Productions; 1986; 95 minutes; rated PG.

*　*　*

In 1917, did the Virgin Mary predict a nuclear chain reaction might destroy the Earth? In 1986's *A State of Emergency*, the answer is "Yes." But despite the film's sincerity, the storyline is too contrived to convince.

Nuclear physicist Alex Carmody and his team conduct a nuclear testing experiment that results in an apparent anomaly. His colleague Ken Parrish cites this experiment in public and says, "There is a possibility that a single missile or bomb could set into motion an unlimited chain reaction that would in effect ignite the atmosphere." Unhappy with Parrish, Alex's superiors discipline him. But they let Alex repeat the experiment. The results are frightening, indicating that an explosion at the right temperature could indeed produce a chain reaction. Alex's boss confiscates the results, declares the project top secret and bars Alex from further experimentation.

Taking a leave of absence, Alex tells his worried wife Dianne and a sympathetic Catholic priest that during the experiment, he saw the Virgin Mary's image. He travels to Fatima to speak to Sister Lucia Santos, who saw a vision of the Virgin Mary in 1917 and, Alex believes, predicted the chain reaction he fears. The Catholic hierarchy won't allow him to speak with her.

Returning home, Alex is given permission to repeat the chain reaction experiment, which goes out of control. The high radiation should have fried Alex, but he survives without injury. He tells a group of international politicians and scientists that if Russia conducts a scheduled atmospheric nuclear test at the Arctic,[14] it could result in a catastrophic chain reaction. The two Russian ambassadors at the meeting exchange written messages with each other indicating the Soviet Union should cancel the test.

Family-friendly, *A State of Emergency* depicts a warm relationship between Alex and his wife and son. Also, the movie champions faith, for though Alex appears to be a lapsed Catholic at the beginning, by movie's end, he is a believer.

In the latter sense, the movie appears to be a religious tract. Alex does his best to speak with Sister Lucia, who as a child in 1917 reportedly heard the Virgin Mary give her a secret that the Catholic Church hasn't revealed; she won't speak with Alex, but relays a message to him to pray for guidance. Later, Alex impossibly survives intense radiation that should have killed him, and he regards this as a miracle. Before addressing an international assembly, he is a practicing Catholic again.

Of course, this movie (or any movie) doesn't show beyond doubt that Roman Catholicism is or isn't real. You can substantiate anything in a fictional script, because you can create incidents and scenarios that favor your viewpoint. Alex's vision of the Virgin Mary, his reignited faith and his surviving lethal radiation exposure don't "prove" Roman Catholicism is true, for these incidents were all invented by the writers. You could just as easily "prove" the opposite by depicting Alex having no visions, no miraculous survival, no reinvigorated faith.

And while the movie does include factual information regarding the 1917 Fatima incident and its aftermath, such as Lucia Santos becoming a Carmelite nun, the notion of the third secret predicting a nuclear chain reaction is sheer speculation. The actual wording of the third secret offers religious symbolism but no apparent direct prophecy, certainly not one of nuclear annihilation by unfettered chain reaction.[15]

Regarding the science behind *A State of Emergency*, I plead ignorance. It sounds plausible in the movie, but perhaps a nuclear physicist might label the film's nuclear assertions pseudo-scientific. In any event, in the almost four decades since the movie was released, a nuclear chain reaction has not destroyed the Earth.

The acting is natural and convincing, the characters believable, and the story plays like a mild nuclear thriller. The score is lush, featuring choral interludes. In addition, the pacing flows smoothly.

A State of Emergency means well, and it is non-offensive, but the storyline is too contrived to be taken at face value.

* * *

Thunder Run

DIRECTOR: Gary Hudson; WRITERS: Charles Davis, Carol Heyer (screenplay); Clifford Wenger, Sr., Carol Lynn (story); MUSIC: Jay Levy, Matthew McCauley; CINEMATOGRAPHER: Harvey Genkins; EDITOR: Burton Lee Harry; PRODUCER: Carol Lynn.

CAST: Forrest Tucker (Charlie Morrison); John Ireland (George Adams); John Shepherd (Chris); Alan Richins (Carlos).

PRODUCTION: Lynn-Davis Productions, Panache Productions; 1986; 86 minutes; rated PG-13.

* * *

Thunder Run marks the last chance to see Hollywood veteran Forrest Tucker in action. Some of you may shrug. But anyone who enjoyed TV's *F Troop* in the 1960s might want to watch.

Thunder Run is a nuclear threat movie in which terrorists plan to steal a plutonium shipment. The government authorizes businessman George Adams to arrange to haul a shipment of plutonium to the Air Force's Neville Test Facility, supposedly to flush out terrorists.

George asks his old army buddy Charlie Morrison to make the haul. Charlie could use the money, so he agrees to take the shipment and buys a new rig outfitted with special defenses. Charlie's teenage grandson Chris stows away aboard. Though initially angry, Charlie accepts Chris' help.

Terrorists try their best to snatch the plutonium shipment, employing gunfire, explosives, a roadblock and small heat-seeking rockets (mounted atop customized VW Beetles no less). Charlie and Chris leave most of these bad guys roasted or otherwise incapacitated, thanks to the rig's unusual defenses (which include side flamethrowers and Molotov cocktails launched from the rear).

Carlos, perhaps the boldest bad guy, roars up in his own semi. Charlie ditches his semi, then from the back of Charlie's cab, Chris drives his yellow pickup (which has the plutonium shipment), and Charlie climbs aboard. With seconds to spare, he and Chris get a code that lets them enter the test facility's tunnel entrance. Meanwhile, Carlos crashes his rig.

George tells the soldiers that Charlie and Chris have clearance, and he gives Charlie the money owed. And then, Charlie asks George why he set them up. Actually, the viewer is wondering that too: What was in it for George? He was the guy in the helicopter orchestrating the attacks on Charlie, but why? Charlie socks George. The FBI then arrests George, and Charlie and Chris take off with the loot.

Thunder Run attempts to combine youth movies and action flicks. It also tosses in a large helping of nuclear threat with the plutonium heist plot. The first half-hour features the usual John Hughes–style PG-13 teenage twaddle, and the last hour settles for Mad Max–ian road mayhem. Predictable? You bet. Dopey? Sure. Worthwhile? That all depends on your movie sensibilities.

As noted earlier, oldtimers might enjoy seeing Forrest Tucker's last film. Tucker had an extensive Hollywood career in both movies and television. When it comes to genre movies, fans probably recall Tucker in *The Abominable Snowman*, *The Cosmic Monster* (aka *The Strange World of Planet X*) and *The Crawling Eye* (aka *The Trollenberg Terror*). On TV's *F Troop* (1965–67), Tucker displayed his comedic abilities, teaming well with co-star Larry Storch. A tireless performer, Tucker worked all the way up to his death on October 25, 1986.[16]

John Ireland, who plays the two-faced villain George, also had a major career in film and television. For 1949's acclaimed *All the King's Men*, he was nominated for Best Supporting Actor. Ireland passed away on March 21, 1992.[17]

*   *   *

When the Wind Blows

DIRECTOR: Jimmy T. Murakami; WRITER: Raymond Briggs, based on his graphic novel; MUSIC: Roger Waters; EDITOR: John Cary; PRODUCER: John Coates.
CAST: Peggy Ashcroft (Hilda Bloggs); John Mills (Jim Bloggs).
PRODUCTION: Meltdown Productions, British Screen, Film Four International, TVC London, Penguin Books; British; released in the U.K. on 24 October 1986; (released in the U.S. on 11 March 1988; 84 minutes; not rated.

* * *

Days after a nuclear attack, a middle-aged woman complains about blood in her stool, and her husband assures her it's hemorrhoids. She also notes lesions on her legs, and he passes them off as varicose veins. This man will do anything to cling to his belief that Emergency Services will arrive at any moment, despite the desolate post-nuke world surrounding him and his wife. These two are the core of the animated British feature *When the Wind Blows*.

Jim (voice of John Mills) and his wife Hilda (voice of Peggy Ashcroft) live in a modest country home. When a radio announcer says that war with the Soviet Union may start in three days, Jim springs into action. Using a government pamphlet on nuclear attack preparation, he employs the house's doors to construct a living room lean-to. He is appalled to hear that his son Ron is ignoring the government's instructions to prepare for the coming war. Ron lives in London, and apparently believes that he and his family will die once the bombs hit.

Jim moves food and other supplies into the lean-to, and tells Hilda that the grocery store had no bread due to "panic buying." But Hilda is far more interested in day-to-day house upkeep than a possible nuclear attack. Meanwhile, Jim paints the windows white, apparently to deflect heat from an atomic blast.

When the radio announces that missiles will strike momentarily, Jim and Hilda take refuge in the lean-to. A nuclear explosion occurs not far away, its shock wave obliterating much of the surrounding rural world, damaging but not entirely destroying Jim and Hilda's home. Hilda frets over the mess, but Jim insists she stay in the lean-to, per the government pamphlet's instructions.

Eventually they get back to their normal routines, with Jim insisting that the

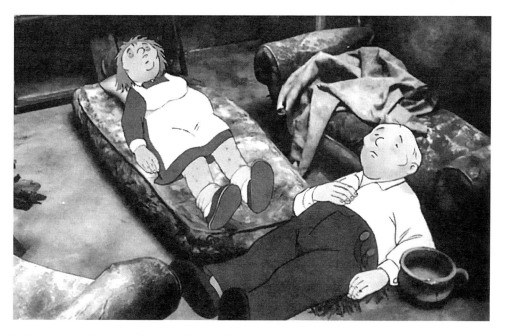

Following a nuclear attack on England, elderly couple Hilda Bloggs (voice of Peggy Ashcroft) and Jim Bloggs (voice of John Mills) succumb to radiation poisoning in the 1986 animated film *When the Wind Blows* (Meltdown Productions).

authorities will arrive soon. He and Hilda express profound ignorance about radiation, believing you can see it, and soon they show symptoms of radiation poisoning. A stroll through the dead gray world outside their home fails to jolt them back into reality.

Hilda displays advanced signs of radiation sickness, including lesions and hair loss. Jim assures her all will be fine. Both become so weak that they retreat to the lean-to. Hilda asks Jim to pray, an activity with which he is clearly unfamiliar. He jumbles together parts of a wedding invocation, Psalm 23 and "The Charge of the Light Brigade." After hearing the word *death*, Hilda says, "No more, love. No more." We don't have to guess Jim and Hilda's fate.

When the Wind Blows uses its premise—an elderly British couple coping with the aftermath of a nuclear attack—to make statements about life, hope, denial and the nuclear threat. The film focuses solely on Jim and Hilda, narrowing its scope from even that of *Testament*'s lone family. The British couple exhibits a muddled view of history and the present. Depending on your viewpoint, their confusion either protects them from the nuclear aftermath's horror or keeps them from dealing with its reality.

While Jim tries to keep up with the news, Hilda's concerns are smaller. Her world revolves around housekeeping and the like, and she ignores the news. Regarding the newspapers Jim reads, she says, "Oh, those things, full of rubbish. I never look at them." We see how far her insularity goes when, after the radio announces missiles will fall in three minutes, she frets that her cake will burn.

Jim struggles to keep informed, though his knowledge of science and history contains blank spots. Maintaining an unfailing faith in the government, he takes the official pamphlet "Protect and Survive" as gospel. His philosophy can be summed up in one of his statements: "We must look on the bright side." This maxim locks him into a level of denial deeper than the Marianas Trench.

For example, after the nuclear blast, he maintains that Emergency Services will arrive any minute. When he finds the water and electrical power are off, he reasons that the authorities have curtailed them due to emergency conservation. He likewise dismisses Hilda's (and his) clear radiation poisoning symptoms. Indeed, he probably perishes from his radiation sickness still believing the authorities will momentarily arrive to set everything right.

Regarding the upcoming war, he and Hilda wax nostalgic about World War II when they were children. They recall the shelters, the blackouts and all the rest with relish. As Jim says, "Those were the days." Funny, but I doubt survivors of Germany's concentration camps saw the war the same way.

Jim and Hilda can't (or won't) comprehend that the impending nuclear war will be nothing like World War II. They speak of Russian soldiers invading Britain. The level of death and destruction an all-out nuclear war would wreak dwarfs their imaginations.

Of course, the couple views history through a foggy lens. For example, Hilda talks about Stalin being "a nice chap," unaware that he was responsible for the murders of millions. While she and Jim recall clearly the "Big Three" from World War II—Churchill, Stalin and Roosevelt—they can't recall the current political leaders.

At the half-hour point, the film's nuclear blast scene excels. The shock wave flips cars, lifts a sheep, derails a train, obliterates the town—and finally, reaches Jim and Hilda's home. This was more imaginative than had the movie shown us the usual mushroom cloud billowing over a major city.

The film likewise features a wonderful lyrical sequence just before the blast hits the couple's home. A wedding picture hangs on a wall, and we witness Jim and Hilda wed and cavort as young people—until the shock wave hits, shattering the picture just as it has shattered their world.

Given its grim bent, the film unexpectedly manifests a wry humor at times. About the imminent attack, Jim says, "It'll all be over in a flash." After he and Hilda have unknowingly ingested radioactive rainwater, he posits that Emergency Services will soon arrive with an antidote to make them "right as rain." And in the wake of the nuke aftermath, Jim remarks that a local merchant would rather be dead (as he almost certainly is) than not show up at his store.

David Bowie provided the title song, and Roger Waters of Pink Floyd wrote the score. The soundtrack includes several 1980s music artists, including Genesis, Paul Hardcastle, Squeeze and Hugh Cornwell.

Critically, *Where the Wind Blows* rates 88 percent fresh on Rotten Tomatoes on both its tomatometer (professional reviewers' critiques) and audience scores. Vincent Canby (*The New York Times*) wrote, "James and Hilda Bloggs are a most unlikely hero and heroine, and *When the Wind Blows* is a most unlikely entertainment. Here is an animated film (with live-action inserts) about the end of civilization."[18] More recently, Mick Martin and Marsha Porter wrote, "[The couple's] ignorance of the facts and innocent faith in the 'powers that be' make this a touching and moving statement about the nuclear Armageddon."[19]

Baby boomers and Gen Zers are apt to recognize older relatives (parents, grandparents, uncles, aunts) in the characters of Jim and Hilda. Despite their shortcomings and Hilda's hint of racism, the couple means well.

Jim and Hilda's incessant nostalgia about World War II and the old days may puzzle some viewers. After all, no one born from the '60s on pines for the Vietnam Conflict or the Afghanistan War or sentimentalizes them. Yet Jim and Hilda's denial is just as relevant today as it was in the '80s. As I write this, international events have revived the specter of nuclear war, but few seem to actually fear it. Of course, maybe, like Jim, they are just looking on the bright side.

CHAPTER NINE

*   *   *

1987

Amazing Grace and Chuck

DIRECTOR: Mike Newell; WRITER: David Field; MUSIC: Elmer Bernstein; CINEMA-
TOGRAPHER: Robert Elswit; EDITOR: Peter Hollywood; PRODUCER: Roger M.
Rothstein.

CAST: William Petersen (Russell); Jamie Lee Curtis (Lynn Taylor); Joshua Zuehlke
(Chuck Murdock); Alex English (Amazing Grace Smith); Gregory Peck (President);
Lee Richardson (Mr. Jeffries).

PRODUCTION: Rastar Pictures, Delphi IV Production, ML Delphi Premier Productions, Turnstar Pictures; 1987; 114 minutes; rated PG.

* * *

A Little League baseball player wields so much power that the president of the
United States seeks his help. No, this isn't a kid superhero premise, but rather 1987's
Amazing Grace and Chuck, a mostly forgotten nuke film.

In Montana, star Little League pitcher Chuck Murdock regularly strikes them out.
He and his class visit a Minuteman III missile silo, a field trip that opens Chuck's eyes
to the terror of nuclear weapons. At the next Little League game, Chuck refuses to pitch,
saying, "I can't play because of nuclear weapons."

Amazing Grace Smith, a pro basketball player, reads Chuck's story and resigns
from the NBA. Soon a wave of professional athletes joins Chuck and Smith, refusing
to play while nuclear weapons exist. For the good of Soviet-American negotiations, the
president beseeches Chuck to abandon his crusade, but Chuck refuses.

When his friend Smith dies in a plane explosion, Chuck chooses to become mute,
his silence inspiring children worldwide to stop talking. The president tells Chuck the
Americans and Soviets have agreed to 15 percent reduction of nuclear weapons over
seven years. This seems too tentative to Chuck. In the end, the president and the Soviet
Union's General Secretary negotiate a deal for total nuclear disarmament, which Chuck
accepts. As Amazing Grace Smith had said earlier in the film, "Wouldn't it be nice."

This movie evokes the cinema of filmmaker Frank Capra, who specialized in sentimental films championing the "little guy." One key example is 1946's *It's a Wonderful Life*,
but his film classics also include 1936's *Mr. Deeds Goes to Town* and 1939's *Mr. Smith Goes
to Washington*. Naysayers often derided Capra's work as "Capracorn," a term Capra fans
consider a compliment, and *Amazing Grace and Chuck* is Capracorn for the nuclear age.

All the elements are on hand: thick-sliced Americana, family values (note grace
said at the dinner table), one man (in this case child) bucking the odds, a villain out

to stop Chuck's crusade, a final victory for human decency. *Amazing Grace and Chuck* could have stayed family-lite, but like Capracorn at its best, instead chooses to include dark elements, such as angry town residents harassing Chuck and his family and major industrialist Mr. Jeffries engineering Amazing Grace Smith's death.

Could this have happened in real life? With apologies to glass-half-full enthusiasts, no. The notion that a Little Leaguer could start a movement resulting in Russia and America's nuclear disarmament has more holes in it than a prairie dog town. Even if it could have happened, the script ignores some of the premise's unpleasant shortcomings.

For example, early on, one of the football players who's signed with Chuck will be living in the "protest" barn in Montana. But what about his responsibility to his wife and kids who live in another state? Also, on TV at one point, we hear that pro sports are dead in America. What about all the "little people" this would hurt? The vendors, ticket sellers, restaurant workers, hotel employees and many others who would be unemployed?

On the other hand, as a parable, the film works. The movie even opens with the on-screen words "Once upon a time there was a boy...."

The finale delivers sweeping nuclear disarmament for America and Russia. Okay, but what about China? It has nukes. What about India? Pakistan? And in today's world, we'd have to add North Korea. And check out the final scenes at the Little League baseball game when the president and Soviet general secretary are sitting beside each other. Possible in a fairy tale, but not reality.

The performances shine. Joshua Zuehlke convinces as Chuck. Jamie Lee Curtis gives an excellent (albeit brief) performance as Amazing Grace Smith's agent, and there's a touching moment between her and Smith. Gregory Peck likewise excels as the

Star Little League pitcher Chuck Murdock (Joshua Zuehlke) says he can no longer pitch because of nuclear weapons. His protest starts a nationwide trend among professional athletes in 1987's *Amazing Grace and Chuck* (Rastar Pictures).

president. In 1959, Peck starred in the nuclear threat movie *On the Beach*, which many at the time considered a shattering look at humankind's final days following a nuclear war.[1]

Critical reaction to *Amazing Grace and Chuck* varied. *The New York Times'* Janet Maslin called its story "preposterous. The screenplay ... starts with a simple premise and winds up spiraling away more crazily than the wildest science fiction."[2]

But the *Los Angeles Times'* Charles Champlin said,

[T]he best of *Amazing Grace and Chuck* is first-rate, and this includes a very strong and characterful portrait of a good, gentle, tough-minded President by Peck, an easy and ingratiating performance by Alex English [as Amazing Grace], strong and emotional moments by Curtis as the athlete's agent, and some quietly intense work by William Petersen as Chuck's confused father.[3]

Upon this film's 1987 release, I rolled my eyes. It sounded like one of the most ridiculous scenarios I'd ever heard. But when I viewed it recently, I did find it often heavy-handed, but I also discovered its virtues. Though flawed, *Amazing Grace and Chuck* attempts to approach the nuclear anxiety of the '80s from a fresh perspective. And fresh Capracorn always beats stale cynicism.

*   *   *

Creepozoids

DIRECTOR: David DeCoteau; WRITERS: David DeCoteau, Buford Hauser; MUSIC: Guy Moon; CINEMATOGRAPHER: Thomas Callaway; EDITOR: Miriam L. Preissel; PRODUCERS: David DeCoteau, John Schouweiler.
CAST: Linnea Quigley (Bianca); Ken Abraham (Butch); Michael Aranda (Jesse); Richard S. Hawkins (Jake); Ashlyn Gere (Kate).
PRODUCTION: Full Moon, Empire Pictures, Beyond Infinity, Titan Productions. Released 1987; 72 minutes; rated R.

*   *   *

With no sense of shame, *Creepozoids* steals from both 1979's *Alien* and 1974's *It's Alive*. The film tosses in a post-nuke milieu, giving audiences another 1980s bargain basement chiller.

In 1992, World War III scorched the world into a barren wasteland. Six years later, small, roving bands struggle to survive. A group of five unfortunates—Jake, Jesse, Kate, Butch and Bianca—enter what appears to be an abandoned warehouse and decide to stay.

Jesse finds out from the bunker's computers that the former tenants engaged in dangerous genetic research—obviously bad news. Next, an Alienesque monster assaults Jesse. But soon we see him sitting at the dinner table with his four friends. So the monster didn't kill him. What's up? Almost everybody's lunch when Jesse morphs into a disgusting mutant and dies in a welter of gunk.

Kate gets on the computer and discovers that their presumed shelter was intended to be "a containment vessel." The former occupants' research discovered a way for the human body to manufacture its own amino acids, hence ridding humans of the need for food. Because Jesse was eating, his body experienced an overload of amino acid production which caused his death. Yet the monster that assaulted him is still around.

Bianca blunders into a hanging skeleton and screams. Also, a giant rat—a prop so stiff, it appears to suffer from premature rigor mortis—attacks and bites Butch. As only team leaders can, Jake wastes the mutant rodent. Jake decides that he and Butch will embark on a search-and-destroy mission while the women stay behind (shades of 1950s gender politics). The monster nabs Butch. In the waiting room, Kate and Bianca fret. Bianca reveals her fear of rats, and right on cue, a *second* rat shows up and attacks her. The rodent injures Kate, and Jake tends to her.

The monster sprays Butch with black ick, and he transmutes into a grotesque hurling mutant and dies like Jesse. The movie's Main Monster attacks again, and Jake fires his ray gun at it, to no avail. Meanwhile, Bianca discovers that Kate has turned into a snarling, zombie-like mutant (apparently from the rat's bite). In self-defense, Bianca kills Kate. The Main Monster in turn kills Bianca and engages Jake in a violent battle. After Jake stabs it with a hypo, the creature gives birth to a horrific baby, the spitting (or should that be puking?) image of Rick Baker's prosthetic newborn from 1974's *It's Alive*. After the expected struggle, Jake dispatches the terrible tyke. But a final shot reveals that the tot still lives.

If not for its 1980s R-rated touches such as brief nudity, sex, language and graphic violence, *Creepozoids* would resemble a 1950s Grade-B sci-fier. The film's stiff rat prop cheerfully calls to mind the puppet monster head from 1959's *The Killer Shrews*, and of course, that's all to the good. As for the brief nudity and shower sex, "gratuitous" is overused, so I'll go with "tasteless." The graphic violence gives us the usual. The special effects succeed most of the time. However, poor lighting gives the monster baby away, and the searching closeups don't help.

The characters live up (or down) to their respective stereotypes. For example, at the beginning, the quintet of survivors has just entered the large building. Anyone—or anything—could be in there. So Butch helpfully calls out, "Hello! Anybody home?" Obviously, he is not Rhodes scholar material.

Creepozoids reveals that the five protagonists deserted the Army. You wonder when this happened. World War III occurred six years earlier. Did the protagonists know missiles had been launched and thus flee their military posts? Or did they engage in combat with foreign soldiers? The movie doesn't tell.

Reviews are mostly unkind. John Stanley gave the movie one and a half stars out of four and wrote, "The effects are really bad, the rat and the monster obviously puppets pushed around by hand."[4]

Due to its excesses and microscopic budget, many may find *Creepozoids* off-putting. But at its best, it recalls the spirit of 1950s sci-fi monster movies, and that can't be all bad.

* * *

Death Run

DIRECTOR-WRITER-PRODUCER: Michael J. Murphy; MUSIC: Graham Hunt, Philip Love, Urbreaker & Cature.

CAST: Rob Bartlett (Paul Saunders); Debbi Stevens (Barbara); Eddie Kirby (Hero); Patrick Olliver (Messiah); Wendy Parsons (Jenny).

PRODUCTION: Murlin Films; British; 1987; 70 minutes; not rated. Alternate title: *Mutant City*.

* * *

Death Run's typical post-nuke milieu offers no surprises, and the filmmakers appear to be on autopilot. It's a run-of-the-mill film.

When nuclear war breaks out, a scientist places her adult son Paul and his girlfriend Jenny into suspended animation. A quarter of a century later, a power shortage causes them to awaken. Alas, they discover that post-nuke society teems with surly bikers, monstrous mutants and badly dressed women. The bikers jail Paul and toss Jenny into the Messiah's harem, where she becomes an unwilling concubine. The Messiah is a cultivated British type who talks like a James Bond villain, listens to scratchy vinyl records and incessantly complains about his boredom. He also forces prisoners to participate in what is called the "Death Run," a fate awaiting Paul.

Barbara helps Paul and Jenny escape. A mutant kills and feasts on Jenny. Along comes Hero, the only man ever to have survived the Death Run, and he trains Paul to ace the coming ordeal. Paul does complete the Death Run, and he and Hero dispatch the Messiah's cronies. The Messiah's concubines, clutching knives, stab him repeatedly, and Paul delivers the *coup de grâce*.

Amazingly, Paul experiences a character arc: At first, he's unable to kill but in the end he's dispatching the bad guys with relish. The film also touches on his grief following Jenny's death, a sincere attempt at pathos. But for the most part, the movie employs the standard low-budget post-nuke basics, its direction, script and performances all perfunctory.

The film tries to make the mutants look disgusting, but their appliances and "breathing" bladders are fairly obvious. After all the build-up, the Death Run itself disappoints. It's just a guy handcuffed to an electrified wire while dispatching strategically placed mutants.

The unrated *Death Run* would probably receive a PG-13 for adult content, brief nudity, violence and language.

* * *

Equalizer 2000

DIRECTOR: Cirio H. Santiago; WRITERS: Frederick Bailey (screenplay); Frederick Bailey, Joe Mari Avellana (story); MUSIC: Edward Achaoso; CINEMATOGRAPHER: Johnny Araojo; EDITOR: Pacifico Sanchez, Jr.; PRODUCER: Leonard Hermes.
CAST: Richard Norton (Slade); Corinne Wahl (Karen); William Steis (Lawton).
PRODUCTION: Premiere Productions; released directly to U.S. video on 19 May 1987; 85 minutes; rated R.

* * *

One of *Equalizer 2000*'s taglines is, "A weapon without limits." However, the movie featuring this armament revels in limits, careful to keep within its post-nuke action cliché boundaries.

A hundred years after a nuclear war, Alaska has become a desert. The Ownership hoards oil resources and rules North Alaska, though rebels in the region challenge them.

Slade once fought for the Ownership, but due to its ruthlessness, he struck out on his own. A group of marauders catch him, but he escapes and, later, comes to the aid of Karen. He's injured, and she takes him to an outsider compound to treat him. Slade marvels over the Equalizer 2000, a multi-purpose weapon.

A group of Ownership commandos encounter the Mountain People, who fight their battles using bows and arrows. The Mountain People overcome the soldiers, and their leader sends one Ownership commando back with the message to leave the Mountain People alone. The Ownership's villainous Lawton chooses not to shoot the messenger; instead, he has him fried with a flamethrower.

Lawton wants Slade and the Equalizer 2000. Naturally, a major battle erupts between the Ownership and the rebels. Overwhelmed, the rebels retreat. Lawton gets his hands on the Equalizer 2000 as well as Karen. But Slade rescues her and returns her to the rebels.

Another major battle ensues, but this time the Mountain People join the rebels in fighting the Ownership. During the fracas, Lawton kills Karen. Slade attacks and kills Lawton. The rebels and the Mountain People win their battle.

In one of the final scenes, Slade dashes the Equalizer 2000 against a rockface, inspiring some of the Mountain People and rebels to toss their weapons into a fire. Presumably, this ending was supposed to be a statement about war's futility.

Another lesson the movie teaches is that if you're a bad guy like Lawton in a post-nuke world, you will appear unkempt (note his scraggly beard) and spindly. But if you're a good guy like Slade, you will appear well-groomed (note his neatly trimmed beard) and strapping.

The central notion that the Equalizer 2000 is some kind of ultimate armament fails to convince. Yes, it's a tweaked assault weapon, but not much deadlier than conventional war arms. Speaking of conventional, the movie is a typical post-nuke action adventure in every way. Its director, the prolific Cirio H. Santiago, was no novice in the post-nuke genre, having already churned out 1983's *Stryker* and 1985's *Wheels of Fire*. His directorial approach appears to be all commerce and fleeting (if any) art. Basically, if a movie met its exploitation movie goals, regardless of quality, Santiago seemed to be satisfied, which is the case with *Equalizer 2000*.

Still, to its credit, the movie doesn't litter the post-nuke

The DVD packaging for 1987's *Equalizer 2000* (Premiere Productions) depicts hero Slade (Richard Norton) holding the titular weapon with Karen (Corinne Wahl) posed behind him. Note "Roger Corman's Post Nuke Collection" banner at top.

landscape with zombies or mutants. It tries to stay within the margins of the possible, albeit in Grade-B action movie terms. Or maybe the filmmakers simply couldn't afford the makeup for zombies or mutants.

*   *   *

The Fourth Protocol

DIRECTOR: John Mackenzie; WRITERS: Frederick Forsyth (screenplay); George Axelrod (story); based on Forsyth's novel *The Fourth Protocol*; MUSIC: Lalo Schifrin; CINEMATOGRAPHER: Phil Meheux; EDITOR: Graham Walker; PRODUCER: Timothy Burrill.

CAST: Michael Caine (John Preston); Pierce Brosnan (Major Valeri Alekseyevich Petrofsky); Ned Beatty (General Pavel Petrovich Borisov); Joanna Cassidy (Irina Vassilievna).

PRODUCTION: Fourth Protocol, Rank Organisation; British; released in the U.K. on 19 March 1987; released in the U.S. on 28 August 1987; 119 minutes; rated R.

*   *   *

Having embarrassed the acting head of Britain's MI5, agent John Preston is assigned to cover airports and seaports. He discovers that an accidentally killed Russian seaman had in his effects a polonium disk, which serves as a detonator for an atomic bomb. The ailing MI5 director Sir Hemmings and his MI5 associate Sir Irvine tell Preston to investigate.

Top Russian KGB agent Major Petrofsky settles into a U.K. residence near an American Air Force base. He plans to help build a 1.5-kiloton atomic bomb, making its explosion appear to be America's fault. This will strain relations between the U.K. and the U.S. and bolster the anti-nuke movement in England, all to Russia's advantage.

KGB agent Irina Vassilievna joins Petrofsky in the role of his wife and oversees the A-bomb construction; she estimates it will kill from 2000 to 5000 people. Though the bomb has been set to detonate two hours after its button is pushed, unbeknownst to Petrofsky, Irina changes the setting to zero, meaning that the bomb will explode the moment he activates it. Petrofsky sleeps with Irina and then, per orders, kills her.

Preston and fellow British agents track Petrofsky down and move in on him. The Soviet agent plans to trigger the A-bomb and flee, but he checks and sees the timer has been set at zero. Preston subdues Petrofsky, but one of the other U.K. operatives shoots and kills the KGB agent, and tells Preston that he was ordered to do so.

In a bitter denouement, Preston discovers that Soviet General Karpov and the MI5's Sir Irvine, whom Preston thought was an ally, schemed to make sure that Preston and his men would find and stop Petrofsky. This resolution works to further the careers of both Karpov and Irvine.

The Fourth Protocol hits all the right Cold War buttons. The presentation bristles with old-fashioned spy movie ambience. For example, in the scenes with only Russians, they all speak English when, amongst themselves, they should be speaking Russian.

Fourth Protocol's acting rates high on the thespian proficiency scale. Pierce Brosnan scores as the merciless KGB agent with a cadaver-cold soul. As always, Michel Caine gives a masterful performance. He breathes life into all the facets of John Preston, from arrogant smart-aleck to expert operative to widowed dad. Preston's scenes as doting father to his young son get him audience sympathy. The Christmas scene—the fireplace burning, dad and son relaxed on the couch, the Christmas tree aglow in the background—is pure Norman Rockwell.

Far from James Bond, *Fourth Protocol* attempts to keep its spies grounded. We see underhanded politics at work in the U.K. secret service. Among the Russians, things are even worse. And while the movie seems to champion democracy over Communism, the ethical line between the agents of both systems blurs. Still, you can't imagine Michael Caine nuking Russian civilians.

Not everything in the film works. For example, Preston stumbles upon Petrofsky's scheme because his boss has demoted him to monitoring ports, a coincidence that feels contrived. Petrofsky has minor involvement with an obnoxious American airman and the man's wife; the latter wants to sleep with Petrofsky. But this subplot goes nowhere and could have been axed, though perhaps its purpose is to show that Petroksfy's dedication won't allow him to compromise his mission for sex.

The A-bomb plot was a common device for movies and novels in the 1970s and 1980s. Here, atomic terrorism appears frighteningly simple. However, it's notable that in real life, the West has never suffered an act of nuclear terrorism, so perhaps it is more difficult to pull off than *Fourth Protocol* presumes. Of course, the film also has the A-bomb plan thwarted, perhaps suggesting that real-life attempts have always been foiled.

The movie is rated R for language, adult content, brief nudity and violence.

Reviews for *The Fourth Protocol* are generally positive. Roger Ebert wrote that the movie "is first-rate because it not only is a thriller, but it also pays attention to its characters and shows how their actions grow out of their personalities."[5] For Allentown's *Morning Call*, Paul Willistein called the movie "a showcase for Michael Caine…. Director John Mackenzie (*The Long Good Friday*) pulls out all the stops to make *Fourth Protocol* an action-packed, as well as psychological, thriller."[6]

The Fourth Protocol is the only movie in which two acclaimed actors who played Bruce Wayne's butler Alfred appear together. They are Michael Gough, Alfred in the Tim Burton–directed *Batman* (1989) and *Batman Returns* (1992), and Michael Caine, Alfred in Christopher Nolan's *Dark Knight* trilogy.

* * *

Interzone

DIRECTOR: Deran Sarafian; WRITERS: Clyde Anderson, Deran Sarafian; MUSIC: Stefano Mainetti; CINEMATOGRAPHER: Gianlorenzo Battaglia; EDITOR: Kathleen Stratton; PRODUCER: David Hills.

CAST: Bruce Abbott (Swan); Beatrice Ring (Tera); Teagan Clive (Mantis); Kiro Wehara (Panasonic); John Armstead (Balzakan).

PRODUCTION: Filmirage; Italian; 1987; 97 minutes; rated R.

* * *

Interzone is standard post-apocalyptic fare from the land of the Roman Coliseum.

Swan, one of those typical post-nuke wanderers, blunders into unexpected adventure when he meets Panasonic, a mind-reading priest who recruits Swan to protect the Interzone's treasure. The Interzone itself is, as Swan tells us, a "300-square-mile area of radioactive-free land." The villainous Mantis, her consort Balzakn and their raiders covet the treasure, but priests generate a force field that keeps them out—that is, until the villains discover a weakness in the barrier.

Though Panasonic unexpectedly dies by absorbing Swan's lethal injuries, Swan not only keeps Mantis from nabbing the treasure but gets to see it: a collection of sculptures, art, books and a video message left by one of the last humans alive as the world was consumed in a nuclear war.

The film suffers from several technical problems. The worst is the muddied sound. The swelling background music sometimes renders the dialogue unintelligible. There's also padding to spare, including an irrelevant opening scene in a post-nuke tavern. Action of course rules the day, some of it okay, some of it awful. The acting varies, from Teagan Clive's hammy Mantis to Bruce Abbott's tongue-in-cheek Swan. The film has a good music score.

Having priests serve as the treasure's guardians is a nice touch, though perhaps not surprising considering Italy's proximity to the Vatican.

Interzone is rated R for adult content, nudity and violence.

* * *

Mr. India

DIRECTOR: Shekhar Kapur; WRITERS: Salim Khan and Javed Akhtar; MUSIC: Laxmikant Pyarelal; LYRICS: Javed Akhtar; CINEMATOGRAPHER: Baba Azmi; EDITORS: Waman Bhonsle, Gurudutt Shirali; PRODUCER: Boney Kapoor.
CAST: Anil Kapoor (Arun Verma); Sridevi (Seema Sohni); Annu Kapoor (Mr. Gaitonde); Amrish Puri (Mogambo).
PRODUCTION: Narsimha Enterprises; India; 1987; 179 minutes; not rated.

* * *

In the made-in-India *Mr. India*,[7] the link to nuclear peril movies is the villain's threat to blast India with four ICBMs. Bollywood is the nickname of India's movie industry, and *Mr. India* spotlights Bollywood conventions such as frequent singing and dancing as well as colorful clothes and backgrounds. For many Westerners, *Mr. India* requires some cultural adjustment.

The temptation is to diss the melodramatic plotting, broad slapstick and generous blending of different genres and tones. As *Shock Cinema* reported in 1998, "[T]he story is awash in plot twists so heartwarming that you'll want to puke; but there are also so many lovably asinine moments that it's difficult not to enjoy (particularly with the aid of a Fast Forward button)."[8]

Mogambo is an evil criminal genius out to subjugate India. He schemes from an island headquarters where he demands absolute obedience from his henchmen, such as casually ordering three of them to yell "Hail Mogambo!" then jump into a flesh-dissolving acid vat. (Obviously, Mogambo's staffers need a union.)

Meanwhile, Arun Verma is a humble violinist struggling to feed and clothe ten orphans. To help purchase groceries, he rents his house's top room to journalist Seema Sohni. He soon comes into possession of his late father's invisibility wrist band, with which he can become transparent.

When bad guys threaten Seema, Arun turns invisible and punches them out, announcing he is Mr. India. But he keeps his real (visible) identity secret. A national superhero, Mr. India develops an appreciative following as he champions the cause of ordinary Indians.

This doesn't sit well with Mogambo, who disguises bombs and plants them all over India. Young Tina, one of Arun's orphans, picks up a bomb disguised as a toy; it explodes and she is killed. Mogambo's men nab Arun, Seema and the orphans, and the villain demands the secret of invisibility, not realizing that Arun is actually Mr. India. After a flurry of action—some silly, some serious—Arun takes on Mogambo one on one. The villain has vowed to use four ICBMs to turn India into a nuclear wasteland. Will Arun–Mr. India win in the end?

In its home country, *Mr. India* is highly esteemed. According to *Eastern Eye*, the film "has been named in pretty much every 100 greatest Bollywood film list published in the last few decades."[9] When talk of a sequel emerged, the original film's assistant director argued against it.[10]

On first viewing, I found the movie's first hour okay and the second hour difficult given its surfeit of slapstick. But the third hour rounds out the film to a satisfying conclusion. For example, orphan Tina's hospitalization and subsequent death evoke pathos. And bad guy Mogambo gets the beating every viewer knows he deserves. I find the film somewhat endearing, not unlike an old stuffed toy. Plus, I realize if I had grown up in Indian culture, I would no doubt appreciate those aspects of the film I find too broad.

Perhaps *Mr. India*'s most entertaining aspect is Amrish Puri's flamboyant portrayal of Mogambo. From his malevolent smile to his delight at hearing his minions salute him, he bats James Bond's Blofeld out of the bad guy park. For Indians, a famous film quote is *Mr. India*'s evil megalomaniac purring *"Mogambo khush hua"* (meaning "Mogambo is pleased").[11]

As Mr. India, Anil Kooper seems not only to be invisible but also super-strong. Plus, as a meek violinist, where did he learn the hand-to-hand combat with which he wastes the bad guys? His voice is amplified when he is transparent. But these are minor issues in a movie that frequently and cheerfully violates reality (such as having one of the orphans, probably all of eight years old, punch out a couple of adult bad guys).

One of the song-and-dance numbers briefly shows Indians in blackface. Apparently, this wasn't considered wrong in India in 1987, but it is of course offensive. Different movie cultures learn more slowly than others.

Mr. India was intended as a family-friendly film. Apparently it is legendary in India, not unlike *Superman* in the West. But it appears that Mr. India's debut was also his swan song.

* * *

Plutonium Baby

PRODUCER-DIRECTOR: Ray Hirschman; WRITER: Wayne Behar; MUSIC: Mark Knox; CINEMATOGRAPHER: Peter Clark; EDITORS: Briton J. Petrucelly, Keith Reamer.

CAST: Patrick Molloy (Dr. Drake); Danny Guerra (Young Danny); Ciaran Sheehan (Adult Danny); Marion Crane (Emily).

PRODUCTION: PB, Troma Team; 1987; 85 minutes; not rated. Alternate title: *The Mutant Kid*.

* * *

Can a mad scientist trapped in a radioactive steel drum for ten years without food or water survive? If you answered no, count yourself lucky; that means you've never seen low-grade horror drivel like *Plutonium Baby*.

Dr. Drake experimented on Emily with radiation, and she gave birth to a mutant child. To silence her, Drake had her sealed in a radioactive steel drum. Twelve years later, her mutant son Danny frees her. She goes on a rampage, finds Dr. Drake, and stuffs him in the drum.

Ten years later, two teenage morons open the drum—and out pops Dr. Drake sporting unimpressive radiation monster makeup. He seeks revenge against Danny while the audience would probably like to seek revenge against the filmmakers.

Plutonium Baby is sick, zero-budget tripe, badly written and staged. For example, as a radiation monster, Emily savages her victims, disemboweling one of them. There are also several exploitative sex scenes, all needless. The dumb, predictable ending doesn't help, but it does signal the movie is mercifully over. By the way, despite the title, you never see Danny as an infant.

The performances? Let's just say the cast tried.

Unrated, *Plutonium Baby* would obviously merit an R for language, sex, adult content and graphic violence.

*   *   *

Robot Holocaust

WRITER-DIRECTOR: Tim Kincaid. CINEMATOGRAPHER: Arthur D. Marks; EDI-
  TOR: Barry Zetlin; PRODUCERS: Charles Band, Cynthia DePaula.
CAST: Norris Culf (Neo); Nadine Hart (Deeja); Michael Downend (Jorn); Valeria (Ange-
  lika Jager).
PRODUCTION: Taryn Productions; Italian-U.S.; 1987; 79 minutes; not rated.

*   *   *

For once, it's not a nuke war, but rather a future revolt of robots that has destroyed society and released massive amounts of radiation. However, that's about as far as this movie's ingenuity travels.

Neo, one of those patented wasteland loners, happens upon human slaves being forced to work for someone (or some*thing*) called the Dark One. Jorn, the creator of a device that can counteract the Dark One's atmosphere weapon, has been kidnapped and taken to the evildoer's Power Plant. There, the villainous Valeria tortures Jorn, but he won't talk.

Neo and his robot sidekick join Deeja and several others to rescue Jorn. They encounter various menaces, including vicious fanged hand puppets popping out of wall holes. However, the Dark One has forced Jorn to merge with him—the film's one macabre scene—so Neo shoots and kills the hybrid being.

Robot Holocaust is a good example of poor technique in almost all departments. Some of the staged swordfighting transcends the word "unconvincing." The various obstacles likewise tilt to below zero on the Plausibility Meter. The pacing often drags, and the production values seem to be on loan from a thrift shop. However, there is one nice matte painting, and the scene in which the Dark One absorbs Jorn is effectively grisly.

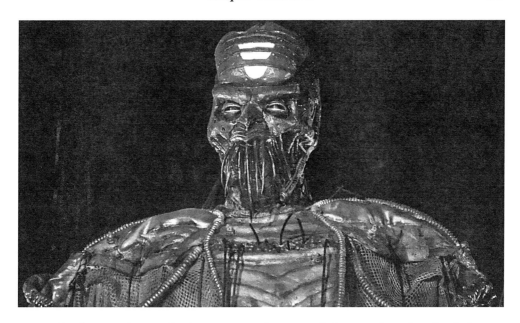

Torque (Rick Gianasi), an evil robot, menaces the post-nuke heroes of 1987's *Robot Holocaust* (Taryn Productions).

Unrated, this film would likely receive an R for adult content, brief nudity and graphic violence.

Mystery Science Theater 3000's *Robot Holocaust* send-up was enjoyed by fans of the series, and that should tell you everything you need to know.

* * *

Steel Dawn

DIRECTOR: Lance Hool; WRITER: Doug Lefler; MUSIC: Brian May; CINEMATOG-RAPHER: George Tirl; EDITOR: Mark Conte; PRODUCERS: Lance Hool, Conrad Hool.

CAST: Patrick Swayze (Nomad); Lisa Niemi (Kasha); Anthony Zerbe (Damnil); Christopher Neame (Sho); Brion James (Tark); Brett Hool (Jux).

PRODUCTION: Vestron Pictures in association with Silver Lion Films; 1987; 100 minutes; rated R. Alternate title: *Desert Warrior*.

* * *

In what kind of Western does a villain hire an assassin to kill a heroic loner, and both the loner and the assassin use swords instead of six-guns? In a post-nuke Western such as *Steel Dawn*.

America has suffered multiple wars, the first of which was nuclear (according to the film's official trailer which states "Out of the ruins of a nuclear war … a legend is born"). Nomad, a former soldier, now wanders the wasteland the U.S. has become. He finds work on a purification farm run by widow Kasha. Her young son Jux also lives there.

Villainous Damnil dominates the farms surrounding the settlement of Meridian. Kasha and Nomad discover that Damnil's men have damaged Kasha's farm equipment.

In turn, Nomad and farm foreman Tark sneak into Damnil's compound and steal a water pump that Kasha's farm needs.

Damnil hires Sho—an assassin who killed Nomad's mentor—to kill Nomad. During a fight in town, Sho slays Tark and injures Nomad. The climax features an epic fight between Sho and Nomad. Naturally, Nomad kills Sho as well as Damnil, and all is once more right with the world. Kasha can now fulfill her dream of building a city. Loner that he is, Nomad leaves to again wander the wastelands.

Sporting a higher budget than most 1980s post-nuke action films, *Steel Dawn* benefits from a slick production gloss. The characters are all "types," but the script's character development works. Brian May's music score is good and the action scenes are fair.

Steel Dawn is derivative not only of post-nuke action films, but also of the traditional Hollywood Western. Certain storyline aspects suggest parallels with 1953's oater classic *Shane*. You have a woman in distress, a boy who idolizes a heroic loner, a hired gun, a fight between the loner and the hired gun (the loner wins) and the boy running after the loner as he leaves at movie's end.[12]

Patrick Swayze convinces as the laconic Nomad, a Man with No Name for the post-apocalyptic genre. Anthony Zerbe as Damnil portrays his usual sneering villain, which he could probably play under deep sedation. The other leads fare okay.

The background story lacks clarity. We hear of plural "wars" and of Nomad and Sho being soldiers, but neither of them (or anyone else) has firearms, instead brandishing swords and knives. We also hear of a "council," of "enforcers," and of "peacemakers," implying an organized government, but how this regime works remains unknown. On the other hand, Kasha clearly speaks of her H_2O source as supplying "uncontaminated water," and presumably contaminated water would be tainted by radiation.

The film's opening teems with "sand people," humanoid mutants (caused by radiation?) who live under the desert and attack anyone who stumbles onto them, such as Nomad, whose encounter results in a memorable action sequence. Later, Nomad's mentor refers to "half-men," presumably the sand people, but they vanish for the rest of the movie.

Thematically, the film ends on a hopeful note, with the expectation that a city will be built and farms will flourish. It also hints that Nomad may return for a *Steel Dawn 2*. The film tanked at the box office, quashing any sequel plans.

In 1987, Swayze also appeared in *Dirty Dancing*, the movie that catapulted him to stardom. After this, he had a stellar Hollywood career, appearing in such diverse films as 1989's *Road House*, 1990's *Ghost* and 1991's *Point Break*. He and fellow *Steel Dawn* star Lisa Niemi were married from 1975 until Swayze's death in 2009 from pancreatic cancer.[13]

Most critics disdain *Steel Dawn*. Mick Martin and Marsha Ported gave it a turkey rating: "Brainless bore set in the post-apocalyptic future."[14]

Steel Dawn is better than most 1980s post-nuke action films, but far from a classic. Still, Swayze fans and genre enthusiasts might want to check it out.

* * *

Superman IV: The Quest for Peace

DIRECTOR: Sidney J. Furie; WRITERS: Lawrence Konner, Mark Rosenthal (screenplay); Christopher Reeve, Lawrence Konner, Mark Rosenthal (story); MUSIC: John

Williams, adapted and conducted by Alexander Courage; CINEMATOGRAPHER: Ernest Day; EDITOR: John Shirley; PRODUCERS: Menahem Golan, Yoram Globus. CAST: Christopher Reeve (Clark Kent/Superman); Gene Hackman (Lex Luthor [also the voice of Nuclear Man]); Mark Pillow (Nuclear Man); Sam Wanamaker (David Warfield); Jackie Cooper (Perry White); Mariel Hemingway (Lacy Warfield); Jon Cryer (Lenny Luthor); Margot Kidder (Lois Lane); Marc McClure (Jimmy Olsen). PRODUCTION: Cannon Group, Golan-Globus; 1987; 90 minutes; rated PG.

* * *

Some movies are almost universally reviled by critics and audiences alike, and *Superman IV: The Quest for Peace* is one of them. On Rotten Tomatoes, it ranks a mere 10 percent fresh score from professional reviewers, 16 percent from the audience. That said, I confess I like this movie.

A sequel to 1983's *Superman III*, *Superman IV* finds Clark Kent returning to Smallville where his parents' farm is up for sale. In the barn, he finds a green energy module from Krypton, and his mother's voice tells him it can be used only once.

Meanwhile, disreputable scandal sheet tycoon David Warfield buys the *Daily Planet*, fires long-time editor Perry White and replaces him with his (Warfield's) daughter Lacy.

Superman, moved by a boy's request that he save the world from nuclear weapons, gathers all nukes into a gigantic net, which he swings into the sun.

Lex Luthor's nephew Lenny Luthor, a real '80s child, has broken Lex out of jail. Realizing that the sudden absence of nukes makes black market atomics a growth industry, Lex joins other reprehensible nuke dealers and steals a strand of Superman's hair from a museum. The nuke with the hair is launched, and like the selfless superhero he

On the moon, Superman (Christopher Reeve, left) faces Nuclear Man (Mark Pillow) in 1987's *Superman IV: The Quest for Peace* (Golan-Globus). The film received strongly negative reviews.

is, Superman hurls it into the sun. This causes the hair to mutate into Nuclear Man, who flies to Earth with one goal: destroy Superman.

Nuclear Man battles Superman from the Great Wall of China to Europe to New York. At one point, Nuclear Man scratches him on the back of the neck. Sickened by the scratch, the Man of Steel goes into hiding. A *Daily Planet* headline suggests that he has died. This proves too much for reporter Lois Lane, who takes Superman's cape (which the hero lost during the battle) and gives it to an ailing Clark Kent. Kent returns to his parents' Smallville farm and employs the one-use-only Krypton energy module to cure his radiation poisoning.

Proving that even supervillains have hormones, Nuclear Man finds himself pining for Lacy. The next Superman–Nuclear Man battle takes them to the moon, where Nuclear Man pounds Superman into the lunar soil. Returning to Earth, Nuclear Man kidnaps Lacy and takes her into outer space. Superman recovers from his moon defeat and pushes the moon in front of the sun, causing a total eclipse. Cut off from his solar energy source, Nuclear Man weakens. Superman flies Lacy to Earth, retrieves the now dormant Nuclear Man and hurls him into a nuclear power plant's core, which destroys him.

Metropolis bankers loan Perry White enough money to give him the controlling interest in *The Daily Planet*. Superman delivers a speech in which he declares he was wrong to attempt to give the world "the gift of freedom from war" by destroying all nuclear weapons. He says, "It's not mine to give." Instead, he indicates that the world will be war-free (and presumably nuke weapons–free) when *the people* pressure their governments into peace.

As a final act, Superman admits Lenny Luthor to Boys Town, and deposits Lex Luthor back on the prison farm.

I've admitted that I like this movie, but I won't argue that it isn't flawed. The budget wasn't sufficient for the scope the movie was attempting, and at a mere 90 minutes, the film seems abbreviated. This is due to budget cutting: It was originally slated to cost $32 million, but the Cannon Group experienced money trouble which made them drop the budget to $17 million.[15] This affected the quality and frequency of the film's special effects, keys to any movie spectacular. A test screening proved troublesome, and director Sidney Furie wound up cutting a half-hour from the film.[16] Star Christopher Reeve disdained the results; in his memoir, he wrote, "*Superman IV* was simply a catastrophe from start to finish."[17]

I don't find it a catastrophe. I think it retains the spirit of 1978's *Superman* and 1981's *Superman II*, if not their spectacle. And it boasts an intriguing premise.

Regarding the familiar cast, seeing the series actors who have played Lois Lane, Perry White, Jimmy Olson and (yes) Clark Kent kindles warm nostalgia. Toward the end, Clark exits after noting he has forgotten his tape recorder. Jimmy quips, "Same old Mr. Kent. He'll never change." Lois replies, "I hope not." A sentiment that could apply to Superman as well.

This was Reeve's last appearance as the Man of Steel. He once again gives it his all, lovable as the deliberately awkward Clark Kent, noble as the one and only Kal-El of Krypton. Still, it's sad that his last Superman movie couldn't have boasted a sky-high budget and a crackerjack script.

Superman IV's theme of Superman choosing to rid the world of nuclear weapons was a timely one. Too often, superheroes of old seemed to ignore major real-world problems, so having Supe confront the nuclear threat front and center was refreshing.

However, this theme goes underdeveloped. We understand Supe hurls all nuclear weapons into the sun because they have the potential to destroy civilization. But in his speech at the end, he says he was wrong to want to obliterate nukes; it's up to the people of each country to champion peace by pressuring their government leaders.

Earlier, we heard him note in his Fortress of Solitude, "The Earth is threatened with the same fate as Krypton." But the image of one of his planet's elders informs him that if Earthlings put their fate in the hands of one man, they will be betrayed. Again, why? Because the one man will fail them? Because this is giving one man too much power, and power tends to corrupt?

Apparently, at film's end, Superman has decided he agrees with Krypton's elders, and he chooses to honor the same non-interference attitude with which he's approached Earth's other major events, similar to *Star Trek*'s Prime Directive. But is it always okay for a super-being to say "hands off"? No, or Superman wouldn't battle supervillains and thwart Lex Luthor's schemes. So is it a matter of scale? It's okay to save citizens from events like a runaway subway (*Superman IV*) but not larger causes of human suffering like genocide? This "not my problem" thesis for super-folks definitely needs fine tuning.[18]

The film could have beefed up its nuclear theme using pertinent imagery. Perhaps while contemplating what to do, Superman might encounter a Hiroshima survivor at a memorial. He might look through horrendous photos of A-bomb victims. Or he might meet a grown woman, herself radiation-scarred, her parents killed in the Hiroshima bombing. Perhaps he could have had a dream filled with images of the aftermath of

Superman (Christopher Reeve) addresses the United Nations about nuclear weapons in 1987's *Superman IV: The Quest for Peace* (Golan-Globus). Reeve contributed to the film's story idea.

Hiroshima's bombing, including blast-ravaged civilians. Any or all of these ideas would have given more weight and relevance to Superman's nuclear ruminations.

As for Nuclear Man, his fate appears gloomy. Superman calls him a "creature" and dispatches him into a nuclear power plant's core as though he was a wad of garbage. But if Superman's hair strand gave birth to Nuclear Man, he would be just as alive, and would have just as much of a soul, as the Man of Steel. After all, imagine the reaction if Superman had discarded Lex and Lenny Luthor into a nuclear power core.

Superman IV marked Lex Luthor's fourth appearance in the Reeve Superman series, and he was starting to wear out his welcome; it was past time to root around in Superman's DC Comics chest and see what other supervillains could cinematically challenge the Man of Steel.

Logic issues abound in *Superman IV*. For example, Nuclear Man soars into outer space with Lacy. Lacy isn't wearing a spacesuit and there's no hint that Nuclear Man is shielding her in a force field. Within 15 seconds, Lacy should have been dead, either from asphyxiation or freezing. Also, wind exists neither in space nor on the moon, despite Superman's flapping cape.

Given the film's many problems, the movie unsurprisingly tanked at the box office. It grossed only $14.5 million stateside and $36.7 million worldwide. This pretty much obliterated any plans for a sequel. (The next Superman movie appeared in 2006.[19]). The critics were unmerciful. Reviewer Jeff Strickler wrote, "It's a bird. It's a plane. It's … a bomb."[20]

Superman IV's savaging happened even in the "safe" environs of the science fiction film community. For example, *Starlog Science-Fiction Video Magazine* #1 (1988) gave the film a one-star rating, lamenting the "incomprehensible editing and frighteningly cheap special effects … [T]he very competent FX crew fell victim to budget-slashing that left the picture an embarrassment of obvious blue screen and matte lines."[21]

But the film is not unlistenable, with John Williams' stirring Superman cues embedded throughout. The music, in this case, is better than the film it supports, but it calls to mind the best of the Man of Steel heroics. That may be meaningless to Superman skeptics, but wide-eyed zealots like me are always susceptible.

Getting back to that underdeveloped nuclear threat theme, two of the film's closing lines intrigue:

Lex Luthor asks Superman, "Is the world going to be vaporized?" Superman replies, "No, Luthor, it's as it always was, on the brink, with good fighting evil."

The Man of Steel's response probably wasn't intended to be prophetic, but here we are, decades later, and we still remain on the brink.

*   *   *

The Survivalist

DIRECTOR: Sig Shore; WRITER: John V. Kraft; MUSIC: Tony Camillo; CINEMATOGRAPHER: Benjamin Davis; EDITOR: Darrell Hanzalik; PRODUCERS: Steven Shore, David Greene.

CAST: Steve Railsback (Jack Tillman); Sandra Lea (Sally Ryan); Tara Trimble (Kim Tillman); Cliff De Young (Dr. Vincent Ryan); Marjoe Gortner (Lieutenant Youngman); Jason Healey (Danny Tillman).

PRODUCTION: Precision Films, Skouras Pictures; 1987; 93 minutes; rated R. Alternate title: *Jack Tillman: The Survivalist*.

* * *

Twenty-first century reviews for *The Survivalist* either denounce the film as right-wing propaganda or praise it as pro-survivalist gospel. The film is not based on Jerry Ahern's novel series *The Survivalist* which started in 1981. However, this movie shares a similar theme.

When a suitcase nuke explodes in an uninhabited region of Siberia, Russia blames the U.S. Looting and panic spread across America, and the president declares a national emergency, freezing all bank accounts, forbidding travel, and deploying the National Guard to keep order.

Survivalist Jack Tillman will have none of it. When two National Guardsmen stand watch before the bank, Jack orders them at gunpoint to move. They do, and he uses a caterpillar tractor to smash into the bank and asks for his safety deposit box. Why he needs it is unclear. But the movie makes it abundantly clear that the National Guard are Bad Guys, presumably because they represent big government.

Jack pays the banker for the damage he has caused, but what about the fact that he has made the bank vulnerable to anyone who wants to charge in and steal? What about the jeopardy this puts the on-duty banker in? Apparently, not Jack's problem.

Going home, Jack discovers that criminals have killed his wife and shot his daughter Kim. He rushes Kim to the hospital, where his friend Dr. Vincent Ryan is unable to save her. Vincent wants to stay in the hospital to care for his patients, but Jack knocks him cold and takes him and his wife Sally, a nurse, out of town. They head for northern mountains where Jack's young son Danny lives.

The trio encounters a police roadblock enforced by two surly lawmen who refuse to let strangers into their county. No sweat—Jack quietly sneaks up on them and, at gunpoint, makes them handcuff themselves to their police car and pull their pants down, the latter apparently to let the lawmen know who's boss. Sally finds this amusing. Could it be she's falling for Jack?

Arrogant Lieutenant Youngman, epitomizing the movie's negative view of the National Guard, gets clearance from his commanding officer to hunt Jack down and make an example of him. Of course. Chasing a survivalist would obviously be the National Guard's key priority in a county where dozens are looting and rioting.

To find Jack, Lieutenant Youngman gathers a band of National Guardsmen who resemble extras from a Hell's Angels movie. They zoom forth on their motorcycles, for no reason running an innocent couple's truck off the road, killing them.

Jack, Vincent and Sally stop briefly at a country gas station and enjoy hospitality from Dub (excellent character actor David Wayne). On TV, the president's press secretary declares that "a limited nuclear war is imminent."

Vincent and Sally engage in a war of their own: Sally does not want to go with Vincent to help at a local hospital, but instead wants to stay with Jack. Though Vincent has acted like a good guy up to this point, he now becomes nasty, telling Sally, "I used to be the boss, remember … and you liked it, you were Mrs. Doctor" and "Now you're into trigger-happy rednecks?" This outburst has turned Vincent into a bad guy, meaning Jack can now bed Sally with a clear conscience. (Also, never mind that Jack's wife died just a couple of days earlier.)

Now on his own, Vincent picks up a young couple who turn out to be heartless villains. They kill Vincent and steal his pickup. But hey, Vincent had defied Jack, so he got what was coming to him.

Sally quickly seems to forget all about departed (and now dead) hubby Vincent. Apparently, she now only has eyes for Jack. Speaking of same, Jack finds Danny in an agreed-upon hiding place in the mountains and sadly delivers the news about the passing of his (Danny's) mom and sister.

As Lieutenant Youngman trails Jack in a helicopter, the squad of cycling National Guardsmen comes barreling Jack's way. Jack evades them, eventually confronting Lieutenant Youngman and another law officer when they disembark from the chopper. Jack kills the second officer, then goes for Youngman, who now holds Danny at gunpoint. But Danny escapes, and Jack terminates Youngman with extreme prejudice.

In the helicopter, Jack takes Sally and Danny airborne to parts unknown.

An interesting film could have been made about responsible preppers, but instead, *The Survivalist* peddles propaganda, its manipulative script constantly "proving" that Jack is always right. Part of that is the forementioned conversion of Dr. Vincent Ryan into a heel, which clears the way for Jack and Sally's adultery. Also, making the county roadblock lawmen nasty to the core; that way, Jack can feel perfectly justified shackling them to their police car. But wait a minute. That leaves the county town they were guarding open to criminals and junkies who will no doubt pillage the place.

Of course, the movie couldn't have shown the two roadblock lawmen as regular guys who are just trying to protect their town and loved ones. That might make Jack look bad. And we couldn't have any hint of such ethical complexity in a radical survivalist tract.

Even more heinous, the film vilifies the National Guard. Sure, a few bad apples no doubt reside among their ranks, but they are mostly regular guys and ladies who believe in their country and are striving to do the right thing. The two Guardsmen stationed in front of the bank aren't doing anything wrong. And Jack's smashing into the bank isn't warranted. But in uber-survivalist think, the Guard represents big government, so defying Guardsmen isn't only justified, it's required.

I have nothing against anyone who has prepared or is preparing for the possibility of a national emergency. Our technology makes us vulnerable to a number of threats, some from other countries, some from domestic terrorists, some from nature itself. But it's one thing to sensibly prepare for the worst, and quite another to hope an apocalypse happens, which seems to be the case with some radical survivalists, the type who might enjoy *The Survivalist*.[22]

On a technical level, the movie founders, lacking the budget to successfully depict wide-scale looting and rioting. The direction wobbles, and some of the acting is shaky, though the three leads—Steve Railsback, Susan Blakely and Cliff De Young—fare well. The film's inconclusive ending suggests a possible sequel.

A political tract, *The Survivalist* tilts to the far right, an unusual specimen in Hollywood. Your reaction may depend on your views about surviving catastrophes such as a limited—or unlimited—nuclear war.

* * *

Survivor

DIRECTOR: Michael Shackleton; WRITERS: Bima Stagg (screenplay); Bima Stagg, Martin Wragge (story); MUSIC: Adriann Strydom; CINEMATOGRAPHER: Fred Tammes; EDITOR: Max Lemon; PRODUCER: Martin Wragge.

CAST: Chip Mayer aka Christopher Mayer (Survivor); Richard Moll (Kragg); Sue Kiel
   (The Woman).
PRODUCTION: Matrix Motion Pictures; South African; released to U.S. via Vestron
   Video in 1988; 86 minutes; not rated.

*   *   *

Near *Survivor*'s end, the villain tells the hero, "Apply the ancient truth 'an eye for
an eye,' or find a new truth for a new reality?" You won't find much new in this film, but
you may find much that is ancient.

When an American astronaut known only as Survivor launched an anti-missile
laser system, World War III broke out. He returns from space to find the Earth a
nuke-devastated wasteland. After wandering for years and finding a handful of others
(all of them less than neighborly), he finds a woman (simply known as "The Woman").
They engage in a padded and gratuitous sex scene.

A bad guy kidnaps Woman. Survivor trails her and discovers an underground
power station integrated with an underground settlement. There, the international
locals inform Survivor about the villainous Kragg, who has kidnapped all the women so
that he can have his way with them. Survivor tells one of the locals, "So kill him."

The local replies, "You kill him."

Survivor obliges. First, of course, he takes on some of Kragg's ineffectual assassins.
Next, he confronts Kragg—or so he thinks. Kragg proceeds to lecture Survivor for what
feels like at least an hour, proving himself to be windier than a platoon of Texas torna-
does. Kragg shares such choice wisdom as, "Homo so-called sapiens, man of wisdom …
we live on a blank canvas dying for a masterpiece—Homo realitas."

Eventually, Survivor takes an axe to Kragg (at this point, you may find yourself
wishing he'd done so earlier), and they fight until Survivor plunges a knife into Kragg's
skull, killing him. Survivor and Woman return to her boat and watch the sun set. The
actors were probably hoping their agents haven't signed them to a sequel.

Survivor starts fairly well, but goes off track about midway. Like a bad art film, its
final half becomes pretentious.

Survivor paints a bleak picture for the post-apocalyptic Earth. Not only is radiation a hazard, but the ozone layer has been stripped away, the soil nutrients depleted, the
Earth blown off its axis. This sounds like several *Twilight Zone* premises crammed into
one movie. It also calls into question the blissful finale for the film's two lovebirds. If the
Earth is falling towards the sun, it's only a matter of time before the sunset becomes the
sunscorch.

Unrated, the film would probably merit a PG-13 for language, violence and adult
content.

With a better script and a less verbose second half, *Survivor* might have worked. As
is, it fails to survive as a worthwhile nuclear threat film.

*   *   *

Unmasking the Idol

DIRECTOR: Worth Keeter; WRITERS: Phil Behrens (screenplay), Robert P. Eaton
   (story); MUSIC: Dee Barton; CINEMATOGRAPHER: Steven Shaw; EDITOR: Matthew Mallinson; PRODUCER: Robert P. Eaton.

CAST: Ian Hunter (Duncan Jax); C K Bibby (Star); Shangtai Tuan (Sato); Shakti Chen (Scarlet Leader).
PRODUCTION: Polo Players Ltd.; 1987; 90 minutes; rated PG.

*   *   *

What secret agent could break into a heavily guarded island and save the day from World War III? James Bond, you say? Sorry—007 was apparently out on loan, so instead *Unmasking the Idol* presses imitation spy Duncan Jax into service.

The villainous Scarlet Leader plans to exchange gold for nuclear warheads with which he will threaten to start World War III. The deal is scheduled to go down on Scarlet Leader's heavily fortified Devil's Crown Island. To thwart him, secret agent Duncan Jax gathers a group of ninja combatants, one of whom is Boon, Jax's pet baboon. (Do I smell comedy relief ahead?)

The film unashamedly exploits 007 movie conventions, such as the opening theme song that harkens back to Bond's '60s epics. In addition, one of the villains is named Goldtooth. A sort of combination Blofeld/Dr. No, Scarlet Leader often laughs maniacally, and his pastimes include dumping defenseless elderly couples into pools teeming with piranhas. Still in Bondian mode, the movie tosses in a couple of twists, but alas, not of the Chubby Checker variety.

Ian Hunter fares well as Duncan Jax, smoothly delivering his lines. The supporting cast provides decent performances. The action is okay, if usually less than convincing. But the film has a tired, been-there-done-that feel that might put off viewers. For example, a maniacal bad guy who wants to threaten World War III was nothing new in 1988, nor was it particularly compelling.

Unmasking the Idol is rated PG for adult content and violence.

Overall, this James Bond wannabe proves imitation is not necessarily the sincerest form of flattery.

*   *   *

Urban Warriors

DIRECTOR: Joseph Warren aka Giuseppe Vari; WRITER: Piero Reanoli; MUSIC: Paolo Rustichelli; CINEMATOGRAPHER: Sergio Rubini; EDITOR: Giuseppe Vari; PRODUCER: Pino Buricchi.
CAST: Karl Landgren aka Bruno Bilotta (Brad); Alex Vitale (Mutant Leader); Bjorn Hammer (Maury); Maurice Poli (Stan).
PRODUCTION: Immagine Productions, Immagine S.r.l.; Cannon (distributor); Italian; 1987; released to U.S. VHS (NTSC) on 5 April 1989; 90 minutes; not rated.

*   *   *

Low-rent mutants menace the protagonists in *Urban Warriors*, another Italian post-nuke action flick.

A nuclear war starts. Three survivors—underground laboratory workers Brad, Maury and Stan—escape to the surface, greeted by a barren landscape and a distant city in remarkably good shape considering it was recently nuked. The men find a place in the city to sleep. The nuke war happened only a day or so earlier, yet all three seem oblivious to radiation danger.

Stan literally loses his head thanks to a band of decapitating mutants who prey on normal people for spinal marrow. The Mutant Leader fatally shoots Maury. Brad meets a woman named Julie who says she survived in a bomb shelter, and both hide out and make love. (Cue the objectifying nudity for the woman.) But it turns out Julie is a mutant who's after Brad's spinal marrow—definitely an argument against casual sex. In no time, the Mutant Leader kills her and has Brad imprisoned. Brad, his cellmate Angela and a female mutant judge escape. Only Brad and Angela survive, hoping to bring new life into the world.

The mutants are about as low-budget as you can get. They look like non-mutants, i.e., no makeup required. In another cost-cutting move, the film employs stock footage from previous Italian post-nuke flicks, particularly 1984's *The Final Executioner*. Waste not, want not.

Inexplicably, radiation has in mere hours turned people into homicidal mutants who devour spinal cords. They also organize themselves into a government within less than a week, and were supposedly "voted" into these positions!

Unrated, *Urban Warriors* would merit an R for the explicit sex scene and gory violence. It's just more of the same, tired, post-nuke twaddle cranked out in droves during the 1980s.

* * *

World Gone Wild

DIRECTOR: Lee H. Katzin; WRITER: Jorge Zamacona; MUSIC: Laurence Juber; CINEMATOGRAPHER: Don Burgess; EDITOR: Gary Griffin; PRODUCER: Robert L. Rosen.

CAST: Bruce Dern (Ethan); Michael Paré (George Landon); Catherine Mary Stewart (Angie); Adam Ant (Derek Abernathy); Alan Autry (Hank).

PRODUCTION: Apollo Pictures. Released in Italy on 27 October 1987; released in the U.S. on 22 April 1988; 95 minutes; rated R.

* * *

When veteran actor Bruce Dern appears in a movie, that may be the sole reason to see it. Such is the case with *World Gone Wild*, a post-nuke action flick.

In the far-future year of 2022, superpowers begin a 15-year war using nukes. Afterwards, rain doesn't fall for 50 years. But in 2087, residents of the small community of Lost Wells have access to water thanks to their enigmatic leader Ethan.

One day, religious cult leader Derek leads his converts to trash Lost Wells, killing residents and kidnapping others. Derek declares he will return. Consequently, Ethan recruits four out-of-town mercenaries—including his old partner-in-crime George—to defend Lost Wells.

One mercenary, Hank, tries to rape schoolteacher Angie, but George stops him. Hank rides off on a cycle and tries to join forces with Derek. Derek has his followers torture Hank to death (offscreen).

Derek makes good on his threat to return to Lost Wells, but he doesn't know the mercenaries have set booby traps for him and his followers. His forces overwhelmed, Derek calls for retreat.

Bu it appears Lost Wells' watering hole has dried up. The mercenaries, promised

The enigmatic Ethan (Bruce Dern) oversees Lost Wells, a small post-nuke community, in 1987's *World Gone Wild* (Apollo Pictures).

water as pay, express disgust, but say they will stay to fight Derek and his cohorts anyway. Ethan then literally turns on the water for the watering hole, saying he had shut it off as a test of the mercenaries' commitment.

Derek & Co. return, and the mercenaries again fight them. George takes on Derek, who ultimately burns to death. Ethan announces he's leaving and sets fire to his dwelling. But lightning crackles and rain pours from the sky to the joy of everyone, including Ethan.

World Gone Wild uses 1954's *Seven Samurai* plot, that of recruiting mercenaries to defend a besieged settlement. *The Magnificent Seven* (1960) and its 2016 remake also use this storyline. So did 1980's *Battle Beyond the Stars*, a more enjoyable film than *World Gone Wild*.

World Gone Wild is sometimes tongue-in-cheek, sometimes on the level. The film displays too much unpleasantness to be fun, and instead comes off as a low-wattage, post-apocalyptic actioner. Its major virtue is Bruce Dern, who wisely milks his role as Ethan for all its worth, applying his patented droll spin to line after line. No newcomer to genre films, Dern had previously appeared in 1971's *The Incredible Two-Headed Transplant* and 1972's *Silent Running*. These two films alone demonstrate Dern's range, from a wide-eyed mad scientist (*Transplant*) to a low-key ecologist (*Silent Running*).

In addition, rocker Adam Ant (remember his hit "Goody Two Shoes"?)[23] plays the insane religious cult leader Derek with relish (and with his cultured British accent). Catherine Mary Stewart instills sensitivity into her under-written schoolteacher role.

Leonard Maltin wrote, "*The Seven Samurai* meet *Mad Max* in this marginally successful, futuristic action yarn."[24]

*   *   *

CHAPTER TEN

1988

Akira

DIRECTOR: Katsuhiro Ôtomo; ANIMATION DIRECTORS: Yoshio Takeuchi, Hiroaki Sato; WRITERS: Katsuhiro Ôtomo, Izô Hashimoto, based on the graphic novel *Akira* by Katsuhiro Ôtomo; MUSIC: Shôji Yamashiro; CINEMATOGRAPHER: Katsuji Misawa; EDITOR: Takeshi Seyama; PRODUCERS: Shunzo Kato, Ryohei Suzuki.

CAST (voice actors: Animaze/Pioneer 2001 English Dub) Johnny Yong Bosch (Shōtarō Kaneda); Joshua Seth (Tetsuo Shima); Wendee Lee (Kei); James Lyon (Colonel Shikishima); Simon Prescott (Doctor Ōnishi); Bob Buchholz (Ryūsaku aka Ryu); Sandy Fox (Kiyoko, No. 25); Cody MacKenzie (Takashi, No. 26); Travis Weaver (Masaru, No. 27).

PRODUCTION: Akira Committee Company Ltd.; Japanese; released in Japan on 16 July 1988; released in the U.S. on 25 December 1989; 124 minutes; rated R.

*   *   *

Every subgenre boasts core classics, and often one film in that subgenre can bring to mind all the category has to offer. For anime, it might be—and for many fans is—*Akira*.

On July 16, 1988, a nuclear explosion destroys Tokyo and World War III breaks out. Thirty-one years later, Japan's capital city has been rebuilt as Neo-Tokyo, a gleaming metropolis rocked by social and political turmoil. Tetsuo, a young member of a motorcycle gang, crashes into an ESPer, and Colonel Shikishima has Tetsuo taken to a hospital. There, Doctor Ōnishi discovers that Tetsuo has strong mental powers, similar to those of the departed Akira, the ESPer who initiated Tokyo's destruction in 1988.

Fearful of Tetsuo's ability to destroy Tokyo, three child-like ESPers attempt to kill him, but he overcomes them and escapes the hospital. In his search for what became of Akira, Tetsuo destroys the military forces the colonel rallies against him. Tetsuo finds Akira's remains buried beneath a stadium, nothing but various organs in glass containers.

Kaneda, Tetsuo's best friend, tries to stop him, to no avail. The colonel has an orbital weapon attack Tetsuo, shearing off one of his arms. Tetsuo destroys the orbital weapon and creates a new arm out of the metal and wires littered about the landscape. However, he loses control of his powers and morphs into a bloated, blob-like monster that attempts to absorb Kaneda, the colonel and Tetsuo's own girlfriend Kaori.

The three ESPers help resurrect Akira, who creates an energy expansion similar to a nuclear explosion. Tetsuo and Kaneda are sucked into another dimension, followed by the three ESPers who, along with Akira, send Kaneda back to our plane of existence. Kaneda reunites with his girlfriend Kei while Tetsuo expands into what appears to be a new universe.

Visually, *Akira* dazzles. Inspired by 1927's *Metropolis* and 1982's *Blade Runner*, *Akira*'s futuristic Neo-Tokyo becomes a character in and of itself, its gleaming skyscrapers a stark contrast to the chaos below. Searchlights nervously scan the heavens, though they might be better trained on the streets. Anarchy breaks out constantly, from student protests to terrorist bombings to motorcycle gangs randomly terrorizing citizens. Social order appears to be membrane-thin. Neo-Tokyo's exquisite architectural skyline masks the cancer metastasizing in its guts below.

The film excels in richly delineating its environs—for example, the ice crumbling off the vault door to Akira's resting place. Also, the background visuals are awe-inspiring, especially those of row after row of Neo-Tokyo high-rises. The film's scope is astounding, its attention to detail impressive.

Akira bristles with action, yet it provides interludes between the violence, allowing viewers to catch their breath and learn more about the characters and the expansive plot. Its take on politics is intriguing: A corrupt executive council runs Neo-Tokyo and the colonel, a sympathetic character, leads a *coup d'état* against it.

For a film that only briefly includes a monster (Tetsuo as the inflated blob), *Akira* includes more urban destruction than many kaiju movies. And it wallows in human destruction as well, from widening pools of gore to bullet-riddled bodies. Thematically, some may fault *Akira*'s metaphysical ponderings. Indeed, in one sense, *Akira*'s finale suggests the old thought "There is a universe in each of us—worlds within worlds." When I was an adolescent, this theme filled me with wonder. Later, I learned better about the origin of the universe, but the wonder remained.

A more tangible theme, one stronger than *Akira*'s metaphysics, is friendship. We learn that Kaneda has always been Tetsuo's mentor, and that Tetsuo has mixed feelings about his surrogate big brother. After Tetsuo escapes the hospital, he steals Kaneda's motorcycle and talks gruffly to his girlfriend, apparently trying to imitate Kaneda's toughness. Close to the end, the now super-powerful Tetsuo taunts Kaneda, his resentment at full throttle. Yet when Tetsuo loses control of his powers and bloats into the blob, in desperation he calls out to Kaneda for help, and Kaneda answers that call.

Akira reviews, both at the time of its American release and more recently, are mostly positive. On Rotten Tomatoes, the film receives a 90 percent fresh rating based on 51 professional reviews. For *The New York Times*, Janet Maslin called the movie "a phenomenal work of animation with all the hallmarks of an instant cult classic."[1] In *The Sci-Fi Movie Guide*, Chris Barsanti called *Akira* "an exciting, impressive spectacle … [C]onceptually it tends to wander at times, [but] it still packs a punch with its awesome visuals."[2]

Akira is rated R for language, brief nudity and strong graphic violence.

Though *Akira* may appear to only graze the nuclear threat theme, primarily because of the opening destruction of Tokyo followed by World War III, it embraces an atmosphere of doomsday. And doomsday, or the threat of it, is what makes nuke threat movies tick.

*   *   *

C.A.T. Squad: Python Wolf

DIRECTOR: William Friedkin; WRITERS: Robert Ward (teleplay); Gerald Petievich, William Friedkin, Robert Ward (story); MUSIC: Ennio Morricone; CINEMATOGRAPHER: Guy Dufaux; EDITOR: Jere Huggins; PRODUCER: David Salven.

CAST: Joseph Cortese (Richard Burkholder); Jack Youngblood (John Sommers); Steve James (Bud Raines); Deborah Van Valkenburgh (Nikki Pappas); Miguel Ferrer (Paul Kiley); Brian Delate (Colonel Vincent Trask); Alan Scarfe (Bekker).

PRODUCTION: NBC Productions; broadcast on NBC-TV on 23 May 1988; 93 minutes; not rated.

* * *

In 1980s TV-movies, patriotism juts out its unblemished square jaw—except in made-for-TV grit-fests like 1988's *C.A.T. Squad: Python Wolf*. A sequel to 1986's *C.A.T. Squad*, it features the four-member top secret team thwarting a plutonium heist in South Africa.

American operative Bud Raines purchases plutonium from two smugglers, then he and fellow agent Richard Burkholder arrest them. Bud and Burkholder and their fellow two C.A.T. members discover South African vigilantes want the plutonium.

On one front, C.A.T. agent Nikki Pappas pretends to be the lover of Paul Kiley and keeps him interested by forking over classified documents. On another front, the Air Force orders C.A.T. agent John Sommers to fly a reconnaissance mission over South Africa. Before he leaves, he and Nikki marry.

Sommers' reconnaissance plane is shot down, and he and his surviving crew members are imprisoned in a labor camp run by South African vigilantes. But the U.S. government covers up the incident.

Nikki, Bud and Burkholder learn that Colonel Vincent Trask is in charge of the secret program Python Wolf. Trask claims that Sommers and his crew did not survive the plane crash. Meanwhile, Paul Kiley discovers that Nikki is a federal agent and kills her. Bud tapes Colonel Trask plotting to wipe out the South African labor camp holding Sommers and his crew in order to erase the botched operation. But instead of Trask flying to South Africa, Burkholder and Bud do. The labor camp's personnel have fled, leaving behind the prisoners' massacred remains. But Sommers has survived.

Bekker, who ran the prison camp and ordered the massacre, attempts to steal plutonium from a power plant. Burkholder, pretending to be a plant employee, sets off a false meltdown alarm. Bekker doesn't buy it and attempts to shoot Burkholder, who blasts hot steam into Bekker's face. Bekker falls into power plant circuitry that electrocutes him.

C.A.T. Squad: Python Wolf rates well above average. Its complex story unfolds amidst a grim atmosphere. Three examples: Paul murders Nikki in one quick knife thrust, shocking her and leaving him whistling as he strolls away. The vigilantes holding Sommers and his crew burn one of them as the man screams. When U.S. Senators learn of Trask's plan to raze the labor camp to cloak the botched reconnaissance operation, one senator sympathizes with Trask's approach.

The performances all hit the mark, with standout work from Joseph Cortese as Burkholder and Miguel Ferrer as Paul. In the second half, the powerhouse action slams forward, no surprise considering this TV-movie was directed by Hollywood veteran

William Friedkin, who won a Best Director Oscar for 1971's *The French Connection*, a paean to in-your-face violence.

The complicated Cold War America the movie portrays defies easy categorization. It isn't above rationalizing or sacrificing patriots. But it still wants to hit one out of the park for Uncle Sam, even if that hurtling ball takes out an innocent bystander along the way.

C.A.T. Squad: Python Wolf proves that TV-movies can be just as dynamic as their cinematic counterparts.

* * *

Delta Force Commando

DIRECTOR: Frank Valenti aka Pierluigi Ciriaci; WRITER: David Parker, Jr. aka Dardano Sacchetti; MUSIC: Elio Polizzi; CINEMATOGRAPHERS: Al Bartholomew, Adolfo Bartoli; EDITOR: Fiorenza Muller; PRODUCER: Milos Antic.
CAST: Brett Clark (Lieutenant Tony Turner); Fred Williamson (Captain Samuel Beck).
PRODUCTION: Realtà Cinematografica; Italian; 1988; 99 minutes; rated R.

* * *

If you read the words *Delta Force* in this entry's title and thought "Chuck Norris," think again. The movie in question is not *Delta Force* but rather *Delta Force Commando*, an Italian action picture with a touch of nuclear threat tossed in. But rest assured gunfights and explosions are still the order of the day.

In Puerto Rico, terrorists steal a nuclear bomb from a U.S. military base. During the fray, a terrorist kills the pregnant wife of Lieutenant Tony Turner. Turner seeks revenge by forcing military pilot Captain Samuel Beck to fly into Nicaragua, where the nuclear device has been taken.

Turner and Beck ditch the out-of-fuel plane and take on the Nicaraguan army. Unbelievably, Turner mows down bad guy after bad guy without a single one of them being able to hit him, despite the fact he's usually standing out in the open firing his weapon. Turner implausibly finds the terrorist who killed his wife and wastes him. It turns out that the stolen nuclear bomb is a dud, a prop used for American military maneuvers. A Delta Force rescue mission ferries Turner and Beck out of Nicaragua, with Turner implying he might use his knife against his superiors.

This tedious, unconvincing action movie quickly wears out its welcome. It's basically the same thing over and over: Turner shooting up the enemy. Attempts at "buddy movie" camaraderie between Turner and Beck don't work. Worst of all, the nuclear threat angle turns out to be bogus.

Delta Force Commando is rated R for adult content, language, and graphic violence. Skip this one and watch a good military movie like 2001's *Black Hawk Down*.

* * *

Desert Warrior

DIRECTOR: Jim Goldman; WRITERS: Bob Davies, Carl Kuntze; MUSIC: Marita A. Manuel; CINEMATOGRAPHER: Fred Conrad; EDITOR: Rene Tucker.
CAST: Lou Ferrigno (Zerak); Shari Shattuck (Racela); Kenneth Peer (Baktar); Mike Monty (Dr. Creo).

PRODUCTION: Silver Star Film Company; made in the Philippines; released in the U.S. on 1 January 1988; 86 minutes; rated PG-13. Alternate title: *Sand Wars*.

* * *

They did their best.

Sometimes, filmmakers are saddled with such tiny budgets and tight shooting schedules that making a good film becomes almost impossible. No doubt most if not all of the cast and crew of *Desert Warrior* tried. However, the movie did get released as a professional product that consumers paid money to see, and they deserved better.

Twenty years after a nuclear war, nomads roam the barren land. Baktar, ruler of a tribe afflicted with radiation, worries that he will never have a non-mutant son.

Non-contaminated survivors called Drones live underground. Racela, daughter of a prominent Drone, escapes the subterranean world and rushes past the Drones' forbidden boundary. Captured by marauders, she is freed by Zerak, Baktar's second-in-command. Racela nurses the injured Zerak. Baktar's tribesmen ferry Zerak and Racela to their compound. Because Racela is radiation-free, Baktar plans to unite with her to produce non-mutant children. Racela's reaction to his plan is less than enthusiastic.

Racela's father and his two assistants rescue Racela but leave Zerak behind. Baktar decrees that Zerak must be killed. But like any good feminist heroine, Racela rushes back and frees Zerak. Problem is, if Racela returns to the Drones with Zerak, she will die, since Drone law dictates that if anyone goes past the boundary and returns, they must be executed—in her case, by a firing squad.

Dr. Creo to the rescue. The scientist has discovered a way to rejuvenate radiation damage, and via so-so special effects, he restores Zerak's disfigured blind eye. Thus, like a defanged Abominable Snowman, the Drone boundary no longer poses a danger, and the Drones won't have to waste Racela after all.

Baktar's tribesmen spoil this happy plot development by attacking the Drones. After plenty of explosions and gunfire, Zerak calls a truce so he can talk to Baktar. The two converse, and Zerak shows Baktar his healed eye, meaning Dr. Creo can cure the radiation afflictions of Baktar's people. Next thing you know, Zerak and Baktar are bear-hugging like two long-lost buddies, and Baktar's tribe shouts exuberantly like a sports arena cheer section. All is sweetness and light—so much so that Zerak and Racela walk hand in hand into a golden sunset as a typical 1980s love song plays in the background.

Technical issues plague *Desert Warrior*. The sound reeks, and sometimes the dialogue is unclear. Lou Ferrigno and Shari Shattuck fare okay as Zerak and Racela, but the rest of the cast members needed drama lessons.

To its credit, unlike most 1980s post-nuke action flicks, *Desert Warrior* makes clear that the recent nuclear war still seriously affects the majority of the survivors. For example, early on, Baktar says, "We're all dying of nuclear contamination."

It's nice to see Lou Ferrigno in the lead. Most classic TV fans know he played the Hulk in the CBS-TV series *The Incredible Hulk* (1977–82) plus three reunion TV movies (1988–90). From 2005 to 2007, he appeared regularly on the TV sitcom *The King of Queens*.[3]

Desert Warrior often seems like a desert itself. Completists will want to take a look; others, probably not.

* * *

Disaster At Silo 7

DIRECTOR: Larry Elikann; WRITER: Douglas Lloyd McIntosh (teleplay); Mark Carliner, Douglas Lloyd McIntosh (story); MUSIC: Mark Snow; CINEMATOGRA-PHER: Roy G. Wagner; EDITOR: Peter V. White; PRODUCER: Julian Krainin.

CAST: Michael O'Keefe (Sgt. Mike Fitzgerald); Perry King (Major Hicks); Patricia Charbonneau (Kathy Fitzgerald); Peter Boyle (General Sanger); Joe Spano (Sgt. Swofford); Joe Urla (Pepper).

PRODUCTION: Mark Carliner Productions for ABC-TV; aired on ABC 27 November 1988; 96 minutes; not rated.

* * *

On September 19, 1980, near Damascus, Arkansas, a Titan II missile exploded in its silo, and the missile's nuclear warhead was hurled 200 feet. Fortunately for Arkansas, it remained intact. But Senior Airman David Livingston died and 21 others were injured.[4] This incident inspired the TV-movie *Disaster at Silo 7.*

On a Texas ICBM base, Sgt. Mike Fitzgerald and his crew discover that recycled fuel is not pumping into the missile (or, in their lingo, they "don't have flow"). Sgt. Fitzgerald fixes the problem. He and Sgt. Swofford get into an argument because Swofford found Pepper, one of Fitzgerald's men, asleep during duty hours.

Inside the missile silo, two soldiers doing routine upkeep find they don't have the proper wrench to perform a maintenance job. Instead of fetching the correct wrench, they use the wrench they have. A wrench socket falls into the missile shaft and hits the fuel tank, causing a leak. Fitzgerald is called in to fix the situation.

SAC's General Sanger worries about the nuclear warhead crowning the missile, and

An ICBM missile silo from 1988's *Disaster at Silo 7* (Mark Carliner Productions). In the film, an accident causes the Titan II missile to explode in its silo, and its nuclear warhead lands somewhere nearby. The film is based on an incident that occurred in Damascus, Arkansas, on September 19, 1980.

fears that the missile's first stage may fail. Fitzgerald goes into the silo and checks the readings, which indicate that the missile may soon explode. Major Hicks orders Swofford to relay the readings to SAC.

Fitzgerald runs a plan by Major Hicks, who gets SAC approval for it. Fitzgerald and his best friend Pepper venture into the missile shaft to get new readings. However, the condition of the vapor-filled missile won't allow them to do so. After Fitzgerald and Pepper leave the silo, Pepper thinks he hears on his headset an order from Swofford to activate the silo fan. He does so, and the missile (but not the warhead) explodes, seriously injuring Fitzgerald and Pepper.

Major Hicks orders an evacuation of the base. Medics find Fitzgerald and Pepper, both badly burned, and ferry them via helicopter to a hospital. Fitzgerald survives, but Pepper dies. An Air Force search crew finds the missile's nuclear warhead, still intact.

Disaster at Silo 7 is a respectable TV-movie that tells its story soberly and without fanfare. The major suspense section deals with whether the Titan II missile will explode. Once it does, the next suspense section concerns the lost nuclear warhead. Authorities order civilians miles from the site to evacuate, for the warhead may be leaking radiation. Of course, it may also explode, and the movie has established that the nuke blast from the warhead would be 700 times greater than the explosion that leveled Hiroshima.

The film's teleplay fleshes out the main characters to the extent possible in 96 minutes. Some of the players are TV veterans: Peter Boyle as General Sanger, Dennis Weaver as Sheriff Harlen, Perry King as Major Hicks, Joe Spano as Sgt. Swofford. As Sgt. Fitzgerald, Michael O'Keefe gives an outstanding performance. When he steps into Pepper's hospital room and mourns his friend's death, his grief seems genuine, and is genuinely touching. Otherwise, he plays his somewhat risk-taking character as a fun-loving extrovert.

The viewer knows the missile will explode, and yet when it does, it will surprise you. The explosion itself and its aftermath completely convince.

The film includes a spiritual aspect unusual for television movies. We learn that the sheriff is a faithful churchgoer, and Fitzgerald's wife Kathy goes to church with her and Fitzgerald's kids. Kathy's daughter asks if God will protect her dad the way God protected Daniel in the Old Testament. Fitzgerald tells Kathy he isn't wired to be spiritual. Yet for all this, the movie's religious subtheme goes nowhere.

Except for by-the-book Sgt. Swofford, the movie refreshingly includes no villains, just decent, concerned people, from General Sanger to Sheriff Harlen. The sheriff tries to learn as much as he can so he can safeguard the county's citizens. The airmen are regular guys duty-bound to keep information secret until they receive clearance to do otherwise.

At the end, the movie tells us that the military no longer uses Titan II missiles (this was 1988). Yet the film features a Titan II missile as its threat. Perhaps it should have featured a Minuteman (in use then) to have increased the suspense.

Overall, *Disaster at Silo 7* is a minor nuclear threat film capably done.

* * *

Empire of Ash

DIRECTORS: Lloyd A. Simandl, Michael Mazo; WRITERS: John Ogis (screenplay), Lloyd A. Simandl (story), Saul Urbonas, Michael Mazo; MUSIC: Tom Lavin;

CINEMATOGRAPHER: Nathaniel Massey; EDITOR: Michael Mazo; PRODUCERS: Lloyd A. Simandl, John A. Curtis.

CAST: Melanie Kilgour (Danielle); Thom Schioler (Orion); Frank Wilson (Shepherd); Ann Louise Meyer (Jasmine).

PRODUCTION: North American Pictures; Canadian; released in the U.S. in February 1989; 86 minutes; not rated. Alternate title: *Empire of Ash II*.

* * *

The low-budget *Empire of Ash* is a post-apocalyptic action movie strung together by an episodic storyline.

The aftermath of "the Great Fire" (nuclear war) has altered America, and a strange government mixing religion and survivalism has taken over. Due to a plague, paramilitary Raiders scour the land for antibody-free survivors, unfortunates whose uncontaminated blood is siphoned out and infused into government-sanctioned citizens.

When Raiders kidnap the uncontaminated Jasmine, her sister Danielle teams with loner Orion to find her. Late in the movie, the focus occasionally shifts to two ex-military good old boys who trade barbs while they blast Raiders. All these two are missing is a chaw of tobacco in their cheeks. Yet for all their swagger, they come off as likable.

Fans of low-budget post-apocalyptic action flicks get all the familiar trappings: gun battles, big explosions, leather outfits, mistimed stunts. And what cheap post-nuker would be worth its weight without some 100 percent gratuitous female nudity? In this regard, the movie's disrespect for women is as unsurprising as it is repugnant.

But even in a mostly low-wattage letdown like this, there is a brief shining moment of genuine after-the-holocaust angst. In a cave at night, Orion and Danielle are talking beside a fire. After examining Orion's talisman, Danielle says, "Family. My sister is all I have left of family." Orion replies, "Nothing makes much sense any more, does it?" This is followed by a long, firelit pause.

Unrated, *Empire of Ash* would probably receive an R for language, sex, nudity and violence. Except for the subplot of the two ex-military rednecks, the reflective moment between Orion and Danielle, and some fair action scenes, *Empire of Ash* is typical 1980s Exploitation cinema with a capital E.

* * *

FireFight

DIRECTOR AND PRODUCER: Scott Pfeiffer; WRITERS: Scot Pfeiffer and Butch Engle; MUSIC: Ren Klyce; CINEMATOGRAPHER: Craig A. Patterson; EDITOR: Richard Bansbach.

CAST: James Pfeiffer (Barry Rader); Janice Carraher (Elaine Rader); Jack Turner (Grandpa); Mark Chaet (Kit).

PRODUCTION: San Rafael Pictures, Trans World Entertainment; 1988; 86 minutes; not rated. Alternate title: *Fire Fight*.

* * *

At one point, the villain of *FireFight* tells an underling, "Don't you ever call me crazy!" Which leaves the underling with a wealth of synonyms he can substitute for crazy, such as "irrational," "insane," "nuts."

This wee-budgeted nuker opens with Middle Eastern tensions heading towards a nuclear confrontation between the U.S. and the Soviet Union. Meanwhile, Elaine Rader announces to husband Barry that she wants a divorce. He tells her, "It's out of the question." From a phone conversation, we learn that he's involved in some illegal South American business dealings. On the line, he tells his accomplice, "Keep your mouth shut. I got a few things to take care of at the office." Those "things" include garroting a co-worker to death.

Soon after the nuclear war breaks out, Barry becomes the psycho leader of a group of escaped convicts—the Raiders—who terrorize the countryside. Elaine joins forces with the good guys—the Traders—who oppose Barry. Crusty-faced mutants shamble about. When one is unlucky enough to run into Barry, he's blown to kingdom come.

In between much atomic age melodrama, the Traders and Raiders engage in gun battles, and no viewer will be surprised when the good guys win and bad guy Barry buys it. The film ends optimistically, with Elaine and her new beau Kit declaring they will raise an orphaned newborn. Kit says, "Maybe it's time for a little hope." Or a better movie.

FireFight appears well-intended, but the photography is oily, the action murky, the script subpar. The depiction of a post-nuke world two months after the nuclear war fails to convince.

The addition of mutants strains credibility, and their facial disfigurement makeup is mostly amateurish. This might not matter so much except that *FireFight* seems to desperately want viewers to believe its after-the-Bomb tale could really happen. On the plus side, the music score isn't bad.

The movie is most effective during the initial atomic attack scene. A stock footage nuclear explosion is well-integrated with newly shot footage in which the blast's light flash and turbulence assail various characters.

FireFight is mostly tough sledding, even for professional bad movie sledders.

* * *

Future Hunters

DIRECTOR: Cirio H. Santiago; WRITERS; J.L. Thompson (screenplay); Anthony Maharaj (story); MUSIC: Ron Jones; CINEMATOGRAPHER: Ricardo Remias; EDITOR: Bass Santos; PRODUCER: Anthony Maharaj.
CAST: Robert Patrick (Slade); Linda Carol (Michelle); Richard Norton (Matthew).
PRODUCTION: Lightning Pictures; produced in the Philippines released on U.S. video in March 1989; 96 minutes; rated R. Alternate title: *Deadly Quest.*

* * *

Future Hunters features an unusual plot point: the Spear of Destiny. But otherwise, this post-nuke action adventure scores below this subgenre's already low standards.

In 2025 after a nuclear war, a loner named Matthew clutches the spearhead of the Spear of Destiny, supposedly the tip of the spear that pierced Jesus Christ's side. The spearhead transports him to 1986—a year in which neo–Nazis plan to seize control of all nuclear weapons and spark a nuclear holocaust. But the Spear of Destiny can thwart their ambitions.

Matthew gets the spearhead to a young couple, ex–Marine Slade and anthropology student Michelle. The Nazis plan to stop them from reuniting the spearhead with the spear, the latter located in a jungle. Thus begins a quest showcasing chases, tiresome plot developments, gratuitous martial arts matches, chortling Nazis, fierce Amazons and brave little people. Naturally, Slade and Michelle accomplish their mission, with Michelle triumphantly reuniting spearhead and staff and thus saving the world.

Future Hunters anemically mimics better films such as 1979's *Mad Max* and 1981's *Raiders of the Lost Ark*. Despite all the action, I wanted to skip to the end, but as this book's author, I knew that would be unethical.

Star Robert Patrick went on to bigger and better things, such as the role of the T-1000 in 1991's *Terminator 2: Judgment Day*. This led to a wealth of other movie and TV appearances, including a stint (2000–2002) on *The X-Files*. Patrick has fared well in everything I've seen him in—except this movie, in which he yells most of his lines as though he's at a sporting event.

Future Hunters is rated R for language, brief nudity and violence.

*   *   *

In the Aftermath

DIRECTOR: Carl Colpaert; WRITERS: Carl Colpaert, Mamoru Oshii, animation based on the original story "Angel's Egg" by Mamoru Oshii, Yoshitaka Amano; MUSIC: Anthony Moore; ANIMATION: Yasuyoshi Tokuma, Mamoru Oshii; ANIMATION PRODUCER: Yasuyoshi Tokuma; CINEMATOGRAPHER: Geza Sinkovics; EDITOR: Kevin Sewelson; PRODUCER: Tom Dugan.
CAST: Tony Markes (Frank); Rainbow Dolan (Angel); Feliz Tully (Doctor Sarah); Kenneth McCabe (Goose).
PRODUCTION: New World Pictures; American-Australian-Japanese; 1988; released in the U.S. in 1988; 72 minutes; not rated. Alternate title: *In the Aftermath: Angels Never Sleep*.

*   *   *

Probably the most offbeat movie this tome covers, *In the Aftermath* combines animation from a 1985 Japanese anime film with newly shot "live action" scenes. The result is surprisingly effective.

Angel's brother Jonathan is teaching her the ropes of angelhood, and he tells her she must judge who is and isn't worthy to receive her egg's blessing.

Elsewhere, Earth has experienced a recent apocalypse. The air is contaminated, and gas-masked soldiers Frank and Goose search for an oxygen source in a demolished facility. A desperate survivor knocks Frank out, then kills Goose and steals his equipment. Frank awakens in a hospital and meets Dr. Sarah, who tells him they are the only two people in the hospital, and that their room contains good air.

Frank sketches Angel (whom he saw earlier in the guise of a young human girl). He considers venturing outside to find her. Jonathan destroys her egg because she fell asleep, and angels must never sleep. Yet as the fairy of second chances, Jonathan gives her a new egg.

Frank dons protective equipment and goes outside to find Angel in the form of the human girl. This selfless act makes him worthy of accepting Angel's egg, and she gives it to him, saying it offers his "chance to shine again." When Sarah finds Frank, he gives her the egg, which miraculously decontaminates the air. The brackish clouds melt into a blue, sunlit sky, and Sarah and Frank remove their gas masks, no longer needing them.

Producer Tom Dugan said that once New World Entertainment purchased the 1985 Japanese animated film *Angel's Egg* at a bargain price, they didn't understand the tale.[5] Consequently, New World decided to film a new live-action storyline involving a post-apocalyptic America, then splice in appropriate segments of *Angel's Egg*, essentially giving the latter a new story.[6]

New World being New World, the live-action segments were shot on the cheap. But the movie does a decent job of depicting a collapsed civilization. Frank and Goose find a few corpses in good condition, indicating that they died recently. The tainted air implies either chemical or radiological toxicity. At one point, Sarah notes that outside the hospital, the "contamination level is very high." This implies radiation.[7]

The animation segments dazzle, brimming with grand architecture and eerie topography. The world of the angels seems bizarre, their depiction miles from the West's traditional bird-winged, halo-topped messengers of God.

Almost every "patchwork" movie displays some frayed seams, and such is the case for *In the Aftermath*. The animation segments remain mysterious and sometimes seem disconnected from the film. Given they are separate elements, the frequent switching from animation to live-action sometimes jars. But the film supplies fairly effective bridge elements: the white feather, Frank's sketch of Angel, Angel appearing as a live-action human child.

In the Aftermath is one of the more unusual takes on the 1980s nuke threat genre. *Vive la différence.*

* * *

The Incredible Hulk Returns

DIRECTOR-WRITER: Nicholas Corea; MUSIC: Lance Rubin; CINEMATOGRAPHER: Chuck Colwell; EDITORS: Janet Ashikaga, Briana London; PRODUCER: Daniel McPhee.

CAST: Bill Bixby (David Banner); Lou Ferrigno (The Hulk); Jack Colvin (Jack McGee); Steve Levitt (Donald Blake); Eric Kramer (Thor); Lee Purcell (Maggie Shaw).

PRODUCTION: Bixby-Brandon Productions, New World Television; broadcast on NBC-TV on 22 May 1988; 100 minutes; not rated.

* * *

You won't like him when he's angry.

Before the Hulk became a movie star in the Marvel Cinematic Universe, he was a TV star from 1978 to 1982. On *The Incredible Hulk* TV series, Bill Bixby played scientist David Banner who, exposed to gamma radiation bombardment in an experiment, becomes the Hulk whenever he becomes upset. On the run until he can find a cure for his condition, Banner embarks on a number of adventures. *The Incredible Hulk Returns* is a 1988 TV reunion movie.

Still seeking a cure, Banner is employed as David Bannion at a respected research institute, where he has spearheaded a team that has created the Gamma Transponder. Banner believes it can rid him of the Hulk. But Donald Blake, a former student of Banner's, enters his life along with Thor, a Norse superhero beholden to Blake. Naturally, the Hulk and Thor clash, but they soon make peace.

A criminal element kidnaps Banner's girlfriend Dr. Maggie Shaw and demands the Transponder in return for her life. Banner damages the Transponder so it cannot be used as a weapon—or a source that could free him from the Hulk. At the bad guys' hideout, the Hulk and Thor mop the floor with gun-toting gangsters and rescue Maggie. Banner spends one last evening with Maggie, who's figured out he is secretly the Hulk, and then leaves.

The Incredible Hulk Returns makes good use of its assets—a fine cast, a serviceable script, a capable director. Like on the TV show, Bixby expertly humanizes Banner, who hopes to be able to live a normal life with his newfound love Maggie. But fate, plus the possibility of a sequel, leaves Banner once again a lonely man.

This movie also served as a pilot for a Thor TV series that didn't materialize; that's too bad since Eric Kramer plays a spirited Thor. As on the *Hulk* TV show, budget and special effects constraints keep the action modest, but still effective. As always, Lou Ferrigno shines as the Hulk, a not-so-jolly green giant ready to knock heads.

The nuclear threat angle is the gamma radiation that created Banner's counterpart. This implies that nuclear forces, even harnessed for a well-intended experiment, may lead to tragedy and spiral off in dangerous, unintended directions. (Similarly, in the character's 1962 comic book origin, radiation from a nearby "gamma bomb" explosion creates Banner's alter ego.)

Bixby and Ferrigno returned in two more reunion movies, 1989's *The Trial of the Incredible Hulk* and 1990's *Death of the Incredible Hulk*.

*   *   *

Iron Eagle II

DIRECTOR: Sidney J. Furie; WRITERS: Kevin Elders, Sidney J. Furie; MUSIC: Amin Bhatia; CINEMATOGRAPHER: Alain Dostie; EDITOR: Rit Wallis; PRODUCERS: Sharon Harel, Jacob Kemeny, Jacob Kotzky.

CAST: Louis Gossett, Jr. (Colonel "Chappy" Sinclair); Mark Humphrey (Captain Matt "Cobra" Cooper); Stuart Margolin (General Stillmore); Colm Feore (Yuri Lebanov); Sharon Brandon (Valeri); Jesse Collins (Major Bush).

PRODUCTION: Carolco Pictures, Alliance Entertainment, Canadian Entertainment Investors Number One and Company Limited Partnership, Harkot Productions; 1988; 105 minutes; rated PG.

*   *   *

When Hollywood churns out a sequel, this usually means the original film killed at the box office. However, 1986's *Iron Eagle* cost $18 million but grossed only $24,159,872.[8] Nevertheless, that was considered good enough to launch 1988's *Iron Eagle II*, a movie that, unlike its predecessor, boasts clear nuclear threat ties.

Pulled from reserve duty, Colonel Charles "Chappy" Sinclair is chosen to go to Israel and oversee a military operation involving American and Soviet fighter pilots. An undisclosed Middle Eastern nation has built a nuclear weapons base capable of launching missiles at either the U.S. or the U.S.S.R. Chappy has two weeks to whip the pilots into shape, for by then, the Middle Eastern base will be ready to launch nukes.

During training, pilots Matt Cooper and Yuri Lebanov aggravate each other, inevitably moving into a confrontation. Meanwhile, Matt courts Russian pilot Valeri. An overconfident Major Bush dies during mission training, and General Stillmore scuttles the operation. Chappy discovers that Stillmore deliberately chose difficult pilots so the operation would fail. Consequently, Chappy ignores Stillmore's order to end the operation and soldiers on.

During the mission, ground forces will disable anti-aircraft weapons while F-16s fire one or more missiles down the enemy base's ventilator shaft. Problems arise, and Chappy calls off the mission. But Matt and his wingman press forward, clashing with enemy jets. Yuri and Valeri arrive to help, and Valeri fires a missile that destroys the enemy compound.

The film ends with Chappy turning down an offer to work for General Stillmore—and telling Matt that the young pilot will be meeting Valeri again at an upcoming Russian parade.

Iron Eagle II is a by-the-numbers military action movie. Clichés abound, and the first half provides plenty of "audience pleasing" manipulation. The second half likewise manipulates, but does so more smoothly.

Louis Gossett, Jr., scores as Chappy, and the supporting cast members earn their wings as well. The action scenes hum, boasting fine effects and photography. The film never drags.

In the context of 1988, the movie portrays Russians as "regular folks." Of course, American grievances against the Soviet Union in the 1980s weren't aimed at the Russian people, but rather at the Russian political and military leaders, some of whom advocated nuclear war (as did some U.S. hawks).

In *Iron Eagle II*, both Americans and Russians contribute to taking out the Middle Eastern missile base before it goes online. In this way, the film depicts Russians and Americans both being anti-nuke—at least when it comes to loose-cannon Middle Eastern nations.

* * *

Colonel Chappy Sinclair (Louis Gossett Jr., center) prevents pilot Matt Cooper (Mark Humphrey) from clashing with pilot Yuri Lebanov (Colm Feore, far left) in 1988's *Iron Eagle II* (Carolco Pictures). In the film, Soviet and American pilots join forces to take out a shared enemy's nuclear missile base.

The Sisterhood

DIRECTOR: Cirio H. Santiago; WRITER: Thomas McKelvey Cleaver; MUSIC: Jun
   Latino; CINEMATOGRAPHER: Ricardo Remias; EDITOR: Edgar Viner; PRO-
   DUCER: Anna Roth.
CAST: Rebecca Holden (Alee); Chuck Wagner (Mikal); Lynn-Holly Johnson (Marya);
   Barbara Hooper (Vera).
PRODUCTION: Santa Fe; 1988; 75 minutes; rated R.

*   *   *

Some movies, such as *The Sisterhood*, seem to run out of money as you watch, and
you can't help but feel sorry for the filmmakers.

The opening narration tells us, "The Final War leveled the old world to the ground."
What we're left with are wastelands, raiders, mutants, the obligatory Forbidden Zone
and the legendary Sisterhood, a band of independent women, each bosting a specific
paranormal power. Mikal, a marauder for hire, nurses an unjustified vendetta against
the Sisterhood.

Eighteen-year-old Marya joins two Sisterhood members, Alee and Vera, in their
quest to rescue women held captive in Calcarra—"Sin City" for the post-apocalyptic
crowd. Mikal kidnaps Vera. In their resolve to free their sister, Alee and Marya battle the supposedly fearsome mutants we've heard about, many of whom look as they
were only dabbed with makeup, some looking as though they dodged the makeup chair
completely.

Alee and Marya happen upon an underground nuclear bunker and commandeer
a "war wagon" (how could it still run after all this time?) as well as military rifles, and
Vera returns to them. They attack Calcarra and shoot scores of men. The "Reverend
Mother" materializes, frees all captive females, and teleports the women to safety outside Calcarra. In addition, Mikal decides the Sisterhood is now okay in his book.

The movie seems to want to champion women, but the scenes of toplessness clash
with that intent. The acting seesaws, with Chuck Wagner and Lynn-Holly Johnson coming off best. The explosions, swordplay and gun battles are okay, but the movie suffers
from uneven direction, a lackluster script, repetition and, yes, a minuscule budget.

The Sisterhood is rated R for adult content, language, nudity and violence. It could
have been a much better film, one actually tuned into its more honorable intentions.
Perhaps a female writer and director would have helped.

CHAPTER ELEVEN

*   *   *

1989

Curse II: The Bite

DIRECTOR: Fred Goodwin aka Federico Prosperi; WRITERS: Susan Zelouf, Federico Prosperi; MUSIC: Carlo Maria Cordio; CINEMATOGRAPHER: Roberto D'Ettorre Piazzoli; EDITOR: Claudio M. Cutry; PRODUCER: Ovidio G. Assonitis.
CAST: Jill Schoelen (Lisa Snipes); J. Eddie Peck (Clark Newman); Jamie Farr (Harry Morton).
PRODUCTION: Trans World Entertainment (TWE), VIVA Entertainment, Towa Production, Trihoof Investments; 1989; 98 minutes, rated R. Alternate title: *The Bite*.

* * *

Snakes terrify three out of every ten Americans,[1] so it's no surprise these slithering reptiles star in horror films like *Curse II: The Bite*.

The film opens with two men in hazmat suits snaring a snake on the Yellow Sands Nuclear Base. Later, a gas attendant tells a young couple, Clark and Lisa, to avoid the Yellow Sands area, but of course they go that direction anyway. After driving through a mass of snakes covering the road, Clark is bitten by a mutated snake. His hand turns into a serpent hungry for victims, and several cast members fill the bill. At the end, Clark becomes a serpent repository from which snakes pour.

While the film does feature good special effects and acting, it is defeated by inconsistent logic and unsatisfying dramatics. For example, the sheriff believes Clark is smuggling drugs, but while he leaves the police car and relieves himself, Clark's snake hand shoots into his deputy's mouth and yanks out his heart. Later, even after the sheriff has seen his dead deputy, he still thinks Clark is smuggling drugs, seemingly oblivious to the bizarre way in which Clark killed the deputy.

Clark attacks several good folks—killing the earnest doctor and the religious father who takes him in, and blinding the latter's wife. Yet for unclear reasons, even though he faces Harry Morton in the hospital, Clark doesn't kill him. But Morton, not even a real doctor, had given Clark the wrong antidote, so why does Morton get off bite-free?

Despite the 1980s gore and other R-rated touches, the movie's method of converting Clark into a snake-man—a bite from a radioactive serpent—harks back to 1950s atomic mutant movies. The basic idea here is that radiation creates monsters who, even when human-sized, could serve as metaphors for the dangers of nuclear contamination.

Curse II: The Bite is rated R for language, adult content, sex, and graphic violence. If you want to see a good were-snake movie, watch 1966's *The Reptile* instead.

* * *

Deadly Reactor

DIRECTOR-WRITER: David Heavener; MUSIC: Brian Bennett; CINEMATOGRA-
   PHER: David Hue; EDITOR: Brian Evans; PRODUCER: Fritz Matthews.
CAST: Stuart Whitman (Duke); David Heavener (Cody); Darwyn Swalve (Hog).
PRODUCTION: Action International Pictures; released in the U.S. to video in May
   1989; 88 minutes; not rated. Alternate title: *Reactor.*

*   *   *

Deadly Reactor's production company, Action International Pictures, has the ini-
tials AIP, and many Baby Boomers will recall the AIP logo from the '50s, '60s and '70s.
Then, however, AIP stood for American International Pictures, a company that released
a wealth of genre movies and youth films. Had the company still existed in 1989, it might
very well have released a low-budget action opus like *Deadly Reactor.*

Following a nuclear war, Cody runs into bad guys who shoot him and leave him for
dead. Duke, a quintessential cowboy type, nurses Cody back to health and mentors him
in the ways of the Westerner.

The peaceful Agape People live in a nearby small town, where Hog and his thugs terrorize them. After one of Hog's goons kills Duke, Cody sets out to avenge his mentor and
save the Agape People. He teaches them how to shoot (most have been pacifists) and prepares them for battle. After a prolonged gunfight, Cody and the Agape People win. But
wait—a new jerk just drove into town vowing to tear it apart. Cody stands his ground.

Unfortunately, so does misogyny. *Deadly Reactor*'s first half features plenty of
objectifying female toplessness and wallows in rape culture both in terms of behavior
and dialogue. This would be inexcusable even if the rest of the movie was first-rate—and
make no mistake, it's not.

On one level, the film tries to be a Western. Duke, played by Stuart Whitman,
seems to have popped out of a 1950s cowboy classic (Stuart in fact played a Western mar-
shal in the TV series *Cimarron Strip* [1967-68]). Meanwhile, Cody's look and behavior
are obviously styled after Clint Eastwood. Even some strains of the music score recall
Eastwood's Italian Westerns.

The film makes a few nuke references. For example, one of the characters warns her
daughter that the lake water they bathe in is radioactive. Cody tells Duke that a nuke
killed his wife and children. Otherwise, except for the modern-day autos, we could be
back in the Old West.

Unrated, *Deadly Reactor* would merit an R for nudity, sex, rape, language and
graphic violence.

My advice: Forget this would-be "modern" Western and watch the real thing, such
as 1962's *Ride the High Country* or one of its classic oater kin.

*   *   *

Godzilla vs. Biollante

DIRECTOR: Kazuki Omori; WRITERS: Kazuki Omori, Shinichiro Kobayashi; MUSIC:
   Koichi Sugiyama, Yuki Saito; STOCK MUSIC: Akira Ifukube; CINEMATOGRA-
   PHER: Yudai Kato; EDITOR: Michiko Ikeda; SPECIAL EFFECTS: Koichi Kawakita;
   PRODUCER: Tomoyuki Tanaka.

CAST: Kunihiko Mitamura (Kazuhito Kirishima); Yoshiko Tanaka (Asuka Okouchi); Masanobu Takashima (Major Sho Kuroki); Kôji Takahashi (Dr. Genichiro Shiragami); Manjot Bedi (SSS9); Megumi Odaka (Miki Saegusa).

PRODUCTION: Toho; Japanese; released in Japan on 16 December 1989; released in the U.S. (to video and cable TV) on 25 November 1992; 104 minutes; rated PG.

* * *

After Godzilla's rampage through Tokyo in 1984, the monster has been sealed in Mount Mihara. However, patches of Godzilla's skin are found in the Tokyo ruins, and everybody wants them—the Japanese, the American company Biomajor, and the (fictional) Middle Eastern nation of Saradia.

Thanks to Saradian agent SSS9, Saradia gets the G cells and employs the brilliant Dr. Shiragami to use them to develop grain that will thrive in the desert. But a terrorist bomb obliterates his lab and kills Shiragami's daughter Erika. Shiragami grafts some of Erika's DNA into a rose. Next, using the G cells, he injects Godzilla's DNA into the Erika-rose hybrid so that it will become immortal.

Elsewhere, Biomajor threatens to blow up Mount Mihara if they don't get the G cells, but agent SSS9 thwarts the handoff between Japan and the American corporation. Biomajor's bombs unleash Godzilla, who proceeds to once again terrorize the Land of the Rising Sun. Japan's airborne warship *Super-X2* takes on the atomic dragon, to no avail.

Meanwhile, the Godzilla-Erika-rose hybrid has grown into the giant, stationary plant-monster Biollante, which fights Godzilla. The Big G wins. Or does he? We see Biollante dissolve into glittering particles that float skyward. Fairy dust?

Later, Anti-Nuclear Bacteria (ANB), created using G cells, is shot into Godzilla. Then Biollante spores rain from the sky and form a monstrous new incarnation of Biollante, this one ambulatory and boasting a cavernous maw studded with sharp teeth and a wealth of fanged tentacles. After a fierce struggle, Godzilla—weakened by the ANB and Biollante's attacks—crashes into the sea and appears to be down for the count.

Back to the human plot: After Dr. Shiragami watches Biollante's spores stream heavenward, agent SSS9 kills him. Then one of the energy pads intended to attack Godzilla vaporizes the assassin.

Godzilla mysteriously revives (he is, after all, the sacred beast of the apocalypse) and wades into the ocean.

Godzilla vs. Biollante, the seventeenth Toho Godzilla film, injected new energy into the Big G series. The two men responsible were writer-director Kazuki Omori and special effects supervisor Koichi Kawakita.

Omori, formerly a medical doctor, stuffed his script with ideas: genetic engineering, nuclear politics, international terrorism, scientific ethics. So many characters populate the story that a first-time viewer might feel overwhelmed. Multiple characters, a blizzard of ideas and subplots galore became the hallmark of Omori's Godzilla scripts for what is known as the Heisei Series (Big G movies made between 1984 and 1995). Omori wrote four of them: *Godzilla vs. Biollante*, 1991's *Godzilla vs. King Ghidorah* (which he also directed), 1992's *Godzilla and Mothra: The Battle for Earth* (aka *Godzilla vs. Mothra*) and 1995's *Godzilla vs. Destoroyah*.

Meanwhile, starting with *Godzilla vs. Biollante*, special effects director Koichi Kawakita improved the series' visual effects. He employed a wealth of camera angles when photographing giant monsters. For Godzilla, he employed a cable-controlled robot from the torso up that used the same mold as the man-in-suit costume, thus assuring a perfect match. The robot Godzilla head was quite expressive, allowing facial nuances never before seen in a Big G movie. For *Godzilla vs. Biollante*, Kawakita gave the Big G a fierce, animalistic look with ominous eyes and a double row of teeth.

Kawakita also excelled at "mecha," such as the sleek and impressive *Super-X2* in *Godzilla vs. Biollante*. He was likewise no slouch when it came to miniatures and opticals. Though hampered by lower budgets than those for American effects movies, Kawakita didn't go unnoticed; for example, Western special effects ace Richard Edlund of ILM lauded his work.[2]

Godzilla vs. Biollante is certainly flawed. With so many characters coming and going, the film lacks focus. Some subplots are not satisfactorily developed.

Despite Koichi Kawakita's special effects panache, the movie does utilize old-school effects, such as Godzilla being a man-in-a-monster-suit, known as suitmation, and a bevy of miniatures. This may be off-putting to some, but the film's use of suitmation is among the best examples of this practical effects technique, with suit actor Kenpachiro Satsuma making Godzilla appear more animalistic than anthropomorphic.

In addition, *Godzilla vs. Biollante* is one of the Heisei Series' most atmospheric entries. For example, a thunderstorm breaks out as Dr. Shiragami prepares to inject the Erika-rose hybrid with G cell DNA. Appropriately, lightning flashes and thunder booms as he creates his Frankenstein Monster.

One of the movie's most interesting notions, Anti-Nuclear Bacteria (ANB), ties in with the nuke threat movies of the 1980s. Kirishima and a Japanese VIP discuss the very real possibility that ANB could "neutralize nuclear missiles. Nuclear weapons would be rendered useless." Yet ANB would "only be used in case of a nuclear emergency that would threaten the country." In this regard, the Japanese employ ANB in their attempt to defeat Godzilla, but at movie's end, the Big G seems to have shrugged off the genetically engineered bacteria.

Disappointingly, the movie doesn't explore what would happen if Japan used ANB to nullify all the world's nukes, particularly those of the United States and the Soviet Union. Such a move would have alarmed the superpowers. In fact, nukes made harmless might have made Russia and America more careful—or on the other hand, emboldened either or both to take greater risks. If one's country cannot be vaporized in return, why not wage a conventional war to resolve irreconcilable differences?

After *Godzilla vs. Biollante*, the Godzilla series simply forgot about ANB. You'd assume the Japanese Special Defense Forces might try it again against the Big G, this time with a mega-dose. But such was not to be.

In America, *Godzilla vs. Biollante* went directly to video and cable TV in 1992. Reviews from G-friendly sources are mostly positive. Rotten Tomatoes gives the movie a 71 percent fresh rating based on seven reviews, and the audience score is 72 percent. *Sci-Fi Movie Guide* author Chris Barsanti called it "visually lush, with a moody and even poetic sensibility featuring a truly unforgettable monster."[3] Japanese movie scholar Stuart Galbraith IV wrote that it was a "more than worthy entry in the series."[4] J.D. Lees (editor of *G-FAN Magazine*) and Marc Cerasini opined that the movie "is a very different Godzilla film, perhaps the most poetic of the series. And Biollante is a very different foe for Godzilla."[5]

Throughout the Heisei Series, Godzilla's nuclear aspect was never forgotten. In fact, it was front and center in *Godzilla vs. Destoroyah*, the last Heisei film. In that one, the Big G literally melts. But fans who shed a tear over Godzilla's demise needn't have worried; like Arnold Schwarzenegger, he came back.

* * *

Miracle Mile

DIRECTOR-WRITER: Steve De Jarnatt; MUSIC: Tangerine Dream; CINEMATOGRA-PHER: Theo Van de Sande; EDITORS: Stephen Semel, Kathie Weaver; PRODUCERS: John Daly, Derek Gibson.

CAST: Anthony Edwards (Harry Washello); Mare Winningham (Julie Peters); Denise Crosby (Landa); Robert DoQui (Fred); Lou Hancock (Lucy); John Agar (Ivan); Raphael Sbarge (Chip).

PRODUCTION: Hemdale, Miracle Mile Productions; 1989; 87 minutes; rated R.

* * *

Miracle Mile begins as a love story between Harry Washello and Julie Peters. Then about 20 minutes into the movie, Harry receives a phone call meant for someone else, and the caller says that nuclear war is a little over an hour away. At that point, the movie changes tone from light romantic comedy to terrifying nuclear thriller.

After meeting at Los Angeles' La Brea Tar Pits, musician Harry and waitress Julie spend the day together, quickly falling in love. Harry plans to pick her up for a date at midnight, but the power shorts out and he doesn't awaken until hours later.

He hurries to Julie's diner, but she has already left. From a phone booth, Harry calls her and leaves an apology on her answering machine. Then the phone rings. Harry answers and hears a distressed message from a soldier who thinks he's calling his dad: The soldier says that America will launch its ICBMs in 50 minutes, guaranteeing a Russian response.

Distraught and confused, Harry tells the folks in the diner, including Landa (Denise Crosby), an upper-income patron. She makes some quick phone calls and decides that Harry's phone caller was probably on the level. Quickly, she and the diner's manager, staff and a few customers (including Harry) are speeding to the airport in the diner's van.

But Harry leaves the van because he's determined to rescue Julie. Gun in hand, he gets into several dangerous scrapes. He finds Julie and spirits her to the heliport atop the Mutual Benefit Life Building (Landa had reserved a helicopter shuttle to LAX).

By this time, the news about an impending nuclear war has spread throughout L.A. and panic engulfs the city. The chopper takes off, but an EMP caused by a nuclear explosion cripples it and it crashes into the La Brea Tar Pits. Harry tells Julie that a direct hit might turn them into diamonds. After the couple submerges, there is a direct hit.

Miracle Mile delivers the goods as intensely as any 1980s nuclear threat movie. While Harry listens to the phone call from Chip (Raphael Sbarge), who thinks he's calling his dad, emotions wash across Harry's face: bafflement, curiosity, fear, shock. Harry hears gunfire over the phone, implying that Chip has been shot, and then a voice tells him to forget what he's heard. This provides the ideal punctuation to this tense sequence.

Upon hearing Harry's story about the phone call, the diner customers react in disbelief and terror. The movie gets across how chilling it would be to hear, out of the blue,

In 1989's *Miracle Mile* (Hemdale), Harry Washello (Anthony Edwards) learns in a phone call that the U.S. is launching its ICBMs in 50 minutes.

that your world will be nuked in a little over an hour. It also plumbs the fear bubbling under most Americans' psyches during the 1980s. For example, after Harry delivers the bad news, manager Fred (Robert DoQui) says, "I knew they'd do something stupid just like this one day." Toward the end, the panic gripping L.A. residents becomes palpable, displaying the worst in human behavior.

The movie also plays up the power of rumors. As Julie tells Harry, the story of his phone call is what's caused L.A.'s pandemonium, and no evidence backs up his story. Harry wonders if he's a modern Chicken Little. During a newscast, a correspondent gets shot live on the air; confusion and horror engulf Harry's face: Did he cause the correspondent's death? And the deaths of others amidst L.A.'s civil breakdown?

But mostly, Harry's goal is selfless: save Julie. The film emphasizes the importance of relationships. When Harry tells others about the imminent nuking, many of them want to save a loved one. The film makes you wonder what you would do if you suddenly heard missiles would be falling within the hour.[6] In my case, all my relatives live hundreds of miles away. And most likely, smartphones would be down. But if you have a spouse or children or a significant other, you would probably want to spend the end with them, and could if they lived or worked in the same area.

Miracle Mile's one redemptive story is that of Julie's grandparents, Lucy (Lou Hancock) and Ivan (John Agar), who haven't spoken to each other in 15 years. But on the eve of nuclear annihilation, they reconcile and plan to spend their last moments together at Lucy's favorite diner.

The film has flaws. For example, a scene in which Harry searches for a helicopter pilot teeters on borderline parody. He dashes into a gym, and what do you know: In minutes, he finds said pilot.

In the first 20 minutes, Harry comes across as an easygoing charmer, though he can also be careless (he inadvertently causes the small fire that shorts out his apartment building's power). It's fascinating watching him change from laid-back smoothie

Harry Washello (Anthony Edwards, left) stands in shock as panicked LA residents, fearing nuclear attack is imminent, rush through the streets in 1989's *Miracle Mile* (Hemdale).

to revved-up dynamo, his reckless edge showing itself. Actor Anthony Edwards nails the transformation.

The movie paints a dark picture of the United States. For example, when Harry hears gunfire over the phone, it's obvious that someone has shot Chip, probably his military superior or an MP. Not exactly Reagan's "Morning in America."[7]

Reviews were mostly positive. In a 1989 critique, Roger Ebert praised the film's "diabolical effectiveness" and added, "[T]here is real terror in a scene where word of the possible attack begins to spread through the city, and there are riots in the streets."[8] About a decade later, reviewer James O'Neill called the film a "great, underrated end-of-the-world movie … [The film] really knows how to build tension and suspense."[9] In 2000, John Stanley wrote, "Offbeat cautionary tale (call it pre–Armageddon) that scores for mood and unpredictable plot…. Compelling viewing."[10]

Interestingly, the film begins and ends in the La Brea Tar Pits. At the opening, we see skeletons, sculptures and paintings of the various extinct mammals trapped in the tar. At the end, Harry and Julie are sinking into it, perhaps fated to join the mammals as exhibits at some future date, with sightseers pondering the lives of these two skeletons before nuclear war annihilated their hopes, dreams and futures.

*　*　*

The Package

DIRECTOR: Andrew Davis; WRITER: John Bishop; MUSIC: James Newton Howard; CINEMATOGRAPHER: Frank Tidy; EDITORS: Billy Weber, Don Zimmerman; PRODUCERS: Beverly J. Camhe, Tobie Haggerty.

CAST: Gene Hackman (Johnny Gallagher); Joanna Cassidy (Eileen Gallagher); Tommy
    Lee Jones (Thomas Boyette); John Heard (Colonel Glen Whitacre); Dennis Franz
    (Milan Delich); Pam Grier (Ruth Butler).
PRODUCTION: Orion Pictures; released 25 August 1989; 108 minutes; rated R.

*   *   *

Once upon a time, the two leading superpowers decided to discard their nukes and
peaceably co-exist. That's the premise of 1989's *The Package*. Such an event's probability
in the 1980s? About as likely as politicians submitting to lie detector tests during political debates.

When it comes to nuclear weapons, I do consider myself a realist. Nuke reduction
between the 1980s superpowers was possible and in fact in the late '80s it did happen. But
the Soviet Union and the U.S. ditching their nukes in one fell swoop? Paging the men in
white coats.

After all, what about the other countries that had nukes in 1989—China, Britain,
France, Israel, India, Pakistan and South Africa? Would they have given theirs up in a
show of solidarity with Russia and America? Or would they see nuke-free superpowers
as an opportunity to achieve their geopolitical goals?

In *The Package*, the U.S. president and the Soviet general secretary plan to sign a
treaty calling for nuclear disarmament. However, a renegade group of American and
Soviet generals want to keep the Cold War going, and they conspire to assassinate the
general secretary in Chicago. Army Master Sergeant Johnny Gallagher unknowingly
brings the assassin, who has assumed a real soldier's identity, into the U.S.

To figure out what's going on, Johnny teams with his ex-wife Lieutenant Colonel Eileen Gallagher. Johnny tracks down and kills the would-be assassin as the latter
aims a sniper rifle. He has also figured out that Colonel Whitacre masterminded the
assassination plot, and the disgusted sergeant vows to expose the colonel to the powers that be.

The Package takes the established thriller template and fleshes it out with all the
right ingredients: a likable protagonist, a hissable villain, a fast pace, a suspenseful
unease, an effective music score, a looming deadline. The stakes are the highest, for the
protagonist's failure to stop the assassination plot will leave the world on the nuclear
brink.

Heading an exemplary cast, Gene Hackman *becomes* Sergeant Gallagher, a military professional caught up in espionage crosshairs. In the initial meeting between
Johnny and ex-wife Joanna Cassidy, both actors convey volumes about the couple's
multi-layered relationship, both in the past and the present. Dennis Franz gives excellent support as a world-weary police veteran, the kind of role he was born to play.

The renegades want to prevent the abolition of U.S.–U.S.S.R. nuclear weapons
because the disposal of nukes would mean a return to conventional warfare. John Heard
tells Hackman that American troops would be fighting Russians in the streets of Washington. True, having nukes did mean that the two superpowers did not engage in a conventional war, and thus the military did not entail thousands or millions of casualties.
But having nukes also meant that either by accident or design, a nuclear war could devastate both nations, killing not only soldiers but civilians as well, tens or hundreds
of millions of them. And that's not counting the millions who would die during the
radiation-saturated aftermath.

The Package is rated R for language and violence.

Despite the less than believable premise, the movie is a good bet for thriller fans.

* * *

The Trial of the Incredible Hulk

DIRECTOR: Bill Bixby; WRITER: Gerald Dipego; MUSIC: Lance Rubin; CINEMA-TOGRAPHER: Chuck Colwell; EDITOR: Janet Ashikaga; PRODUCERS: Robert Ewing, Hugh Spencer-Phillips.

CAST: Bill Bixby (David Banner); Lou Ferrigno (The Hulk); John Rhys-Davies (Wilson Fisk); Rex Smith (Matt Murdock/Daredevil); Marta DuBois (Ellie Mendez).

PRODUCTION: Bixby-Brandon Productions, New World Television; broadcast on NBC-TV on 7 May 1989; 100 minutes; not rated.

* * *

David Banner turns into the Hulk on the witness stand, disrupts the courtroom, and even strangles a lawyer. But regrettably, it's only a dream midway through this TV movie. Despite the title, Banner and the Hulk never appear in court.

On a city subway, a thug accosts a woman, and David turns into the Hulk and saves the day. The woman, Ellie Mendez, first says that David attacked her, then declares him innocent after she's almost killed in a hospital. She is abducted by the forces of Wilson Fisk, a criminal kingpin who has corrupted the city.

Lawyer Matt Murdock has taken an imprisoned Banner as a reluctant client. Banner dreams of becoming the Hulk in court, then awakens and actually becomes the Hulk, breaking out of prison.

Murdock and Banner work together and learn each other's secret identity. Murdock moonlights as Daredevil, an acrobatic crimefighter. (Radiation blinded him at a young age, but gave him extra-sensory powers.) Together, Daredevil and Banner rescue Ellie and thwart Fisk's plans to become the head of a nationwide crime syndicate. Both living lives transformed by radiation, Murdock and Banner part as "brothers."

The tone for this *Incredible Hulk* retread is standard 20th century TV superhero fare. The performances pass muster, but the story and presentation are uneven. Daredevil's black costume is realistic, but lamentably looks nothing like the comic book's red getup. As the villain, the usually dependable John Rhys-Davies lacks charisma; his performance is flat.

Hulk-wise, it's nice to see Banner have a fellow super-being with whom he can bond. This Hulk TV movie also served as a pilot for a proposed Daredevil series that never happened. Pity.

* * *

Warlords

CO-PRODUCER–DIRECTOR: Fred Olen Ray; WRITER: Scott Ressler; MUSIC: William Belote; CINEMATOGRAPHER: László Regos; EDITOR: William Shaffer; PRODUCER: Harel Goldstein.

CAST: David Carradine (Dow); Dawn Wildsmith (Danny); Sid Haig (The Warlord).

PRODUCTION: American Independent Productions; 1989; 87 minutes; rated R.

*   *   *

There's a talking head in this one, but unfortunately, it's not David Byrne.[11] Instead, it's the painfully unfunny mutant sidekick of David Carradine. Carradine plays a clone in search of his wife.

All the ingredients of post-nuke action movies are on hand: stock nuclear explosion, gunfights, hand-to-hand combat, mutants, desert wasteland, blood and an evil warlord, this time actually named the Warlord in an apparent attempt at humor. The film fulfills the genre's usual expectations, with one minor twist: When Carradine finds his wife, it turns out she wasn't kidnapped but is having an affair with the Warlord.

Nothing works. The script strains for laughs here and there, but they're mostly DOA. The mutants stay in gas masks throughout, no doubt because the film couldn't afford monster makeup. Unsurprisingly, the movie treats women with the usual disrespect (plenty of toplessness).

Fred Olen Ray's direction is unimaginative and dull, just what you'd expect from a filmmaker who cranks out cheapies by the dozen. (To be fair, he does have a fan following.) The actors try, but have little to work with. Carradine seems dispirited, and Dawn Wildsmith appears to be doing a Margot Kidder impression—a good one by the way. Old-time genre fans may be surprised to see Robert Quarry (1970's *Count Yorga, Vampire* and others) in a minor role.

The film is rated R for language, adult content, nudity and violence.

*   *   *

CHAPTER TWELVE

1990

By Dawn's Early Light

DIRECTOR: Jack Sholder; WRITER: Bruce Gilbert, based on the novel *Trinity's Child* by William Prochnau; MUSIC: Trevor Jones; CINEMATOGRAPHER: Alexander Gruszynski; EDITOR: Tony Lombardo; PRODUCER: Thomas M. Hammel.

CAST: Powers Boothe (Major Cassidy); Rebecca De Mornay (Captain Moreau); James Earl Jones (General Charlie, callsign "Alice"); Martin Landau (President of the United States); Peter MacNicol (Tom Sedgwick).

PRODUCTION: Home Box Office, Paravision International, S.A.; released 24 April 1990; 100 minutes; rated PG-13. Alternate title: *The Grand Tour*.

* * *

During an escalating nuclear conflict, two U.S. fighter jets are ordered to shoot down an American B52 bomber that has veered from its Russian target. Both fighter pilots call this "shit duty." And there probably couldn't be a clearer sentiment describing military action of any kind on the day World War III breaks out.

From Turkey, dissident Russians fire a non–NATO nuclear missile at the Soviet Union, destroying the city of Donetsk. The self-activating Soviet defense system launches a number of ICBMs at America. The Soviet head of state explains the situation to the U.S. president (Martin Landau), noting that he cannot recall the ICBMs already in the air, and that they will kill from six to nine million Americans. The Soviet leader welcomes a U.S. strike that will mean similar casualties for Russia, followed by a cessation of hostilities from both countries.

Strategic Air Command verifies that Russia has sent a second wave of nukes. Reluctantly, the president authorizes a phased, full-scale nuclear response against the Soviet Union. But it turns out that second Soviet strike was directed at China, not the U.S. Before the president can turn the situation around, a nearby nuclear explosion causes his helicopter to crash.

From here, the movie plays out between two sets of protagonists: the crew of B52 bomber *Polar Bear 1*, piloted by Major Cassidy (Powers Boothe) and Captain Moreau (Rebecca De Mornay), flying towards Russia to deliver nuclear ordnance; and the U.S. political and military authorities.

Polar Bear 1 scrambles into airborne action, and the crew learns that war is underway. Their Air Force base is nuked; the white flash blinds Captain Moreau in one eye; the shock wave kills a crew member.

After the president is assumed dead, the Secretary of the Interior (Darren McGavin) is sworn in as the acting president and takes the codename Condor. In flight aboard *Night-hawk*, Condor ignores an admiral urging him to work with Russia to stop the war before it becomes bigger. Instead, Condor falls under the spell of ultra-hawk Colonel Fargo (Rip Torn), who urges Condor to escalate hostilities so the U.S. can "win" this nuclear war.

Condor contacts the Looking Glass plane and speaks to its commander codenamed Alice (James Earl Jones), ordering him to send in more U.S. bombers. Alice reluctantly complies.

Aboard *Polar Bear 1*, the crew has decided to defy orders and turn around. Crewman Tyler (Glenn Withrow) becomes distraught and assaults Major Cassidy. He next attempts to shoot Cassidy and Captain Moreau, but sets off an ejection seat that pulls all the crew out of the plane except for Cassidy and Moreau.

The original president is found, injured by his helicopter's crash. He manages to speak with the Soviet head of state, both agreeing to cease hostilities for at least 60 minutes. The president talks to Alice, who turns the American bombers around but doesn't have the codes to do so for U.S. submarines. For that, the president will have to speak with Condor.

The president talks on the phone with Condor, who believes the caller could be an imposter. Condor orders his plane's crew to tell the submarines to fire their missiles. To prevent the subs from receiving this command, Looking Glass deliberately crashes into Condor's plane, destroying both aircraft.

Sanity is restored, and America and Russia cease hostilities. But Cassidy and Moreau, still airborne, have no idea what comes next.

After choosing not to bomb their Russian target, pilots Captain Moreau (Rebecca De Mornay, left) and Major Cassidy (Powers Boothe) find U.S. Navy jets escorting their aircraft with orders to shoot them down in 1990's *By Dawn's Early Light* (HBO).

Though debuting at the tail end of the Cold War nuke movie cycle, *By Dawn's Early Light* shines with the best of them. Intense and fast-paced, it benefits from a canny script that fleshes out its characters through dramatic shorthand. Naturally, it helps that every actor delivers an effective performance, the standouts being Martin Landau as the president, James Earl Jones as "Alice," Rip Torn as Colonel Fargo and Darren McGavin as Condor. Story-wise, perhaps Cassidy and Moreau's romance isn't necessary, but it doesn't damage the film.

Though the filmmakers didn't have the budget to show detailed widespread destruction, we do see long shots of burning ruins in Washington, D.C., and Baton Rouge. All of the aircraft effects pass muster, from *Polar Bear 1*'s B52 to the Russian bandits. However, we see only one long shot of a mushroom cloud.

The film's message seems to be that if a nuclear weapon is used inadvertently and leads to the possibility of a limited nuclear war, the nations involved should agree to stop escalation as soon as possible. Otherwise, you get the nightmare aftermaths depicted in *The Day After* and *Threads*.

The film places a heavy emphasis on how different personalities could influence a confused nuke war scenario. For example, Moreau leads Cassidy and the *Polar Bear 1* crew to abandon their orders to drop nuclear ordnance in Russia. Had she not been Cassidy's co-pilot, perhaps he would have continued; his romantic feelings for her no doubt tipped the scales in favor of aborting the mission. But at what price? Was this an act of treason? Or was this a case of following your conscience despite the consequences?

Similarly, "Alice" defies Condor at one point, and Condor fires the general. But "Alice" will not follow orders that could lead to a war killing hundreds of millions when it is still possible to negotiate a ceasefire. "Alice" is a general who eschews the notion of a "winnable" nuclear war. James Earl Jones expertly embodies the man's grit.

However, Colonel Fargo is the type of hawk who embraces triumphant World War III scenarios. And Condor allows Fargo to seduce him into the notion of old-style military "victory," despite the reality that all-out nuclear war would prevent America from being able to dominate anyone, much less Russia, which would also be in ruins. In such a case, what would the U.S. win?

As the acting president, Darren McGavin captures Condor's bluster and power-grabbing pleasure.

By Dawn's Early Light includes many memorable touches, and one of the best is the pilot of Condor's plane saluting Looking Glass, and Looking Glass's "Alice" returning the salute before his plane slams into Condor's. This tragic sacrifice, the intentional destruction of both planes, calls to mind 9/11's Flight 93 in which the passengers rallied to stop the terrorists, resulting in the plane crashing and all on board dying.

There's an insightful touch when Cassidy and Moreau turn their bomber around. Moreau says, "Maybe we ought to face reality."

"If we're lucky," Cassidy replies, "reality is a firing squad."

"And if we're unlucky?"

"*Planet of the Apes*, darlin'."

And that is where an all-out nuclear war would leave all of us.

But even with the limited atomic combat of *By Dawn's Early Light*, millions of Americans would be dead, the country's infrastructure would be in shambles, and the healthcare system would be inundated by a flood of survivors needing medical attention.

Reviews for the HBO movie are mostly positive. *USA Today*'s Matt Roush called it

"Alice" (James Earl Jones), the Air Force general in control of the EC-135 Looking Glass, in a pensive moment in 1990's *By Dawn's Early Light* (HBO).

"a white-knuckled thriller about the impending end of the world ... [W]ith its mutinies and reversals and sacrifices keeping you guessing till the end, it succeeds as a fail-safe, flat-out–entertaining doomsday fantasy."[1] According to Baltimore's *Evening Sun*, "Even though it was made for cable's Home Box Office, this hard-edged thriller can compete with the best of theatrical films."[2]

The movie ends inconclusively, with Cassidy and Moreau flying into the morning sun. Cassidy's final words are cryptic: "Welcome to tomorrow."

Welcome indeed.

*   *   *

The Death of the Incredible Hulk

DIRECTOR: Bill Bixby; WRITER: Gerald Di Pego; MUSIC: Lance Rubin; CINEMA-TOGRAPHER: Chuck Colwell; EDITOR: Janet Ashikaga; PRODUCERS: Robert Ewing, Hugh Spencer-Phillips.

CAST: Bill Bixby (David Banner); Lou Ferrigno (The Hulk); Elizabeth Gracen (Jasmin); Philip Sterling (Dr. Ronald Pratt); Anna Katarina (Bella); Barbara Tarbuck (Amy Pratt).

PRODUCTION: Bixby-Brandon Productions, New World Television; broadcast on NBC-TV on 18 February 1990; 95 minutes; not rated.

*   *   *

If you feel a distinct sense of *déjà vu*, you're not alone. Anyone familiar with the *Incredible Hulk* TV series or its two previous reunion TV-movies has seen this plot before: Banner works at a major lab, finds a scientist whose work may cure him, the process is interrupted, Banner becomes the Hulk, trounces the bad guys, turns back into Banner, and walks away. But this time, that final plot point is missing.

While pretending to be mentally challenged, Banner works at a research institute where scientist Ronald Pratt is developing theories similar to Banner's. Once Banner reveals his true identity to Dr. Pratt, the scientist believes he can cure Banner and put the Hulk to rest once and for all.

During the procedure, Jasmin, a spy, breaks in to steal Dr. Pratt's work. In the confusion, the lab catches fire. David becomes the Hulk and carries Dr. Pratt to safety, then flees.

Pursued by spies, Banner finds refuge with Jasmin. She's done with spying, and in a secluded cabin, she and Banner fall in love.

Bella, Jasmin's sister, has her men kidnap Dr. Pratt and his wife Amy and take them to an airfield. Federal agents and the police storm the airfield, getting into a firefight with Bella's agents. During the fray, Dr. Pratt and Amy find safety, while Banner turns into the Hulk. Bella and one of her agents attempt to escape in an airplane, but the Hulk smashes on board as it takes off. The Hulk forces Bella's gun hand to shoot the fuel tank, and the plane explodes.

The Hulk falls, buckling the concrete when he lands. Once he has transformed into a fatally injured Banner, Jasmin tells him they can be free now. To which a dying Banner replies, "Jasmin, I am free."

In this final entry, cast to crew turns in professional work. Some might have wanted the green goliath's last adventure to perhaps have tugged more at the heartstrings. But Banner's death is wisely underplayed, and this time when you hear the series' familiar "Lonely Man" theme, it takes on a plaintive finality, especially considering the fact that Bixby has also passed on.

Thanks for the memories, Bill and Lou.

* * *

The Final Sanction

DIRECTOR-WRITER: David A. Prior; MUSIC: Tim James, Garm Beall, Steve McClintock; CINEMATOGRAPHER: Andrew Parke; EDITOR: Christopher Reynolds; PRODUCER: David Marriott.

CAST: Ted Prior (Sgt. Tom Batanic); Robert Z'Dar (Sgt. Sergi Schvackov); Renée Cline (Lieutenant Tavlin); William Smith (Major Galashkin); David Fawcett (General Royston).

PRODUCTION: Action International Pictures; released to U.S. video on 30 November 1990; 85 minutes; rated R.

* * *

It's 1990, you have a minuscule budget, but you want to stage a conflict between the United States and the Soviet Union. What to do? Scale down the battle to just one American and one Russian.

The Final Sanction begins well with a limited nuclear war waged between the U.S. and the U.S.S.R. We hear that 15 American military bases have suffered direct hits, and that tens of thousands have died. This sequence includes that best friend of low-budget filmmakers, stock footage, which includes often-seen images of ICBMs lifting off, as well as a government test area suffering nuclear blast damage. A bit of *The Day After* is thrown in to provide an honest-to-Oppenheimer mushroom cloud.

After this modest but not-bad opening, the film quickly fizzles. Sgt. Tom Batanic will represent America against a Soviet soldier in a one-on-one battle to determine which nation wins, thus preventing the countries from resorting to further nuclear engagement. Batanic is a smart-aleck jerk, while Sgt. Sergi Schvackov, the Soviet fighter, embodies the motherland.

They wage war on a 20-acre section of Virginia. Lieutenant Tavlin serves as Batanic's online assistant, tracking his opponent's whereabouts. The Yank and the Russian clash like the movie combatants they are: lots of shooting, explosions, chasing, cursing and, from the Russian, much throwing of garden spades (yes, you read that right). Somewhat unbelievably, neither Batanic nor Schvackov wear body armor, helmets or protective clothing. Instead, their minimal combat attire flaunts their bulging biceps, making them appear to be extras in a new Rambo movie.

It was all for naught: American General Royston and Russian Major Galashkin reveal that this duel was a ruse; it was to be declared a draw so neither nation would face dishonor. However, Batanic and Schbackov have survived the immense explosions the general thought had killed them. Accordingly, the FBI arrests the general, putting a damper on his power-grabbing schemes.

The film's main idea isn't bad; 1990's *Robot Jox* employs a variation of the concept. In addition, a 1970 ABC made-for-TV movie called *The Challenge* uses the premise, with Darren McGavin and Mako fighting each other as surrogates for America and China.

As antiheroes go, Batanic brings to mind the ill-mannered Snake Plissken from 1981's *Escape from New York*. Batanic and his female combat assistant Lieutenant Tavlin start out squabbling but wind up dating by movie's end. This overly familiar subplot should be relegated to the movie cliché waste-bin, but I admit I fell for it.

The Final Sanction wants to be an action flick and a nuke thriller—but it fails on both counts.

* * *

Flight from Paradise

DIRECTOR: Ettore Pasculli; WRITERS: Lucio Mandarà, Ettore Pasculli; MUSIC: Michel Legrand: CINEMATOGRAPHER: Alfio Contini; EDITOR: Ruggero Mastroianni; PRODUCERS: Luciano Luna, Claudia Mori.
CAST: Fabrice Josso (Theo); Inés Sastre (Beatrice); Horst Buchholz (Thor).
PRODUCTION: Iduna Film Produktiongesellschaft, Azzurra Film, Cinémax, RAI Radiotelevisione Italiana; Italian-French-German; 1990; 112 minutes; not rated. Alternate titles: *Escape from Paradise*, *Fuga dal Paradiso*.

* * *

The last thing I expected from this European post-nuke drama was narration by classic movie veteran Van Johnson,[3] a major Hollywood star in the 1940s and 1950s. I also didn't anticipate seeing the bad guys riding camels instead of horses. And their weapons of choice were flamethrowers. However, fans of this subgenre will find the movie's other post-nuke elements familiar.

In the future, nuclear war (evidenced by a parade of stock footage mushroom clouds) and ecological havoc have caused uncontaminated humans to live in underground vaults safe from the irradiated surface world. Most families live in separate quarters, only seeing and communicating with others on a viewscreen. Such is the case for teenagers Beatrice and Theo, in love but unable to touch each other. However, after the couple secretly watches a video-disk showing pre-apocalyptic society, they escape from their quarantined vaults and touch for the first time, then flee to the outside world.

There, they discover choking clouds, city ruins and ragtag survivors. Thor, their underground world's policeman, is hot on their trail. Thor eventually captures Theo, but friendly surface survivors spirit Beatrice away. Eventually, Theo and Beatrice reunite, for though Thor threatens to kill Beatrice, he frees her instead. Beatrice and Theo join the surface survivors on a ship sailing for parts unknown.

Flight from Paradise gives us an overlong look at teenage love in a post-apocalyptic world, with Theo and Beatrice serving as a sort of nuclear age Romeo and Juliet. The acting varies from reasonably collected to arm-waving hysteria. Interestingly, Beatrice and Theo's romance remains chaste—we never see them sleep together. Still, we assume they marry shortly after the movie's finale.

Unrated, the film would probably receive a PG for adult content and very brief nudity.

* * *

Hardware

DIRECTOR-WRITER: Richard Stanley; MUSIC: Simon Boswell; CINEMATOGRA-PHER: Steven Chivers; EDITOR: Derek Trigg; PRODUCERS: Paul Trybits, Joanne Sellar.

CAST: Dylan McDermott (Moses "Mo" Baxter); Stacey Travis (Jill); John Lynch (Shades); Iggy Pop (Angry Bob); Carl McCoy (Nomad); Mark Northover (Alvy); Lemmy (Taxi Driver).

PRODUCTION: Unlimited Palace Productions; British Screen; British Satellite Broadcasting (BSB), Wicked Films; British; 1990; rated R.

* * *

Science fiction films don't customarily begin with a Bible passage, but 1990's *Hardware* starts with a title card saying, "'No flesh shall be spared,' Mark 13." Of course, after watching the movie, you may feel the passage should be changed to "No viewer shall be spared."

The film begins in a city of the future after a nuclear war. The sky is reddish-pink, the wastelands scrap-littered, the city a crumbling mess. As DJ Angry Bob tells his listeners regarding good news, "There is no effing good news!"

Military man Mo buys assorted robot parts from a nomad and sells this junk, minus the robot head, to salvage merchant Alvy. Mo gives the head to his artist girlfriend Jill as a Christmas present, and she immediately sets it atop a scratch-built sculpture. The head is the key component of a defective M.A.R.K. 13 robot and it still functions.

Alvy summons Mo to warn him about the robot head, but it's too late: The metallic skull has already cannibalized metal and electronics from Jill's apartment to turn itself into an ambulatory killing machine. It gorily dispatches a voyeuristic neighbor, then traps Jill in her kitchen.

Mo and reinforcements assault the robot with heavy weapons fire. It appears to be finished—but of course, it's not. Mo attacks it, but the robot injects him with a slow-acting toxin. His mechanical hand somehow links to the M.A.R.K. 13, and when Jill patches into the robot's head, what's left of Mo tells her about the robot's weakness: humidity. Jill ends up in the shower with the robot and turns on the water, shorting out the homicidal automaton.

The following morning, DJ Angry Bob announces that the defense department is allowing an electronics company to mass-produce the M.A.R.K. 13, whose purpose will be to massacre a number of humans to "solve" the overpopulation crisis.

Admittedly stylish, *Hardware* is also repugnant. The production design gives life to a grungy post-nuke world. Indicative of the film's heinousness is a scene in which a sexual voyeur delights in his depravity while "Silent Night" plays. The scene comes off as sick and offensive, as was apparently intended. *Hardware*'s world is one in which innocence has breathed its last.

Hardware's post-nuke milieu intrigues on a number of levels. Despite the generally decrepit state of the buildings, technology seems to be functioning fairly well. TVs work, and electricity seems to be available. This suggests that the nuclear war—or wars, as the case may be—was limited.

What little we see of this age's TV programs is disturbing. Also, Jill frequently gets high via apparently government-supplied drug cigarettes. We see Mo's friend Shades give himself over to an elaborate drug ritual. Obviously, this is a society seeking escape.

In addition, we hear that the government is trying to solve the overpopulation crisis. But after a limited nuclear war, would overpopulation be a problem? In a limited nuke exchange, possibly millions, and at least thousands, would die. Then again, perhaps the government of *Hardware* wants to reduce the number of radiation-caused birth defects. Or perhaps it only has limited supplies (food, medicine, etc.).

Jill tells Mo that the government wants to pass a bill to levy fines and take away ration coupons, to force people to have fewer children, as well as sterilize those who have been exposed to high radiation doses. This means a centralized government seems to be functioning, albeit one more draconian than most today. M.A.R.K. 13's mission to exterminate humans suggests a dystopian government gone berserk.

The film pours on the sex and violence. The sex, in fact, appears to give a sense of Mo's and Jill's desperation in this joyless post-nuke milieu, as well as epitomizing Mo's transient commitment. For example, after Jill makes a remark about the possibility of having radioactive children, Mo says, "I stopped thinking about kids a long time ago."

As for the violence, the movie initially received the MPAA's × rating for excessive carnage. After excising a portion from a scene of a man cut in two, it received an R.[4] If *Hardware* could be said to have a worldview, it appears to be nihilism. Yet there is the odd scene of Mo reading a Bible and contemplating the Gospel of Mark 13. If the Bible belongs to him, maybe it provides some modicum of comfort despite his pessimism. Of course, the Bible passage also ties into the M.A.R.K. 13 robot, as well as the army of these homicidal automatons that will soon assail humankind.

Hardware received mixed reviews. *Variety*: "A cacophonic, nightmarish variation on the post-apocalyptic cautionary genre, *Hardware* has the makings of a punk cult film."[5] Richard Harrington of *The Washington Post* opined, "While it's obvious that [writer-director Richard] Stanley has seen a lot of genre films, he's not yet learned how to make one, though his shortcomings are less visual than dramatic and narrative."[6]

Hardware wallows in its perversity. It presents a post-nuke society more disturbing than those depicted in *Mad Max* clones, one headed straight for Hell.

* * *

The Hunt for Red October

DIRECTOR: John McTiernan; WRITERS: Larry Ferguson, Donald Stewart, based on the novel by Tom Clancy; MUSIC: Basil Poledouris; CINEMATOGRAPHER: Jan de Bont; EDITORS: Dennis Virkler, John Wright; PRODUCER: Mace Neufeld.

CAST: Sean Connery (Captain Marko Ramius); Alec Baldwin (Jack Ryan); Scott Glenn (Commander Bart Mancuso); Sam Neill (Captain Borodin); James Earl Jones (Admiral Greer); Tomas Arana (Igor Loginov); Joss Ackland (Andrei Lysenko); Richard Jordan (Jeffrey Pelt); Peter Firth (Ivan Putin); Tim Curry (Dr. Petrov).

PRODUCTION: Paramount Pictures, Mace Neufeld Productions, Nina Saxon Film Design; 1990; 134 minutes; rated PG.

* * *

You've got trouble, right here in Paramount Studios: It's March 1990 and you're about to release the Cold War thriller *The Hunt for Red October*. But in real-life Russia, the Communists have been ousted from government. Even before its release, your movie

Soviet submarine Captain Marko Ramius (Sean Connery) plans to defect to the U.S. despite dangerous obstacles (such as the Russians trying to sink his sub) in 1990's *The Hunt for Red October* (Paramount), an adaptation of Tom Clancy's best-selling novel.

has become dated. What to do? Insert a screen crawler stating that the film takes place in 1984 instead of the present day. This post-production strategy literally paid off: The film cost $30 million but got $122 million domestically and $200 million worldwide.[7] Of course, some (or a lot) of that can probably also be credited to the film's star power.

Marko Ramius, the captain of *Red October*, a new Russian ballistic missile submarine, plans to defect to the U.S. His submarine officers are in on the scheme. However, the Soviet leadership is aware of Ramius' intentions and they deceptively tell the Americans that Ramius is a madman who plans to launch a nuclear missile at the U.S., something he can do clandestinely because *Red October* has a new propulsion drive that sonar cannot detect.

CIA agent and former Marine Jack Ryan knows Ramius' psychology and asserts to his superiors that Ramius doesn't want to start World War III, but rather to defect. The National Security Adviser gives him three days to prove it.

Ryan boards the American submarine *Dallas*, which is tracking *Red October* because *Dallas*' sonar officer has found a way to "listen" to the Russian sub's propulsion signal. Ryan convinces *Dallas* commander Bart Mancuso to communicate with Captain Marius, who confirms his intention to defect.

Staging a faked nuclear reactor accident, Ramius has his men evacuate the sub in lifeboats; once *Red October* has re-submerged, Ryan and several others board the vessel via a rescue submarine. The Soviet sub *Konovalov* attacks *Red October*, but a deft move on *Red October*'s part causes the attack torpedo to destroy the *Konovalov*.

The U.S.'s official cover story is that *Red October* was destroyed and that it's at too great a depth to examine the wreckage. Meanwhile, Ramius and Ryan, aboard *Red October*, arrive in the Penobscot River in Maine. Ramius tells Ryan he defected because *Red October* was created for one reason: to make a nuclear first strike against the U.S.

The Hunt for Red October provides over two hours of savvy political thriller excitement. The complex storyline never gets in its way, instead maintaining an admirable clarity throughout. The direction propels the movie at a satisfying pace—never too fast, never too slow.

The dramatic highpoints are handled with slick precision, such as the saboteur's attack on Ryan & Co. near the movie's end, and also the suspenseful sequence in which it appears an attack torpedo will waste *Red October*. A last-second command moves the sub out of harm's way and the torpedo strikes the Russian sub that launched it.

However, the presentation of the Russians' dialogue disappoints. For example, at the beginning of the movie, we hear Sean Connery and Sam Neill's characters speaking in Russian, but a short time later, they and the other Russians start speaking English (still supposed to be Russian), an awkward transition. But having Connery, Neill and the other Russian submarine cast members speak in Russian throughout would have been problematic, and a disappointment to Connery fans.

Also, Ryan's penchant for being both right and lucky occasionally strains credulity. He doesn't have much evidence beyond speculation that Marius wants to defect. And his luck, such as guessing that Marius would go starboard, proves too convenient.

Connery brings Captain Marius to life; Connery not only looks the part, he *is* the part. The rest of the cast deliver professional performances, especially James Earl Jones as Admiral Greer.

The American Film Institute noted, "A week before the film's release, the Soviet newspaper *Izvestia* released confirmation of previously unverified reports describing a mutiny on a Russian anti-submarine destroyer in Nov[ember] 1975."[8] Apparently, a Russian naval officer planned to take the ship to Sweden and declare it free of Communist control. Some have assumed that this partially provided the basis for author Tom Clancy's novel, but the author maintained that his tale was merely fiction.[9]

Captain Marius's reason for defection—refusing to be the first wave of a Russian nuke attack against America—clearly connects the movie to the nuclear threat, and shows a military professional placing humanity above his country. His defection also serves as a chilly reminder that some Soviet and U.S. military leaders actually considered "first strike" strategies in the 1980s. Leonard Maltin gave the film three and a half out of four stars and opined "Exciting, complex thriller from the best-seller by Tom Clancy ... another direct hit."[10]

Intelligently conceived and executed, *The Hunt for Red October* is a model of its Cold War thriller genre.

* * *

Robot Jox

DIRECTOR: Stuart Gordon; WRITER: Joe Haldeman (screenplay); Stuart Gordon (story); MUSIC: Frederic Talgorn; CINEMATOGRAPHER: Mac Ahlberg; EDITORS: Ted Nicolaou, Lori Scott Ball; VISUAL EFFECTS: David Allen; PRODUCER: Albert Band.

CAST: Gary Graham (Achilles); Anne-Marie Johnson (Athena); Paul Koslo (Alexander); Robert Sampson (Commissioner Jameson); Danny Kamekona (Dr. Matsumoto); Hilary Mason (Professor Laplace); Michael Alldredge (Tex Conway).

PRODUCTION: Empire Pictures; 1990; 85 minutes; rated PG.

* * *

Robot Jox was one of the last gasps for the special effects technique known as stop-motion model animation. It was also one of the last gasps for Cold War–inspired nuke movies.

Fifty years after a devastating nuclear holocaust, the two major superpowers are the America-dominated Market and the Russia-dominated Confederation. They have banished conventional war, and now giant robots represent each nation. Piloted by techno-gladiators called "robot jox," the robots battle for territory.

The Confederation's Alexander has just won his ninth match, killing his Market opponents. Achilles, the Market's reigning champion with nine matches under his belt, is Alexander's next opponent.

Alexander and Achilles' gargantuan automatons clash. Alexander fires a rocket fist that accidentally hurtles towards the match's bleachers. Achilles' robot stops it, but the impact knocks him into the bleachers, killing over 300 spectators.

Devastated, Achilles announces his retirement. But when it is reported that Athena, a genetically engineered pilot, will take his place, Achilles changes his mind and announces that he will fight Alexander after all.

The Market's ace trainer Tex Conway tells Achilles the Confederation is winning its matches because a Market spy is feeding them insider information. In private, Dr. Matsumoto accuses Tex of being the spy. Tex shoots him and tells his superiors that Matsumoto confessed to being a spy and killed himself.

Athena, who (surprise) is in love with Achilles, is determined to fight the match. She gives Achilles a sedative she says will wear off in a few hours. Warding off attempts to stop her, she boards the Market robot and reaches its control center.

Matsumoto's video about the robot's newest weapon is seen in both the Market robot and control room; it also includes Tex's shooting of Matsumoto. Before Tex can be captured, he takes his own life by flinging himself down the elevator shaft.

Alexander's robot clashes with Athena's, besting her. The referees declare Alexander has won the match, but he refuses to stand down. Achilles takes over the Market robot, and the Market and Confederation automatons take their battle into outer space. Soon, Achilles crash-lands back on Earth, followed by Alexander. Alexander attacks Achilles' robot, forcing Achilles to flee on foot. But Achilles manages to rig Alexander's severed robot fist so that it launches toward Alexander's machine, destroying it. The robot jox fight *mano a mano*. But Achilles says to Alexander, "We could both live." He hurls aside his metal staff. Alexander drops his rock, and both men fist bump robot jox–style as soaring music swells.

Robot Jox features an unlikely set-up: two (improbable) giant robots duking it out in place of warring armies. The opening narration tells us the nuclear war half a century earlier almost obliterated humankind. Yet in the future the movie portrays, we see no signs of that past epic conflict. However, its sheer brutal scope has inspired the superpowers to find something other than nuclear brinksmanship to solve disputes.

But the film quickly dispenses with this grim setup and instead opts for bubblegum sci-fi action territory (with plenty of swearing). This movie apparently inspired Guillermo del Toro's 2012 *Pacific Rim* and its 2018 sequel *Pacific Rim: Uprising*. In addition, *Robot Jox*'s battles between skyscraping robots evoke an undeniable comic book spirit.

Stop-motion fans will savor the film's effects. Said visuals may recall "the good old days" when model-animated

This poster for 1990's *Robot Jox* captures the movie's comic book spirit.

monsters and mythical creatures ruled movie screens. (Starting more or less with 1993's *Jurassic Park*, CGI has replaced stop-motion ... for better or worse.) David Allen, an ace animator of old, served as *Robot Jox*'s visual effects supervisor. His résumé includes such goodies as 1981's *Caveman* and 1989's *Honey, I Shrunk the Kids*. In 1972, he animated a clever Volkswagen TV commercial featuring a model-animated King Kong harkening back to the 1933 feature.[11]

Director Stuart Gordon and screenwriter Joe Haldeman, a science fiction author best known for 1974's award-winning *The Forever War*, clashed over *Robot Jox*'s tone like two of the movie's warring robots. Initially, Gordon had told Haldeman he wanted a science fiction movie based on *The Iliad*. But Gordon stunned Haldeman by requesting non–Homerian concepts such as evil Communists and Godzilla-sized robots. Haldeman recalled, "I really wanted to write a movie, and I was sure I could talk Stuart out of the worst parts—the same attitude that most doomed marriages begin with."[12]

After considerably more drama and rewrites (one by a different writer), Haldeman found himself rewriting some scenes as the movie was being filmed. But he felt the film drastically uneven, since he didn't rewrite all of the scenes. "Most of the scenes that I worked on with Gary [Graham] and Anne-Marie [Johnson] look like a normal movie; many of the others look painfully cartoonish."[13]

Robot Jox includes lapses in logic. For example, Tex tells his fellows that Matsumoto killed himself, but Tex's fingerprints would be all over the gun (he didn't wear a glove). Also, due to the angle of the gunshot and the nature of the fatal wound, forensics would ascertain that Matsumoto did not commit suicide.

The movie features a subplot of genetically engineered "gen jox" bred to pilot the warring robots. Tellingly, they have been saddled with the derisive nickname "Tubies." But we don't find out much about them.

The finale doesn't ring true when Achilles convinces Alexander to set aside their differences and choose to live rather than fight to the death. We haven't seen anything in Alexander's sadistic character that suggests he would, out of the blue, choose pacifism over violence.

The Washington Post's Roger Hurlburt offered this apparently unintended compliment: "For pre-teens, ... *Robot Jox* might be considered really 'neat' entertainment."[14] *The Encyclopedia of Science Fiction* more favorably opined, "[T]op-of-the-line effects by David Allen in the robot combat, but low-budget interiors and a few wobbly matte fringes.... [Director Gordon] gives the film a pleasantly uncluttered comic-bookish look, while [Joe] Haldeman's sf-writer touch can be traced in the neat background details."[15]

Robot Jox has developed something of a cult following. It's a relic of its age, both in terms of special effects and Cold War politics. But those open to its appeal will have fun.

*   *   *

Sons of Steel

DIRECTOR-WRITER-MUSIC: Gary L. Keady; CINEMATOGRAPHER: Joseph Pickering; EDITOR: Amanda Robson; PRODUCER: James Michael Vernon.
CAST: Rob Hartley (Black Alice); Roz Wason (Hope); Jeff Duff (Secta).
PRODUCTION: Big Island Pictures; Australian; 1990 (Australian release; played at Cannes in 1998); 104 minutes; not rated.

*   *   *

Some movies are dumb unintentionally, but some are deliberately daft. Such appears to be the case with the nuke threat rock-musical *Sons of Steel.*

In the near-future, Oceana is a military dictatorship and a nuclear-free zone. But the latter will change when a nuclear submarine sails into harbor. Enter Black Alice, a body-builder rock star (think Ozzy Osbourne with pecs) who heads a national peace movement.

After multiple songs sandwiched between frenetic action, mad scientist Secta sends Alice 113 years into the future. There, Alice discovers a nuclear wasteland which he inadvertently caused. He returns to the present to prevent a ferry of peace activists from colliding with a nuclear submarine, which will atomize Oceana and start a nuclear war.

Sons of Steel may be foolish and pseudo-artsy, but no one can say it's pokey: It moves like a cinematic cheetah. Colorful visuals dazzle the viewer, but the movie plays like an overlong music video. The songs are for the most part appealing. I especially liked the film's cover of Thunderclap Newman's 1969 hit "Something in the Air."

Sons of Steel fails to make a serious or even satirical case against nuclear weapons. Yet it does feature one striking post-nuke visual: human skeletons melted together. It also posits a prehistoric future for those who have survived on the surface.

Unrated, the film would probably receive an R for strong language, adult subject matter, kinky content, nudity and violence.

Given all the worthwhile 1980s nuke threat movies, *Sons of Steel* doesn't merit even a single viewing.

*   *   *

Ultra Warrior

DIRECTORS: Augusto Tamayo, Kevin Tent; WRITERS: Len Jenkin, Dan Kleinman; MUSIC: Kevin Klingler, Ed Tomney, Terry Plumeri; CINEMATOGRAPHER: Cusi Barrio; EDITOR: Dan Schalk; PRODUCER: Luis Llosa.

CAST: Dack Rambo (Kenner); Clare Beresford (Grace); Meshach Taylor (Elijah); Ramsay Ross (Uncle Lazarus); Orlando Sacha (Bishop).

PRODUCTION: Concorde-New Horizons; produced in Peru; released on 16 March 1990; 81 minutes; rated R.

*   *   *

By 1990, the post-nuke action genre was wheezing its last, its collapse epitomized in *Ultra Warrior.*

A space-based defense system malfunction causes nuclear destruction that kills millions, with millions more dying from fallout. A familiar society has risen from the ashes: Rich folks live in cities run by dolts; poor folks have largely become mutants, or "Muties," constantly on the run from feudal factions who enslave and abuse them.

Enter our hero Kenner. His superior orders him to trek to Oblivion (once the Atlantic Ocean coast) and take the radiation readings on the zirconium there. It seems the rich folks are battling space-faring aliens who want to turn all the planets in our solar system into stars, and only zirconium bombs work against the alien ships. (At least this is a different, if ridiculous, wrinkle in a post-nuke action film.)

En route to Oblivion, Kenner fraternizes with a group of Muties, especially Grace. Uncle Lazarus, the Muties' leader, passes the leadership torch off to a reluctant Kenner.

He leads the Muties against a group of bandits ruled by the Bishop. Unsurprisingly, the Muties defeat the Bishop's henchmen, and the Bishop turns out to be a Mutie himself.

Kenner, who by now has fallen in love with Grace, reports to his superiors that the zirconium repositories are still too radioactive to mine—a deliberate lie. He and Grace take off for the Oblivion.

Ultra Warrior is one of the weakest of its era's post-nuke action flicks. To save money, stock footage stuffs the movie, much of it from 1980's *Battle Beyond the Stars*. Also, the film manages to be—by turns—cheap, tawdry, dull and pretentious.

To its credit, it features a quick (and clever) cameo by Roger Corman. In addition, it includes a bona fide character arc for Kenner, as he changes from cynical mercenary to benevolent good guy. His character metamorphosis is simplistic, yes, but it's still worth noting, given that most of this era's post-nuke action movies eschew character development.

To its discredit, the film delves into soft porn territory. The two explicit sex scenes definitely objectify women, appealing to the worst in male viewers. The second sex scene provokes unintentional laughs: While Kenner and Grace have conjugal relations, a superimposed fire burns at the bottom of the screen. Talk about over-the-top.

Dack Rambo, who plays Kenner, had featured guest roles on many classic television shows, including *Cannon, Wonder Woman* and *Charlie's Angels*. Alongside Walter Brennan, he starred in *The Guns of Will Sonnett* (1967-69). From 1985 to 1987, he played Jack Ewing on TV's *Dallas*. On March 21, 1994, he died from AIDS complications.[16]

Meshach Taylor is probably best-remembered for his role of Anthony Bouvier on the sitcom *Designing Women* (1986–93). A gifted performer, Taylor deserved far better than the thankless role of *Ultra Warrior*'s Elijah. Stricken with cancer, Taylor died on June 28, 2014.[17]

Ultra Warrior is one of those forgotten movies that deserves to be forgotten. Re-discover it at your own risk.

* * *

Epilogue

Do we need a *The Day After* for the 2020s? Some have suggested as much. But are the themes of 1980s nuke threat movies—limited or total nuclear war, nuclear terrorism, nuclear accidents—now overly familiar?

A quick survey of several post–1990 nuke threat movies suggests some answers. *Aftermath* (2014) gives us a traditional nuke war survival tale, familiar but still mesmerizing in its grimness, a sort of mini–*Day After*. *The Sum of All Fears* (2002) delivers a nightmare many a U.S. administration has feared, terrorists setting off a nuclear bomb at a major American event, in this case a pro football game, territory no 1980s nuke threat movie broached. And *Deterrence* (1999) depicts what could happen if an adamant president carried out a nuclear threat against a Middle Eastern country. It's a situation similar to 1984's *Countdown to Looking Glass*, yet one that chillingly remains relevant. Pushing the genre further, 2011's *The Divide* depicts some basement-dwelling nuclear war survivors sliding into psychosis and sadism. It's perhaps the most unpleasant aftermath movie yet.[1]

The themes of these movies coincide with those of their 1980s brethren, demonstrating how easily nuclear war or terrorism could happen and showing or implying the horror such an event would visit upon America. But granted, post–1990 nuke threat films have only appeared sporadically, nowhere near the annual numbers 1980s nuke movies boasted.

Are Americans today as afraid of nuclear war as during the 1980s? Probably not, but as I write this epilogue, current international events have once again shoved the nuke threat into the spotlight. A March 2022 AP-NORC poll asked the question, "How concerned are you about Russia targeting the following with nuclear weapons?" Amazingly, 45 percent of Americans said they were "extremely/very concerned" that Russia might use nukes against the U.S., and another 30 percent said they were "somewhat" concerned.[2] Similarly, a March 2022 Gallup poll asked respondents to rate a series of threats to the U.S. as "Critical," "Important" or "Not important." Seventy-eight percent rated "Development of nuclear weapons by North Korea" as critical, and 76 percent rated "Development of nuclear weapons by Iran" as critical.[3] In both cases, more than three in every four Americans consider nuclear weapons development by questionable international players to be a major worry.

So if it's true that Americans are still open to the nuke threat genre, and studios started making more of them, perhaps especially in the mini-series format, would greater awareness of nuclear war be good or bad?

First, a quick look at nuclear war types: Greater awareness, and thus greater preparation, could be advantageous in a limited nuclear war, but perhaps of little if any advantage in a full-scale nuclear conflict. Similarly, if you live in a rural area, your survival odds are greater than if you live in an urban environment. Of course, rural Americans would probably be subject to nuclear fallout, which could kill many of them as 1983's *Testament* depicts.

Given that survival chances in a nuclear war are not good no matter how you slice it, wouldn't greater awareness needlessly magnify this possible horror? For example, even in the event of terrorists detonating a one-megaton nuclear weapon in an American city of one to two million, the number of burn victims would exceed America's total burn bed capacity.[4] In addition, because of radiation and wreckage hazards, the most severely injured victims would die before rescue teams reached them.[5] Americans more aware of these and other facts might let this anxiety spill over into their daily lives, tainting both work and play. This fear might not only afflict the person, but also their family, friends, colleagues and acquaintances—indeed, society at large.

On the other hand, greater awareness could increase the recovery odds of nuclear attack survivors. For example, informed survivors would know to get inside within 15 minutes, move to a room or basement preferably with no windows, and stay there for at least 48 hours.[6] Greater awareness could also lead to better nuclear weapons policies. If nuclear war became one of the top political issues of the day and received widespread media coverage, politicians would be forced to grapple with the issue beyond vague generalities. This might lead many Americans to be less fearful about this pivotal concern, an optimism that could spill over into their civic, work and personal lives.

U.S. soldiers watch a billowing mushroom cloud that was part of the Hardtack Series I Pacific Tests in 1958. Were they watching a simple nuclear demonstration, or a portent of humankind's destiny in the 21st century?

Still, survival following a major nuclear war would be grim at best, and any advice for post-nuke preparations would have to acknowledge this reality. U.S. government officials would have an edge, as many would be evacuated to a safer area, possibly Raven Rock Mountain Complex, basically a miniature underground city.[7] The super-rich would also have an edge: They would presumably retreat to multi-million dollar survival bunkers.[8] The rest of us would be left on our own; our best shelters would be basements or storm cellars, and many wouldn't even have *that*.

On the other hand, in the case of a single-event nuclear occurrence, such as a stand-alone nuke going off in a city, nuclear event preparations could benefit the survivors. The same could be true in case of a major nuclear accident. But when it comes to full-scale nuclear war, our best preparations would probably make little difference.

Still, as they say, knowledge is power, and it's better to be informed than to live in denial. For example, let's say you are diagnosed as having advanced cancer. Would you want to know your odds of survival? Your options for dealing with the affliction? The pain and discomfort that radiological and other treatments might cause? Or would you prefer that your oncologist smile, pat you on the shoulder, and say, "I wouldn't worry about it if I were you."

Perhaps a *Day After* for the 2020s based on current geopolitical possibilities (for example, North Korea nuking a West Coast city) might serve as both a catharsis and a rallying cry for modern-day America. Of course, rallying cries spoken softly can often be the most effective. A scene from the end of 1959's post-nuke movie *On the Beach* comes to mind. In the film, radioactive fallout will soon kill the nuclear war survivors in Melbourne, Australia. At an outdoor Salvation Army meeting, at which dozens have gathered, a fluttering banner reads, "There's still time, brother."

The same holds true today.

*   *   *

Appendix

The following is a list of ten movies that some readers might have expected to see in this book, but I did not include them because they don't fit the three criteria of a "nuclear threat" movie laid out in my preface.

*   *   *

1990: The Bronx Warriors (1982)

The movie makes no mention of nukes, nuke war, radiation or any kind of war. New York City is completely intact; only the Bronx has changed.

*   *   *

2010: The Year We Make Contact (1984)

This sequel to 1968's *2001: A Space Odyssey* takes place primarily in the planet Jupiter's orbit. About halfway through, there are indications that the Soviet Union and the United States may go to war over a U.S. blockade of Honduras. America has sunk a Russian destroyer, and Russia has retaliated by destroying an American satellite.

However, after the film's climax, in which the Earth now has two suns plus a profound message from the Monolith intelligence, the American and Russian leaders cease hostilities. The film doesn't qualify for the nuclear threat genre because no nuclear weapons are used, nor is a third world war started; in addition, this is a subplot to the film's major thrust (figuring out the mystery of what happened to *2001*'s Jupiter mission).

*   *   *

Barefoot Gen (1983)

This animated Japanese film deals with the 1945 atom bombing of Hiroshima and its aftermath. Because it is not contemporary with the 1980s, but rather historically harkens back, I have excluded it.

*   *   *

Day of the Dead (1985)

This is the third film in director George Romero's "Zombie" series, after 1968's *Night of the Living Dead* and 1978's *Dawn of the Dead*. *Night of the Living Dead* suggests but never confirms that radiation may have caused the flesh-eating undead's reanimation. *Day of the Dead* makes zero reference to anything nuclear, and instead speaks of an infection that takes over a victim bitten by a zombie. This sounds like either a virus or bacteria, certainly not radiation.

Escape from Safehaven (aka Inferno in Safehaven) (1988)

Despite being described in many online sources as "post-apocalyptic," this movie neither mentions nor alludes to nuclear war, nor are there any references to radiation. Instead, the opening narration speaks of "those glorious days before the collapse" and goes on to say that the present is "a land made barren by greed and man's cruelty to his fellow man. All over the country, cities had crumbled, the strong began to rule the weak, and soon the law of the land became the roar of a gun or the hiss of cold steel." Thus, the fall of the U.S. happened due to social and political breakdown, not nuclear war.

* * *

Hell Squad (1985)

The Internet Movie Database categorizes this movie as "Action." I disagree: *Hell Squad* is definitely a comedy. The film concerns a group of Las Vegas showgirls who are recruited and trained to be commandos to rescue a kidnapped diplomat's son. This unbelievable premise only works as comedy. In addition, certain dialogue, most scenes and the ridiculous Scooby Doo–style ending are all clearly intended to be humorous.

* * *

Island Claws (1980)

Some Internet sources claim that radiation spawned this movie's menaces (aggressive normal-sized crabs and one giant crustacean). Yes, *Island Claws* does include a nuclear power plant accident, but this is a red herring. According to the movie, an experimental growth hormone causes a crab to grow as big as a house.

* * *

Land of Doom (1986)

Internet sources, including the IMDb, claim this movie takes place after a nuclear war. However, in the film, the type of war is unspecified. The opening narration says, "I don't know how the Final War began. It doesn't even matter." The narrator also says that the post-war world is "filled with disease and pollution." This suggests a biological or ecological war rather than a nuclear conflict.

* * *

Murder by Moonlight (aka Murder on the Moon) (1989)

According to the IMDb, this movie is set after a nuclear war. That is incorrect. There's dialogue in the movie that indicates that there was *almost* a nuke war between the U.S. and the U.S.S.R., but it didn't happen.

Solarbabies (1986)

Some sources list this film as a post-nuke movie, but it never mentions or alludes to nuclear war. It is a generic post-apocalyptic film.

* * *

Superman II (1981)

Technically, *Superman II* could meet the first criterion of a nuclear threat film: "movies that depict nuclear terrorism, nuclear extortion, nuclear theft or any combination thereof." However, its nuke aspect is a minor subplot dealt with in just the first few minutes: Early in the movie, Superman takes an H-bomb into outer space and hurls it and lets it explode. But the explosion destroys the Phantom Zone, freeing Krypton villains General Zod, Ursa and Non. The H-bomb explosion-nuke threat is then completely dropped. For this reason, I have chosen not to cover *Superman II*.

* * *

Chapter Notes

Preface

1. Alia Wong. "Pandemonium and Rage in Hawaii." *The Atlantic*, 14 January 2018, https://www.theatlantic.com/international/archive/2018/01/-pandemonium-and-rage-in-hawaii/550529/.

2. Here's a focus on what "an extraordinary nuclear aspect" of a film means. In 1987's *Heaven and Earth*, a young girl's grandfather sells land to the Air Force on which they plan to build a missile base, upsetting the girl. The selling of land to the military and the latter's plans to build a missile base are ordinary events, thus, this book doesn't include *Heaven and Earth*. But in 1987's *Amazing Grace and Chuck*, a boy who is a star Little League player says he can't pitch because of nuclear weapons, an act that provokes a nationwide movement. The boy's oath and its repercussions are extraordinary, anything but normal, indicating *Amazing Grace and Chuck* meets the criteria of having "an extraordinary nuclear aspect" and is thus included in this tome.

3. *The Day After* was released theatrically in several countries.

4. Bill Warren. *Keep Watching the Skies! American Science Fiction Movies of the Fifties, the 21st Century Edition*. McFarland, 2010, p. 5.

5. Harry Cockburn. "Russian State TV Host Lists Possible U.S. Nuclear Targets." *The Independent (Daily Edition)*, London, 26 February 2019, p. 30.

6. Daryl G. Kimball. "New Approaches Needed to Prevent Nuclear Catastrophe." *Arms Control Today*, April 2022, vol. 52, no. 3, p. 3.

7. Tyler Parmelee. "The H-bomb in the Swamp: Taking Nuclear War Seriously Again." *Survival*, vol. 63, no. 4, August 2022, p. 181.

Introduction

1. Peter Kerr. "TV Films Will Use More Social Issues." *The New York Times*, 28 February 1984, p. C158.

2. If you're interested in an in-depth analysis of 1950s American giant monster movies in which the title menace serves as a metaphor for the Bomb, see my book *Apocalypse Then: American and Japanese Atomic Cinema, 1951–1967*. McFarland, 2017.

Chapter One

1. A good friend related this incident to me, noting the teacher's panic alarmed him and his second-grade classmates.

2. Spencer R. Weart. *The Rise of Nuclear Fear*. Harvard University Press, 2012, p. 71.

3. *Ibid.*, p. 148.

4. *Ibid.*, p. 150.

5. Richard Rhodes. *Dark Sun: The Making of the Hydrogen Bomb*. Simon & Schuster, 1995, p. 572.

6. Ward Wilson. "Why Are There No Big Nuke Protests?" *Bulletin of the Atomic Scientists*, vol. 71, no. 2, March 2015, p. 57.

7. Weart, p. 232.

8. For all of these time periods, I am excluding comedy films with atomic age themes as well as nuclear documentaries.

9. Weart, p. 152.

10. Sorry, couldn't resist the pun.

11. Weart, p. 230.

12. Ibid.

Chapter Two

1. Gary Arnold. "'The Children': Have You Hugged Your Ghoul Today?" Review of *The Children*, directed by Max Kalmanowicz. *The Washington Post*, 9 July 1980, p. B6.

2. Richard Scheib. Review of *The Lathe of Heaven*, directed by Fred Barzyk and David Loxton. *Moira Science Fiction, Horror and Fantasy Film Review*, no date, https://www.moriareviews.com/sciencefiction/lathe-of-heaven-tv-1980.htm.

3. Chris Barsanti. Review of *The Lathe of Heaven*, directed by Fred Barzyk and David Loxton. *The Sci-Fi Movie Guide: The Universe of Film from Alien to Zardoz*. Visible Ink, 2015, p. 223.

4. *The China Syndrome* concerns the cover-up of a potentially looming nuclear power plant meltdown in California.

5. Mick Martin and Marsha Porter. Review of *Nuclear Run (Chain Reaction)* directed by Ian Barry. *DVD & Video Guide 2005*. Ballantine Books, 2004, p. 184.

6. Stuart Galbraith, IV. *Japanese Science Fiction, Fantasy and Horror Films: A Critical Analysis*

of 103 Features Released in the United States, 1950–1992. McFarland, 1994, p. 263.

7. In 1975, New World Pictures Americanized *Submersion of Japan* into *Tidal Wave*, cutting much of the Japanese original's footage and adding new American-shot footage with Lorne Greene.

8. *The Great Prophecies of Nostradamus* was released in Los Angeles as *Prophecies of Nostradamus*. In 1981, the American home video version was called *The Last Days of Planet Earth*, running 72 minutes. This version also played on American TV.

9. Director Fukasaku specialized in Yakuza films in Japan, but in addition to *Virus*, he also directed the science fiction films *The Green Slime* (1968) and *Message from Space* (1978).

10. *On the Beach*, however, ended with the implied extinction of all humankind.

11. The final credit in 1962's nuclear threat film *Panic in Year Zero!* in fact displays this very message.

Chapter Three

1. Vincent Canby. Review of *Escape from New York*, directed by John Carpenter. *The New York Times*, 10 July 1981, p. C6.

2. Robert Greenberger. Review of *Escape from New York*, directed by John Carpenter. *Starlog Science-Fiction Video Magazine* #1, 1988, p. 62.

3. So too is womanizing, but for my comments on that Bond subject, see my entry for 1983's *Never Say Never Again*.

4. "Roger Moore, Actor: Biography." *TCM (Turner Classic Movies)*, 2022, https://www.tcm.com/tcmdb/person/134821%7C161989/Roger--Moore#overview.

5. Editors. Review of *For Your Eyes Only*, directed by John Glen. *Starlog Science-Fiction Video Magazine* #1, 1988, p. 80.

6. Maciej Pietrzak. "David Avidan's Message from the Future: Nuclear Fantasies of the Galactic Poet." *Images: The International Journal of European Film Performing Arts and Audiovisual Communication*, vol. 28, no. 37, March 2021, p. 129.

7. Edward Gross. Review of *The Road Warrior*, directed by George Miller. *Starlog Science-Fiction Video Magazine* #1, 1988, p. 62.

Chapter Four

1. The title *The Aftermath* is also used for a 2019 film; in addition, the single word *Aftermath* with no preceding article is the name of four other films, released chronologically in 2012, 2014, 2017, and 2021. Of these, the 2014 *Aftermath* deals with nuclear war.

2. James O'Neill. Review of *The Aftermath*, directed by Steve Barkett. *Sci-Fi on Tape: A Complete Guide to Science Fiction and Fantasy on Video*. Billboard Books, 1997, p. 8.

3. John Stanley. Review of *The Aftermath*, directed by Steve Barkett. *Creature Features: The Science Fiction, Fantasy, and Horror Movie Guide.* Berkley Boulevard Books, 2000, p. 5.

4. Missionaries of the Sacred Heart. Review of *Deadline*, directed by Arch Nicholson. *Missionaries of the Sacred Heart*, 18 September 2021, https://misacor.org.au/item/5304-deadline.

5. Peter Taylor. "Six Days That Shook Britain: It Was One of the Events That Defined the 80s—Establishing the SAS's Lethal Reputation and Margaret Thatcher as a Prime Minister Who Refused to Give in to Terrorists." *The Guardian*; London (UK), 24 July 2002, p. 2:2.

6. Michael Blowen. "Right Is Wrong in 'Final Option.'" Review of *The Final Option*, directed by Ian Sharp. *Boston Globe*, 7 October 1983, p. 1.

7. Mick Martin and Marsha Porter. Review of *The Final Option*, directed by Ian Sharp. *DVD & Video Guide 2005*. Ballantine Books, 2004, p. 377.

8. Sean O'Mara. Review of *Future War 198X*, directed by Toshio Masuda, Koji Katsubota. *Zimmert*, 20 September 2016, https://www.zimmerit.moe/most-dangerous-year-future-war-198x/.

9. Sci-Fi-Central. Review of *Future War 198X*, directed by Toshio Masuda, Koji Katsubota. *Sci-Fi-Central*, no date given, https://www.sci-fi-central.com/Database/SF/02/9N/index.php.

10. Demi Moore, interview by James Corden. *The Late Show*, 24 October 2019, https://www.youtube.com/watch?v=wxpRVetn76o.

11. Janet Maslin. "'Parasite,' a Creature in 3-D." Review of *Parasite*, directed by Charles Band. *The New York Times*, 13 March 1982, p. I19.

12. "The Soldier (1982): History." *AFI Catalog of Feature Films: The First 100 Years 1893–1993*, 2019, https://catalog.afi.com/Catalog/moviedetails/56876.

13. "Ken Wahl, Actor: Biography." *TCM (Turner Classic Movies)*, 2022, https://prod-www.tcm.com/tcmdb/person/200464%7C0/Ken-Wahl#biography.

14. "Ken Wahl Biography," *TVGuide.com*, 2022, https://www.tvguide.com/celebrities/ken-wahl/bio/3000062132/.

15. Vincent Canby. Review of *The Soldier*, directed by James Glickenhaus. *The New York Times*, 3 September 1982, p. C11.

16. Jesse Skeen. Review of *The Soldier*, directed by James Glickenhaus. *DVDtalk*, 5 April 2018, https://www.dvdtalk.com/reviews/review/72923.

17. Leonard Maltin. Review of *Warlords of the 21st Century*, directed by Harley Cokliss. *2002 Movie and Video Guide*. Signet, 2001, p. 1499.

18. Technically, some would (and do) call *World War III* a mini-series. It aired over two nights on NBC-TV in 1982 in two-hour time slots with commercials. However, with only two "episodes" equaling three hours and nine minutes, the broadcast fits the bill as a TV-movie. Granted, my reasoning may be somewhat arbitrary, but any TV broadcast with three or more two-hour episodes would, I think, qualify as a mini-series, whereas one with only two two-hour editions would qualify as a made-for-TV movie.

19. Gorbachev and President Ronald Reagan hammered out the Intermediate-Range Nuclear Forces Treaty (INF) in 1987, a meaningful disarmament agreement that called for the dismantling of land-based ballistic missiles. For more information, see this book's entry for 1983's *The Day After*.

20. Rock Hudson appeared in the science-fiction movies *Seconds* (1966) and *Embryo* (1976). He also played a major role in NBC's 1980 mini-series *The Martian Chronicles*.

21. In addition, Soul sang the 1977 *Billboard* Hot 100 #1 hit "Don't Give Up on Us": Joel Whitburn. *The Billboard Book of Top 40 Hits, Revised and Enlarged 7th edition*. Billboard Books, 2000, p. 587.

22. Arnav Manchanda. "When Truth Is Stranger Than Fiction: The Able Archer Incident." *Cold War History*, vol. 9, no. 1, February 2009, pp. 117–120.

23. *Ibid.*, pp. 122–123.

24. Tom Shales. "Apocalypse Wow! It's 'WW III.'" Review of *World War III*, directed by David Greene and Boris Sagal. *Washington Post*, 30 January 1982, https://www.washingtonpost.com/archive/lifestyle/1982/01/30/apocalypse-wow-its-ww-iii/f44b8d24-71a2-4501-a148-0641a233de36/.

Chapter Five

1. Science fiction fans will also of course remember Landau's role in the ABC-TV *Outer Limits* episode "The Man Who Was Never Born" that originally aired on 28 October 1963.

2. Leonard Maltin. Review of *The Being*, directed by Jackie Kong. *Leonard Maltin's 2002 Movie & Video Guide*. Signet, 2001, p. 103.

3. The Telltale Mind. "Radiation's Progeny—*The Being* (1983)." Review of *The Being*, directed by Jackie Kong. *The Telltale Mind*, 24 October 2019, https://thetelltalemind.com/2019/10/14/-radiations-progeny-the-being-1983/.

4. Peter Kerr. "TV Films Will Use More Social Issues." *The New York Times*, 28 February 1984, p. C158.

5. "Silence in Heaven: Looking Back at *The Day After*." *The Day After*, directed by Nicholas Meyer. Disc TV Cut, Kino Lorber, 2018. DVD.

6. While this may make some readers feel old, almost everyone on the panel is now deceased.

7. The Nuclear Freeze movement basically called for the halting of nuclear weapons production and deployment.

8. "'The Day After' Nuclear War/Deterrence Discussion Panel—ABC News 'Viewpoint.'" *YouTube*, 20 November 1983, https://www.youtube.com/watch?v=PcCLZwU2t34.

9. Deron Overpeck. "Remember! It's Only a Movie! Expectations and Receptions of *The Day After* (1983)." *Historical Journal of Film, Radio and Television*, vol. 32, no.2, June 2012, pp. 276–279.

10. *Ibid.*, 279.

11. Sally Bedell Smith. "Film on Nuclear War Already Causing Wide Fallout of Political Activity." *The New York Times*, 17 November 1983, p. A20.

12. Ronald Reagan. "Diary Entry." *White House Diaries of Ronald Reagan*, 10 October 1983, https://www.reaganfoundation.org/ronald-reagan/white-house-diaries/diary-entry-10101983/.

13. Dawn Stover. "Facing Nuclear Reality 35 Years After *The Day After*: A Special Report." *Bulletin of the Atomic Scientists*, 2018, https://thebulletin.org/facing-nuclear-reality-35-years-after-the-day-after/.

14. Ronald Reagan. *Ronald Reagan: An American Life*. Threshold, 2011, p. 586.

15. Stover.

16. "The Intermediate-Range Nuclear Forces (INF) Treaty." *Arms Control Today*, vol. 47, no. 3, April 2017, pp. 14–15.

17. Robert Greenberger. Review of *The Day After*, directed by Nicholas Meyer. *Starlog Science-Fiction Video Magazine* #1, 1988, pp. 30–31.

18. Leonard Maltin. Review of *The Day After*, directed by Nicholas Meyer. *Leonard Maltin's 2002 Movie & Video Guide*. Signet, 2001, p. 323.

19. Judith Crist. Review of *The Day After*, directed by Nicholas Meyer. *TV Guide*, 19–25 November 1983, p. A-7.

20. Robert MacKenzie. Review of *The Day After*, directed by Nicholas Meyer. *TV Guide*, 19–25 November 1983, p. 56.

21. Review of *The Day After*, directed by Nicholas Meyer. *VideoHound's Sci-Fi Experience*. Visible Ink, 1997, p. 71.

22. Roger Ebert. Review of *The Dead Zone*, directed by David Cronenberg. *Roger Ebert's Movie Home Companion 1993 Edition* (originally appeared in *Chicago Sun-Times*). Andrews and McMeel, 1992, p. 194.

23. *Ibid.*

24. Janet Maslin. "Film: 'Dead Zone,' from King Novel." Review of *The Dead Zone*, directed by David Cronenberg. *The New York Times*, 21 October 1983, p. C8.

25. Leonard Maltin. Review of *The Dead Zone*, directed by David Cronenberg. *Leonard Maltin's 2002 Movie & Video Guide*. Signet, 2001, p. 332.

26. Review of *The Dead Zone*, directed by David Cronenberg. *VideoHound Sci-Fi Experience*. Visible Ink, 1997, pp. 74–75.

27. Though featuring different stars than the film, *The Dead Zone* debuted as a TV series in 2002 and ran for six seasons. Anthony Michael Hall played the role of Johnny Smith.

28. Ricou Browning performed the underwater stunt work for Universal's famous in three films—1954's *Creature from the Black Lagoon*, 1955's *Revenge of the Creature*, and 1956's *The Creature Walks Among Us*. In addition to *Never Say Never Again*, Ricou also directed the underwater scenes in 1965's *Thunderball*.

29. "Never Say Never Again (1983)." *The Numbers*, 1997–2022, https://www.the-numbers.com/movie/Never-Say-Never-Again#tab=summary.

30. Janet Maslin. "Sean Connery Is Seasoned James Bond." Review of *Never Say Never Again*, directed by Irvin Kershner. *The New York Times*, 7 October 1983, p. C13.

31. Leonard Maltin. Review of *Never Say Never Again*, directed by Irvin Kirschner. *Leonard Maltin's 2002 Movie & Video Guide*. Signet, 2001, p. 964.

32. Michael Blowen. "Bond Shows His Age." Review of *Octopussy*, directed by John Glen. *Boston Globe*, 10 June 1983, p. 1.

33. Leonard Maltin. Review of *Octopussy*, directed by John Glen. *Leonard Maltin's 2002 Movie & Video Guide*. Signet, 2001, p. 996.

34. "75 Nuke Extortion Cases." *The Telegraph-Herald*, UPI, 15 June 1981, p. 2.

35. Tom Shales. "Bulletin! The Show That Shook NBC." *The Washington Post*, 20 March 1983, https://www.washingtonpost.com/archive/lifestyle/style/1983/03/20/bulletin-the-show-that-shook-nbc/014edc08-362c-414a-8935-ede8c2e46562/.

36. Sally Bedell. "NBC Nuclear-Terror Show Criticized." *The New York Times*, 22 March 1983, p. C15.

37. Patrick Daniel O'Neill. Review of *Special Bulletin*, directed by Edward Zwick. *Starlog Science-Fiction Video Magazine* #1, 1988, p. 67.

38. "Special Bulletin (NBC)." Television Academy Emmys, no date, https://www.emmys.com/shows/special-bulletin.

39. Aljean Harmetz. "NBC Film on Terror Wins Prize." *The New York Times*, late ed., 8 July 1983, p. C19.

40. Roger Ebert. Review of *Testament*, directed by Lynne Littman. *Roger Ebert's Movie Home Companion 1993 Edition* (originally appeared in *Chicago Sun-Times*). Andrews and McMeel, 1992, p. 655.

41. David McDonnell. Review of *Testament*, directed by Lynn Littman. *Starlog Science-Fiction Video Magazine* #1, 1988, p. 69.

42. Kim Newman. *Apocalypse Movies: End of the World Cinema*. St. Martin's Griffin, 2000, p. 240.

43. James O'Neill. *Sci-Fi on Tape: A Complete Guide to Science Fiction and Fantasy on Video*. New York: Billboard Books, 1997, p. 210.

44. *Testament* (Warner/Allied Vaughn, April 5, 2016). Special Feature: "*Testament* at 20." DVD.

45. David L. Pike. "Nuclear Realism and Memories of Extinction in the 1980s: *Testament*, *The Day After*, and *Threads*." *Bright Lights Film Journal*, 23 December 2021, https://brightlightsfilm.com/nuclear-realism-and-memories-of-extinction-in-the-1980s-testament-the-day-after-and-threads/#.YhwZV9_MKUn.

46. Ebert.

47. The theme of only one fertile woman left in a post-holocaust world is expanded upon in 2006's critically acclaimed *Children of Men*.

48. James O'Neill. Review of *2019, After the Fall of New York*, directed by Martin Dolman. *Sci-Fi on Tape: A Complete Guide to Science Fiction and Fantasy on Video*. Billboard Books, 1997, p. 9.

49. Ward Wilson. "Why Are There No Big Nuke Protests?" *Bulletin of the Atomic Scientists*, vol. 71, no. 2, March 2015, p. 57.

50. "WarGames (1983)." *The Numbers*, 1997–2022, https://www.the-numbers.com/movie/WarGames#tab=summary.

51. John Badham interviewed by Robert Kazel. "30 Years After 'WarGames,' Director John Badham Recalls His Nuclear-Brink Blockbuster." *Nuclear Age Peace Foundation*, 12 February 2013, https://www.wagingpeace.org/30-years-after-WarGames-director-john-badham-recalls-his-nuclear-brink-blockbuster/.

52. *Ibid.*

53. Jen Chaney. "The Tricks May Be Dated, But Suspense Is Timeless." *The Washington Post*, 1 August 2008, p. WW29.

54. Chris Barsanti. Review of *WarGames*, directed by John Badham. *The Sci-Fi Movie Guide: The Universe of Film from Alien to Zardoz*. Visible Ink, 2015, p. 422.

55. Fred Kaplan. "'WarGames' and Cybersecurity's Debt to a Hollywood Hack." *The New York Times*, 19 February 2016, p. AR24.

56. Hoffman, David. "Cold-War Doctrines Refuse to Die; False Alert After '95 Rocket Launch Shows Fragility of Aging Safeguards Series: Shattered Shield: The Decline Of Russia's Nuclear Forces Series Number: ½." *The Washington Post*, 15 March 1998, p. A01.

Here's what happened: In 1995, four years after the Soviet Union ceased to exist, a Norwegian satellite-carrying rocket moved into Russian airspace. Although Norway had far in advance alerted Russia of this non-military rocket launch, the word never reached the proper Russian authorities. Hence, Russian President Boris Yeltsin had to decide whether or not the rocket threatened Russia; soon, he clutched his country's nuclear suitcase. Once the rocket veered north, Yeltsin decided it was not a danger to Russia, and thus he did not launch a nuclear missile attack against the United States.

57. Janet Maslin. "'Yor, the Hunter' with a Cave Man Hero." Review of *Yor, the Hunter from the Future*, directed by Anthony M. Dawson (a.k.a. Antonio Margheriti). *The New York Times*, 21 August 1983, p. I54.

58. Leonard Maltin. Review of *Yor, the Hunter from the Future*, directed by Anthony M. Dawson (a.k.a. Antonio Margheriti). *Leonard Maltin's 2002 Movie & Video Guide*. Signet, 2001, p. 1565.

59. James O'Neill. Review of *Yor, the Hunter from the Future: A Complete Guide to Science Fiction and Fantasy on Video*, directed by Anthony M. Dawson (a.k.a. Antonio Margheriti). *Sci-Fi on Tape*. Billboard Books, 1997, p. 242.

60. "Yor, the Hunter from the Future (1983)." *The Numbers*, 1997–2022, https://www.the-numbers.com/movie/Yor-Hunter-From-the-Future#tab=summary.

61. Published by Gold Key Comics, *Mighty Samson* was a comic book featuring the title

character, a cave man who lived in a post-nuclear holocaust world teeming with mutant monsters. His series ran from 1964–1982.

62. *Turok, Son of Stone* was a comic book featuring Turok, a Native American who battled dinosaurs in the Lost Valley. The comic, which ran from 1956–1982, was published by Dell and later by Gold Key.

63. Reb Brown. "Reb Brown Interview" *YouTube*, 23 May 2011, https://www.youtube.com/watch?v=cDsavdR-Mq0.

64. John Stanley. *Creature Features: The Science Fiction, Fantasy, and Horror Movie Guide.* Berkley Boulevard Books, 2000, p. 591.

Chapter Six

1. Jordan Peele, interview by Luria Freeman. "How 'Us' Director Jordan Peele Makes Truly Scary Horror Films." *Now This Entertainment, YouTube,* 25 March 2019, https://www.youtube.com/watch?v=MQOrue_Wuww.

2. James S. Murphy. "The Obscure 80s Horror Film That Unlocks the Meaning of Us." *Vanity Fair*, 25 March 2019, https://www.vanityfair.com/hollywood/2019/03/us-horror-movie-chud.

3. Lawrence Van Gelder. "'C.H.U.D.,' a Tale of Strange Creatures." Review of *C.H.U.D.* directed by Douglas Cheek. *The New York Times*, 1 September 1984, p. 1:10.

4. Steve Schneider. "Cable TV Notes: Nuclear Conflict on HBO's 'Countdown.'" *The New York Times*, 14 October 1984, p. 2:29.

5. In 1964's *Fail-Safe*, an American warplane inadvertently nukes Moscow, causing the Soviet Union to demand the U.S. President H-bomb New York City. For an in-depth look at *Fail-Safe*, see pp. 251–255 of my book *Apocalypse Then: American and Japanese Atomic Cinema, 1951–1967.* McFarland, 2017.

6. A global nuclear war might not kill everyone, but it would put an end to civilization as we know it.

7. "Dreamscape (1984)." *AFI (American Film Institute) Catalog*, no date, https://catalog.afi.com/Catalog/moviedetails/57070.

8. Robert Greenberger. Review of *Dreamscape*, directed by Joseph Ruben. *Starlog Science-Fiction Video Magazine* #1, 1988, p. 33.

9. Janet Maslin. Review of *Dreamscape*, directed by Joseph Ruben. *The New York Times*, 15 August 1984, p. C24.

10. Frank Manchel. "The Man Who Made the Stars Shine Brighter: An Interview with Woody Strode." *Black Scholar*, vol. 25, no. 2, Spring 1995, p. 41.

11. In case you're wondering, it was called "I Need Somebody" and in 1966 peaked at #22 on *Billboard*'s Hot 100: Joel Whitburn, *The Billboard Book of Top 40 Hits, Revised and Enlarged 7th edition*. Billboard Books, 2000, p. 514.

12. "Persis Khambatta, Actor: Filmography." *TCM (Turner Classic Movies)*, 2022 (no monthly

date given), https://prod-www.tcm.com/tcmdb/person/101549%7C0/Persis-Khambatta#filmography.

13. Allen A. Debus. *Prehistoric Monsters: The Real and Imagined Creatures of the Past That We Love to Fear.* McFarland, 2009, p. 209.

14. J. Oberman. "Poetry After the A-Bomb" booklet. *Godzilla.* The Criterion Collection, 2012. DVD.

15. Steve Ryfle. *Japan's Favorite Mon-Star: The Unauthorized Biography of "The Big G."* ECW Press, 1998, p. 235.

16. *Ibid.*, 237.

17. *Ibid.*, 237.

18. David Kalat. *A Critical History and Filmography of Toho's Godzilla Series*, 2nd ed. McFarland, 2010, p. 164.

19. Ryfle, 237.

20. *Ibid.*, 232.

21. Kalat, 160.

22. Ryfle, 234–235.

23. Jason C. Jones. "Japan Removed: *Godzilla* Adaptations and Erasure of the Politics of Nuclear Experience." *The Atomic Bomb in Japanese Cinema*, edited by Matthew Edwards. McFarland, 2015, p. 43.

24. Vincent Canby. "The Screen: 'Godzilla 1985.'" Review of *Godzilla 1985*, directed by Koji Hashimoto and R.J. Kizer. *The New York Times*, 30 August 1985, p. C11.

25. Kalat, 161.

26. Peter Donat. Interview with Bill Warren. *Starlog Magazine*, May 1993, p. 48.

27. Adam Groves. "Eighties Nuke Movies." *The Bedlam Files*, 2022, https://thebedlamfiles.com/commentary/eighties-nuke-movies/.

28. *Ibid.*

29. Alfio Leotta. "When War Imitates Art: Rediscovering *Red Dawn*, the 1984 Movie Inspiring Ukrainian Fighters." *The Conversation*, 18 April 2022, https://theconversation.com/when-war-imitates-art-rediscovering-red-dawn-the-1984-movie-inspiring-ukrainian-fighters-181261.

30. Vincent Canby. "Cockeyed at 'Red Dawn.'" Review of *Red Dawn*, directed by John Milius. *The New York Times*, late ed., 16 September 1984, p. A19.

31. "Wolverines: Ukrainian Graffiti Inspired by 80s Film Sprayed on Wrecked Russian Tanks." *Forces.net*, 22 April 2022, https://www.forces.net/ukraine/wolverines-ukrainian-graffiti-inspired-80s-film-sprayed-wrecked-russian-tanks.

32. Leotta.

33. *Ibid.*

34. *Red Dawn* was remade in 2012, with North Korea invading the U.S. However, this critically-panned reboot has not found cultural traction.

35. Leonard Maltin. Review of *The Terminator*, directed by James Cameron. *Leonard Maltin's 2002 Movie & Video Guide.* Signet, 2001, p. 1370.

36. Jude Rodgers. "Here Come the Bombs: The Making of 'Threads,' the Nuclear War Film That Shocked a Generation." *The New Statesman*, 17

March 2018, https://www.newstatesman.com/-long-reads/2018/03/here-come-bombs-making-threads-nuclear-war-film-shocked-generation.

37. "Audio Commentary with Director Mick Jackson Moderated by Film Writer Kier-La Janisse and Severin Films' David Gregory." *Threads*, directed by Mick Jackson, Severin Films, 2018. DVD.

38. *Ibid.*

39. *Ibid.*

40. Ted Turner. "WTBS Introduction Threads 1985." *YouTube*, 17 July 2015, https://www.youtube.com/watch?v=ZgNsD8iCFvA.

41. Darren Burke. "Threads: Sheffield Nuclear War Drama Named in Top 100 BBC Shows of All Time." *The Star; Sheffield*, 4 May 2022.

42. Leonard Maltin. Review of *Threads*, directed by Mick Jackson. *Leonard Maltin's 2002 Movie & Video Guide*. Signet, 2001, p. 1396.

43. Chris Barsanti. Review of *Threads*, directed by Mick Jackson. *The Sci-Fi Movie Guide: The Universe of Film from Alien to Zardoz*. Visible Ink, 2015, p. 385.

44. James O'Neill. Review of *Threads*, directed by Mick Jackson. *Sci-Fi on Tape: A Comprehensive Guide to Over 1,250 Science Fiction and Fantasy Films on Video*. Billboard Books, 1997, p. 214.

45. Paul Whitelaw. "G2: Film & Music: Reviews: Television: Your Next Box Set: 'Threads.'" *The Guardian*, 22 November 2013, p. 28.

46. "*Threads* Official Blu-ray Trailer." *SeverinFilmsOfficial*, 5 December 2017, https://www.youtube.com/watch?v=EHyNFlhjojM.

47. "Billy Dee Williams, Actor: Biography." TCM (Turner Classic Movies), 2022, https://prod-www.tcm.com/tcmdb/person/206488%7C22113/-Billy-Dee-Williams#biography.

48. *Ibid.*

49. "Morgan Fairchild, Actor: Biography." TCM (Turner Classic Movies), 2022, https://prod-www.tcm.com/tcmdb/person/59286%7C0/Morgan-Fairchild#biography.

Chapter Seven

1. Vincent Canby. Review of *Def-Con 4*, directed by Paul Donovan. *The New York Times*, 28 April 1985, p. 1:65.

2. Leonard Maltin. Review of *Def-Con 4*, directed by Paul Donovan. *Leonard Maltin's 2002 Movie and Video Guide*. Signet, 2001, p. 340.

3. "*Def-Con 4* Reviews." Review of *Def-Con 4* directed by Paul Donovan. *TV Guide*, https://www.tvguide.com/movies/def-con-4/review/2030345569/.

4. See the IMDb user reviews for this movie: https://www.imdb.com/title/tt0089530/reviews.

5. Roger Ebert. Review of *Max Max: Beyond Thunderdome*, directed by George Miller and George Ogilvie. *Roger Ebert's Movie Home Companion 1993 Edition* (originally appeared in *Chicago Sun Times*). Andrews and McMeel, 1992, p. 393.

6. Michał Oleszczyk. "Things to Come: Piotr Szulkin's Homespun Apocalypse." *Roger.Ebert.com*, 16 March 2015, https://www.rogerebert.com/far-flung-correspondents/piotr-szulkins-homespun-apocalypse.

Chapter Eight

1. Richard Bernstein. "Soviet Eye Examines Atom War." Review of *Dead Man's Letters*, directed by Konstantin Lopushanskiy. *The New York Times*, 27 January 1989, p. C11.

2. Kim Newman. *Apocalypse Movies: End of the World Cinema*. St. Martin's Griffin, 2000, p. 223.

3. John Corry. "TV View: Queeg Would Feel Right at Home." Review of *The Fifth Missile*, directed by Larry Peerce. *The New York Times*, 23 February 1986, p. 2:29.

4. "The Manhattan Project (1986)." *AFI (American Film Institute) Catalog of Feature Films: The First 100 Years 1893–1993*, 2019, https://catalog.afi.com/Catalog/moviedetails/57404. See also: "The Manhattan Project (1986)." *The Numbers*, 1997–2022, https://www.the-numbers.com/movie/Manhattan-Project-The#tab=summary.

5. John C. Tibbetts. "Marshall Brickman Interview for The Manhattan Project (1986)." *John C. Tibbetts Interviews*, 9 March 2022, https://www.youtube.com/watch?v=bPFkA48Zud0. This interview was posted on 9 March 2022, but actually occurred many years ago; the date is unknown, but Tibbetts probably interviewed Brickman about *The Manhattan Project* in the latter 1980s or during the 1990s.

6. "Lithgow Finally Gets the Girl," *Chicago Tribune*, 5 September 1985, p. 8L.

7. Tibbetts.

8. Gerald Jonas. "Marshall Brickman Humanizes the Nuclear Arms Race." *The New York Times*, 15 June 1986, p. 2:21.

9. Paul Collins. "The A-Bomb Kid." *Village Voice*, 16–23 December 2003, p. C56.

10. *Ibid.*

11. Vincent Canby. "Screen: *The Manhattan Project*." Review of *The Manhattan Project*, directed by Marshall Brickman. *The New York Times*, 13 June 1986, p. C8.

12. Michael Wilmington. "'Manhattan Project': Bomb Plot." Review of *The Manhattan Project*, directed by Marshall Brickman. *Los Angeles Times*, 13 June 1986, https://www.latimes.com/archives/-la-xpm-1986-06-13-ca-10957-story.html.

13. Roger Ebert. Review of *The Manhattan Project*, directed by Marshall Brickman. *Roger Ebert's Movie Home Companion 1993 Edition* (originally appeared in *Chicago Sun-Times*). Andrews and McMeel, 1992, p. 396.

14. The Limited Test Ban Treaty ratified in 1963 banned the Soviet Union, the U.S., and many other nations from conducting atmospheric nuclear tests.

15. Joe Woodward. "The Fatima Debate: After Decades of Secrecy, the Vatican's Release of the

Fatima Text Fails to Resolve All the Unanswered Questions." *Calgary Herald*, 1 July 2000, p. O10. See also: "The Message of Fatima," both in original language and English translation. *Congregation for the Doctrine of the Faith*, no date given, https://www.vatican.va/roman_curia/congregations/cfaith/documents/rc_con_cfaith_doc_20000626_message-fatima_en.html.

16. Leonard Maltin. "Tucker, Forrest." *Leonard Maltin's Movie Encyclopedia*. Plume Books, 1994, p. 894–895.

17. Leonard Maltin. "Ireland, John." *Leonard Maltin's Movie Encyclopedia*. Plume Books, 1994, p. 433.

18. Vincent Canby. "Animated Black Comedy About Courage as the World Ends." Review of *When the Wind Blows*, directed by Jimmy T. Murakami. *The New York Times*, 11 March 1988, p. C19.

19. Mick Martin and Marsha Porter. Review of *When the Wind Blows* directed by Jimmy T. Murakami. *DVD & Video Guide 2005*. Ballantine Books, 2004, p. 1221.

Chapter Nine

1. If you're interested in reading a review and analysis of 1959's *On the Beach*, see pp. 225–230 of my book *Apocalypse Then: American and Japanese Atomic Cinema, 1951–1967*. McFarland, 2017.

2. Janet Maslin. A review of *Amazing Grace and Chuck*, directed by Mike Newell. *The New York Times*, 22 May 1987, p. C30.

3. Charles Champlin. "'Grace and Chuck': An Amazing Story." A review of *Amazing Grace and Chuck*, directed by Mike Newell. *Los Angeles Times*, 26 May 1987, p. 1.

4. John Stanley. Review of *Creepozoids*, directed by David DeCoteau. *Creature Features: The Science Fiction, Fantasy, and Horror Movie Guide*. Berkley Boulevard Books, 2000, p. 104.

5. Roger Ebert. Review of *The Fourth Protocol*, directed by John Mackenzie. *Roger Ebert's Movie Home Companion 1993 Edition* (originally appeared in *Chicago Sun-Times*). Andrews and McMeel, 1992, p. 231.

6. Paul Willistein. Review of *The Fourth Protocol* directed by John Mackenzie. *Morning Call*, 29 August 1987, p. A60.

7. In the "Introduction," I noted that I was bypassing comedy films for this book. However, some might say *Mr. India* is most certainly a comedy. I disagree. Given its abundant mix of Bollywood film elements, I think *Mr. India* is a whole other case.

8. Steven Puchlaski. Review of *Mr. India*, directed by Shekhar Kapur. *Shock Cinema*, 1998, https://www.shockcinemamagazine.com/india.html.

9. Asjad Nazir. "'Mr. India': 35 Facts About the Cult Film." *Eastern Eye; London (UK)*, 27 May 2022, p. 30.

10. "35 Years of 'Mr. India': Here's Why Satish Kaushik Insists the Classic Shouldn't Be Remade." *Free Press Journal; Mumbai*, 27 May 2022.

11. "Salman Lends His Own Twist to the Immortal Lines of Bollywood Baddies." *IANS English; New Delhi*, 25 September 2022.

12. Walter Goodman. Review of *Steel Dawn*, directed by Lance Hool. *The New York Times*, 6 November 1987, p. C33.

13. "Patrick Swayze Biography (1952–2009)." *Biography*, 27 April 2017, https://www.biography.com/actor/patrick-swayze.

14. Mick Martin and Marsha Porter. Review of *Steel Dawn*, directed by Lance Hool. *DVD & Video Guide 2005*. Ballantine Books, 2004, p. 1056.

15. AFI (American Film Institute). "Superman IV: The Quest for Peace (1987)." *AFI Catalog of Feature Films: The First 100 Years 1893–1993*, 2019, https://catalog.afi.com/Film/57838-SUPERMAN-IVTHEQUESTFORPEACE?sid=25294c53-7642-454a-8c77-95a143365b5c&sr=6.600077&cp=1&pos=0 .

16. *Ibid.*

17. Christopher Reeve. *Still Me: With a New Afterword*. Ballantine Books, 1999, p. 220.

18. The notion of how much superheroes should interfere with the real world has of course been explored in recent superhero movies such as *The Avengers* series (2012–2019) and 2016's *Batman V Superman: Dawn of Justice*.

19. "Superman IV: The Quest for Peace (1987)." *The Numbers*, 1997–2022, https://www.the-numbers.com/movie/Superman-IV-The-Quest-for-Peace#tab=summary.

20. Jeff Strickler. "'Superman IV' So Bad, It Makes '50s Television Series Look Good." *Minneapolis Star and Tribune*, 30 July 1987, p. 06C.

21. Kim Howard Johnson. Review of *Superman IV: The Quest for Peace*, directed by Sidney Furie. *Starlog Science-Fiction Video Magazine* #1, 1988, p. 38.

22. Again, I am not putting down responsible preppers and survivalists. Nor am I putting down owning one or more firearms, though I do believe in practicing gun safety and passing reasonable gun laws. Guess that makes me only a quasi-snowflake.

23. Released in 1982, Adam Ant's single "Goody Two Shoes" peaked at #12 on *Billboard*'s Hot 100: Joel Whitburn. *The Billboard Book of Top 40 Hits, Revised and Enlarged 7th edition*. Billboard Books, 2000, p. 35.

24. Leonard Maltin. Review of *World Gone Wild*, directed by Lee H. Katzin. *Leonard Maltin's 2002 Movie & Video Guide*. Signet, 2001, p. 1557.

Chapter Ten

1. Janet Maslin. Review of *Akira* directed by Katsuhiro Ôtomo. *The New York Times*, 19 October 1990, p. C12.

2. Chris Barsanti. Review of *Akira*, directed

by Katsuhiro Ôtomo. *The Sci-Fi Movie Guide: The Universe of Film from Alien to Zardoz.* Visible Ink, 2015, p. 8.

3. "Lou Ferrigno, Actor." *TCM (Turner Classic Movies)*, 2022 (no monthly date given), https://prod-www.tcm.com/tcmdb/person/61231%7C0/Lou-Ferrigno#overview.

4. Frank Fellone. "Explosive Era: Tour Visits Site Where Titan II Blast in 1980 Sent Warhead Flying." *Arkansas Democrat-Gazette*, 21 September 2015, pp. 1E, 6E.

5. Rich Cross. Review of *In the Aftermath*, directed by Carl Colpaert. *Starburst*, 29 May 2019, https://www.starburstmagazine.com/reviews/in-aftermath.

6. *Ibid.*

7. Another "clue" is that on the cover of the DVD, a mushroom cloud appears in the *Aftermath* letters.

8. "Iron Eagle (1986)." *The Numbers*, 1997–2022, https://www.the-numbers.com/movie/Iron-Eagle#tab=summary.

Chapter Eleven

1. Taylor Orth. "Three in 10 Americans Fear Snakes—and Most Who Do Fear Them a Great Deal," *YouGovAmerica*, 16 June 2022, https://today.yougov.com/topics/society/articles-reports/2022/06/16/americans-fear-snakes-heights-spiders-poll.

2. David Kalat. "Godzilla vs. Biollante." *A Critical History and Filmography of Toho's Godzilla Series, 2nd ed.* McFarland, 2010, p. 176.

3. Chris Barsanti. Review of *Godzilla vs. Biollante,* directed by Kazuki Omori. *The Sci-Fi Movie Guide: The Universe of Film from Alien to Zardoz.* Visible Ink, 2015, p. 164.

4. Stuart Galbraith IV. "Godzilla vs. Biollante (1989)." *Japanese Science Fiction, Fantasy and Horror Films: A Critical Analysis of 103 Features Released in the United States, 1950–1992.* McFarland, 1994, p. 275.

5. J.D. Lees and Marc Cerasini. "Godzilla vs. Biollante." *The Official Godzilla Compendium.* Random House, 1998, p. 62.

6. If land-based ICBMs were headed our way, in most of the U.S., residents would have approximately half an hour. However, submarine-fired nukes could hit U.S. cities in 10 to 15 minutes. Source: Union of Concerned Scientists. "Frequently Asked Questions about Taking Nuclear Weapons Off Hair-Trigger Alert." *Union of Concerned Scientists Fact Sheet,* January 2015, https://www.ucsusa.org/sites/default/files/attach/2015/01/Hair-Trigger%20FAQ.pdf.

7. "Morning in America" is a political ad created for President Ronald Reagan's re-election campaign in 1984. Source: Michael Beschloss. "How Reagan Sold Good Times to an Uncertain Nation." *The New York Times*, Sunday Business, 8 May 2016, p. 5.

8. Roger Ebert. Review of *Miracle Mile*, directed

by Steve De Jarnatt. *Roger Ebert's Movie Home Companion 1993 Edition* (originally appeared in *Chicago Sun-Times*). Andrews and McMeel, 1992, p. 416.

9. James O'Neill. Review of *Miracle* Mile, directed by Steve De Jarnatt. *Sci-Fi on Tape: A Complete Guide to Science Fiction and Fantasy on Video.* Billboard Books, 1997, p.141.

10. John Stanley. Review of *Miracle* Mile, directed by Steve De Jarnatt. *Creature Features: The Science Fiction, Fantasy, and Horror Movie Guide.* Berkley Boulevard Books, 2000, p. 343.

11. David Byrne was the leader of the 1970's, 1980's, and early 1990's rock group Talking Heads.

Chapter Twelve

1. Matt Roush. "HBO Fires Off a Doomsday Thriller." Review of *By Dawn's Early Light*, directed by Jack Sholder. *USA Today*, 18 May 1990, p. 01D.

2. John Singh. "On Video, Nuclear War Always a Possibility." *The Evening Sun*, 10 February 1992, p. C3.

3. In the film, an unidentified European actor dubs Van Johnson's voice.

4. "Hardware (1990)." *AFI (American Film Institute) Catalog: The First 100 Years 1893–1993*, 2019, https://catalog.afi.com/Catalog/moviedetails/58537.

5. Variety Staff. Review of *Hardware*, directed by Richard Stanley. *Variety*, 31 December 1989, https://variety.com/1989/film/reviews/hardware-1200428398/.

6. Richard Harrington. Review of *Hardware*, directed by Richard Stanley. *Washington Post*, 14 September 1990, p. C07.

7. "The Hunt for Red October (1990)." *The Numbers*, 1997–2022, https://www.the-numbers.com/movie/Hunt-for-Red-October-The#tab=summary.

8. "The Hunt for Red October (1990)." *AFI (American Film Institute) Catalog*, 2019, https://catalog.afi.com/Catalog/moviedetails/67290.

9. *Ibid.*

10. Leonard Maltin. Review of *The Hunt for Red October*, directed by John McTiernan. *Leonard Maltin's 2002 Movie & Video Guide.* Signet, 2001, p. 645.

11. Donald Glut. *Jurassic Classics: A Collection of Saurian Essays and Mesozoic Musings.* McFarland, 1999, pp. 219–220.

12. Joe Haldeman. "Interim Report: An Autobiographical Ramble." *Internet Archive Wayback Machine*, 25 October 2004–21 February 2019, https://web.archive.org/web/20110514001111/http://home.earthlink.net/~haldeman/biolong.html.

13. *Ibid.*

14. Roger Hurlburt. "Dueling Robots: It's A Mechanical Affair." Review of *Robot Jox*, directed by Stuart Gordon. *The Washington Post*, 14 September 1990, p. 3E.

15. Review of *Robot Jox*, directed by Stuart Gordon. *SFE: The Encyclopedia of Science Fiction*, 5

April 2020, https://sf-encyclopedia.com/entry/robot_jox.

16. "Dack Rambo, Actor." *TCM (Turner Classic Movies)*, 2022 (no monthly date given), https://www.tcm.com/tcmdb/person/157435%7C34846/Dack-Rambo#overview.

17. "Meshach Taylor, Actor." *TCM (Turner Classic Movies)*, 2022 (no monthly date given), https://www.tcm.com/tcmdb/person/189673%7C0/Meshach-Taylor/#biography.

Epilogue

1. Since 1990, the nuclear threat has also figured into some episodes of 21st century TV shows. For example, on May 3, 2017, *The Goldbergs* aired a Season 4 episode called "The Day After the Day After," in which ABC's showing of *The Day After* in 1983 scares Barry. Also, on May 20, 2018, *Madame Secretary* aired a Season 4 episode called "Night Watch," in which nuclear missiles supposedly have been launched at the U.S. (it turns out to be a false alarm). Then there is CBS's 2006–2008 TV series *Jericho*, whose premise focused on a small Kansas town after a limited nuclear war.

2. "Concerns About Nuclear Weapons." *AP-NORC at the University of Chicago*, 28 March 2022, https://apnorc.org/projects/concerns-about-nuclear-weapons/.

3. Jefrey M. Jones. "Terrorism, Nuclear Weapons, China Viewed as Top U.S. Threats." *Gallup*, 7 March 2022, https://news.gallup.com/poll/390494/-terrorism-nuclear-weapons-china-viewed-top-threats.aspx.

4. Alan F. Phillips. "The Effects of a Nuclear Bomb Explosion on a City." *Peace Research*, vol. 36, no. 2, November 2004, p. 97.

5. *Ibid.*

6. Morgan McFall-Johnsen and Aria Bendix. "How to Survive a Nuclear Bomb Attack: Minute-By-Minute Steps to Protect Yourself." *Business Insider*, U.S. edition, 19 October 2022.

7. Amy Mackinnon, Anushi Rathi, and Mary Yang. "Why You Shouldn't Use Conditioner After a Nuclear Attack." *FP (Foreign Policy)*, 22 July 2022, https://foreignpolicy.com/2022/07/25/nuclear-attack-aftermath-what-to-do-government-response/.

8. Tea Krulos. *Apocalypse Any Day Now: Deep Underground with America's Doomsday Preppers.* Chicago Review Press, 2019, pp. 121–149.

Bibliography

Amen, Carol. "The Last Testament." *Ms. Magazine.* August 1981, pp. 72–74, 82–86.

Arnold, Gary. "'The Children': Have You Hugged Your Ghoul Today?" Review of *The Children,* directed by Max Kalmanowicz. *The Washington Post,* 9 July 1980, p. B6.

Atkinson, Barry. *Atomic Age Cinema: The Offbeat, the Classic, and the Obscure.* Midnight Marquee Press, 2014.

"Audio Commentary with Director Mick Jackson, moderated by film writer Kier-La Janisse and Severin Films' David Gregory." *Threads,* directed by Mick Jackson. Severin Films, 2018. DVD.

Badham, John, interviewed by Robert Kazel. "30 Years After 'WarGames,' Director John Badham Recalls His Nuclear-Brink Blockbuster." *Nuclear Age Peace Foundation,* 12 February 2013, https://www.wagingpeace.org/30-years-after-WarGames-director-john-badham-recalls-his-nuclear-brink-blockbuster/.

Banco, Lindsey Michael. "'Hiroshima Is Peanuts': The Strange Landscape of 'The Day After.'" *The Arizona Quarterly,* vol. 71, no. 1, Spring 2015, pp. 101–128.

Barsanti, Chris. *The Sci-Fi Movie Guide: The Universe of Film from Alien to Zardoz.* Visible Ink, 2015.

Bedell, Sally. "NBC Nuclear-Terror Show Criticized." *The New York Times,* 22 March 1983, p. C15.

Bernstein, Richard. "Soviet Eye Examines Atom War." Review of *Dead Man's Letters,* directed by Konstantin Lopushanskiy. *The New York Times,* 27 January 1989, p. C11.

Beschloss, Michael. "How Reagan Sold Good Times to an Uncertain Nation." *The New York Times,* Sunday Business, 8 May 2016, p. 5.

Bianculli, David. "Nuclear War—In Grisly Detail." *Philadelphia Inquirer,* 12 January 1985, p. C6.

"Billy Dee Williams, Actor: Biography." *TCM (Turner Classic Movies),* 2022, https://prod-www.tcm.com/tcmdb/person/206488%7C22113/-Billy-Dee-Williams#biography.

Blowen, Michael. "Bond Shows His Age." Review of *Octopussy,* directed by John Glen. *Boston Globe,* 10 June 1983, p. 31.

Blowen, Michael. "Right Is Wrong in 'Final Option.'" Review of *The Final Option,* directed by Ian Sharp. *Boston Globe,* 7 October 1983, p. 1.

Boyer, Paul. *By the Bomb's Early Light: American Thought and Culture at the Dawn of the Atomic Age.* University of North Carolina Press, 1994.

Broderick, Mick. *Nuclear Movies: A Critical Analysis and Filmography of International Feature Length Films Dealing With Experimentation, Aliens, Terrorism, Holocaust, and Other Disaster Scenarios, 1914–1989.* McFarland, 1991.

Brothers, Peter H. *Mushroom Clouds and Mushroom Men: The Fantastic Cinema of Ishiro Honda.* CreateSpace Books, 2013.

Brown, Reb. "Reb Brown Interview." *YouTube,* 23 May 2011, https://www.youtube.com/watch?v=cDsavdR-Mq0.

Buchanan, James. Review of *Special Bulletin,* directed by Edward Zwick. *Allmovie.com,* https://www.allmovie.com/movie/special-bulletin-v45967.

Burke, Darren. "Threads: Sheffield Nuclear War Drama Named in Top 100 BBC Shows of All Time." *The Star*; Sheffield, 4 May 2022.

Canby, Vincent. "Animated Black Comedy About Courage as the World Ends." Review of *When the Wind Blows,* directed by Jimmy T. Murakami. *The New York Times,* 11 March 1988, p. C19.

Canby, Vincent. "Cockeyed at 'Red Dawn.'" Review of *Red Dawn,* directed by John Milius. *The New York Times,* late edition, 16 September 1984, p. A19.

Canby, Vincent. Review of *Escape from New York,* directed by John Carpenter. *The New York Times,* 10 July 1981, p. C6.

Canby, Vincent. Review of *The Soldier,* directed by James Glickenhaus. *The New York Times,* 3 September 1982, p. C11.

Canby, Vincent. "The Screen: 'Godzilla 1985.'" Review of *Godzilla 1985,* directed by Koji Hashimoto and R.J. Kizer. *The New York Times,* 30 August 1985, p. C11.

Canby, Vincent. "Screen: The Manhattan Project." Review of *The Manhattan Project,* directed by Marshall Brickman, *The New York Times,* 13 June 1986, p. C8.

Champlin, Charles. "'Grace and Chuck': An Amazing Story." A review of *Amazing Grace and Chuck,* directed by Mike Newell. *Los Angeles Times,* 26 May 1987, p. 1.

Chaney, Jen. "The Tricks May Be Dated, but

Suspense Is Timeless." *The Washington Post*, 1 August 2008, p. WW29.

Church, Steven. *The Day After The Day After: My Atomic Angst.* Soft Skull Press, 2010.

Cockburn, Harry. "Russian State TV Host Lists Possible US Nuclear Targets." *The Independent (Daily Edition)*; London, 26 February 2019, p. 30.

Collins, Paul. "The A-Bomb Kid." *Village Voice*, 16 December 2003, p. C56.

"Concerns About Nuclear Weapons." *AP-NORC at the University of Chicago*, 28 March 2022, https://apnorc.org/projects/concerns-about-nuclear-weapons/.

Cook, Scott. *Rehearsing for Doomsday: Memoir of a Nuclear Missile Crew Commander.* McFarland, 2021.

Corry, John. "TV View: Queeg Would Feel Right at Home." Review of *The Fifth Missile*, directed by Larry Peerce. *The New York Times*, 23 February 1986, p. 2:29.

Crist, Judith. Review of *The Day After*, directed by Nicholas Meyer. *TV Guide*, 19–25 November 1983, p. A-7.

Cross, Rich. Review of *In the Aftermath*, directed by Carl Colpaert. *Starburst*, 29 May 2019, https://www.starburstmagazine.com/reviews/in-aftermath.

"Dack Rambo, Actor." *TCM (Turner Classic Movies)*, 2022, https://www.tcm.com/tcmdb/person/157435%7C34846/Dack-Rambo#overview.

"'The Day After,' Nuclear War/Deterrence Discussion Panel—ABC News 'Viewpoint,'" *YouTube*, 20 November 20,1983, https://www.youtube.com/watch?v=PcCLZwU2t34.

Debus, Allen A. *Prehistoric Monsters: The Real and Imagined Creatures of the Past That We Love to Fear.* McFarland, 2009.

Donat, Peter. Interview with Bill Warren. *Starlog Magazine*, May 1993, pp. 46–48, 69.

"Dreamscape (1984)." *AFI (American Film Institute) Catalog: The First 100 Years 1893–1993*, 2019, https://catalog.afi.com/Catalog/moviedetails/57070.

Ebert, Roger. *Roger Ebert's Movie Home Companion 1993 Edition.* Andrews and McMeel, 1992.

Ebert, Roger. *Roger Ebert's Video Companion 1997 Edition.* Andrews and McMeel, 1996.

Editors. Review of *For Your Eyes Only*, directed by John Glen. *Starlog Science-Fiction Video Magazine #1*, 1988, p. 80.

Edwards, Matthew, ed. *The Atomic Bomb in Japanese Cinema.* McFarland, 2015.

Fellone, Frank. "Explosive Era: Tour Visits Site Where Titan II Blast in 1980 Sent Warhead Flying." *Arkansas Democrat-Gazette*, 21 September 2015, pp. 1E, 6E.

Fields, Alison. "Visualizing Faith and Futility in the Nuclear Apocalypse." *Religions*, vol. 13, no. 2, 3 February 2022, pp. 1–10.

Galbraith, Stuart, IV. *Japanese Science Fiction, Fantasy and Horror Films: A Critical Analysis of 103 Features Released in the United States, 1950–1992.* McFarland, 1994.

Gerani, Gary. *Top 100 Sci-Fi Movies.* IDW Publishing, 2011.

Glut, Donald. *Jurassic Classics: A Collection of Saurian Essays and Mesozoic Musings.* McFarland, 1999.

Goodman, Walter. Review of *Steel Dawn*, directed by Lance Hool. *The New York Times*, 6 November 1987, p. C33.

Greenberger, Robert. Review of *The Day After*, directed by Nicholas Meyer. *Starlog Science-Fiction Video Magazine #1*, 1988, pp. 30–31.

Greenberger, Robert. Review of *Dreamscape*, directed by Joseph Ruben. *Starlog Science-Fiction Video Magazine #1*, 1988, p. 33.

Greenberger, Robert. Review of *Escape from New York*, directed by John Carpenter. *Starlog Science-Fiction Video Magazine #1*, 1988, p. 62.

Gross, Edward. Review of *The Road Warrior*, directed by George Miller. *Starlog Science-Fiction Video Magazine #1*, 1988, p. 62.

Groves, Adam. "Eighties Nuke Movies." *The Bedlam Files*, 2022, https://thebedlamfiles.com/commentary/eighties-nuke-movies/.

Haldeman, Joe. "Interim Report: An Autobiographical Ramble." *Internet Archive Wayback Machine*, 25 October 2004–21 February 2019, https://web.archive.org/web/20110514001111/http://home.earthlink.net/~haldeman/biolong.html.

"Hardware (1990)." *AFI (American Film Institute) Catalog: The First 100 Years 1893–1993*, 2019, https://catalog.afi.com/Catalog/moviedetails/58537.

Harmetz, Aljean. "NBC Film on Terror Wins Prize." *The New York Times*, late edition, 8 July 1983, p. C19.

Harrington, Richard. Review of *Hardware*, directed by Richard Stanley. *Washington Post*, 14 September 1990, p. C07.

Hoffman, David. "Cold-War Doctrines Refuse to Die; False Alert After '95 Rocket Launch Shows Fragility of Aging Safeguards Series: Shattered Shield: The Decline of Russia's Nuclear Forces Series Number: ½." *The Washington Post*, 15 March 1998, p. A01.

"The Hunt for Red October (1990)." *AFI (American Film Institute) Catalog: The First 100 Years 1893–1993*, 2019, https://catalog.afi.com/Catalog/moviedetails/67290.

"The Hunt for Red October (1990)." *The Numbers*, 1997–2022, https://www.the-numbers.com/movie/Hunt-for-Red-October-The#tab=summary.

Hurlburt, Roger. "Dueling Robots: It's A Mechanical Affair." Review of *Robot Jox*, directed by Stuart Gordon. *The Washington Post*, 14 September 1990, p. 3E.

"The Intermediate-Range Nuclear Forces (INF) Treaty." *Arms Control Today*, vol. 47. no. 3, April 2017, pp. 14–15.

"Iron Eagle (1986)." *The Numbers*, 1997–2022, https://www.the-numbers.com/movie/Iron-Eagle#tab=summary.

Johnson, Kim Howard. Review of *Superman IV: The Quest for Peace*, directed by Sidney Furie.

Starlog Science-Fiction Video Magazine #1, 1988, p. 38.

Jonas, Gerald. "Marshall Brickman Humanizes the Nuclear Arms Race." *The New York Times*, 15 June 1986, p. 2:21.

Jones, Jason C. "Japan Removed: *Godzilla* Adaptations and Erasure of the Politics of Nuclear Experience." *The Atomic Bomb in Japanese Cinema*, edited by Matthew Edwards. McFarland, 2015, pp. 34–55.

Jones, Jeffrey M. "Terrorism, Nuclear Weapons, China Viewed as Top U.S. Threats." *Gallup*, 7 March 2022, https://news.gallup.com/poll/390494/terrorism-nuclear-weapons-china-viewed-top-threats.aspx.

Kalat, David. *A Critical History and Filmography of Toho's Godzilla Series, 2nd ed.* McFarland, 2010.

Kaplan, Fred. "'WarGames' and Cybersecurity's Debt to a Hollywood Hack." *The New York Times*, 19 February 2016, p. AR24.

Katz, Ephraim, with Ronald Dean Nolen. *The Film Encyclopedia: The Complete Guide to Film and the Film Industry, 7th ed.* Collins Reference, 2012.

"Ken Wahl, Actor: Biography." *TCM (Turner Classic Movies)*, 2022, https://prod-www.tcm.com/tcmdb/person/200464%7C0/Ken-Wahl#biography.

Kerr, Peter. "TV Films Will Use More Social Issues." *The New York Times*, 28 February 1984, p. C158.

Kimball, Daryl G. "New Approaches Needed to Prevent Nuclear Catastrophe." *Arms Control Today*, vol. 52, no. 3, April 2022, p. 3.

Krulos, Tea. *Apocalypse Any Day Now: Deep Underground with America's Doomsday Preppers.* Chicago Review Press, 2019.

Lees, J.D., and Marc Cerasini. *The Official Godzilla Compendium.* Random House, 1998.

Leotta, Alfio. "When War Imitates Art: Rediscovering *Red Dawn*, the 1984 Movie Inspiring Ukrainian Fighters." *The Conversation*, 18 April 2022, https://theconversation.com/when-war-imitates-art-rediscovering-red-dawn-the-1984-movie-inspiring-ukrainian-fighters-181261.

"Lithgow Finally Gets the Girl," *Chicago Tribune*, 5 September 1985, p. 8L.

"Lou Ferrigno, Actor." *TCM (Turner Classic Movies)*, 2022, https://prod-www.tcm.com/tcmdb/person/61231%7C0/Lou-Ferrigno#overview.

MacKenzie, Robert. Review of *The Day After*, directed by Nicholas Meyer. *TV Guide*, 19–25 November 1983, p. 56.

Mackinnon, Amy, Anushi Rathi, and Mary Yang. "Why You Shouldn't Use Conditioner After a Nuclear Attack." *FP (Foreign Policy)*, 22 July 2022, https://foreignpolicy.com/2022/07/25/nuclear-attack-aftermath-what-to-do-government-response/.

Maloney, Sean M. *Deconstructing Dr. Strangelove: The Secret History of Nuclear War Films.* Potomac Books, 2020.

Maltin, Leonard. *Leonard Maltin's Movie Encyclopedia.* Plume Books, 1994.

Maltin, Leonard. *Leonard Maltin's 2002 Movie & Video Guide.* Signet, 2001.

Manchanda, Arnav. "When Truth Is Stranger than Fiction: The Able Archer Incident." *Cold War History*, February 2009, vol. 9, no. 1, pp. 111–133.

Manchel, Frank. "The Man Who Made the Stars Shine Brighter: An Interview with Woody Strode." *Black Scholar*, vol. 25, no. 2, Spring 1995, pp. 37–46.

"The Manhattan Project (1986)." *AFI (American Film Institute) Catalog of Feature Films: The First 100 Years 1893–1993*, 2019, https://catalog.afi.com/Catalog/moviedetails/57404.

"The Manhattan Project (1986)." *The Numbers*, 1997–2022, https://www.the-numbers.com/movie/Manhattan-Project-The#tab=summary.

Martin, Mick, and Marsha Porter. *DVD & Video Guide 2005.* Ballantine Books, 2004.

Maslin, Janet. "Film: 'Dead Zone,' from King Novel." Review of *The Dead Zone*, directed by David Cronenberg. *The New York Times*, 21 October 1983, p. C8.

Maslin, Janet. "'Parasite,' A Creature in 3-D." Review of *Parasite*, directed by Charles Band. *The New York Times*, 13 March 1982, p. 1:19.

Maslin, Janet. Review of *Akira*, directed by Katsuhiro Ôtomo. *The New York Times*, 19 October 1990, p. C12.

Maslin, Janet. Review of *Amazing Grace and Chuck*, directed by Mike Newell. *The New York Times*, 22 May 1987, p. C30.

Maslin, Janet. Review of *Dreamscape*, directed by Joseph Ruben. *The New York Times*, 15 August 1984, p. C24.

Maslin, Janet. "Sean Connery Is Seasoned James Bond." Review of *Never Say Never Again*, directed by Irvin Kershner. *The New York Times*, 7 October 1983, p. C13.

Maslin, Janet. "'Yor, the Hunter' with a Cave Man Hero." Review of *Yor, the Hunter from the Future*, directed by Anthony M. Dawson (a.k.a. Antonio Margheriti). *The New York Times*, 21 August 1983, p. 1:54.

Mathis, John R. *Atomic Cinema in America: Historical and Cultural Analysis of a New Film Genre That Reflected the Nuclear Zeitgeist of the Cold War (1945–1989).* Salve Regina University Library, PhD dissertation, 2013.

McDonnell, David. Review of *Testament*, directed by Lynn Littman. *Starlog Science-Fiction Video Magazine* #1, 1988, p. 69.

McFall-Johnsen, Morgan, and Aria Bendix. "How to Survive a Nuclear Bomb Attack: Minute-By-Minute Steps to Protect Yourself." *Business Insider*, US edition, 19 October 2022.

McNeil, Alex. *Total Television*, 4th ed. Penguin Books, 1996.

"Meshach Taylor, Actor." *TCM (Turner Classic Movies)*, 2022, https://www.tcm.com/tcmdb/person/189673%7C0/Meshach-Taylor/#biography.

"The Message of Fatima," both in original language and English translation. *Congregation for the Doctrine of the Faith*, no date given, https://www.

vatican.va/roman_curia/congregations/cfaith/documents/rc_con_cfaith_doc_20000626_message-fatima_en.html.

Missionaries of the Sacred Heart. Review of *Deadline*, directed by Arch Nicholson. *Missionaries of the Sacred Heart*, 18 September 2021, https://misacor.org.au/item/5304-deadline.

Moore, Demi, interview by James Corden. *The Late Show*, 24 October 2019, https://www.youtube.com/watch?v=wxpRVetn76o.

"Morgan Fairchild, Actor: Biography." *TCM (Turner Classic Movies)*, 2022, https://prod-www.tcm.com/tcmdb/person/59286%7C0/-Morgan-Fairchild#biography.

Murphy, James S. "The Obscure 80s Horror Film That Unlocks the Meaning of *Us*." *Vanity Fair*, 25 March 2019, https://www.vanityfair.com/hollywood/2019/03/us-horror-movie-chud.

Nazir, Asjad. "'Mr. India': 35 Facts About the Cult Film." *Eastern Eye*; London (UK), 27 May 2022, p. 30.

"Never Say Never Again (1983)." *The Numbers*, 1997–2022, https://www.the-numbers.com/movie/Never-Say-Never-Again#tab=summary

Newman, Kim. *Apocalypse Movies: End of the World Cinema*. St. Martin's Griffin, 2000.

Oberman, J. "Poetry After the A-Bomb" booklet. *Godzilla*. The Criterion Collection, 2012. DVD.

Oleszczyk, Michal. "Things to Come: Piotr Szulkin's Homespun Apocalypse." *Roger.Ebert.com*, 16 March 2015, https://www.rogerebert.com/far-flung-correspondents/piotr-szulkins-homespun-apocalypse.

O'Mara, Sean. Review of *Future War 198X*, directed by Toshio Masuda and Koji Katsubota. *Zimmert*, 20 September 2016, https://www.zimmerit.moe/most-dangerous-year-future-war-198x/.

O'Neill, James. *Sci-Fi On Tape: A Complete Guide to Science Fiction and Fantasy on Video*. Billboard Books, 1997.

O'Neill, Patrick Daniel. Review of *Special Bulletin*, directed by Edward Zwick. *Starlog Science-Fiction Video Magazine* #1, 1988, p. 67.

Orth, Taylor. "Three in 10 Americans Fear Snakes—and Most Who Do Fear Them a Great Deal," *YouGovAmerica*, 16 June 2022, https://today.yougov.com/topics/society/articles-reports/2022/06/16/americans-fear-snakes-heights-spiders-poll.

Overpeck, Deron. "Remember! It's Only a Movie! Expectations and Receptions of *The Day After* (1983)." *Historical Journal of Film, Radio and Television*, vol. 32, no. 2, June 2012, pp. 267–292.

Parmelee, Tyler. "The H-bomb in the Swamp: Taking Nuclear War Seriously Again." *Survival*, vol. 63, no. 4, August 2022, pp. 179–184.

"Patrick Swayze Biography (1952–2009)." *Biography*, 27 April 2017, https://www.biography.com/actor/patrick-swayze.

Peele, Jordan, interview by Luria Freeman. "How 'Us' Director Jordan Peele Makes Truly Scary Horror Films." *Now This Entertainment*,

YouTube, 25 March 2019, https://www.youtube.com/watch?v=MQOrue_Wuww.

Phillips, Alan F. "The Effects of a Nuclear Bomb Explosion on a City." *Peace Research*, vol. 36, no. 2, November 2004, pp. 93–101.

Pietrzak, Maciej. "David Avidan's Message from the Future: Nuclear Fantasies of the Galactic Poet." *Images: The International Journal of European Film Performing Arts and Audiovisual Communication*, vol. 28, no. 37, March 2021, pp. 127–139.

Pike, David L. "Nuclear Realism and Memories of Extinction in the 1980s: *Testament, The Day After*, and *Threads*." *Bright Lights Film Journal*, 23 December 2021, https://brightlightsfilm.com/nuclear-realism-and-memories-of-extinction-in-the-1980s-testament-the-day-after-and-threads/#.YhwZV9_MKUn.

Puchlaski, Steven. Review of *Mr. India*, directed by Shekhar Kapur. *Shock Cinema*, 1998, https://www.shockcinemamagazine.com/india.html.

Reagan, Ronald. "Diary Entry," *White House Diaries of Ronald Reagan*, 10 October 1983, https://www.reaganfoundation.org/ronald-reagan/-white-house-diaries/diary-entry-10101983/.

Reagan, Ronald. *Ronald Reagan: An American Life*. Threshold, 2011.

Reeve, Christopher. *Still Me: With a New Afterword*. Ballantine Books, 1999.

Review of *Future War 198X*, directed by Toshio Masuda and Koji Katsubota. *Sci-Fi-Central*, no date given, https://www.sci-fi-central.com/Database/SF/02/9N/index.php.

Review of *Robot Jox*, directed by Stuart Gordon. *SFE: The Encyclopedia of Science Fiction*, 5 April 2020, https://sf-encyclopedia.com/entry/robot_jox.

Rhodes, Richard. *Dark Sun: The Making of the Hydrogen Bomb*. Simon & Schuster, 1995.

Rodgers, Jude. "Here Come the Bombs: The Making of 'Threads,' the Nuclear War Film that Shocked a Generation." *The New Statesman*, 17 March 2018, https://www.newstatesman.com/-long-reads/2018/03/here-come-bombs-making-threads-nuclear-war-film-shocked-generation.

"Roger Moore, Actor: Biography." *TCM (Turner Classic Movies)*, 2022, https://www.tcm.com/tcmdb/person/134821%7C161989/Roger—Moore#overview

Roush, Matt. "HBO Fires Off a Doomsday Thriller." Review of *By Dawn's Early Light*, directed by Jack Sholder. *USA Today*, 18 May 1990, p. 01D.

Ryfle, Steve. *Japan's Favorite Mon-Star: The Unauthorized Biography of "The Big G."* ECW Press, 1998.

"Salman Lends His Own Twist to the Immortal Lines of Bollywood Baddies." *IANS English*; New Delhi, 25 September 2022.

Scheib, Richard. Review of *The Lathe of Heaven*, directed by Fred Barzyk and David Loxton. *Moira Science Fiction, Horror and Fantasy Film Review*, no date, https://www.moriareviews.com/sciencefiction/lathe-of-heaven-tv-1980.htm.

Scheilbach, Michael. *Atomic Narratives and*

American Youth: Coming of Age with the Atom, 1945–1955. McFarland, 2003.

Schlosser, Eric. *Command and Control: Nuclear Weapons, the Damascus Accident, and the Illusion of Safety.* Penguin Press, 2013.

Schneider, Steve. "Cable TV Notes: Nuclear Conflict on HBO's 'Countdown.'" *The New York Times,* 14 October 1984, p. 2:29.

"75 Nuke Extortion Cases." *The Telegraph-Herald,* UPI, 15 June 1981, p. 2.

Shaheen, Jack G., ed. *Nuclear War Films.* Southern Illinois University Press, 1978.

Shales, Tom. "Apocalypse Wow! It's 'WW III.'" Review of *World War III,* directed by David Greene and Boris Sagal. *Washington Post,* 30 January 1982, https://www.washingtonpost.com/archive/lifestyle/1982/01/30/apocalypse-wow-its-ww-iii/f44b8d24-71a2-4501-a148-0641a233de36/.

Shales, Tom. "Bulletin! The Show That Shook NBC." *The Washington Post,* 20 March 1983. https://www.washingtonpost.com/archive/lifestyle/style/1983/03/20/bulletin-the-show-that-shook-nbc/014edc08-362c-414a-8935-ede8c2e46562/.

"Silence in Heaven: Looking Back at *The Day After.*" *The Day After,* directed by Nicholas Meyer, disc TV Cut, Kino Lorber, 2018. DVD.

Skeen, Jesse. Review of *The Soldier,* directed by James Glickenhaus. *DVDtalk,* 5 April 2018, https://www.dvdtalk.com/reviews/review/72923.

Smith, Sally Bedell. "Film on Nuclear War Already Causing Wide Fallout of Political Activity." *The New York Times,* 17 November 1983, p. A20.

"The Soldier (1982): History." *AFI Catalog of Feature Films: The First 100 Years 1893–1993,* 2019, https://catalog.afi.com/Catalog/moviedetails/56876.

"Special Bulletin (NBC)." *Television Academy Emmys,* no date, https://www.emmys.com/shows/special-bulletin.

Stanley, John. *Creature Features: The Science Fiction, Fantasy, and Horror Movie Guide.* Berkley Boulevard Books, 2000.

Stover, Dawn. "Facing Nuclear Reality 35 Years After *The Day After*: A Special Report." *Bulletin of the Atomic Scientists,* 2018, https://thebulletin.org/facing-nuclear-reality-35-years-after-the-day-after/.

Strickler, Jeff. "'Superman IV' So Bad, It Makes '50s Television Series Look Good." *Minneapolis Star and Tribune,* 30 July 1987, p. 06C.

"Superman IV: The Quest for Peace (1987)." *AFI (American Film Institute) Catalog of Feature Films: The First 100 Years 1893–1993,* 2019, https://catalog.afi.com/Film/57838-SUPERMAN-IVTHEQUESTFORPEACE?sid=25294c53-7642-454a-8c77-95a143365b5c&sr=6.600077&cp=1&pos=0.

"Superman IV: The Quest for Peace (1987)." *The Numbers,* 1997–2022, https://www.the-numbers.com/movie/Superman-IV-The-Quest-for-Peace#tab=summary.

Tall, Richard Whit. "Into Your Life It Will Creep; How the 'Mid-'80s Nuclear War Message Movie' Remains Relevant Today." *National Post,* 10 April 2017, p. B.5.

Taylor, Peter. "Six Days That Shook Britain: It Was One of the Events That Defined the 80s—Establishing the SAS's Lethal Reputation and Margaret Thatcher as a Prime Minister Who Refused to Give in to Terrorists," *The Guardian;* London (UK), 24 July 2002, p. 2:2.

The Telltale Mind. "Radiation's Progeny—*The Being* (1983)." Review of *The Being,* directed by Jackie Kong. *The Telltale Mind,* 24 October 2019, https://thetelltalemind.com/2019/10/14/-radiations-progeny-the-being-1983/.

Testament, Warner/Allied Vaughn, April 5, 2016. Special Feature: "*Testament* at 20." DVD.

"35 Years of 'Mr. India': Here's Why Satish Kaushik Insists the Classic Shouldn't Be Remade." *Free Press Journal;* Mumbai, 27 May 2022.

Threads Official Blu-ray Trailer. *SeverinFilmsOfficial,* 5 December 2017, https://www.youtube.com/watch?v=EHyNFlhjojM.

Tibbetts, John C. "Marshall Brickman Interview for The Manhattan Project (1986)." *John C. Tibbetts Interviews,* 9 March 2022, https://www.youtube.com/watch?v=bPFkA48Zud0.

Turner, Ted. "WTBS Introduction Threads 1985." *YouTube,* 17 July 2015, https://www.youtube.com/watch?v=ZgNsD8iCFvA.

Union of Concerned Scientists. "Frequently Asked Questions about Taking Nuclear Weapons Off Hair-Trigger Alert." *Union of Concerned Scientists Fact Sheet,* January 2015, https://www.ucsusa.org/sites/default/files/attach/2015/01/Hair-Trigger%20FAQ.pdf.

Van Gelder, Lawrence. "'C.H.U.D.,' a Tale of Strange Creatures." Review of *C.H.U.D.,* directed by Douglas Cheek. *The New York Times,* 1 September 1984, p. 1:10.

Variety Staff. Review of *Hardware,* directed by Richard Stanley. *Variety,* 31 December 1989, https://variety.com/1989/film/reviews/hardware-1200428398/.

VideoHound's Sci-Fi Experience: Your Quantum Guide to the Video Universe. Visible Ink Press, 1997.

Warren, Bill. *Keep Watching the Skies! The 21st Century Edition.* McFarland, 2010.

Weart, Spencer R. *Nuclear Fear: A History of Images.* Harvard University Press, 1988.

Weart, Spencer R. *The Rise of Nuclear Fear.* Harvard University Press, 2012.

Whitburn, Joel. *The Billboard Book of Top 40 Hits, Revised and Enlarged 7th edition.* Billboard Books, 2000.

Whitelaw, Paul. "G2: Film & Music: Reviews: Television: Your Next Box Set: 'Threads.'" *The Guardian,* 22 November 2013, p. 28.

Willistein, Paul. Review of *The Fourth Protocol,* directed by John Mackenzie. *Morning Call,* 29 August 1987, p. A60.

Wilson, Ward. "Why Are There No Big Nuke

Protests?" *Bulletin of the Atomic Scientists*, vol. 71, no. 2, March 2015, pp. 56–59.

Wolverines: U31. "Wolverines: Ukrainian Graffiti Inspired by 80s Film Sprayed on Wrecked Russian Tanks." *Forces.net*, 22 April 2022, https://www.forces.net/ukraine/wolverines-ukrainian-graffiti-inspired-80s-film-sprayed-wrecked-russian-tanks.

Woodward, Joe. "The Fatima Debate: After Decades of Secrecy, The Vatican's Release of the Fatima Text Fails to Resolve All the Unanswered Questions." *Calgary Herald*, 1 July 2000, p. O10.

The World Almanac and Book of Facts. Newspaper Enterprise Association, 1983.

"Yor, the Hunter from the Future (1983)." *The Numbers*, 1997–2022, https://www.the-numbers.com/movie/Yor-Hunter-From-the-Future#tab=summary.

Index

Numbers in *bold italics* indicate pages with illustrations

251